INTRODUCTION TO PHILOSOPHY

INTRODUCTION TO PHILOSOPHY

AN INQUIRY

AFTER

A RATIONAL SYSTEM OF SCIENTIFIC PRINCIPLES

IN

THEIR RELATION TO ULTIMATE REALITY

GEORGE TRUMBULL LADD

GYAN

Published by

GYAN

Gyan Publishing House
5, Ansari Road
Daryaganj, New Delhi-110002
Phone: 011-47034999, 9811692060
E-mail: books@gyanbooks.com

Distribution Network
gyanbooks.com
India, USA, Canada, UK, Australia

ISBN: 978-93-6780-185-7 (PB)

First Published, 1890

2nd Impression 2025

Printed at: Gyan Press, Delhi.

INTRODUCTION TO PHILOSOPHY
Author: GEORGE TRUMBULL LADD

INTRODUCTION TO PHILOSOPHY

Introduction to Philosophy

AN INQUIRY

AFTER

A RATIONAL SYSTEM OF SCIENTIFIC PRINCIPLES

IN

THEIR RELATION TO ULTIMATE REALITY

BY

GEORGE TRUMBULL LADD

PROFESSOR OF PHILOSOPHY IN YALE UNIVERSITY

NEW YORK

CHARLES SCRIBNER'S SONS

1891

PREFACE.

IT is not easy to describe the precise purpose of this book in the few words of an appropriate title. I have, indeed, cherished the hope that it may serve to "introduce" some of its readers to the study of philosophy. Undoubtedly the number is increasingly large who recognize, if only vaguely, the existence of "those riddles" — as said Lotze — "by which our mind is oppressed in life, and about which we are compelled to hold some view or other, in order to be able really to live at all." It is these riddles which form the subjects of philosophical investigation. Among the persons who at least recognize their existence are the young in the later years of our higher institutions of learning. I have therefore had them in mind in writing this treatise.

I have not thought it desirable, however, to put my thoughts into the technical form of a book of instruction for beginners in philosophy. In a subject that deals so largely with problems inviting to reflection and ending, at best, in opinion, there seems to me something unbecoming and even repulsive in the textbook form. Yet I believe that the skilful teacher of philosophy will find this book helpful in bringing its problems, and their discussion from whatever point of view, before his classes.

But there are many besides the students in our colleges and seminaries who thoughtfully raise and earnestly pursue the philosophical inquiries. To them, too, I would gladly speak a word of sympathy and cheer, and (if possible) hold out a helping hand. Of no other pursuit is it so true as of philosophy, that it has no "royal road." The profoundest reflections of the mightiest intellects and the daily musings and self-questionings of the plainest men and women have all the fundamental things in common here. Freedom and caution, earnestness and modesty, are alike becoming in all. No costly laboratory, no expensive apparatus, no tiresome journeys of exploration, are indispensable in the pursuit of philosophy.

This book is therefore addressed to the laity, at large, as well as to those who are in processes of education. Though much of its language is somewhat foreign to that of common life, the subjects of which it treats are those which lie upon the minds and hearts of all the thoughtful. If to such any of my thoughts can be an introduction, or a *vade-mecum*, in reflection, my purposes will thus be the more completely attained.

Though this book is called an "Introduction," no special pains have been taken to simplify or popularize its treatment. For those accustomed to think in the lines it follows, its views will, I hope, always be found clearly and candidly expressed. It is not to be expected that these views will all find acceptance with those most competent to judge. For beginners in philosophy some expressions will doubtless seem obscure, or hard to be understood. But, then, reflection is the indispensable method of philosophy; and he who does not learn to reflect over the meanings which the words employed in philosophical writings bear, cannot hope to make progress in philosophical study. For if, when entering upon this study, the plain and thoughtful man needs no special equipment besides his own powers of reflection, the keenest and most showily educated mind cannot dispense with reflection.

Finally, the expert readers — if such the book should find — will not be long in discovering that the so-called "Introduction" is by no means a perfectly colorless affair. Doubtless a system of philosophy (or at least the sketch and protocol of such a system) lies concealed in these pages. If the subject were urged to the point of a confession, it would appear that the author has views of his own to which he wishes to *introduce* his readers. These views are to a certain large extent positive as well as critical. The attempt has been made, however, to prevent their expression in a form unreasonably and offensively dogmatic. Whether they are sound and defensible, each reader must, on due consideration, judge for himself. But a "system of philosophy" has only been suggested and sketched. The expansion and more detailed discussion of its separate departments by the same hand must abide their time.

GEORGE TRUMBULL LADD.

YALE UNIVERSITY, July, 1890.

TABLE OF CONTENTS.

CHAPTER I.

INTRODUCTORY.

HISTORY AND DEFINITION OF THE TERM "PHILOSOPHY."

THE inquiry, "What is philosophy?" cannot be answered by a direct appeal to history. This is true, whether the appeal be taken to a widespreading and confessedly unscientific usage, or to the conceptions and terminology of authorities in philosophy. Popular expression has much misused the word; it has thus tended in no small degree to produce distrust toward the particular discipline which the word represents. But the writers of philosophical masterpieces have by no means been at agreement on this point. This, too, is one reason for the unfavorable attitude of many cultivated persons toward the pursuit of "metaphysics," technically so called. Men eminent in science, literature, or education are accustomed to identify philosophy with metaphysics; and by the latter term they understand the sum-total of unverifiable ontological speculations.

If the fullest reasonable allowance be made for the grounds upon which the foregoing misapprehensions are based, a claim to honorable mention can still be made for philosophy, and also a claim to recognition for philosophical study. Nay, more; we should not despair of showing that this "mother of the sciences" has been scarcely inferior to any other factor in the elevation, ameliorating, and enrichment of the life of literature and of conduct. But even the beginnings of such an apologetic argument must be for the present postponed. It will be a more economical course, first of all, to clear from obscurity the conception of philosophy, and to show how the study of philosophy may be most successfully pursued.

It need not be argued in detail that the exact and comprehensive definition of any form of science or of intellectual discipline is no easy task. Life and reality nowhere draw for us perfectly distinct lines. Even the physical and natural sciences find great difficulty in separating their peculiar spheres, and in limiting their particular ends and objects of pursuit within those spheres. Here lies at least one reason why, if we are to believe Mr. Herbert Spencer, "the sciences cannot be rationally arranged in serial order." In fact, the experts of the "exact sciences" are still at disagreement over important points relating to this matter. Meanwhile, the world of scholars is inquiring whether clearer conceptions of such forms of knowledge as logic and psychology are not possible. A recent writer[1] on the latter of the two has maintained that "psychology cannot be defined at all by reference to a special subject-matter, as can mineralogy and botany."

Philosophy, then, is not necessarily at a great relative disadvantage, if it cannot appeal to common consent in limiting its own domain. Satisfactory definition is one of the latest and finest achievements in the pursuit of any science. Nor is it likely that finished and faultless definition will be reached until human knowledge is itself finished and faultless.

It is not our intention, however, to deny that somewhat peculiar difficulties surround the attempt to formulate a precise conception of the nature of philosophy. Nor do we fear the further confession that the reason for these difficulties is in part the fault of philosophers themselves. For the reason is only *partly* due to them; it is also partly due to the nature of the subject. If we speak of philosophy as a "science" at all,

[1] Dr. Ward in the Encyclopædia Britannica (9th ed.); art. Psychology.

it can only be to lay emphasis upon a correct method for its study, and a certain ideal certainty aimed at in its conclusions. It will be one result of our inquiry to show that philosophy should not be identified with any form of positive science.

The difficulty of fixing upon an independent domain for philosophy is increased by the recent vigorous growth and wonderful diversifying of the particular sciences. Familiar changes in the use of terms illustrate this truth. Intelligent persons are no longer inclined to speak of physics as "natural philosophy;" and yet this term has a legitimate birthright. For the speculative thought in whose line of succession we are standing to-day, had its rise in crude theories as to the ultimate constituents of the physical universe. Some, with Thales, said that all things arose from and consist of water; and some, with Anaximander, that the beginning of all things (*ἀρχή*) was the unlimited (*ἄπειρον*), — that is, "the infinite mass of matter, out of which all things arise." Still others said the ultimate physical principle is air, or "eternally living fire." Others sought a formal or quasi-spiritual "First;" and this they found in number, through which the totality of things becomes a cosmos, — an orderly and beautiful whole; or in One Divine Being, "all eye, all ear, all thought;" or in Mind, "itself mixed with nothing," but acting on matter considered as an inert and compound, but as yet undifferentiated, mass.

It is to physics rather than to metaphysics that inquirers appeal in these days for a speculative solution of questions like the foregoing. But it is nevertheless true that any solution of such questions must always be mingled largely with the prevailing metaphysics. The fact that we assign their discussion to science rather than to philosophy, illustrates the modern tendency to narrow the sphere hitherto occupied by philosophy.

What is true of physics is even yet more true of psychology, as inclusive of both logic and ethics. For this science the complex states of consciousness constitute the problems to be solved. In dealing with these problems psychology presses hard upon philosophy for the right to what the latter formerly considered its peculiar domain. The descriptive and evolutionary science of mind claims the power to explain the genesis of conceptions of real Being and eternal Truth. The ultimate and fundamental forms of thought and belief (*semina scientiæ, semina æternitatis*) are thus brought into the burning focus of the idea of development. In this focus the hitherto stable forms of all Thought and Reality lose their life. Not only Space and Time, but also the ethical and æsthetical Ideals, and even the categories of Thought, are thus apparently reduced to a condition of perpetual change.

With Plato, philosophy moved in the sphere of the Idea. The Platonic Idea (*ἰδέα* or *εἶδος*) was "a pure archetypal essence, in which those things that are together subsumed under the same concept participate." Both æsthetically and ethically, it was the perfect in its kind; to it every individual reality remained far and forever inferior. Of all the ideas, the highest (for they were a kingdom) was the Idea of the Good. This Idea is the real cause of all Being and Knowledge, as the sun in the kingdom of ideas. In this sphere of lofty intuitions of supersensible realities did divine philosophy, according to Plato, have its movement and life. But as astronomy with the telescope has banished from the heavens the fixed and musical spheres of the planets, so have psychology and anthropology apparently banished the sphere of the Platonic ideas.

The very conception which Aristotle held of philosophy was unfavorable to the claim for it of a domain distinct from the particular sciences. Psychology and logic recognize in this great Greek their first progenitor. But they treat the Aristotelian categories, and the four principles of his "First Philosophy," — questions set apart by him for metaphysics, — as subjects falling within their scientific domain.

Through the Middle Ages, and even into modern times, it was theology which was most closely allied with philosophy. During this period the latter was understood to be ancillary to the former, or rather to the reigning dogmas of the Church. In theory and appearance, theology dominated philosophy. In reality, philosophy controlled and guided theology; and, finally, having gained her own freedom, undertook the task of freeing her former mistress from the principle of traditional authority. In the general movement of enlarging and diversifying human knowledge, a so-called "science of religion" has arisen. Theology, too, has at length tardily and feebly felt the modern impulse. It has even claimed to be the "science of sciences." How much more of the sphere once recognized as belonging to philosophy is not in this way forever consigned to the particular sciences?

But is it not the peculiar and indefeasible right of philosophy to transact business with the Absolute? In the construction and defence of this Idea, and in the deduction from it of the forms and laws of all reality, may not philosophy find its legitimate work? But certain of the particular sciences refuse to surrender even this barren right to philosophy. Psychology attempts to bring the very conception of the Absolute into this same focus of analysis. The conception is pronounced negative, a mere abstraction, with no correlate in reality. The deductive process, by which philosophy once sought to pass from this Idea to the world of concrete realities with which science deals, is shown to have the appearance and not the substance of an argument. Ethics, politics, art, and religion pursue their way, regardless of the once proud philosophy of the Absolute. To it is left only those pale ghosts of conceptions that belong to the death-kingdom of abstract thought.

"Philosophy," says Lotze, "is a mother wounded by the ingratitude of her own children." It is not the ingratitude, however, of denying their maternal origin which wounds her most deeply. The history of the particular sciences, even more than the history of philosophy, shows how much they owe to the philosophic impulse and the philosophic reflection of the race. A wound not only deep but deadly would be inflicted, however, if these sciences should quite deprive philosophy of her rightful domain. Yet, after granting all their claims, what is left out of which to constitute this domain?

The conception of philosophy, like the conception of science, implies a living historical development. We cannot wholly intrust to Plato and Aristotle the guidance of our minds into the precise and comprehensive idea we are seeking. But in the search we cannot safely overlook the thoughts of these ancient masters in philosophy. Kant, too, as the first who attempted to mark with precision the boundaries between philosophy and the positive sciences, is entitled to great consideration; and yet we cannot uncritically receive the definition of even so profound a thinker.

The true method of defining the nature of philosophy is therefore perfectly plain. We must consult the history of philosophy and learn the views of its great teachers; but we must maintain the freedom of criticism in our consultation of history. As children of all the ages, we receive with docility the instructions of the past. As children especially of this age, we must recognize our own right to the effort for an independent point of view. This method will be applied in two ways. A brief sketch of the history of the term "philosophy" will serve to indicate what are the important and permanent factors in the conception of philosophy. A more detailed criticism of the principal forms of definition (particularly in the modern era) will then enable us so to combine these factors as to reach the true and comprehensive definition.

The word "philosophy"[1] and its kindred terms do not occur in Homer or Hesiod. Herodotus (i. 30) represents Crœsus as

[1] Further information may be found in the following, among other works: Ueberweg, "A History of Philosophy," and an Article in the "Zeitschrift für Philosophie u. philosoph. Kritik," New Series, vol. xlii., 1863, pp. 185–199; Strümpell, "Einleitung in die Philosophie vom Standpunkte d. Geschichte d. Philosophie;" Article by R. Haym, in Ersch und Gruber's "Encycl. d. Wissen. u. Künste," iii. 24; Lichtenfels, "Lehrbuch zur Einleitung in d. Philosophie;" Stuckenberg, "Introduction to the Study of Philosophy."

saying to Solon: "I have heard that thou hast travelled, *philosophizing*, over many lands." Thucydides makes Pericles use the term "to philosophize" in the Funeral Oration (ii. 40), as a striving after intellectual and scientific culture. A statement, probably mythical, concerning the remote and shadowy personality of Pythagoras, refers to him as the first to designate philosophy by the term "science." The thought ascribed to Socrates is well known. In the Platonic Apology (28 E) he calls by the term "philosophizing" that examination of himself and others by which he aimed to destroy the Sophistical conceit of wisdom; in this he saw the mission of his life. It is with the disciples of Socrates that the term "philosophy" appears with a technical significance. Xenophon refers (Memorabil., I. ii. 31) to certain men who made a business (constituting, perhaps, a school) of "philosophizing."

It is Plato, however, who is the first even to attempt to describe, under the term "philosophy," a definite method and domain of human knowledge, and to give to it by his own labors a comprehensive and systematic treatment. Yet Plato vacillates in his definition, nor does he in practice remain true to any one conception of the subject. In several places[1] he expresses the belief — falsely ascribed to Pythagoras, but probably taught by Socrates — that wisdom belongs to God alone; while it belongs to man to be rather a lover of wisdom. This wisdom (σοφία) is identical with true knowledge[2] (ἐπιστήμη, or — as we should say — with *science*); philosophy is the acquisition of such knowledge.[3] It has to do, not with the sensuous, but with the ideal; and, accordingly, with the eternal and immutably real. Philosophers are worthy, then, to be spoken of as those who "set their affections, in each case, on the really existent;"[4] or as those who "are able to apprehend that which is always self-identical and immutable."[5]

[1] Phædr., 278 d; Symp., 203 e; Lysis, 218 a (ed. Steph.).
[2] Theætet., 145 e.
[3] Euthyd., 288 d.
[4] Rep., v. 480.
[5] Rep., vi. 484 b.

Elsewhere[1] he speaks of philosophy so as to include under it certain branches of knowledge which we should to-day assign to the particular sciences,—he thus speaks, at least, of "geometry and certain other philosophy."

Philosophy has its spring, according to Plato, in a deep and passionate impulse of human nature. Its root is *Eros*,—the effort of mortal man to attain the immortal. To reach its proper aim it must pass from what is sensuous to what is intellectual, from the individual to the universal,—to the intuition and understanding of the Idea.[2] Thus philosophy is the elevation of the entire man out of the senses; it includes all real and valuable knowledge, as well as the pursuit of knowledge in the correct manner. It also secures the fulfilment of moral duties. All other education or culture is merely a preparation for philosophy.[3]

These expressions of Plato are sufficiently vague and shifting; yet they clearly suggest all four of the most important factors in the true conception of philosophy. Two of them, at least, are to be distinguished even previous to the Platonic writings. One of these is the recognition of the profound and noble impulse from which springs the movement of philosophical thought. The truth is indeed expressed by Plato in figures of speech, but it is unmistakably expressed. What is only sensuous as an object, and uncertain opinion as a method, does not satisfy the rational nature of man. He longs, sometimes with the enthusiasm of the lover for his mistress, for communion with the Ideas,—with the eternal verity and real Being which they are.

The world has grown old since Plato's time, and some would have us believe that the passionate but rational impulse to which he appealed has become obsolete. But the philosophic impulse still exists, as vigorous and effective as ever, for its seat is the rational human soul; and until it fails, philosophy

[1] Theætet., 143 d. [2] Symp., 211 d; Phædr., 246–256.
[3] Rep., vii. 514–521 c; 540 a and b.

will not fail to have its devotees and to fulfil its mission in the evolution of mind. Unlike any of the particular sciences, it is of the very nature of philosophy to exist with man. If there were no shells, there would be no science of conchology; if there were no insects, no entomology; if there were no precious metals, the science of political economy would undergo a great change. But wherever finite reason is, there philosophy as a pursuit and discipline must arise, and run a course of development.

Another factor made prominent by Plato in his inchoate conception may be thus stated: Philosophy is a special and peculiarly certain knowledge of reality. Whatever in each case is the really existent, upon that is the affection of the philosopher set. Whatever is eternal and immutable, this constitutes the object which he strives to grasp and hold. The most hardy Realist of the present age does not venture to re-establish, in their ancient Platonic form, the kingdom of Ideas. And not a few students of the particular sciences would have us believe that to-day, at least, knowledge can flourish and justify itself at the bar of Reason without reference to metaphysical reality. It cannot be denied that these sciences may be successfully pursued without bringing to the front the problems with which philosophy deals. Yet each of the greater divisions of science will always have its own peculiar metaphysical assumptions; and the thought that somehow philosophy includes the search after, and the certification of, a higher and more comprehensive Reality, still furnishes an essential factor in the definition of philosophy. This factor certainly entered into the Platonic conception.

Another noteworthy element in Plato's definition of philosophy is emphasized whenever he brings this discipline into relation with character and with the life of conduct. The wisdom in which it consists is not, indeed, primarily and chiefly a matter of character and conduct. Plato identifies it (*σοφία*) with true and certain knowledge (*ἐπιστήμη*), rather than with disposition or sound judgment in practical affairs (σωφροσύνη).[1] Later we come upon the definition of Cicero, which identifies it with that wisdom which is a knowledge of human and divine affairs.[2] And yet with Plato neither the method nor the conclusions of philosophy can be separated from practical life. For its successful pursuit a right disposition is indispensable; when successfully pursued, it is a chief and only effectual means of cultivating a right disposition. To philosophic insight Plato, especially in all his earlier writings, refers the whole round of human virtues. This close connection between philosophical inquiry and the life of character and conduct remains, in spite of all impressions to the contrary, until the present time. It will always endure; for it belongs to the very nature of philosophy, as issuing from its sources in the soul of man.

The fourth factor in the conception of philosophy, implicitly but insufficiently recognized by Plato, is its dependence upon the particular sciences. Between them and it he does not clearly distinguish; and, indeed, this distinction was not clearly made by any writer until centuries after the time of Plato. But the double sense in which the Greek master and his followers employ the word, recognizes both the fact of a distinction and the fact of the reciprocal dependence of these two forms of knowledge.

With Aristotle philosophy (φιλοσοφία, and sometimes σοφία) was identified with science in general; in its most comprehensive meaning it included things so diverse as mathematics and physics, ethics and politics.[3] The "philosophies," or philosophical sciences, of mathematics, physics, and theology, were called theoretical.[4] But these sciences were, after all, not placed upon precisely the same footing with philosophy proper, in the thought and definitions of this writer. There is a "First

[1] Comp. Lichtenfels, Lehrbuch zur Einleitung in die Philosophie, p. 6 f.

[2] Philosophia est studium sapientiæ; sapientia vero est scientia rerum humanarum atque divinarum.

[3] Metaph., v. 1 1026 a.

[4] Metaph., ibid.; comp. Ethic. Nicomach., i. 4 1096 b 31.

Philosophy" (πρώτη φιλοσοφία), and the knowledge of this is the distinguishing pursuit of the philosopher.[1] This pre-eminently philosophical science is the systematic and critical knowledge of the most general and fundamental principles of Being, — the science of Being, as such (τὸ ὂν ᾗ ὄν), and not of any particular kind or department of existences.[2] In brief, it is what many would now call "metaphysics," or "ontology." In contrast with this, the special sciences are to be considered only partial.

It is obvious that two of the four important factors of the Platonic conception have been made more prominent in the definitions of Aristotle. Philosophy has especially to do with the fundamental principles of all Reality; its object of search is more general than that of any of the particular sciences, not even excepting theology. As compared with any of these sciences, it is universal, first, pre-eminent. It therefore involves some special knowledge of the really true and the really existent. As Paulsen says: "Aristotle indeed thinks he philosophizes when he investigates the natural history of animals, or household economy;" but Aristotle does not consider such investigation as constituting philosophy in the highest and peculiar meaning of the term.

And yet — so the vacillation of the great Greek in his twofold use of the term seems to say — philosophy and the particular sciences are intimately interdependent. Moreover, as to subject-matter they must cover a common ground; for Aristotle admits no real kingdom of an ideal order existing apart from the individual and concrete realities with which the particular sciences deal. Philosophy must also follow scientific method; it must be systematic, comprehensive, and yet kept constantly in touch with concrete realities.

After Aristotle, until comparatively recent times, little or no advance was made in the definition of philosophy. The

[1] Metaph., v. 1, 1026 a 24 and 30 ; iii. 3, 1005 a 21.
[2] Ibid., v. 1, 1026 a 31; comp. x. 3 1060 b 31.

movement of thought was in this regard rather retrograde. The boundary which Plato began to draw when he distinguished the doctrine of the Ideas from other forms of knowledge, and which Aristotle made clearer when he distinguished "first philosophy" from the other philosophies and sciences, was again obscured by the Stoics. By philosophy they understood all forms of theoretical knowledge, together with its relations to conduct and to practical morality. The Epicureans also emphasized this aspect and application of philosophy, to the exclusion of other factors in its conception. With Seneca philosophy is the "love of wisdom" (*sapientiæ amor*), or the "zealous pursuit of virtue" (*studium virtutis*) through virtue itself.[1] Epicurus himself is said to have identified philosophy with "the rational pursuit of happiness."[2] Still later, under the Neo-Platonists, the name became synonymous with the esoteric wisdom of sacred myth and theological poetry. Under early Christianity the monks came to be called philosophers, and the doctrines of the Church a philosophy.

The indefiniteness of the term among the Greeks and their somewhat degenerate successors shows — as says Zeller — that the thing itself had scarcely yet appeared as "a specific form of intellectual life." It must be remembered, however, that this lack of definiteness was chiefly due to a failure to distinguish philosophy from the particular sciences. But the conception of "science" also was never clearly formed in the Greek mind. It was indeed rather foreign to their stage of intellectual development. So true is this, that during all the Greek period the conception of philosophy, as respects comprehensiveness and accuracy, was rather in advance of the conception of science. Aristotle was, indeed, a real founder of logic, psychology, ethics, and æsthetics; but it was only in the Alexandrian period that some of the other particular

[1] Epist., 89, 3 and 7.
[2] Sext. Empir. Adv. Math., xi. 169.

sciences attained to the dignity of an independent cultivation.[1] Previously they had all been included in the vague term philosophy. It was centuries after this period, however, before the conception of science was developed.

It would be of little service to our purpose to trace in detail the history of the term "philosophy" from the post-Aristotelian period down to the time of Kant. The Schoolmen did little more than repeat what had been said by Plato and Aristotle. Descartes and his followers, so far as they make any attempt at definition, do not escape the confusion involved in cultivating, not only psychology, but also physics and biology, under the term "philosophy." The three principal works of Descartes himself are a mixture of considerations which would now be ascribed to the theory of knowledge, to theology, and to physics. Spinoza's works made an influential contribution to the speculative treatment of the highest philosophical themes; but their author does nothing to distinguish philosophy from the particular sciences. The belief, which was fundamental with Leibnitz, compelled him everywhere to unite the theological with the mechanical view of the universe. Philosophy is therefore the result of a speculative union of two corresponding sets of ideas; but its nature and scope are nowhere clearly defined. The school of Leibnitz as a distinct development culminated with the writings of Christian Wolff. This philosopher advocates a conception of philosophy wider, but less definite and satisfactory, than that of Aristotle. It is "such knowledge of those things that are, or happen, as enables us to understand why they are or happen;" or it is "the knowledge of things possible, in as far as they are possible."[2]

By Locke, and most of the writers in England who sprung from the movement he originated, psychology and the theory of knowledge were identified with philosophy. The aim of

[1] See Zeller, Pre-Socratic Philosophy, p. 6.

[2] Philos. Ration., Disc. Prælim., §§ 4, 6, and 29.

his philosophical treatise, "Essay concerning Human Understanding," he defines (i. 1, 2, and 3) as the inquiry "into the original, certainty, and extent of human knowledge, together with the grounds and degrees of belief, opinion, and assent." But in the same treatise Locke also calls physics — that is, "the knowledge of things as they are in their own proper beings, their constitutions, properties, and operations" — by the term "natural philosophy." Elsewhere he pronounces philosophy nothing but the true knowledge of things. The followers of Newton and Bacon emphasized, not only speculative, but experimental, physics as philosophy pre-eminently. The former indeed uttered the warning, "Beware of metaphysics;" but himself made large use of metaphysics, and did much to fix the subsequent vague use of the term philosophy by calling his great work "Philosophiæ Naturalis Principia Mathematica." Hobbes defines philosophy as the knowledge of effects or phenomena by their causes, and of causes from their observed effects, by means of legitimate inferences. Thus is philosophy again identified with the whole round of the sciences. In Hobbes's opinion philosophy has to do only with bodies, natural and political; it therefore comprises only the two divisions corresponding to these terms. Yet a *prima philosophia* is in some sort recognized, which is nothing more than a mixture of definitions of the more fundamental conceptions.

Until the present time the same confusion of philosophy with the particular sciences — even with physics, but especially with psychology — has prevailed among English writers. Only recently has much skilled effort been expended upon the necessary distinctions. In a note to his "Encyclopædia," Hegel remarks upon the use of the word in England in his own time. "Among the advertisements of books just published," says he, "I lately found the following notice in an English newspaper: 'The Art of Preserving the Hair, on Philosophical Principles, neatly printed in post 8vo, price seven shillings.'"[1] Hegel adds the remark,—is it with pure sarcasm, or refreshing *naïveté*?—"By philosophical principles for preserving the hair are probably meant chemical or physiological principles." Surely, "thought, and not a mere combination of wood, iron, etc., ought to be called the instrument of philosophy," says he, in commenting upon the practice of calling physical apparatus by the title "philosophical." But to-day England abounds in books, pamphlets, journals, on special topics in experimental physics, that bear the same inappropriate title,—not to speak of uncouth and newfangled toys.

Nor has this country been free from a confusion of thought scarcely less great than that which has maintained itself in England. If the confusion be in any degree less, it is because the pursuit of both science and philosophy, and the institutions connected therewith, are more recent here. They have therefore derived somewhat more benefit from the recent attempts, especially since the time of Kant in Germany, to distinguish between the two.

The precise limitation of the province of philosophy was undertaken by Kant. In his remarks upon the "Architectonic of Pure Reason" this thinker defines the discipline which was his pursuit in life.[2] All knowledge, considered from the subjective point of view, is either historical or rational: the former sets out from empirical data; the latter from principles (*cognitio ex principiis*). Now, again, of this rational knowledge, one kind is based on concepts; the other is based on the construction of concepts. The former alone is philosophical; the latter is mathematical. Thus does Kant, with two strokes, mark out the domain of philosophy, as distinguished from the empirical sciences on the one hand, and on the other from pure mathematics. The "system of all

[1] Encyclopädie der philosophischen Wissenschaften im Grundrisse, Heidelberg, 1827, p. 11.

[2] Critique of Pure Reason, Müller's Translation, ii. 714 f.

philosophical knowledge" (*i. e.*, knowledge starting from rational principles and based on concepts) is called "philosophy." So far the concept of philosophy is *Scholastic*, — "one of the many crafts intended for many objects."

As related to the ends of reason, moral philosophy, which concerns itself with the whole destination of man, and aims at the perfect systematical unity of reason, stands highest. In its "cosmical" concept, as something that must be of interest to everybody, philosophy is "the science of the relation of all knowledge to the essential aims of human reason."

As regards the objects of philosophy, it may be divided into two branches, — the philosophy of nature, which relates to all *that is;* the philosophy of morals, which relates to all that *ought to be.* As regards its method, it may be either pure or empirical. Pure philosophy is either critical, and "inquires into the faculties of reason with regard to all pure knowledge *a priori;*" or it is metaphysic, and "comprehends in systematical connection the whole of philosophical knowledge." Metaphysic is either speculative use of pure reason (the "metaphysic of nature"); or it is practical (the "metaphysic of morals"), and contains the principles which *a priori* determine and necessitate all *doing* and *not doing.*

It is therefore obvious that Kant distinctly separates philosophy from all the positive sciences, including descriptive psychology, logic, and psychological ethics; and that he identifies it with metaphysics, in the more extended use of the latter term. With Kant, criticism of reason is metaphysical, and metaphysics is but the enumeration and systematic arrangement of the conceptions which have already been sifted out of experience by the process of metaphysical critique. Both his definitions and his practice introduce a new era in the conception of philosophy. This fact, however, is not due simply to his consistent attempt to establish some line of demarcation between philosophy and the particular sciences. It is also due to the prominence he gave to a new factor in the conception, and accordingly to a new division of philosophical discipline. With Kant philosophy becomes pre-eminently man's rational *self*-knowledge.

The new department of philosophy brought into prominence by Kant we may call "Theory of Knowledge" (Noëtics, Epistemology, *Erkenntnisslehre, Wissenschaftslehre*); it is the critical investigation of man's power to reach that which philosophy had, previously — as he thought — uncritically assumed to impart; namely, the certified cognition of reality. With him this critical investigation of reason, both as a process and as a summary of results, constitutes the very essence of philosophy. It is because of their involvement, as it were, in pure reason as Ideals that the great themes of God, Freedom, and Immortality are objects of philosophical investigation, by the critical method, in the Kantian system.

With Kant the present era of philosophy began; and with him was completed the entire round of attempts to survey the domain of philosophy. No other important factors in its conception remain to be introduced. As an object of pursuit it may be said to have attained to a clear self-consciousness. Indeed, the essential factors in the true conception have been, for centuries, at least obscurely indicated. But in the Kantian system they are distinctly recognized and expressed.

The failure of the authorities of the last century to agree in their conception of the nature of philosophy has not, then, been chiefly due to ignorance. It has rather been due to bias from the existing philosophical systems. The philosophical tenets of each writer on philosophy have been too much made a part of his definition of philosophy. The very nature of philosophy — since it is held to be concerned, in some special manner, with ultimate Reality — tends toward this result. But the answer to our inquiry, What *is* philosophy? must not be made dependent upon our tenets concerning what the true philosophical system ought to be.

The temptation to incorporate into one's definition of philosophy one's conclusions as to the nature of the ultimate Reality, and as to the possibility of knowledge of such Reality, will always exist. These conclusions are the tenets on which the different schools of thinkers are divided. It is not strange, therefore, that these schools hold different conceptions as to the nature of philosophy. And yet we cannot think that the previous wide differences with respect to the domain common to all schools need continue to exist. What is required for a true definition is that it shall include all the *permanent historical factors* corresponding to the term "philosophy." In this way alone can we place our conception on objective and abiding grounds.

The definitions of philosophy which have prevailed since the time of Kant may be divided into four classes. Each of these classes is inclined to place its own peculiar and exclusive emphasis upon some one or two, only, of the factors necessary to the complete and true conception.

One principal form of the modern conceptions of philosophy has continued to emphasize the factors rendered most prominent by Plato and Aristotle. This makes the essence of philosophy consist in the special and profound knowledge which it furnishes of the really Existent, of that Being which has reality indeed. Such knowledge may well seem to have a somewhat esoteric character; at any rate, it is pre-eminently rational knowledge. But all the objects of the particular sciences are also regarded — however uncritically — as concrete real existences. If, then, philosophy is to be distinguished from these sciences, the Reality with which it concerns itself must be in some way distinguished from those concrete realities with which the particular sciences are concerned. In Plato's thought, this Reality — alone worthy the name — was regarded as the orderly system of Ideas; in the thought of Aristotle, philosophy was the science of the most fundamental forms of all being, — of Being as such. The corresponding modern conception of philosophy emphasizes especially its metaphysical content; it even identifies philosophy with an ontological metaphysics. Philosophy, from this point of view, may be defined as the systematic knowledge of supersensible reality, or of the supreme Reality.

Under this same general conception of philosophy, several of the great systems and schools alike readily fall. Idealism, Realism, and Dualism, disagree fundamentally in the conclusions they advocate respecting the nature of the Reality which philosophy seeks; but they may agree in defining the sphere of search. Matter, Force, "the Idea," Will, "the Unconscious," the "Absolute Ego," or Personal Absolute, "whom faith calls God," are identified by different systems with the One Reality, supersensible and ultimate, which all alike seek.

In his "Encyclopædia"[1] Hegel, while denying that it is possible "to give in a preliminary way a general conception of philosophy," defines it, with reference to his own system, as the "science of the Idea." Logic, which is Hegel's *prima philosophia*, is the "science of the Absolute Idea." Even in the philosophy of nature (of so-called material reality) nothing else is to be discerned except the "Idea;" and all philosophical discipline is to be conducted on the assumption that this Idea and all real Being is identical. For Reason is the substance of the universe, and the Absolute Idea is the identity of the theoretical and the practical.[2]

Schleiermacher, too, found the true sphere of philosophy in the idea of the highest unity of physical and ethical knowledge, — while demanding a realism that shall consider each finite thing as a manifestation of the eternal, and claiming that speculative thinking is reason's highest objective function. In the mind of this quickening thinker, philosophy is the speculative activity of human reason directed toward the transcendent

[1] Encyclopädie der philosophischen Wissenschaften im Grundrisse, p. 25: Wallace's Translation, The Logic of Hegel, p. 23.

[2] See Philosophy of History (Translation, London, 1884, pp. 9 f.), and Werke, (Berlin, 1841): Logik, zweiter Theil, p. 317.

"Ground" of all existences.[1] So does a modern exponent of his views define philosophy as that fundamental science whose form is pure reflective thinking, but whose content is the totality of being as related to its ultimate "Ground,"—to the Absolute.

With essentially the same view of the nature of philosophy Trendelenburg defines it as the "science of the Idea;" while another writer (Lichtenfels) would start the discussion of its nature with the distinction between the supersensible and the sensuously real, and thus make philosophy the rational knowledge of supersensible Reality. "Philosophy," says Schmid, "is the rational science of reality." What is philosophy? It is, says yet another writer, "the science of the supreme and most important realities."

Schopenhauer and Hartmann also, although differing fundamentally from the authorities just quoted, in respect to their solution of the great problems of philosophy, virtually agree with them in identifying it with ontological metaphysics. The question which the former aims, by his entire system, to answer, may be stated thus: What, besides idea, is the World? Schopenhauer's answer to the question is: The World is also "thing-in-itself," a supersensible and superintelligible reality; and, as such, it is Will. In its positive and constructive part, the entire philosophical system of Hartmann is identical with the "metaphysics of the Unconscious,"—namely, of the ultimate and supreme Reality, which is Will and Idea.

This conception of philosophy, however, is apt to be defective in certain important particulars; and these are the particulars most emphasized by definitions of the other three classes. Especially does it fail to consider sufficiently the important critical work of reason with itself, and the resulting progress of rational self-knowledge. Neither does it, as a rule, sufficiently regard the dependence of philosophy upon the particular sciences.

[1] See his Dialektik; Reden über die Religion; and Vertraute Briefe.

But the antiquity of this conception, which identifies philosophy with some special knowledge of ultimate Reality, and its persistent character before the assaults of criticism and scepticism, furnish a preliminary warrant in its favor. The conclusion derived from an unbiassed estimate of modern views confirms that derived from an historical study of the development of philosophy, beginning with the conception of Plato. As long as man aspires to know, with a rational completeness, what is the ultimate content of human experience, there will be a so-called science of Being. We find here, then, an essential truth as to the unchanging nature of philosophy.

The "Critique of Pure Reason" turned the thought of men to a neglected aspect of the human mind; it resulted, as has been shown, in bringing into prominence a new department of philosophy. With Kant himself this self-criticism of reason was the greater part of philosophical discipline. Metaphysics, he holds, can only exhibit the system of conceptions which the critical process discovers; metaphysics, as a pure ontological science, cannot exist. It is this critical conclusion which is emphasized by the second class of definitions of philosophy. This definition identifies philosophy with the science of rational knowledge itself; it is "science of science," science of notions, or theory of knowledge. It may also be called rational self-knowledge, or science of the ultimate contents of consciousness.

Of Fichte, who is the principal representative of this conception, Professor Adamson has truly said: "Philosophy is to him the re-thinking of actual cognition, the theory of knowledge, the complete systematic exposition of the principles which lie at the basis of all reasoned cognition." "This science," says Fichte himself, "can be nothing but the universal knowledge, which has come to know of itself, and has entered a state of light, consciousness, and independence in regard to itself."[1] It is well known that Herbart also made the distinct func-

[1] New Exposition of the Science of Knowledge. Translation by A. E. Kröger, St. Louis, 1869, p. 7.

tion of philosophy to be the elaboration of concepts (*Bearbeitung der Begriffe*). Following in the same line of definition, we find one author[1] (Riehl) declaring that philosophy began with Locke, and that it is the science and criticism of cognition; another (Biedermann) speaking of the whole system of philosophical discipline as the "science of the notion;" and yet a third describing it as the science which has for its object of examination the function of thinking itself. By all these writers the criticism of the processes and presuppositions of all thinking is made identical with philosophy.

Essentially the same conception of philosophy controls the consideration of philosophical themes in the case of two other suggestive modern writers. "Philosophy calls itself," says Kuno Fischer, "knowledge of the Universe (*Weltweisheit*);" but "we call it self-knowledge." For the world is our object, our presentation; "*We ourselves* are the world."[2] This conception must be modified, however, by introducing the principle of development. For all the concepts with which philosophy deals, and the concept of philosophy itself, are developments. Nay, more, "This process of progressing development *is* the human mind." Philosophy, therefore, is the progressive self-knowledge of the human mind.

It might be expected that intelligent advocates of a similar view would arise in England, where, since the time of Locke, philosophy has been so constantly identified with the theory of knowledge. Mr. Shadworth H. Hodgson, in his "Philosophy of Reflection," takes great pains clearly to distinguish philosophy from psychology; and would also make the former include a theory of Being, or Existence. Philosophy he defines, in "contradistinction to Psychological Science," as "the ultimate analysis of states of consciousness in connection with their objective aspects, abstracting from their conditions in the organism."[3]

[1] Philosophischer Kriticismus, ii. 2, p. 15; comp. ii. 1, pp. 2 f.

[2] History of Modern Philosophy, Introduction, chap. i.

[3] See especially the chapter on "Philosophy and Science," vol. i.

In its analytic branch, therefore, — and with Mr. Hodgson this seems its main branch, — it is an analysis of states of consciousness. Even in its constructive branch it is a "philosophized psychology, or the return of Metaphysic upon psychology."

The factors in philosophy chiefly emphasized by such definitions as the foregoing cannot safely be overlooked. Without recognition of them no fruitful discussion of philosophical problems is possible, much less any attempt at a system of philosophy. But we may not assume in our very definition that the criticism of rational processes, and the synthetic representation of the conceptions discovered thereby, cover the whole domain of speculative thinking.

Yet more comprehensive definitions of philosophy are derived by combining these two sets of factors, and by laying a more nearly equal emphasis upon both. In this way does Zeller, by a study of the history of philosophy, arrive at the following statement: "The problem of philosophy is to investigate scientifically the ultimate grounds of Being and Knowledge, and to comprehend all that is actual in its connection with them."[1] Dr. E. Pfleiderer also, after defining philosophy as "the science of principles," remarks: "And so, one of its chief problems is to investigate and establish the fundamental conditions, presuppositions, and norms of cognition, — of scientific activity in general."[2] The view of Dr. William T. Harris should probably be mentioned in this connection. "Philosophy," says this writer, "attempts to find the necessary *a priori* elements or factors in experience, and arrange them into a system by deducing them from a first principle." Von Hartmann, too, with a *naïve* contradiction of his own practice in the "Metaphysics of the Unconscious," expressly declares: "The theory of knowledge is the true *prima philosophia*."[3]

[1] Grundriss der Geschichte der Griechischen Philosophie, p. 1.
[2] Die Aufgabe der Philosophie in unserer Zeit, p. 8.
[3] Preface to the eighth edition of the Philosophy of the Unconscious.

Fearing—and not without reason—that the conception and practice of philosophy may separate their favorite pursuit too far from the life of conduct, the advocates of a third view would put emphasis upon a thought as old as Plato. This thought has been presented somewhat as follows by a modern writer.[1] Philosophy must indeed be science, as defined by its form and method. Thus defined, it constitutes the only means of raising all our most important opinions, and choicest faiths, to the state of invincible conviction. But if philosophy is to be defined as science, then it must be not as a science of mere thinking, but as a total and comprehensive consciousness, a science of the whole personality and of all that stands in connection with it,—that is, of willing and acting, of disposition and conduct of life. It is, then, a living effort, a striving conscious of itself and of its goal, a determinate form of willing. Philosophy, according to form, is science; and according to its content, is wisdom (*Wissenschaftlicher Weisheitswille*). "It is the self-conscious effort of the human spirit after wisdom, in order to actualize the truth."

It would be unhistorical to doubt that this third conception of philosophy makes prominent an ancient and important truth. It is as old as Plato, and it was taught by Kant. In his "Preface to Jachmann's Examination of the Kantian Philosophy of Religion," Kant himself wrote: "Philosophy as scientific theory may, like every other discipline, serve as an instrument for attaining a variety of excellent ends, but has in this regard only a relative value. But philosophy, in the literal meaning of the word as a doctrine of wisdom (*Weisheitslehre*) has an absolute value; for it is the doctrine of the final purpose of human reason."

By all means let it never be forgotten that the choicest issue of philosophy is not merely a system of speculative thinking, but the production also of conduct and character. We will,

[1] Chalybäus, Fundamentalphilosophie, ein Versuch das System der Philosophie auf ein Realprincip zu gründen, p. 5 f.

moreover, follow Kant in the passage just quoted, and address the man who in himself completely meets this theoretical demand, as "the perfect practical philosopher (an ideal)." But we cannot consent to define the doctrine solely by emphasizing its practical aspect; for such a definition fails to distinguish philosophy, as such, from certain branches of psychology and ethics, and even from that fund of sound maxims and correct moral habits which the so-called "wise man" has gathered from the experience of life.

The fourth form of defining philosophy has arisen from that modern development of the particular sciences to which, in its influence on speculative thinking, reference has already been made. Philosophy, say its advocates, is a comprehensive and systematic view of all the particular sciences; it is not so much science of science, or certified knowledge as such, but — as it were — science of all the sciences.

The dependence of philosophy upon the particular sciences was emphasized by Auguste Comte in such manner as to amount to a denial that it has any domain of its own. The so-called "Positive Philosophy," with a dogmatic scepticism which Kant came forever to condemn, uncritically excludes all metaphysical problems as insoluble. In his "Problems of Life and Mind," Mr. Lewes, after pronouncing this exclusion "somewhat arbitrary and injudicious," pleads the cause of a philosophy which is metaphysics detached from, and not distributed among, the sciences from which its data are drawn. This metaphysics, which is the sum-total of philosophy, he understands to be a "codification of the laws of Cause." "Its object is the disengagement of certain most general principles, such as Cause, Force, Life, Mind, etc., from the sciences which imply these principles, and the exposition of their constituent elements, — the *facts*, sensible and logical, which these principles involve, and the relation of these principles."[1] That philosophical theory of cognition is a necessary correlated

[1] Problems of Life and Mind, * pp. 67 f, 73 f.

branch of inquiry, this writer recognizes — though not very clearly — by giving to metaphysics the title "Objective Logic." In this meaning of the word "philosophy" it may be recognized as "a possible branch of science."

With much firmer grasp and clearer vision does a recent German thinker expound and defend this conception of philosophy as a science of all the positive sciences. Its purpose, says Wundt,[1] is to be found in the attainment of such a summary of the particular cognitions, in our view of the world and of life, as shall satisfy the demands of the intellect and the needs of the heart (*des Gemüthes*). Philosophy is, then, "the universal science which has to unite the cognitions, obtained by the particular sciences, into a consistent system." This is *scientific* philosophy; and its divisions are to be determined by the general scheme of the positive sciences.

A correct conception of philosophy must undoubtedly recognize its dependence for development, as a distinct discipline, upon the particular sciences. For its best growth this noblest child of reason requires not only to be kept in contact with all the forces that sway the popular life of feeling and conduct, but also to be trained in all the schools where certified knowledge of fact and law controls, where method is strictly limited, and where theory is constantly recalled to the test of experience. History amply demonstrates this necessity. The future of philosophy depends upon the intelligent and consistent recognition of the same necessity.

And yet philosophy should not be defined solely by stating its relation of dependence upon the particular sciences. This would involve too wide a departure from the historical point of view. Philosophy was cultivated, and the most essential factors of its right conception recognized, for centuries before its relation to the particular sciences was clearly discerned. The progress of its history shows that important elements in its definition and important developments in its pursuit exist

[1] System der Philosophie, Leipzig, 1889, pp. 2, 21 f.

apart from the considerations which are emphasized by the definitions of Lewes and Wundt.

We make, then, a provisional attempt to gather into a single sentence all the essential truths emphasized in the preceding four classes of conceptions. The relations of philosophy to the practical life, however, can be only indirectly expressed in the definition, through its relations to the sciences of conduct, — to psychology, ethics, and the science of religion. *Philosophy* — we define to be — *the progressive rational system of the principles presupposed and ascertained by the particular sciences, in their relation to ultimate Reality.*

1. Philosophy treats all its material of principles with a view to determine their relation in a Unity of Reality; it seeks to know the nature of this One ultimate Reality, if such reality there be. It is then the science of Being as such.

2. Philosophy is a progressive and rational system of those principles assumed or taken for granted in the particular sciences. It is critical of all the pre-suppositions of each form of positive knowledge. It is itself without pre-suppositions, besides the self-conscious existence of reason as an unfolding life. It is science of Knowledge, as such, — a theory of cognition.

3. Inasmuch as there are sciences which consider the phenomena of ethical, æsthetical, and religious life, of conduct, character, social relations, religious aspiration, worship, etc.; and inasmuch as there are principles presupposed or ascertained by these sciences which apparently stand in a peculiar relation to ultimate Reality, — philosophy involves the effort to actualize the truth of these sciences in wisdom. It "deals with those riddles by which our mind is oppressed in life;" it is practical, and cannot be divorced from disposition, faith, hope, and ethical conviction.

4. But philosophy is in certain aspects strictly dependent, for its legitimate domain and successful cultivation, upon scientific spirit and scientific method; it draws from and deals with the whole round of the positive sciences. It may be

defined with Ueberweg as "the science of the Universe, not according to its details, but according to the principles which condition all particulars;" or as the science of the principles of what is knowable by means of the special sciences.

This definition of philosophy, thus justified by an appeal to the history of the term and to the different classes of current conceptions, will serve to guide our subsequent inquiries.

CHAPTER II.

THE SOURCES OF PHILOSOPHY, AND ITS PROBLEM.

THE answer to the question, Whence comes philosophy? must be framed in accordance with our conception of the nature of philosophy. Now, since philosophy is a progressive and rational system, its fundamental impulses must belong to the life and growth of reason itself; and since it seeks to know both the highest and the most fundamental verities, it must spring from the noblest and most strenuous of rational impulses. It is not sufficient, however, to refer the origin of philosophy in a general way to the reason of man, and to affirm that it is inseparable from the activity and development of reason, — although this is a remark which frequently occurs in the history of human thought.

Plato found the main root of philosophy in *Eros*, a deeply seated and passionate longing of man for communion with the world of eternal realities. At the beginning of his Metaphysics, Aristotle declares that "all men by nature reach after knowledge."[1] In the opening words of his "Convito," Dante translates with approval the declaration of the Greek thinker.[2] This sentence Mr. Shadworth Hodgson[3] echoes by declaring that "the need to philosophize is rooted in our nature as deeply as any other of our needs." Starting from the scientific point of view in the formation of his conception, we have seen how Wundt affirms that a philosophical view of the world is necessary "to satisfy the demands of the intellect and the needs

[1] Πάντες ἄνθρωποι τοῦ εἰδέναι ὀρέγονται φύσει.

[2] Tutti gli uomini naturalmente desiderano di sapere.

[3] Time and Space, p. 14.

of the heart." The purpose of philosophy, says another modern German writer, is the satisfaction of our metaphysical needs, — "the effort, namely, which dwells in all men, but in most unconsciously, after the knowledge of the Being and the Connection of things!"[1] And Lotze, in the Introduction to his "Encyclopædia of Philosophy," warns us against supposing that philosophy is a discipline so peculiar in its nature and methods as to be adapted only to the pursuit of the few. The rather is it nothing else than "the strenuous effort of the human spirit" to find a solution for those riddles about which we are all compelled to hold some view in order to live at all.

But why plead that philosophy is essentially and thoroughly human, and that without its pursuit much of the noblest and most rational part of human nature must be left unsatisfied? Only unworthy ignorance or invincible prejudice will be found ready to deny so obvious a truth. It is not, however, a sufficient answer to the inquiry, Whence does philosophy spring? to refer it in general to the nature of man as a rational being; some more detailed and analytic account of its origin is required. The influence of the more important particular activities in that complex of forms of thinking, feeling, and willing which we are accustomed to call the "human reason" must be traced with some detail. Moreover, it would be a serious mistake to suppose that philosophy lives and grows simply as the result of definite intellectual aims. It has indeed, during modern times, defined more clearly than ever before the problems which it feels the need of pursuing; it has also acknowledged, with more than traditional modesty, its dependence upon the general advance of human knowledge in the form of the particular sciences. And yet if, by speaking of "rational" impulses as furnishing the fundamental and imperishable sources of philosophy, we mean solely to emphasize

[1] Köber, Das philosophische System E. von Hartmann's, p. 1 (in express agreement with Schopenhauer).

the fondness of man, natural or acquired, for speculative thinking, we cherish far too narrow a view of the right answer to this inquiry. By thought man lives, and yet not by thought alone. It is only by recognizing the truth, that the *rational* being penetrates and transforms the entire life, — sensation, motion, perception, instinct, feeling, æsthetical and ethical ideation and emotion, as well as choice, — that we can fully account for the origin of philosophy by referring it to "human reason."

One of the more primary sources of philosophy is that *naïve* or more intelligent wonder with which man stands — as antecedent to philosophical reflection, and yet a principal stimulus of such reflection — before the phenomena of nature. For the average man the phrase "phenomena of nature" signifies an exceedingly narrow domain. The special student of the physical sciences thinks of nature as a realm of entities and forces, to the uniformities of whose relations he is learning to give an ever-increasing accuracy of mathematical expression. To such an one the most pressing need of philosophical treatment for the deeper problems of nature customarily comes only as an indirect result; it arises after the insufficiency of the particular sciences to deal with these problems has become matter of recognized experience.

The case of the untutored man, if he have a mind at all reflective, is favorable for realizing in its most primitive form the energy of this particular impulse toward philosophy. He stands face to face with a little world of natural objects, and of happenings among those objects. For most of these things and events he knows of no so-called "scientific" explanation. The inducement to discover the invariable sequences among the phenomena is not large. He may exist in mingled dependence upon nature and mastery over it, by attributing the direction and flight of his arrow to the structure of his bow and the pull of his arm, his sensations of warmth to the sun or to the fire, the coming of children to the act of procreation, the drift of his canoe to the currents of water and wind.

Beyond these and similar few and simple inductions he feels little need, and makes little use of *science*, however crude and inchoate. But he wonders why things exist and happen as they do; for the very structure of his mind impels him to interest in the beings and events about him, and to inquiry after their causes. Why does his child sicken and die? Why does the lightning strike here rather than there? How does the corn grow in the ground, and the bones of his offspring in the womb of its mother? It is to a metaphysical rather than a scientific answer to these inquiries that his need impels and compels him. He knows nothing of microbes and atoms, of storm-centres and electrical fluids. He does not wait to approach the solution of these problems after having gone through the temple of an inductive physics, physiology, or meteorology. His *naïve* wonder, joined to that necessary and rational impulse to explain which is recognized by philosophy in the so-called universal "principle of sufficient reason," drives him forward upon the road of speculative thinking. He adopts the metaphysical explanation; and all that is left unexplained by his meagre list of uniform physical sequences he perhaps ascribes to some one entity, — spirit like himself, or blind, unreasoning force. And since with him the *causæ occultæ* so vastly outnumber the causes which are known as established uniformities, the sphere of his metaphysics covers far more of his mental life than the sphere of his scientific knowledge. He does not systematize, however.

It was partly in the way just described that, as a matter of history, philosophy had its source in human nature as a crude and primitive cosmological speculation. In modern times — itself a science, in acknowledged dependence upon the culture and attainments of all the particular sciences — it makes use of essentially the same human interest and human activities, though in a different way. The realm of occult causes is not banished, but rather more firmly established, by the physics of to-day. We now know the "why" of many things before unknown; and doubtless physical science will continue its conquests in this domain. And yet by these conquests the realm of occult causes is not even narrowed, but constantly enlarged. Nor can we say that this realm is removed farther from us, whether in time or in space, by the progress of the particular sciences. For occult causes are here and now present in every phenomenon, no matter how fully *explained* it may be said to be by all the results of modern physical discoveries.

The relation of the physical sciences to philosophy is not such, however, as to exclude the latter from the possibility, and even from the right, of considering every natural phenomenon from its own point of view. When the appearance of *naïveté* has departed from the wonder with which man contemplates nature, the strength of the wonder and the philosophical impulse which it imparts are not also necessarily gone.

Explanation, indeed! and yet how much in every case left unexplained! May not the more cultivated man feel all the more strongly the temptation, at every point, to strike into the realm of natural phenomena with a metaphysical faith, or postulate, or reasoned theory, which shall hold out the attractive promise of showing to him the more interior mechanism, or the real meaning, of this realm?

But it is with the individual in his development as it has been with the history of the race. The reflections in which philosophy chiefly consists do not concern the origin, nature, and destiny of things. It is in the consciousness of self, rather than in objective consciousness, — or rather, it is in the reflective consciousness which converts the inner stream of life into an object, — that the more vigorous sources of philosophy are to be found. Whence do I come, and whence come the living men who surround me? For I cannot avoid believing them to be the possessors, with myself, of those intellectual and emotional interests and aptitudes which make man the so-called rational one among the animals. Whither, too, are we in common going? And what in reality is this being I call myself, — its connection with reality in general, its significance, and its value?

When such inquiries as the foregoing are once raised by man's mind, he stands face to face — at first with a simplicity of wonder akin to that which possesses the untutored mind when it looks upon the realm of external nature — with a world of another kind. To the impulse from wonder, joined with reason's unceasing demand for more complete explanation, is now added the unsurpassed interest which man takes in his own conscious life. Even uninstructed observation serves to unite under the principle of uniformity the rise of the body of the individual — its racial, family, and individual characteristics — with his progenitors. This body comes from the parents by a process which is natural, and which affords a visible explanation of its own appearance in the world of things. But whence comes the conscious life, the subject to which the changing states are referred, the one I call myself? When, at a certain stage in the mental evolution of the individual and of the race, this question is first intelligently propounded, an added impulse is given to philosophical inquiry. This question, at a certain stage in all unchecked development, is sure to be propounded. It at once gathers to itself all the interest which the Ego feels in whatever concerns its own life.

Ordinary observation also furnishes every man with material for the induction that he, like the others of his kind around him, is going to die. This is a mystery which, on first reflection, seems to the mind to involve in itself the contradiction of being and not-being at the same time. Others who have already died are not sensibly existent — to me, to their friends or to their enemies, until the end of time. And yet I cannot picture to myself the dying of myself, if by this be meant the cessation at once and forever of all my conscious life. Doubtless my body will continue, visibly and tangibly, to be, for a time (as have the bodies of other dead persons), after the mystery of death has come to me. Some sort of separation is then possible, at least in imagination, between this body and what I am entitled to call "myself." The question of destiny thus becomes for the primitive man, in its natural and most interesting form, the inquiry: Whither do we *go* at death?

To the questioning of the human spirit concerning its own origin and destiny, certain of the particular sciences attempt to furnish an answer. Histology, embryology, and physiology approach the question of origin, and deal with it more or less successfully, on the physical side of the twofold being of man. Biology strives to reduce to terms of a general mechanical theory the phenomena of life,—such as those of metabolism, propagation by fissure, and the "amœboid" movements of bioplasm. This general theory it attempts to apply to the body of man. Embryology traces the evolution of the human offspring from the impregnated egg until its outfit of organs is complete; it tells the marvellous story how by segmentation and proliferation of cells, by deposit and differentiation of layers of cells,—*epiblast*, *mesoblast*, and *hypoblast*,—and by progressive changes of these layers, under mechanical and vital conditions, the new-born infant has come to be. That is, it aims to give the complete description of the history of the "becoming" of the individual body. Physiology then essays to finish the work of explanation. To accomplish this, it employs the aid of histology and general molecular physics and chemistry.

Thus does modern physical science attempt to push its researches toward the ultimate secrets that concern the genesis of human life.

The childlike theological views of the ancient Hebrews, in common with those of all the great Oriental nations, connected the divine interest and agency in some special way with the origin of human life. In their thought, God was pre-eminently the author and disposer of all life; he was the giver of the new life of every new-born child. To this feeling, that the genesis and growth of man are not wholly explained by appeal to visible acts and processes, the heart of the untutored man everywhere responds. Nor do the utmost efforts of the modern sciences succeed in removing this impression; with its thoughtful student, life, over and above and underneath all scientific explanations, calls attention to the presence of the Unexplained. This presence is brought so near to all our interests, and it seems, by the complexity and apparent freedom of the phenomena, so to baffle the utmost conceivable extension of scientific methods, that the bare recognition of it becomes a strong stimulus toward philosophical research. Indeed, modern biology is one of the most important handmaids of modern philosophy.

What is true of the genesis of man's bodily life is more obviously true of his mental being and development. Whoever has attained a certain stage of psychological development, infallibly distinguishes — whether scientifically or unjustifiably, whether for his intellectual weal or woe — between himself and his body. No scientific explanation which applies merely to the genesis of the body will then satisfy the inquiry: Whence do *I* come? Doubtless with most men in the earlier stages of the mental evolution of the race, and with every man in the earlier stages of his individual evolution, the two questions are not clearly distinguished. But they certainly come to be distinguished whenever a certain stage is reached in the development of both race and individual. Biology, psychophysics, and psychology therefore essay to treat scientifically the genesis of consciousness and of self-conscious rational life.

It is not easy for the ordinary man, even after he has somewhat clearly conceived the inquiry into the origin of consciousness and of the higher rational activities, to understand what is meant by ascribing it to *physical* processes. And indeed the expert student of biology and physiological psychology is little better off. How does consciousness come to be, as the result of physical processes? How does human reason arise — with its discourse about "metempirical" entities and "transcendental" causes, about freedom, ideal beauty, immortal life, the "ought" with its categorical imperative, and the grand ideal Reality called God — as the result of similar processes?

From the strong impulse to inquire into the origin of self-conscious and rational life, and from the powerlessness of the particular sciences to answer the inquiry, philosophy receives much assistance. It becomes the refuge of disappointed and eager questioners. It may fail, in its turn, to satisfy the difficult conditions required of the answer to any of this questioning, but in the questioning itself resides one of the principal sources of its own life.

At a certain stage in the development of the individual and of the race, inquiry arises — and with how great interest to the reflective soul! — as to the destiny of the life of self-consciousness. Obviously, with death the more tangible and visible evidence of the body is at an end. So intimately associated is this bodily life with the entire conception of existence, and even with the possibility of existence, that the more primitive reflections of man indissolubly connect the two. But the appropriate physical sciences show beyond question that death terminates that organic and vital union of the physical elements on which the bodily life depends. Death, says science, ends the body, by returning its constituent material, from the highly complex forms of elaboration it had attained to lower and more stable combinations. But does death end all? Is it the destiny of that self-conscious and rational subject, a conception of which the man has succeeded in detaching from the flowing stream of sensations and perceptions, — is it the destiny of the *Ego* also to cease to be? To form a positive conception of the total cessation of the life of conscious feeling and thought is plainly impossible. This impotency — if one please so to call it — acts, not as a rational argument, but as a blind impulse, so as to favor the belief in a continued existence for the soul. But the same positive sciences which aim to explain the genesis of mind and the cessation as well as the genesis of the body, also aim to treat the question of its mortality. They thus speedily come, not only upon many unsolved psycho-physical problems, but also upon certain considerations derived from departments of human knowledge and human feeling with which they are not fitted to deal. Their lack of success reinforces the impulse to philosophical reflection which is derived from man's natural interest in the destiny of the life of self-conscious feeling and thought.

For the question of the so-called "natural" immortality of the mind is not primarily a question for theology, nor is it chiefly a question for physical science. It is primarily and chiefly a psychological and philosophical inquiry. For it is psychology, descriptive and theoretical, which inquires into the *nature* of mind; and it is philosophy which attempts to discern the more ultimate relations in which Mind stands to Matter, Time, Space, and that ultimate Reality which philosophy knows as the Absolute, but which religious faith receives as the Heavenly Father, God. The interest which every self-conscious reason takes in its own continued existence gives reflective earnestness to the question: Whither am I going? It thus lends impulse to philosophical inquiry; it is a source of that product of reflection which is called philosophy.

More maturity of reflective analysis is implied in the inquiry, *What* am I? than in the inquiries, Whence do I come? and Whither am I going? The problem of the metaphysical nature of mind arises late in the history of mental evolution. Yet when once raised, this later inquiry proves itself even more provokingly difficult and baffling, though scarcely less interesting as viewed from both the theoretical and the practical points of view.

Simply to be conscious and sentient, this seems to most men a sufficiently accurate statement in answer to all inquiry after the real nature of the mind. And, indeed, the most thoroughly reflective and consistent thinking has difficulty in saying much more. The intelligent child, or the adult of untutored but thoughtful mind, first makes answer to the question, What am I? by a psychical or physical gesture directed toward certain of the more obvious bodily parts. The precise meaning of this demonstration is not, I am my heart, my head, or the viscera I call mine; much less is it that any of these organs or all of them combined constitutes the whole of what I call "*myself*." The gesture means rather, by indicating some of the more prominent forms of localized sensibility, to insist upon the primary but indescribable actuality of the life of conscious feeling and thought. To the question, What are you? the strong inclination of the earlier stages of the development of reflective consciousness is to respond, *Here* am I. But the presence of the Ego with itself is never undifferentiated or abstract; it is always a definite and concrete presence in some particular form of sentient life. The *sentio* or *cogito, ergo sum,* is not simply equivalent to *sentiens* or *cogitans sum;* it is rather equivalent to the declaration of an existing complex of feeling and ideation, in which the more persistent and prominent factors are localized bodily sensibility.

It is true that, by the process of the mind's unfolding, there comes to exist, in the case of the more reflective members of the race, a conception of the "self" that is highly abstract and separated from all the more obvious references to bodily activities. The formation of this conception is helped forward by reflection upon the problems of the origin and destiny of man. If a scientific description of the physical processes in which the body begins and ceases to be, is not a satisfactory answer to the question, Whence do I come? and Whither do I go? it would also seem that a satisfactory answer to the inquiry, What, in real essence, am I? cannot consist of a simple appeal to localized bodily sensibility.

There are other more obvious reasons, however, why the reflecting mind of the adult is not satisfied with the child's answer to the inquiry, What am I? The progress of experience, through abstracting and relating thought, eliminates one by one from the conception of the "self" the factors of the general conception of the body. Two conceptions come, therefore, to be formed, — distinct, and yet in their genesis and growth curiously interrelated. My body is *mine*, and not *myself*. I am; and I have a body. But then, what *am* I that have, but am not, my body? To this question the more cultivated stage of reflection, when unaided by philosophy, makes direct and uncritical answer in the form of a conception of the soul or spiritual principle. The conception itself is of course only a complex mental product, having its ground in memory-images of past concrete experiences. The answer amounts, then, simply to saying, I am — what I remember myself and others of my kind to have thought, felt, and done. But this answer seems plainly inadequate to the now aroused and inquiring mind.

The sciences of biology, psycho-physics, and psychology proffer their assistance in completing the answer to the inquiry after the essential nature of man. The first of these sciences describes the particular form of life which man possesses in its relation to its environment and to other living forms. But this description fails to satisfy wholly the self-conscious rational soul when it inquires after the essence of its own life. Psycho-physics further explains man as the fortunate owner of an incomparably superior central nervous organism, and as stimulated, conditioned, and compelled to the forth-putting of sentient life by the action of physical forces within and upon this organism. And then psychology — descriptive, non-metaphysical, and "without a soul" — essays a similar task. It gives, with all the details made possible by introspection and modern experimental methods, the history of the formation of the conception of "self." It regards this very conception as the result of a process of evolution. The conception is, therefore, in its very nature subject to change, different for different individuals and for different epochs in the development of the race, —

different also for the same individual under different circumstances and at different times.

The effort of descriptive psychology to discover some fixed kernel of reality, as it were, in the midst of this shifting complex of images so loosely united under the common term "myself," seems to meet with an insufficient reward. And this excites small surprise in one who admits the truth of considerations which Herbart[1] has especially emphasized. *I am myself*, is the sole answer which, it would seem, can be given by psychology, thus pursued, to the inquiry, Who, or what, am I? For all perception in time is a process; hence, by "perception in time I can never find myself at all, as the one who I really am." And all my effort is but a waltzing about in a circle, where the Ego representing itself and the Ego represented by itself form a mysterious couple, — a one that dissolves itself into two, that unite themselves again into one. I am, then, a process; and all my conceptions of selfhood, personal identity, reality of being, are shifting moments and elements of the process.

But this answer of scientific psychology is least of all satisfactory to the inquiry of self-conscious rational man. For man is a metaphysical being. He postulates and confides in reality, although he may not find himself able to comprehend reality, or even to explain the genesis and significance of his own postulate and belief. And if there be reality anywhere, how could it fail to be embraced in man's own self-conscious rational life? How, otherwise, should he even postulate and believe in reality? Thus is the mind of man driven by the impulse of its primitive or more mature inquiry after the nature of what he calls his "soul," his ego, his "self," to the pursuit of philosophy. In the form of rational psychology, or the metaphysics of mind, philosophy at least promises a further and more searching criticism of these important conceptions.

The considerations just mentioned have brought us near to

[1] Psychologie, Königsberg, 1824, i. 85 f.

the border-line of more distinctively ethical, æsthetical, and religious feelings and thoughts. "What called forth Greek philosophy," says Zeller, "was originally not so much the desire for knowledge as the feeling of dependence upon higher powers and the wish to secure their favor." [1] Not among the Greeks alone, but also among all primitive peoples, the impulses to religious faith, doctrine, and worship have been also sources from which philosophy has sprung. And not only so; for many of those more obscure forms of feeling and ideation that lie at the base of the beliefs and practical life of morals, art, and religion are important impulses toward philosophical reflection as well.

There naturally arise, even in the experience of the most unreflecting, certain vague and indefinite feelings which impel toward the search for the Invisible and toward an effort for the establishment of right relations toward the Invisible. Fears of injury to the person, to the dwelling, or to the relatives of the primitive man stir an obscure consciousness of the presence of some power that can make for his weal or woe, but cannot be guarded against by sensible barriers or weapons, or by the precautions which suffice for dealing with the objects of ordinary sensible experience. Out of this feeling of fearful dependence or of awe springs one of the roots of religious faith and life. The same feeling is also a root for the growth of philosophy as well. As knowledge of the sources of danger and of the means for guarding against them increases, the reasons for fear and awe are not removed from the heart of man. The realm of the dreadful that is also the mysterious is scarcely diminished at all by the development of our experience of those things that are visible, tangible, and calculable. Here, then, is an unceasing intimation of the presence of a mysterious unknown Cause of disaster or of success with which man is interested to come to a reckoning. He worships in propitiation of

[1] Grundriss der Geschichte der Griechischen Philosophie, § 2. (Translation: Outlines of the History of Greek Philosophy, New York, 1886.)

it, and speculates as to what it is, and as to what are the relations to it in which it will be possible and best for him to stand. Not alone among the sensitive ancient Greeks and among other primitive peoples in less degree, but also in the case of the most cultivated modern nations, philosophy springs, with religion, from this common root.

There are other higher and more distinctively ethical forms of feeling and ideation which give rise both to philosophy and to religion. These fruits of the ethical being of man were produced long before even the blossoms were put forth which may some day develop into a science of ethics. Such a science on the sociological side and as studied under the guidance of the idea of evolution, has now only just begun to collect its "data;" it will doubtless be some time before it will be a science in anything more than name. As studied from the individual and introspective points of view, ethics is not an independent science at all; it is only a branch, or rather an aspect, of psychology. But the existence of attempts at a moral philosophy is as old as the beginnings of reflective thought; and at its beginnings this existence has its sources in common with those of religion.

Among the more important of those forms of ethical life in which philosophy finds an originating impulse, are the idea of "the ought" and the feeling of moral obligation. Something of that unconditional and absolute character which Kant claimed for this idea doubtless belongs to it in the mind of men in all times and stages of their evolution. *What I ought,* I may learn by consultation of my parents, my companions, my ecclesiastical, social, or political connections; or from my own impressions and judgments relative to my position, opportunities, etc. But that *I ought at all,* — this is a unique fact of the mind's life which seems to demand another kind of explanation.

The idea of the Ought, and its correlated feeling of obligation, doubtless impel men, both uncritically to believe in and intelligently to search for, a "ground" in reality on which the idea and the feeling may rest. The belief is in itself a source of religion. The belief and the rational search for its more clear and objective determination give rise to moral philosophy.

Now, it is conceivable — at least, we will for the present assume it to be conceivable —that evolutionary ethics will some time dispel the almost universal confidence of mankind that a "ground" exists in the ultimate Reality for distinctively ethical feelings and ideas. But such a result, if it could be placed on scientific grounds, would be difficult to reconcile with the rational interpretation of certain historical facts. Men have turned, in faith or fear, toward gods many and toward one God under influence from the feeling of moral obligation. Under the same influence have they been impelled to inquire into the nature of that absolute Being to which the feeling in themselves corresponds; and also into the relations in reality, sustained by themselves and others, toward this Being. Is the ultimate Reality ethical or non-ethical in its essence? Is the obligation, which appears in human consciousness as a restless feeling or vague perception of a bond between man and the Absolute, sure to be exacted in the realm of reality? If so, what is its guarantee; and what, in case of payment or failure, is its outcome in invisible spaces and far distant times? There can be no doubt that men have been driven to reflective thinking and to its issue in philosophy by a strong and imperishable interest in questions such as these.

The statement just made is in some sort true, not only of the worshipper of the fetich who aims by physical propitiation to forestall his dues with the unseen Reality, but also of the modern writer of polished essay who courteously acknowledges the existence of a "Power not ourselves which makes for righteousness." No theist could undertake to show with more ardor and elaboration than does Schopenhauer that the "Ground" of all reality is to be regarded as the philosophical account of the life of human character and human conduct. With him it is Will as "thing-in-itself," — timeless, unconscious, unknown, except that it is *will*, — which is the alone free, eternal in justice and benevolence. And has not Mr. Spencer himself spoken of ethical and religious beliefs and institutions as "modes of manifestation of the Unknowable;" and has he not appealed, in justification of his own belief, to the Unknown Cause who produced the belief in him, and thereby "authorized him to profess and act out that belief"?

It is for reasons such as these that "moral philosophy," or the metaphysical treatment of the grounds and nature of duty and obligation, is far older in history and more deeply rooted in rational impulses than is any empirical science of ethics so called. This statement may not be to the taste of the modern student of ethical phenomena from the evolutionist's point of view. But the facts on which one may rely for making the statement are no unimportant part of the phenomena. They show at least the truth of our reference to the ethical being of man as a principal source of philosophy.

There exist also certain distinctively æsthetical feelings and obscure forms of ideation in which philosophy has its source. To whatever seems beautiful in perception or imagination, — to the graceful, the harmonious, the sublime, — the heart of man responds with emotions and thoughts which, when developed in their finer and more cultured forms, are not improperly held to be activities of "reason" itself. The object of this feeling for the beautiful is considered to have an unconditioned value. The thoughts prompted by intuition of the beautiful object lead to a postulated ground for themselves and for the emotions in some ultimate and supreme Reality. With such activities of human nature both art and religion are concerned; both look to such activities for an explanation of their own origin and significance. Art and religion, though far from being the same, have many common roots struck down deep into the feeling and ideating of man. They both customarily assume the existence, *extra*-mentally, of that which is surpassingly beautiful and sublime. In the unreflecting forms of union which they have oftentimes agreed to assume in history, they have not always by any means served the interests of a purer morality, but they have borne witness to a certain real affinity of origin. This is true alike of the debased worship of beauty in connection with heathen temples and of the "beauty of holiness" that, as a controlling idea, moulded the temple of Jehovah. And when our modern art, under the name of "realism," in painting, sculpture, prose or poetic romantic literature, disregards or offends the power of ethical ideals with the claim to a peculiar relationship with divinity, its action is the more mischievous because its claim has at its basis so much of undoubted truth. Indeed, the invincible persuasion of man that whatever is most grand and beautiful in his own ideal world must be existent in the world of Reality, is one of the strongest supports of religion. It is the very essence and life of several of the strongest "arguments," so called, for the being of God.

But the attempt of reflection to justify by thought the feelings and obscure forms of mental representation to which reference has just been made, constitutes also a source of philosophy. That the Being, out of whose nature and action all physical phenomena and all experience of mind are to be derived, is grand and sublime, seems to follow upon the most primitive consideration almost as a matter of course. The theory of "the beautiful," as a definite and carefully cultivated form of philosophical discipline, has no doubt had a far less notable place in history than the theory of "the ought." "The Good" of the Platonic philosophy was, however, æsthetically as well as ethically good. And all along the course of the development of speculative thought certain considerations, appertaining more fitly either to æsthetics alone or to ethics alone, have been treated without distinction of the field in which they belonged. This treatment has resulted in confusion. But the fact of its existence enforces the claim that the æsthetical being of man must be recognized as a principal source of philosophy.

We should gain little for our present purpose by tracing the sources and development of particular eras, schools, or national types of philosophy. This work belongs rather to the writer on the history of philosophy, or on the philosophy of history. The philosophical position and growth of any age or people is an exceedingly complex result. The account of it includes a multitude of particular influences. The physical and commercial conditions of any people, its educational and especially its political and religious status, act strongly upon the rise and cultivation of philosophy. In every age and among all peoples, the prevalent views on philosophical subjects are also to be regarded in their connection with the preceding and surrounding stream of reflective rational life. Especially is it true of modern times and nations that the sources of any particular development of philosophy cannot be successfully considered as existing apart from the general current of the world's thought. In regard of them, Kuno Fischer's conception of philosophy is emphatically true, — it is the progressive self-knowledge of the human mind; an evolution of the self-conscious reason of the race. In each case, too, — no matter how close the connection with other eras and peoples may appear to be, — if there is a fresh uprising of mind and a marked development of speculative thought, an unexplained residuum of causes, as it were, will be left to be assigned to the genius of great individuals, or of the time, or of the people at large (the *Zeitgeist*).

Doubtless, too, the action of those permanent and universal sources of all philosophy in reason itself, the more precise nature of which we have been trying to determine, is different in different cases and at different epochs in the evolution of the race. Some individual thinkers and some communities of reflective minds — schools or epochs or national types — resort to philosophy chiefly from the ethical or religious interest; others from the more purely intellectual, in the determination to attain a scientific system for their views of nature, mind, conduct, life, and all Reality. To say this, is essentially the same thing as to say that the various main sources of philosophical discipline are not always operative with the same absolute or relative strength of impulse. That these sources always exist and operate as the main sources, and that the foregoing analysis of them is correct, the progress of the discussion will show. Indeed, the true and complete division of the departments of philosophical discipline follows directly from the analysis of its sources.

A writer of some fifteen years ago[1] declared that, for us and for the epochs preceding ours, "philosophy is no longer a pre-eminently Quietistic mode of contemplating the universe, but is rather an essentially restless and active principle for the many-sided shaping of life." Philosophy is then the development of the highest form of the consciousness of the world and of life. Doing and thinking, willing and knowing, active transformation and passive mirroring of the world, are the two sides of this consciousness. This view of philosophy contains important truth; it is truth, however, which is recognizable, not only in the modern epoch, but also in all epochs of the development of rational life. For the essential nature of philosophy as a precise form of rational activity is unalterably determined by the nature of its sources in the rational being of man.

As long, however, as the pursuit of philosophy is ascribed simply to the undisciplined action of certain constitutional impulses, its highest and most truly scientific development is not secured or explained. The modern conception of philosophy aims to make it more amenable than it has hitherto been to scientific tests and to the scientific method. This form of rational life may difference itself from the particular sciences if it can; but it may not advance its speculations or alleged intuitional truths and postulates in disregard of these sciences. It may go forth undismayed into the realm of the unknown, even beyond those unseen and intangible entities called atoms and energies, with which physical science underlays the world of

[1] Dühring, Cursus der Philosophie als streng wissenschaftlicher Weltanschauung und Lebensgestaltung, p. 1 f.

phenomena; it may go into the most profound depths and most transcendent heights of speculation; but it must not lose its vital touch with the concrete and verifiable facts and realities that secure soberness and certainty to physical science. Its walk may be with the Infinite and the Absolute, but the solid ground of admitted experience must be beneath its feet. It must show its humility not only before God, but also before the students of the positive forms of human knowledge.

The justice of such demands is, with us, not simply a confession, it is rather an indubitable inference from the very nature of philosophy; for however we may be inclined to make distinctions between science and philosophy, we cannot forget that both are the outcome of the same human nature placed in the same environment. The need of explanation — the need to know, not only for the sake of knowing itself, but also for the sake of satisfying the demands of the heart and of basing the conduct of the individual and of society in verifiable principles — gives rise to both. And if philosophy is to make good its claim to a domain of its own, and to freedom of control within that domain, it must acknowledge in a more than merely theoretical way its dependence upon the positive sciences. But it must also prove its power to furnish reasonable grounds for the hope of a fuller satisfaction of this need than can be afforded by these sciences.

The inquiry, What is the Problem of Philosophy? admits of various answers, dependent upon somewhat different views taken of the nature, sources, and method of philosophy. Looked at in the light of the two most prominent factors in the customary conception of philosophy, it may be said that its problem is to discover and establish a true metaphysics, in its two branches of ontology and theory of knowledge. To avoid the odium attached to the word "metaphysics," we may state essentially the same problem in a number of different ways. Thus we have seen that Zeller declares that the function of the philosopher is not simply to investigate the ultimate grounds of Knowledge and

Being, but also to comprehend all that is actual in its connection with them. And after Brodbeck, following Schleiermacher, has shown that philosophy, as pure thinking, seeks the perfect agreement of thought with the whole domain of being, in so far as being is knowable, he hastens to explain: its problem is to make the *organism of thinking* a true representative of the *organism of the world*.

Both the foregoing definitions of the problem of philosophy contain the postulate of some unity of real being and life extending through the world of nature and of mind. And, indeed, without such a postulate no worthy and comprehensive conception of this problem can be framed, no significant attempt at its solution can be made. It is, of course, the business of philosophy to clarify and defend this postulate; but without the postulate, I repeat, even the conception of the problem of philosophy cannot be formed. This position must be maintained in opposition to those who would restrict philosophy to a theory of knowledge, and so make its sole problem the establishment of such a theory in satisfactory philosophical form.

Those who desire to emphasize the practical benefits of philosophy would define its problem as pre-eminently the attainment of true wisdom, the actualizing of truth in life. This very definition (if we may call so loose and indefinite a statement a "definition") leads us, however, though by a more indirect path, to the same postulate. For by this definition the ideal side of philosophy, as it were, and the departments of Ethics, Æsthetics, and Philosophy of Religion are brought into especial prominence. But it is the philosophy of the ideal, in these three departments belonging to it, which most peremptorily demands the postulate of a unity of life and reality as the "Ground" of the whole world. If philosophy do not furnish a critical examination and defence of this postulate, if it do not even consider how the basis of human ideals of duty, of beauty, and of supreme rational and self-conscious life is possibly or certainly to be laid in a unity of real being, it misses entirely its own peculiar problem. The practical life of conduct, of art, and of religious faith may exist without such critical examination, but not the cultivation of ethical and æsthetical philosophy, or of the philosophy of religion.

Nor is it necessary for philosophy to define its problem as purely or chiefly practical, in order that it may have the most salutary and effective influence upon the life of conduct. Like all science, it seeks primarily the truth for the truth's sake. Its spirit is far enough removed, however, from that idolatrous worship of concrete facts and exact formulas which does not shrink from ruthlessly sacrificing to them, as to gods, all the finer and choicer ethical, æsthetical, and religious feelings of the sensitive soul. This is not simply because philosophy is always bound to remember that these feelings are themselves *facts*, and that they are no less certainly facts, and no less potent in influence and worthy of rational regard, although they do not admit of easy reduction to the terms of the mathematical and physical sciences. It is rather because the very essence of philosophical reflection on ethical, æsthetical, and religious phenomena consists in regard for the *ideals* of duty and of beauty, and for that Ideal-Real which religion calls God. Through this process of reflection philosophy becomes more fully and profoundly conscious of the effort to apply and verify its postulate of a unity in reality for the world of nature and of mind,—a unity higher than any of the positive sciences are competent to describe.

That conception of the nature of philosophy which regards it as a "possible branch of positive science," or even as a universal science, readily defines the problem of philosophy from the point of view of its relation to the particular sciences. The task which Mr. Lewes sets for himself he defines as "the transformation of metaphysics by reduction to the method of science."[1] The problem of philosophy—that is, of metaphysics thus reduced to a science—is, then, to discard all metaphysical

[1] Problems of Life and Mind, vol. * part i.

elements, and thereupon to handle certain scientific conceptions with which it is inconvenient for any of the positive sciences to deal. But according to Wundt's much profounder view, its problem is "to unite the general cognitions obtained by the particular sciences into a consistent system." But in this view also we find necessarily involved the postulate of a possible *system*, "consistent" and able to serve as a basis of union, a ground of unity, for the particular sciences.

Moreover, unless we enter upon the study of philosophy with the dogmatic rejection of that assumption which, in uncritical form at least, is made by all the sciences, we must regard this consistent system of the general cognitions obtained by them as having its possible "Ground" in some really existent Unity. It belongs, to be sure, to philosophy, as critical of all assumptions and as interested in a wholly rational theory of knowledge, to examine thoroughly this assumption. Philosophical criticism may greatly change the crude form in which the presupposition is held by the particular sciences. But in the very examination it is accompanied by the presence and constantly feels the power of this same postulated Unity of all Reality. Reason at the bar of reason is the same reason which sits as judge. Whatever theory of cognition the philosopher may accept, — and in this regard it is of the very nature of scientific and critical philosophy to claim the freedom of reason, — he cannot understand his main problem, or even state it, without use of the postulate. To say this is the same thing as to say that, while the particular sciences may possibly disregard all inquiry as to the ultimate basis on which they individually rest, and on which reposes the connection existing between them, philosophy cannot so do. On the contrary, it is along this fundamental level that its peculiar inquiries lie. Its one great problem concerns the existence and nature of this fundamental principle.

We may then affirm in a general way that the problem of philosophy is to discover and comprehend a certain kind of unity. This unity involves some connection in reality of the principles of all being and the principles of all knowledge; for philosophy deals with both. It is not merely a critical or positive ontology, nor is it merely a critical or dogmatic theory of knowledge. This unity must also serve as a rational basis for the principles of ethics, æsthetics, and religion. Philosophy seeks a unity, not only for the realities of thought, but also for the ideals of moral conduct, art, and the religious life. It further aims to bring the general principles of being and of rational knowledge into connection and harmony with these ethical and æsthetical ideals. That is, philosophy strives to find for all these principles a unity of being and life, an ideal Real, a realized Idea. In other words, philosophy implies the search, in rational confidence and hope, after some sort of a unity, in which all real processes may have, as it were, an ideal side, a side of sentient, æsthetical, and ethical life, and in which the fundamental forms, not only of rational cognition, but also of æsthetical and ethical ideals, may have existence in reality.

There is, however, no such thing possible as an immediate knowledge of either the real or the ideal independently of those concrete acts and objects of particular knowledge with which the positive sciences deal. Each of these sciences implies the existence and activity of human reason, upon the basis of its fundamental postulates and according to its most general laws. But each of them also involves the gathering and sifting of definite material of experience; each of them, therefore, takes for granted the general postulate that they are all dealing with reality, and proceeds to tell how particular forms of reality actually behave. The sciences of ethics, æsthetics, and religion describe further how certain great ideals — as of duty, beauty, and God — are formed within the mind of the individual and of the race. When further reflection is given to the results of these various branches of positive science, both physical and psychological, it is found that their most mature and well-verified conclusions serve to suggest still other problems, which are unsolved and which lie beyond the power of any form of science to offer for them a solution. These problems become the problem of philosophy. They must be pursued in dependence upon the positive sciences for the forms, as ascertained principles or general presuppositions of these sciences, in which they are, as it were, handed over to philosophy. As parts of the philosophical problem, however, they can neither be solved by the sciences, nor can they be solved by philosophical reflection in disregard of or opposition to the sciences. They must be considered and solved, if at all, in such manner as to tend toward the formation of the sum-total of knowledge by reflection into a harmonious system. The problems thus become parts of one problem, — the problem of philosophy.

At this point we discover again the presence of the great postulate to which reference has already repeatedly been made. There is ultimate and fundamental unity of being to be assumed as the only conceivable or possible ground for a harmonious and consistent rational system of the positive sciences. From this point of view, then, we may say that to convert assumption into a rational conviction, to explore the nature of such ultimate being and its relations to the thoughts and ideals of reason, and so to discern and apprehend the true unity of all the sciences, is the problem of philosophy.

CHAPTER III.

RELATION OF PHILOSOPHY TO THE PARTICULAR SCIENCES.

NOTHING is in these days more important for the true conception and successful pursuit of philosophy than to determine precisely its relation to the particular sciences. The entire history of speculative thinking enforces this truth. History reveals the suffering of philosophy from its failures, in the ancient and mediæval eras, to distinguish itself from the more positive forms of human knowledge. It reveals also the great influence which modern scientific methods have already exercised, and it prophesies the yet greater influence which they are destined to exercise in the future, for the correction and improvement of philosophy. Even a measure of the strong contempt prevalent among devotees of physical science for so-called metaphysics has been a real service to the same cause.

It is no longer possible to cultivate philosophy in virtual disregard of the conclusions reached by observers in the different classes of physical and psychological phenomena. The new physics and the new psychology both demand a hearing at the court which claims to have supreme and final appellate jurisdiction. But who is sufficient to sit as judge in that court? Certainly not the man who has been educated amidst invincible ignorance of both the new physics and the new psychology.

Yet further: the expert students of the particular sciences cannot avoid the enterprise of passing judgment upon the problems which belong, in a peculiar way, to speculative thought. The man of the Scholastic or the strictly Hegelian development, in his day, felt himself competent to deduce the principles of the positive sciences from the laws of absolute existence. And was it not his peculiar business to be familiar with those laws? But the tables are now turned upon philosophy. Who now feels himself competent to pronounce with reference to philosophical secrets, — to solve problems of Freedom, God, and Immortal Life, and to discern the inmost being of the really existent, whether it be blind Force, "the Unconscious," the "mysterious something" which we rightly call "Matter," or the self-conscious Universal Reason, — unless it be the students of empirical physics and psychology?

There is danger, then, that the favor of this potent mistress of thought, called modern science, may become more embarrassing to philosophy than her disfavor has been. Hence, in part, the necessity of determining more carefully the natural and necessary relations of the two.

Our previous investigations enable us at once to reject certain views as to the distinction between philosophy and the positive sciences. Four ways of drawing this distinction are enumerated by Mr. Hodgson,[1] preliminary to the statement of the one which he himself adopts. We agree with him in rejecting them all. The line between philosophy and science cannot be drawn so as to assign to the former only those unverifiable guesses at truth which precede the correct methods and verifiable truths of positive science (view of "English Positivism"). Nor can the chief or distinctive work of philosophy be held to consist in simply co-ordinating and systematizing the many different branches into which advancing science differentiates itself ("Comtian Positivism"). Nor can we make the latter view adequate by adding, as does Mr. Lewes, the task of "disproving and keeping out of science all ontological entities." All those three ways of regarding the relation of philosophy and science destroy the independent existence and value of philosophy; they arise from a total misconception of either its true problem or its correct method, or of both. But

[1] Philosophy of Reflection, i. 28 f.

the view which maintains that philosophy, being the discovery of Absolute Existence, is so related to the sciences that it imparts to them their scientific character, by making their principles deductions from the laws of this Existence ("the Hegelian view"), is also summarily to be dismissed. The disproof of this view is not more firmly embodied in the claims and achievements of modern science than in the woful failures which it has occasioned to the pursuit of philosophy.

Philosophy owes its origin and justification, in its modern form as a distinct discipline and pursuit, to the failure of each and all of the positive sciences to satisfy the most profound and imperative demands of human reason.[1] This failure has respect to three things, — to comprehensiveness, to certainty, and to ethical and æsthetical significance. The positive sciences do not attain, and from their very nature cannot aim at reaching, the ideally most comprehensive view of the world. From their very nature they are *particular* sciences. But philosophy, from its very nature, deals with the most general conceptions; it postulates the possibility of regarding all the conclusions of the sciences in the light of a unity of reality; and from this point of view it strives to transcend what is most particular in each of them, and to reach what is universal and common to them all. It thus offers to rational inquiry the hope of attaining a comprehensiveness of knowledge, for lack of which the forms of more concrete knowledge fail wholly to satisfy the heart and mind.

The different positive sciences, as forms of *science*, possess a particular degree and kind of certainty. But they all involve a host of presuppositions, — of unverified conceptions, postulated entities and relations of entities, assumed modes of the being and behavior of things. Upon the basis of these presuppositions they move onward toward the discovery of further empirical truths. It is not their business to consider the reality

[1] Compare Spir, Forschung nach der Gewissheit in der Erkenntniss der Wirklichkeit, Leipzig, 1869, p. 1 f.

of the basis, or the grounds of certainty with which affirmations or denials can be made touching its reality and its nature. The "truths" of science are the uniform sequences of phenomena which have been discovered by fortunate guessing, and verified by application of the methods of scientific induction. The certainty of science is never more than a higher or lower degree of probability, — of probability that, *if* something of definite sort has been or has happened, *then* something else of a definite sort has been or happened, or is being or happening, or will be or will happen. But philosophy, with its claim to investigate the grounds of all reason, and the universal forms and laws of being, holds out the hope of a more nearly absolute certainty of knowledge.

The different positive sciences do not, as forms of science, necessarily concern themselves with the analysis, criticism, and justification of the ideals of reason. This is true of ethics, æsthetics, and the science of religion, as well as of physics and psychology. These pursuits also, as long as they concern themselves only with particular classes of phenomena, leave much to be desired. It is only when they cease to be strictly empirical sciences, and enter upon inquiry as to the value and existence in reality of such ideals as the Good, the Beautiful, and God, that they seem to attain their highest significance. But when they do this, they cease to remain within the legitimate sphere of science; they pass over, though it may be while retaining the same names, into the domain of the philosophy of the Ideal. They then seem, and truly, to the reflecting mind to surpass, in meaning and value, all the particular sciences, and to gain an existence that is distinctly superior to the basis of scientific induction upon which they dependently rest.

Help toward the fuller comprehension of the relation of philosophical discipline to the positive sciences may be gained by considering under what conditions science and philosophy appear as distinct stages of development in the life of the individual and of the race. Both are related to ordinary non-scientific cognition as being alike the result of the secondary and more elaborate forms of observation and reflection. It may be said, then, that progress toward the highest possible organization of experience into a unity of thought has three principal stages. The first of these is that stage which is marked by such a knowledge of things and events as constitutes ordinary experience. The second and third stages are those of science and philosophy. In the development, both of the individual reason and of that of the race, these three stages are, of course, not preserved apart; nor do they ever exist without direct and reactionary influences upon each other. Neither does all noteworthy construction of philosophical system wait, in the history of the evolution of mankind, until both the popular and the scientific modes of cognition have reached their highest development; nor is it possible to say at just what point ordinary and non-scientific knowledge passes over into the more strictly scientific; or where is the precise dividing-line, in some of the sciences, between their scientific content, strictly so called, and the philosophical elements and tenets which they contain.

It is nevertheless possible to distinguish, though in a somewhat rough and uncertain way, three main stages of knowledge, whatever the subject-matter of the knowledge may be. To know that yeast raises bread, or that mother-of-vinegar converts cider into vinegar, and how to bring about these desirable changes, may be called ordinary, or non-scientific, knowledge. To know how the yeast and vinegar plants appear under the microscope, to what classes of other minute plant-life they are most closely allied, what are the precise thermic, chemical, and mechanical conditions favorable to their propagation, etc., is to have a more scientific knowledge of the same subject. To know that by exciting the nerves of sense, sensations are produced in the mind; that if the sun is shining, the stars are, by a law governing the action of stimulus on the nervous system, obscured; and that injury to the mass of the brain by wounds and tumors paralyzes the power of feeling or motion in the extremities, — this is, indeed, to be better informed than Aristotle; but for our generation it may be called quite ordinary knowledge. To know that the mechanical or chemical action of stimuli on the end-organs of sense starts a mysterious molecular commotion in the axis-cylinders of the centripetal nerves, and that this commotion propagates itself, as a process of an uncertain character, to the central nervous mass, and there, as a process yet more mysterious, lays the physical basis for a special forth-putting of the life of conscious sensation; to know that Weber and Fechner consider an increase in geometrical proportion of the strength of the stimuli necessary to an increase in arithmetical proportion of the strength of the resulting sensation, but that other explorers have probably disproved the exactness of this alleged law; to know that Ferrier locates the so-called "centre of sight" chiefly in the *gyrus angularis*, while Munk considers this *gyrus* the cortical region for the tactile sensations of the eye, and locates the chief centre of sight in a limited area of the occipital lobe, while Goltz flouts at the conclusions of both, — to know these things, and the grounds on which they rest, is to be scientific as respects physiological and psycho-physical questions of the most important kind.

None of the foregoing species of knowledge would be called "philosophical" in any admissible sense of the word. There is, however, a science which aims to compass the most general laws of all life. It is called biology. It is comparatively new in its equipment of method, instruments of research, and masses of material calling for scientific treatment. It is intensely interesting, for its subject of investigation is *life*, — as such, and in all its forms. And it is as ambitious as it is interesting. It is no longer satisfied merely to classify and so to build up more and more minute and elaborate accounts of the related forms of life; its principal questions are no longer morphological.

What is it to live; or rather, to be alive? It is this question which biology essays to answer. But the inquiry after the origin of life, — the question, "Whence does life come?" is regarded with no less interest by this same science of biology. It is true that for the present there is an almost complete cessation from scientific attempts to answer this question. The hot strife over theories of *biogenesis* and *abiogenesis* has largely subsided; the attempt to decide by scientific experimentation between the two theories has been temporarily abandoned. So far as we know, *Omne vivum e vivo*, is the true statement of fact. Biology therefore becomes the science of the origin of life only in so far as it can, by study of embryology and of different living forms under the light of evolution, describe in what manner and by what stages one living being follows from another being also alive.

But biology cannot forever abandon the hope of tracing the existing forms of life beyond the first living germs to their genesis from non-living matter. Meantime, it is at liberty to comfort itself by pushing the origin of those much-needed first particles of living protoplasm out into infinite space as well as back into infinite time. Sir W. Thomson's hypothesis, or some equally unverifiable form of guessing, may in the mean time fill the place vacant of truly scientific information: germs of living things — we will conjecture — have been transported to our globe from some globe unknown. In the future, however, biology will certainly return to the inquiry after the real genesis of life. It will then give attention to this question with vastly increased resources for its successful treatment, and from a far-advanced point of view. Suppose it were at that time to attain a truly scientific knowledge of the origin of life, and were even able, from non-living material particles, to manufacture to order bits of living protoplasm: what then would be left in the realm of living beings for philosophy to do?

In answer to this question there is no escape from the admission that, so far as what we call "life" is a series of physical processes and of related material forms, the whole subject in all its aspects must be left to science, in distinction from philosophy. Morphology and physiology, but both as studied under the conception of evolution, are the twin branches of biology which cover the whole domain of life,—of life, however, only so far as it consists of related physical processes and material forms. But life, we might go on to argue, is not all mere physical processes and material forms. Sentience is perhaps connected, in some degree, with the least highly differentiated of these vital processes and living forms. Upon the more highly developed bodily organisms a complex psychical development is dependent,—a life of soul goes with the life of organism. In the case of that supreme animal called man, life has become self-conscious, rational, free, and spiritual,—whatever meaning we may attach to these and similar terms. Now, if philosophy is forbidden to concern itself with the question of life in its physical aspects and manifestations, may it not appropriate the consideration of those aspects and manifestations which are called spiritual? This separation of spheres between science and philosophy is the one proposed by certain strenuous advocates of the claims of philosophy. "Philosophy of nature," says Lichtenfels, "is a contradiction; philosophy of spirit a pleonasm." [1]

But the modern science of life is not satisfied to leave an uncontested field to philosophy, even after the latter has modestly retreated from the consideration of all questions of morphology, physiology, and the physical evolution of living forms. Biology follows philosophy in its attempted retreat. It claims the right to consider, as falling under general biological laws, the phenomena of sentient, and even of rational or spiritual, life. For are not sentience and reason forms and processes of life; and is not biology (as the very title signifies) the science of the most general principles of all life? We are invited then to listen to discourse of a "physiology of the soul," of a "morphology of

[1] Lehrbuch zur Einleitung in die Philosophie, p. 10.

concepts," of an "evolution of reason" from the irrational life of the brute, of a "development of perceptions" out of sensation-complexes which are themselves highly elaborate "aggregations" and "agglutinations" of simple sensation-elements, which are in turn the subjective correlates of undifferentiated nervous shocks. In fact, a scientific biology is ambitious (and shall we say impudent?) enough to claim that psychology is only a dependent branch of its own native stock.

It is plain from the foregoing considerations that no valid distinction between science and philosophy can be based upon the present limitations of success in the attempt to reduce to scientific form any special group of phenomena. We cannot assign the inquiry into the forms and laws of actual life to science, and the speculative determination of the genesis of life to philosophy. Nor can we say that the nature, laws, and genesis of sentient, rational, and self-conscious life — it being withdrawn from the domain of science — are the peculiar property of philosophy.

There are sciences which lawfully treat, with more or less strictly scientific methods, the various classes of the phenomena of sentient and rational life. Among them are psychology (in the narrower sense of the word), psycho-physics, ethics, and sociology. They may be somewhat imperfectly grouped together and called the psychological sciences, or "psychology," in the more general sense of the word. The relations which the science of general psychology sustains to philosophy are so peculiar and so important that to distinguish clearly and sharply between the two is not easy. One important department of philosophy is called rational psychology, or the philosophy of mind. Other departments are called ethics, æsthetics, and the philosophy of religion. But there is a science of ethics as well as a science of theology and of comparative religions; there is also perhaps a science of æsthetics. If then it is a "pleonasm" to speak of the philosophy of spirit, how shall we distinguish between philosophy and the psychological sciences, even after it has been admitted that it is a "contradiction" to speak of the philosophy of nature?

We will not for a moment admit that philosophy has no place or rights in the domain of physical phenomena. It is no more a contradiction to speak of the "philosophy of nature" than it is a pleonasm to speak of the "philosophy of spirit." We must rather speak of the philosophy of nature and the philosophy of spirit as the two branches of the great department of metaphysics in philosophy, — and this without either contradiction or pleonasm. To illustrate and enforce the possibility of such a distinction between science and philosophy as shall secure the rights of both in the domain of both matter and mind, it will be helpful subsequently to recur to the case of biology. This case affords in some respects the best possible illustration, because biology is the crowning general science of physical phenomena; because, also, it has such peculiar and important relations to the other great groups of phenomena with which the psychological sciences deal.

The distinction between "science" and such ordinary knowledge as we should hesitate to dignify by this term cannot — as we have seen — be drawn by a hard and fixed line. This fact has important bearings upon the attempt to distinguish between science and philosophy. The observations and inductions of the average man have different degrees of approach to the more strictly scientific method and to scientific accuracy. The physical and natural sciences are justly proud of the wonderful apparatus, due to the advances in telescopy, microscopy, photography, chemical analysis, etc., which they are able to use in the observation and discrimination of related phenomena. But not a few of their most important discoveries have been made by observers who had at command little more than the ordinary means of observation. The inductions of science, too, are supposed to be clearly superior to those of common life, not only because of their use of the superior means of observation which science possesses, but also because the successive steps of induction are much more skilfully prepared and carefully guarded. It would be difficult, however, to say just what amount of the rules of induction — agreement, difference, and concomitant variation — is needed in each case in order to impart to the conclusions reached, the right to be called "scientific." And there are subjects where we may (whether rightly or wrongly, we will not say) still prefer the declarations and predictions of men of so-called non-scientific experience to those of professed scientific experts. Not a few pleasure-seekers, for example, take counsel of the weather-wise farmer or sailor with more confidence than of their morning newspaper.

Furthermore, when we ask the students of science themselves to name the distinguishing marks of that kind of knowledge to which they lay special claim, we do not receive a wholly unequivocal and satisfactory answer. The feeling of this inability it doubtless was which led Professor Huxley to define science as "organized common-sense." If we were to gather Mr. Herbert Spencer's conception of the nature of science from his essay on "The Classification of the Sciences," we should say that he regards it as the "*interpretation*," either "*analytical*" or "*synthetical*," of the different principal groups of similar phenomena. But Mr. Spencer apparently does not give us any rule for telling precisely how much of "interpretation" is necessary to the existence of "science," as distinguished from ordinary non-scientific cognition. At the same time, no one holds more firmly than he to a distinct place for philosophy as a sphere or kind of interpretation beyond that of science. Science, Mr. Spencer regards as "partially unified knowledge;" but "philosophy is completely unified knowledge."[1] That "interpretation" of phenomena which seeks the complete unification of knowledge is doubtless philosophy. But since all attempts at philosophy are only "partially" successful, the distinction between science and philosophy becomes in its turn a matter of degree.

[1] First Principles, p. 539.

Considered with reference to its object of pursuit, Helmholtz[1] defines science to be "the knowledge how, at different times, under the same conditions, the same results are brought about." Defining more loosely, and yet from the same point of view, Professor Tait declares: "The object of all pure physical science is to endeavor to grasp more and more perfectly the nature and laws of the external world." And Helmholtz expands his conception of science when he proceeds to say: "Our desire to *comprehend* natural phenomena . . . thus takes another form of expression, — that is, we have to seek out the *forces* which are the *causes* of the phenomena."

In accordance with the spirit of the foregoing definitions and of the entire body of scientific investigation, we describe the work of modern science as follows: It is the systematizing of experience, by classifying the different like groups of phenomena through exact and comprehensive observation, and by explaining them through the discovery and verification of the existing uniform relations. Its formula is: If this happens, that will happen; or if this has happened, that has also happened, — everywhere and every time.

All knowledge implies the progressive systematizing of experience; this is as true of that which is esteemed ordinary knowledge as of that which is praised for its highly scientific character. Indeed, it might be said that the growth of experience itself is but a progressive formation of system amongst the different elements and individual items of experience. Science is superior to the unscientific growth of knowledge, in respect both of the accuracy and extent of its observations, and of the discovery and verification of so-called forces and laws. Its observations are rendered more accurate by the use of special means of observation, — telescope, microscope, and all the improved means of making physical measurements and calculations, — in the hands of trained and expert observers. Its explanations far surpass those of the men of ordinary knowledge,

[1] Popular Lectures on Scientific Subjects, pp. 370 f. and 393 f.

because they consist in the application of a well-compacted body of acknowledged facts and laws to the discovery of new facts; and either to the further verification of forces and laws already known, or to the establishment of new knowledge of forces and laws. Thus understood, however, science differs from ordinary non-scientific knowledge in degree rather than in kind of knowledge.

But thus understood, science is invested on either hand by knowledge, or rather by a potentiality — we will say — of knowledge, from which it differs in kind as well as in degree. On the one hand, it assumes (oftentimes with a *naïveté* as great as that which characterizes the men of only ordinary experience) certain conceptions, forms of general judgment, or other principles, which it does not feel itself bound or competent critically to examine. Or if it does subject these postulates of all its procedure to critical examination, it concerns itself only with the shape which they must take as tenable scientific hypotheses. It regards the postulates as instruments for the successful treatment of phenomena by the methods of classification and discovery of so-called laws or uniform relations. But if science ventures upon a discussion of the applicability in reality of these postulates, or of the relation they sustain in reality to the unity of the world and of all experience, it abandons its own peculiar sphere; for such discussion is not scientific, and does not admit of scientific proof or disproof, in the stricter meaning of these words. Such discussion is metaphysics, — that is, a branch of philosophy. And this is equally true whether it be metaphysics of mathematics, or of physics, or — again — of psychology.

On the other hand of the legitimate sphere of scientific research stands another class of inquiries which are its limits, and at the same time the boundaries of philosophy. These are the inquiries into the relations of the different groups of phenomena, with which the particular sciences deal, to the Ideals of reason, and to the Unity of Reality in which these Ideals are held by philosophy to have their ground. The truth of science is fact and law, — the latter being understood as the verified uniform concomitances and sequences of facts. How these can have, or whether they do have, the value which reason attaches to what is true (in the philosophical sense of the word), beautiful, and morally good, science does not inquire. Or if it does enter upon this inquiry, it passes beyond the limits of the particular sciences, and enters the proper domain of the philosophy of the Ideal. It becomes, no longer science, but philosophical ethics or æsthetics, or the philosophy of religion.

The general distinction which has just been made we will now apply to biology; and since the foregoing considerations have had particular reference to the relation of philosophy and the physical and natural sciences, we will now consider biology as only one of these sciences. What then, we may ask, remains in the sphere of physical life for philosophy to consider, if biology as a science is entitled to claim as its own the discovery and verification of the most general laws, not only of the evolution, but also of the genesis, of all life? There remains for philosophy, we reply, no less than the consideration of the most interesting, difficult, and in some regards most important, of all the inquiries touching the general subject-matter of biology.

What is the significance, in reality, of life? Is it to be found in the supreme form of life, in the self-conscious striving, the thinking and planning, the joy and suffering, of rational mind; or in an unconscious principle called Matter, Absolute Ego, Will, or Will conjoined with Idea and yet not conscious of itself?

What significance in reality, moreover, shall we attach to the development of living forms? Biological science deals with the evolution of life in the individual, the species, the family, — in all interconnected forms of life. But with its aid alone the law of evolution can never attain to anything more than the place of a working hypothesis, adapted to the systematizing of the groups of observed or inferred phenomena. Is this great law itself valid in Reality; or is it good for use only as a seeming (*Schein*)? May we speak of the Absolute (of God) as in a process of becoming? Or if not, in what relation do the law of evolution and the living forms evolved stand to the supreme Reality we try to express by that word? What, further, do we mean when we proclaim, in the name of biological science, the *goodness* of the result attained through the struggle of species, as higher and yet higher forms, leading up to self-conscious rational life, appear to view? What is this standard by which we attempt to difference ideally the living forms and arrange them in series, with man at their head? Is it a matter simply of complexity of mechanical contrivances and processes, leaving all conscious life out of the account? Or is it a matter of more or less in the gross amount of sensuous or other forms of happiness and misery? Or, finally, is it not also a matter of approximation to certain ideals of reason, to the beautiful and the morally good? And what reality does our standard of good possess; or is the standard itself mere seeming good (*Scheingut*)?

Now, it cannot be claimed that the consideration of questions such as the foregoing is not in a large measure distinct from strictly scientific inquiry after the physical relations under which the genesis and evolution of particular living forms take place. This distinction would, moreover, continue to hold if biology were a much more highly developed physical science than it can at present pretend to be. Nay, more: the distinction would not cease to be important if biology had finished all the work that, as an exact science (?), it can ever hope to finish. If the description of all the observed forms of life were, in all their stages, made complete, and if the genesis and interrelated growth of these forms were so mastered that all the facts could be brought under general laws, the services of biological science to philosophy would be greatly enlarged. But the peculiar task of philosophy with reference to the problems of life would not be accomplished. Indeed, it would not necessarily be even rightly begun. For the consideration of the relation in which all these living forms, with the generalized statements of fact respecting their physical genesis and development, stand to the world's Unity in Reality, and to the ideals of reason,— the beautiful, the morally good, and that supreme object of religious adoration whom faith calls God,— would still remain untouched. Such consideration is for philosophy to attempt.

It may be maintained that philosophy can answer none of the foregoing questions, or that it can cope with only a few of them, and with these only with a partial success. So it may be maintained (and truthfully) that biology can at present give a strictly scientific solution to almost none of its own more important problems, and that its most strenuous efforts to bring the phenomena of life under the law of the conservation and correlation of energy, and under the form of a general mechanical theory, have resulted only in unverifiable guessing. But such a claim does not work the destruction of the science of biology so-called; nor does it prevent our setting apart for its researches, (albeit so difficult, and restricted in exact results) a distinctive sphere. In like manner, the claim that philosophy has achieved small success in solving the problems assigned to it, does not destroy its claim to a distinctive work within a somewhat definitively recognized sphere. Perhaps if our knowledge of the principles of all life becomes more scientific, the philosophical consideration of these principles will become more satisfactory to biologists themselves. Certainly, at present, neither the student of biological science, nor the thinker who would give to the phenomena of life a philosophical treatment, is entitled to despise the work of the other.

Nor can it be maintained that the special form of biological inquiries, with which philosophy attempts to deal, is not worthy of consideration. So narrow an interest in the phenomena of life would be as unbecoming to science as to philosophy.

Besides the special philosophical problems which attach themselves to biology as a positive science, there are others which are common to it and to the other physical sciences. The relation of biology to all these sciences is such that it founds itself upon them all. It is the crowning science among the system of sciences, — pre-eminently complex, sensitive, and dependent, and yet supremely interesting on account of its connections with practical and philosophical, as well as strictly scientific problems. Its springs and currents of discovery and speculation swarm with postulated physical entities, forces, and laws, of a kind to promote a large extension of metaphysical theory.

The modern science of biology is not chiefly a system of classifications. Besides morphology, it depends upon histology, embryology, and physiology; and it receives and appropriates the results of all three of these sciences as studied in the light of the theory of evolution. But each of these sciences makes use of microscopy and of the general mechanical theory; especially does each rely upon the conclusions and methods of chemistry and molecular physics. In accepting these methods and conclusions, biology accepts the postulated entities, forces, and laws which enter into them all. It explains the phenomena of life by reference to their causes in invisible and intangible beings of a material sort, called "atoms" and "molecules;" and between these beings it assumes or demonstrates relations of attraction and repulsion, of changing position or motion, of affinity and synthesis or its contrary, and the like. And since a general theory of molecular physics best explains the likenesses and unlikenesses in the groups of phenomena, which refers them to the reciprocal influence of the elementary beings (*i. e.*, of the atoms and molecules), such theory ascribes to these beings "natures" according to which they are arranged into hypothetical kinds, either like or unlike. It distinguishes at present more than sixty of such kinds. The natures of these beings are, moreover, said to be determined by the forces inherent in them; these forces, science declares, may nevertheless be modifications of one and the same force. Possibly the number of entities needed for the explanation of the phenomena may be found to be more than is now thought requisite; or — what seems rather to be desired, and likelier to turn out true — the present number may ultimately be greatly reduced.

All observed changes in biological phenomena are therefore referred, for their ultimate explanation, to occult changes in the invisible realm of molecular entities, forces, and laws. The science of the genesis and growth of living forms regards them thus. Life and death are alike in this respect, that they both consist of observed changes, which are to be referred for their explanation to the occult influence of the same molecular beings, with their wonderful equipment of related forces, acting under law. Thermic, electric, chemical, and other mechanical energies have their bearing on the phenomena of life through the same invisible world of atoms with their ceaseless changes of relation in space.

How does the science of biology come into possession of this equipment of mysterious entities and forces? What is the nature of the knowledge it has lawfully gained of atoms and molecules, original natures of atoms, forces of molecular attraction and repulsion; also of occult causes, and of the hypothesis of universally regnant law? It borrows this knowledge from the other physical sciences on which it depends. What, furthermore, have the sciences on which biology depends to do with the same metaphysical pre-suppositions? Much, if the pre-suppositions are used simply as working hypotheses; nothing, if they require to be validated as belonging to the world of reality.

To the sciences, in so far as they are *merely scientific*, all consideration of the world of entities, forces, and causes has only the value of good or bad working hypotheses. To them the existence and nature of the atom is an hypothesis, valuable according as it does, or does not, serve to explain the phenomena by aiding the discovery and verification of their uniform concomitances and sequences. To them the *extra*-mental reality of the causes and forces — thought of as existing "in" the atoms, or "between" them, or presiding "over" them — is of no immediate concern. For to them causes and forces also are only hypotheses, useful in the classification, and reduction to uniform relations, of the phenomena.

The sciences on which biology more immediately depends themselves rest on a lower and broader basis of physical science. Along the general level of this basis, although at somewhat different relative heights, are such sciences as astronomy, geology, meteorology, and especially physics, in the more limited meaning of the word. Lower still lies mechanics, as the most general science of the action of forces in the production of motion or of strain. This science, as Professor Tait tells us in the last edition of the "Encyclopædia Britannica," "treats of the action of Force upon Matter;" but is more correctly (is this because of the hope thus to escape from the metaphysical implications of words like "force" and "action," etc.?) "the *Science of Matter and Motion*, or of *Matter and Energy*." Matter, Motion, and Energy, — these are words burdened with the survivals of centuries of metaphysical doctrine, and utterly and forever incapable of being wholly cleared of a metaphysical investment and reference.

What, we might ask, is this "Matter" with which it is the business of the science of mechanics especially to deal? Is it the only matter which is concretely and definitively known; namely, matter subjective, the synthesis in experience of localized sensation-complexes, of remembered images of sensation-complexes, of inferences from such images, and of the *naïve* metaphysical postulate of an unknown objective ground for the phenomena? This can scarcely be so, for we are told in this connection that a better name for mechanics would be *abstract* dynamics, and that the science is what is called "pure." Is then the "matter" of which mechanics treats a concept merely, albeit a concept of the very highest form of generalization, and equivalent perhaps to the "mysterious something" by which all this (the processes and evolution called "physical") is accomplished? Now, the type of this matter with which mechanics deals is a single particle, without nature, character, instinct, will, or idea. But, in reality, where exists any such particle? In *reality*, of course, each particle is an atom, or a congeries of atoms, full of manifold potentialities and forms of energy, found at the beginning, and always known, only in the most complicated processes of changing relations toward other like or unlike particles.

Let not mechanics, that science so "pure" and "abstract," think to escape the need of help from philosophy by substituting for the metaphysical term "force" such words as "motion" and "energy." For what are we to understand by the motion of which it is the science, if it be aught more than a particular time-series of differently localized sensation-complexes, — as when a shooting-star passes over the field of my vision, or a fly crawls over the skin of my cheek or hand? Is there motion, in reality? Can there be motion without some reality to Space, in which, as we say, motion takes place; or without some reality to Time, within which (in another meaning of the word "within") motion occurs? Can there be motion without some real being to move? What is the relation in which all motion stands to the ultimate Reality, after whose nature philosophy seeks? Does this Reality itself change; and how can it be the ground of change of relations in space among those elements of material kind whose existence physical science assumes as its working hypothesis? These are among the problems handed over, as it were, to philosophy from the *naïve* and uninstructed presuppositions with which this so-called science of motion deals.

It has been fashionable for some time past to reject the word "force" from the discussions of the exact sciences. and to substitute for it the word "energy." To this no objection can be raised if the end desired be to obtain and employ a term, in a hypothetical way, which shall be better capable of fulfilling the requirements of exact science. It would be vain, however, to hope by a change of words to free physical science from its natural dependence on reason, or from its obligations to that higher use of reason at which philosophy aims. If we adopt the new word, all the old philosophical problems at once recur, and attach themselves with equal persistence to it. What is this "energy," whose conservation and correlation is a postulate of all modern physical science, and with the most general laws of which, as productive of motion, it is the business of "abstract dynamics" to deal? Let a colleague of Professor Tait in the same literary work make answer. "Energy," says Mr. William Garnett, "may be defined as the power of doing work." But in this definition the metaphysical conception is returned to philosophy for its consideration anew. For what is "power," potential or kinetic, apart from all implication of force? What also is it "to do," and "to do work," unless the influence of one part of real being on another, and the occurrence of reciprocally dependent changes in reality, and the reality of some unity in causal relations, be somehow implied.

Undoubtedly it would not do to affirm that mechanics cannot exist and grow, as an exact and pure science, without consciously resting on some basis of philosophical doctrine, more or less intelligently adopted. The contrary is true. As pure *science*, and unmixed with definite metaphysical doctrine, it need not consider the foregoing fundamental problems at all. It is meant rather to affirm that mechanics, like every form of physical or natural science into which mechanics enters, actually involves certain assumptions, the criticism and systematizing of which it is the business of philosophy to undertake. When, then, mechanics and the other mechanical sciences employ words like "Matter," "Motion," and "Energy" or "Force," they are to be understood as legitimately extending the field of science by use of certain universal hypotheses. But the student of mechanics, as a student of science merely, can go no farther than to say, *if* by matter, motion, and force we mean thus and so, *then*, under certain circumstances (also — it is likely — wholly hypothetical), the uniform concomitances and sequences of phenomena will be of the following order and kind. Whenever the student of science enters upon the discussion of the nature and validity, in reality, of the hypotheses he feels compelled to make, he departs from the sphere of science strictly so called. He becomes a metaphysician, a philosopher in one of the most abstruse and difficult departments of philosophy. He is not by any means necessarily saved by his scientific training and resources from being a bad metaphysician, although within the sphere of scientific hypotheses. He is not rendered able to extricate himself, or his science, from need of the helping right-hand of philosophy.

All the abstract and pure sciences, like mechanics, as *sciences*, have only the value of a consistent arrangement of conceptions under a number of most general hypotheses. The validity which they seem in themselves to have is due to their consistency. Nor is even the consistency, which these sciences are obliged to maintain, as necessary to their successful prosecution, of the highest kind. It is not necessary, for example, that the conception of Space which is held by the student of mechanics should be consistent with the truths of psychological development, or with the highest doctrine of that unity which belongs to the world of reality. The student of mechanics may adopt the crudest realism; he may even regard space as itself an existent entity, an indefinitely spread-out actuality; he may feel unable to imagine the Infinite as independent of the relations and limitations of space. He may speak of energy as though it were something which could actually be stored up, and passed over from one atom or mass to another. He may make his atoms into gods, and bow down and worship them, while denying all power in philosophy or theology to bring to man the knowledge of God, the Father Almighty. Such crudities and vagaries of philosophical thought would not, however, of necessity injure the cogency or completeness of his reasoning in the sphere of his science. The highest success here is possible, if only the few conceptions to be systematized be kept consistent with one another, under the conditions imposed by the fundamental hypotheses.

Much of what has already been said concerning the relation of mechanics to philosophy is also true of pure mathematics. The latter science has sometimes been called distinctively metaphysical. The designation is to a certain extent correct, because the entities and ratiocinative processes of mathematics, like those of metaphysics, appear before the mind as independent of verification from concrete and individual experiences. But in the course of thought we are now following, mathematics, of all the sciences, stands most remote from metaphysics. It involves comparatively few of those assumptions touching the existence and nature of known reality with which metaphysics is concerned. We are reminded, however, that an ancient system of philosophy made number of the very essence of reality. Great is the power of this same conception of number in the modern mechanical theory of the world; great also in respect to the questions it opens before us as to the possibility — for example — of space of *n* dimensions, and as regards the application of all arithmetical and geometrical formulæ to the ultimate being of things. And here the problems of mathematics and metaphysics begin to coincide at so many points that the lines of the movement of the two seem to become identical.

Is the Absolute a unity, or in fact can we apply at all the conceptions and relations of number to the ultimate Being we designate by that word? And if the Absolute is One, how shall we conceive of the nature of that unity which the Absolute has or is? What kind of unity do the elements of material reality, the so-called atoms, have? How shall we, by indefinite subdivisions into minuter parts, reach a real physical unity? How, indeed, can there be Unity in consistency with the variety of the really Existent? What bond in idea or actuality ties the infinite multiplicity of things and atoms into the oneness of being which the real world has?

The answer to such questions as the foregoing may be far and difficult to seek, or even impossible to find. But the questions themselves spring forth with ever-new freshness and power from the human reason. They are not proposed as the useless puzzles of a few disturbed brains. They perpetually recur along the path of scientific and rational evolution. They ask themselves, as it were, and keep insisting upon consideration, although the complete answer to them has never yet been found. Mathematics, as a science pure or applied, cannot entertain, not to say answer them. They do not fall within the legitimate sphere of any of the physical and natural sciences. Yet these sciences all contain the fundamental conceptions, the reflective analysis and the attempted synthesis of which give to philosophy some of its hardest problems.

It is not simply for the detection and criticism of their presuppositions, both general and special, that the physical sciences are dependent upon philosophical analysis; they are also dependent upon synthetic philosophy for certain supreme generalizations which may be given to the highest principles that have been discovered empirically. And, in turn, philosophy is dependent upon the particular sciences for its own subject-matter in the form of their highest scientific generalizations. All the more comprehensive results of induction, as they are afforded by these sciences, are contributions to the material of philosophy. The very life and growth of philosophy as a scientific system depends upon its appropriation of this material. Only in this way can the results of speculative reflection keep constantly in touch with concrete and living realities. Only in this way can philosophy be saved from the fate of deceiving itself with the synthesis of barren abstractions, — mere fragments of incomplete analysis, mingled with conjectural entities and forces, and bound together into a totality that has only the consistency and unity of pleasant dreams.

The attitude of direct dependence in which philosophy stands toward the positive sciences might be illustrated by many examples. Indeed, the entire history of modern philosophy does but afford a series of illustrations. The Hegelian system, as left by its founder, fell into disfavor, not more because of the general defectiveness of the dialectical method and the inability of its conclusions to satisfy the needs of the heart, than through the contempt which the positive sciences threw upon its manner of treating the choicest results of their inductions. Every new attempt at philosophical system has first of all to reckon with the positive sciences. If it passes by their discoveries in silence, the present age is sure to consider it inadequate and insufficiently founded. If it contradicts these discoveries, it is itself immediately subjected to so great contempt as not even to be thought worthy of argument. If it seems to show higher speculative reasons for the validity of scientific discoveries, or illustrates them by pointing out new and valuable relations in which they stand to the Ideals of Reason and to the Ultimate Being of the world, it wins, so far forth, some claims to recognition and to respect at the hands of science. Nor do we for a moment think of complaining of all this. On the contrary, this is precisely as it should be. There can be no philosophy of nature which is not securely founded upon the principles established by the inductive science of nature. There is no philosophy of mind which is not dependent for its material upon the empirical pursuit of the psychological sciences. The favor shown to those speculative thinkers who give plain signs of the endeavor to bring their philosophical conclusions at every possible point of contact to the test of the widest and most certain generalizations of the positive sciences, is thus explained. It is largely for this reason that Herbert Spencer,

Von Hartmann, and other writers on philosophy, who avowedly build their synthesis on an inductive basis, attract so large a following among the students of these sciences.

The law of the conservation and correlation of energy, and the various laws which enter into the general theory of evolution, form conspicuous instances at present of the truth which has just been stated. The philosophy of nature and every other department of philosophy feels the influence of these vast but vague scientific generalizations. Who would venture to put forth a system of philosophy or to deal freely with philosophical problems, and leave these generalizations out of the account? No philosophy can become current that neglects them. Indeed, the greater danger to speculative thinking arises just now from a too hasty and complete acceptance of these supreme working hypotheses of all natural science, rather than from a tendency to treat them with disrespect or neglect. And what is true of such supreme principles, in so many and important regards, is true in fewer and less important regards of all the minor generalizations of the natural sciences.

Science is knowledge, as the very word of course signifies. It is knowledge of perception and inference, — knowledge rendered comprehensive and exact by special methods, and rendered systematic and rational by extension to a vast multitude of cases under general laws. But as knowledge, science is ever dependent upon the activity and the constitution of the knowing mind. Perception and inference are processes of knowledge, the nature, genesis, and evolution of which may be made the subjects of scientific research. The comprehensive term for the science resulting from this kind of research is "psychology." As thus employed, the term includes also the empirical pursuit of logic, ethics, and æsthetics. Concepts, judgments, and inductive and deductive argument are all processes of the psychological kind; the description and explanation of the genesis, nature, and development of logical processes and logical products belong to the science of psychology. Nor is the case at all essentially different if the concepts, judgments, and arguments are of duty or of beauty; that is, if they belong to the so-called science of ethics or of æsthetics. As positive sciences, ethics and æsthetics, as well as logic, are only branches of psychology.

But processes of knowledge or phenomena of cognition do not exhaust the variety of the modes of behavior which we attribute to the principle called "soul" or "mind." Psychical life shows a richness of phenomena too great to be grouped under the one rubric of ideation. Phenomena of feeling, desire, volition, also require scientific treatment; the exact classification and explanation, by tracing their genesis and development, of these phenomena also belong to psychology.

Within the very *penetralia* of psychological science, as it were, arise the forms with whose more intimate and profound acquaintance philosophy is specifically concerned. The effort to explain the phenomena of psychical life, leads at once to the detection of certain constitutional mental modes (the so-called "categories") that, in their native aspect, lay claim to a universal significance and validity. Among these phenomena are certain of a peculiarly shadowy and evanescent sort; but they seem to testify to the presence and exciting influence upon the emotions and volitions of supreme ideals. These are the ideals of duty, of beauty, and of the One whom men call God.

In natural as well as in developed and scientifically reflective self-consciousness, there emerges a persistent diremption of the complexes of psychical life. There is a distinction established which seems, as regards its logical value and significance, to lie at the basis of all distinguishing activity. There comes to be recognized the "Ego" (*I*), as the subject of all the states, and the states which are all alike to be called mine. Still later in the development of mind, whether naïvely or with the intelligence of the trained psychologist, I come to speak of *my* body, and of the world that is *not me*, in contrast to which *I am* as thinking, feeling, willing mind.

Who does not recognize in such considerations as these the call of introspective and experimental psychology upon philosophy for its help? Further reflection upon these considerations — reflection of the more distinctively philosophical order — leads to the development of several departments of philosophical discipline. Such departments are the theory of knowledge and theoretical psychology, or the philosophy of mind. By combination of similar material with material drawn from positive sciences other than the strictly psychological, the philosophy of ethics, of æsthetics, and of religion arise. All these branches of philosophy are so closely intertwined with different branches of psychology, or rather they seem so to spring forth from one root in psychological inquiry, that their treatment apart becomes a matter of peculiar difficulty. Not a few have, therefore, either explicitly admitted or in practice implied that psychology and philosophy cannot be distinguished.

The relations of psychological science to philosophical discipline are so important as to demand a separate detailed treatment. It is enough at present to insist that the same characteristic traits of philosophy distinguish it from the psychological and the physical sciences. Psychology, as a science in the widest legitimate use of the term, is concerned only with the classification of psychical phenomena and with their explanation through the discovery and verifying of the uniform relations existing among the psychical phenomena, and between the psychical and certain physical phenomena. But the psychological sciences, as well as the physical, have a body of principles, presupposed or ascertained, with the systematizing of which in their relation to ultimate Reality philosophy must deal. The presuppositions are to be discerned and handled with that free, reflective analysis which characterizes philosophical method. The discovered principles of psychological science afford philosophy the material of synthesis for which it is dependent upon the positive sciences.

It is now obvious that the relation which, so far as material for systematic treatment is concerned, exists between philosophy and the particular sciences, is precisely that which was provided for in the definition of philosophy. Philosophy *is* the rational system of the principles presupposed or ascertained by the particular sciences. But philosophy regards all these principles from its own point of view, and with its peculiar final purpose bearing upon them all. It endeavors to reduce them to system,—by considering them all in their relation to a Unity of ultimate Reality.

CHAPTER IV.

PSYCHOLOGY AND PHILOSOPHY.

THAT a peculiar relation exists between the science of mind and the conclusions of philosophical study, may be argued from the nature of both and from the history of their development. Some difficulty has, indeed, always been experienced in clearly distinguishing certain branches of philosophy from the more closely correlated forms of the positive sciences of nature. In the practice of experts themselves metaphysics has hitherto mingled freely with mechanics, physics, chemistry, and biology. But we have seen that these and similar empirical or more nearly "pure" departments of human knowledge retain their strictly *scientific* character only so long as they confine their aims to the classification of phenomena, and to explanation by the discovery and verification of uniform relations between phenomena. All the particular sciences, however, involve certain principles, which are either presupposed by them or else are the highest generalizations reached in the course of their development. The ultimate source and validity in reality of the presuppositions is not a matter for scientific inquiry. The generalizations do not require to be validated in reality, or connected with generalizations of other sciences in the unity of a rational system, by the particular sciences that make them. These limitations by which their pursuits are lawfully bound, and the need of subjecting their principles to a more penetrating analysis and a higher rational synthesis, are now generally recognized by the most thoughtful and candid students of physical science.

But the case between psychology and philosophy is not precisely the same; nor is it so clear, whether it be viewed in the light of history, or of a satisfactory division of the fields of scientific and philosophical inquiry. From time immemorial, but especially since Descartes, the analysis of consciousness and the statement of conclusions based upon this analysis have been largely dominated by metaphysical points of view. With English authors, since Locke and until the present generation, psychology has controlled and absorbed philosophy. In England, indeed, philosophy has scarcely existed otherwise than in the form of a mixture of empirical and metaphysical observations — interesting, stimulating, yet perplexing — that have rambled over the fields of a descriptive science of related states of consciousness, philosophical theory of knowledge, ontology of mind, philosophy of ethics, and theology. Recently, however, the empirical science of psychology has striven, with commendable success, to establish for itself an independent existence. The philosophy of religion has been more clearly distinguished from dogmatic and biblical theology; and moral philosophy, properly so-called, has recognized many of its points of contact and of contrast with the science of ethical phenomena. A still more vigorous and intelligent development of the different connected branches of philosophical system, as dependent upon psychology and upon all the particular sciences, is doubtless near at hand.

The philosophy of Locke is chiefly an "Essay concerning Human Understanding." This essay has been pronounced "the most important offspring of modern philosophy." It is, however, described by its author as an inquiry "into the original, certainty, and extent of human knowledge, together with the grounds and degrees of belief, opinion, and assent."[1] From the more modern point of view these words would be understood as proposing a mixed psychological and philosophical inquiry. This the "Essay" of Locke really is. The philosophy of his

[1] Book I. chap. i. 2.

great successor, Berkeley, is confined for the most part to a psychological and metaphysical treatment of a single problem of cognition,—the problem, namely, of perception by the senses. Hume justifies his discussion of the more profound and difficult philosophical problems, in a "Treatise of Human Nature," by observing that "all the sciences have a relation, greater or less, to human nature;" and that "in pretending, therefore, to explain the principles of human nature, we in effect propose a compleat system of the sciences." In this way psychology, if it be understood as the science which explains the principles of human nature, appears to include not only all philosophy, but also all the other particular sciences.

More recently, John Stuart Mill and the associational school generally have dominated philosophical discussion almost completely with a special psychological theory of the origin and laws, in combination, of the ideas. The "Scottish" school, including Sir William Hamilton,[1] have constantly confused the psychological investigation of the problem of perception with the effort to establish a peculiar form of realism against all rival claimants in the general field of philosophy. With the same object in view, the most distinguished living representative of this school, Dr. McCosh, identifies metaphysical philosophy throughout with the systematic arrangement of the so-called "intuitions," as determined—it seems to us—by an insufficient psychological analysis.

On the Continent, and especially in Germany, somewhat different relations have been maintained between psychology and philosophy. But everywhere the established relations between the two have been intimate and influential for the fate of both. By reflective analysis Descartes laid the foundations of modern philosophy in an ultimate psychological fact. But every student of Cartesianism knows how unsatisfactory was the metaphysical structure, regarding Mind and Matter, and the connection of

[1] See the Article of Professor Seth on Philosophy, Encyclopædia Britannica ninth edition.

the two, and regarding God and his relation to the world, which Descartes and his disciples proceeded at once to build upon these foundations. The monadology of Leibnitz is a beautiful and inspiring dream in metaphysics as controlled by *naïve* psychological intuition. It is the type of all subsequent attempts (like that made, for example, by Fechner in his "Nanna, or the Soul-life of Plants") to transfer, with little enough of criticism, the diminishing degrees of man's self-conscious life to the diverse forms of reality.

Wolff is said to have been the first to make that distinction of psychology into empirical and rational which holds, substantially unchanged, until the present time. To empirical psychology he assigned the description and systematic arrangement of psychical processes; to rational psychology the explanation of these processes by reference to the real nature of the mind itself. But the Wolffian empirical psychology was defective in that it substituted classification for scientific explanation. The Wolffian rational psychology had no sufficient basis in empirical science, and was also devoid of critical quality. Moreover, the distinction introduced by Wolff must be employed (after being corrected and expanded) to separate the empirical science of psychology from the philosophy of mind, rather than simply to emphasize a division in psychology.

With Kant a new department of philosophy sprang out of the more penetrating and comprehensive application of reflective analysis to psychological phenomena. The "Critique of Pure Reason" proposes a problem in the theory of cognition; this problem is to be pursued without a critical reconstruction of the conclusions of empirical psychology and in contempt and despair of rational psychology. Plainly, the Kantian theory of knowledge is itself dependent upon certain views of the psychical processes that only partially command the support of inductive science, while it involves conclusions that constitute a special metaphysics of mind, and have the widest and most profound influence on all subsequent philosophical system.

Since Kant, in Germany, three not very distinctly separable ways of regarding the relations of psychology and philosophy have been prominent. One of these is the precise opposite of that prevalent among English writers. In Germany, the great philosophical systems have too often dominated the scientific study of the phenomena of man's sentient life. The tendency has been to deduce the nature and modes of the behavior of the mind from some supreme principle, reached by philosophical speculation rather than by inductive science. Hegel's "Phenomenology of Spirit," for example, is not a psychology established upon a scientific basis of observed psychical facts, and inferences from such facts; it is rather a comprehensive but somewhat incoherent survey of different phases in the intellectual growth of the race, from a peculiar speculative point of view. It is, says Dr. William Wallace,[1] "the picture of the Hegelian philosophy in the making, — at the stage before the scaffolding has been removed from the building." From Fichte and Schelling, as well as Hegel, and from Schopenhauer and Hartmann, we get no scientific handling of psychical phenomena. Whatever light these writers throw upon such phenomena comes under the shadow of their theories respecting the nature of reality in general. The science of mind is made dependent upon a special way of the speculative solving of philosophical problems.

One of the most fruitful of the attempts made in modern times to subject the phenomena of mind to a strictly scientific treatment arose with Herbart. This great psychologist and his followers have persistently introduced metaphysics into the study of the psychical processes. But their point of view has been distinctly different from that maintained by the advocates of systematic philosophical Idealism. The Herbartians have rather made use of metaphysics in psychology, tentatively and as a working hypothesis, to assist in the detailed explanation of the genesis and development of observed states of consciousness.

[1] Article on Hegel in Encyclopædia Britannica, ninth edition.

Herbart himself announces on the titlepage of his work[1] the intention to treat psychology as a "science;" although he will found it anew, not only on experience, but also upon "metaphysics and mathematics." The consummate product of the Herbartian development, Volkmann von Volkmar, in his admirable work on Psychology,[2] defines its problem as follows: "To explain the general classes of psychical phenomena by means of processes of ideation (*Vorstellungen*) as empirically given, *and from the speculative concept of ideation in accordance with the general laws of the life of ideation.*" The philosophy of this school of psychologists is avowedly realistic. Its influence is designedly made prominent in the discussion of psychological problems. Each of these problems is to be considered as having, so to speak, a twofold aspect. It is a question of the relation of states of consciousness as empirically given (a problem in psychological science); but it is also a question for the correct deductive application of the laws of the soul's life, as growing out of the very nature of that entity we call soul.[3]

Now, in view of the almost uniform practice of the physical sciences in dealing with phenomena under terms of hypothetical entities,—such as atoms, ether, electricity (as an essence), etc.,—it is difficult to see why psychology should be forbidden to speak, at least hypothetically, of the entities and forces which it seems to find necessary for the explanation of its own peculiar phenomena. But may it not thus speak with a clear understanding of the fact that it is using appropriate hypotheses? And may it not defer to that broader and more penetrating

1 Psychologie als Wissenschaft, neu gegründet auf Erfahrung, Metaphysik und Mathematik, Königsberg, 1824.

2 Lehrbuch der Psychologie vom Standpunkte des Realismus und nach genetischer Methode, last edition, Cöthen, 1884.

3 Thus Herbart himself declares: "The whole series of the forms of experience must be investigated twice over, metaphysically and psychologically. Both investigations must lie side by side, and be compared together long enough for every one to see their complete difference so plainly as never to be in danger of confusing them again."

analysis which philosophy provides for the more complete interpretation of its hypotheses?

The third form of regarding the relations of psychology and philosophy which has prevailed in Germany is that of which Beneke[1] may be regarded as the chief forerunner and representative. It contends for the possibility of separating psychology from metaphysics, and of studying it as a *natural* science by the methods appropriate to such a science. Experience is rationally elaborated through science. The peculiar experience to which psychology, by methods common to it with all natural science, attempts to give rational elaboration is, "What thou findest in thee, or what thy self-consciousness shows to thee." But although Beneke would have us avoid founding psychology upon metaphysics, he himself developed several branches of philosophy upon the basis of his own psychological doctrines. Moreover, as Ueberweg declares, the guiding thought in all the investigations of Beneke is this, "that through self-consciousness we know ourselves psychically just as we really are." The external world, however, we can know only indirectly, by supposing "analoga of our own psychical life" to underlie its phenomena. The masterly effort of this thinker to establish a distinction between psychology and philosophy, by freeing psychology from metaphysics, serves further to illustrate how intimate and pervasive are the relations of the two.

The development of psychology in attempted independence of metaphysics, and by the methods of the natural sciences, has now gone far beyond the point at which it was left by Beneke. Even the modest, tentative hypothesis of a soul, and of its development as the life of a real being, has been rejected by many as a prejudice harmful to the freedom of scientific inquiry. But no examination of so-called psychical processes can be prose-

[1] For Beneke's own view, see his Lehrbuch der Psychologie als Naturwissenschaft, 1ste Aufl., 1833; 4rte Aufl., 1877. Also Pragmatische Psychologie, 1850; Die neue Psychologie, etc.; System der Metaphysik, p. 68 ff.; and the supplement; Der streng naturwissenschaftliche Character der neuen Psychologie, in the Archiv für die pragmatische Psychologie, iii. 495 ff.

cuted long without bringing the inquirer face to face with a certain conception of peculiar value and peculiar claims to validate itself, in some sort, on reality (with the conception, that is, of the Ego, which is the permanent subject of states, and yet not itself a state); accordingly, the *science* of psychology seems to itself confined within limits too narrow for its own comfort and success as a science, if denied the thorough analysis of this conception.

The extreme followers of this empirical tendency, in Germany and in France, have proclaimed the possibility and necessity of a science of "psychology without a soul." But how shall we understand this phrase? Does it mean that even such reality of being as consciousness itself commonly attaches to the word "soul" is to be understood by the science of psychical phenomena as merely hypothetical? Then it belongs either to psychology, or to some more nearly ultimate form of reflective analysis, to clear up this hypothesis. Does it mean to deny that any conception such as that called the "soul," with even its alleged hypothetical reference to reality, is actually to be found among the psychical phenomena? Then the examination and analysis of these phenomena has hitherto been most amazingly lacking in scientific thoroughness and exactness. Does it mean that, for the hypothesis of a soul, scientific psychology requires that we should substitute the hypothesis of no-soul, — the negative or sceptical conclusion that the subject to which the states of consciousness are referred has no existence in reality? Then psychology, in the name of exact science, has gone beyond the avowed rights of such science. It has substituted one metaphysical hypothesis for another; it has assumed the so-called positivistic, or materialistic, instead of the so-called spiritualistic position.

So difficult is it wholly to bar metaphysics out of psychology that those who claim to approach the psychical phenomena from the purely empirical and physiological point of view are not infrequently chief sinners in respect of metaphysical hypotheses. Their whole language convicts them of this. For explanation of the processes observed in self-consciousness, they freely refer to hypothetical and inferred entities that lie wholly and forever beyond consciousness. The existence of occult *metempirical* (to borrow Mr. Lewes's word) beings, far removed from any possible or conceivable experience, is assumed to account for psychical phenomena. Only the metaphysics of physics, in its most uncouth and untried forms, can be admitted, it would seem, into the exact science of psychology. Psychical phenomena are not allowed to appear in their naked reality, undisguised with the war-paint and war-feathers of some momentarily dominant physiological or physical hypothesis. To such a result have certain devotees of science been led by the attempt to set psychology free from its intimate relation to philosophy.

There can be no doubt that the reasons for the difficulties which have so constantly accompanied the attempt to distinguish psychology and philosophy, lie deep in the nature of the case. Psychology, in the widest meaning of the word (as including the sciences of logic, ethics, and æsthetics), cannot be mechanically separated from philosophy. For psychology is the only normal, and the chief necessary, propædeutic of philosophy. All the problems of philosophy first emerge to clear view in the study of psychical processes. Psychology starts and shapes these problems; from its hands philosophy receives them for further analytic treatment, and for constructive use in the elaboration of philosophical system. Psychology represents the first and scientific stage of reflective analysis, and of the theoretic synthesis of experience. But philosophy is the stage beyond and ultimate. Philosophy involves the further and most complete possible reflective analysis of the problems prepared for it by psychology. It aims at a theoretical synthesis which shall include the supreme generalizations based not only upon the psychological sciences in their widest range, but also upon all the sciences.

But the principles with which philosophical analysis and synthesis deal must, in their turn, penetrate and modify the results of psychological science. Every one of these principles has a two-fold aspect, as it were. It may be considered as a conception or judgment built up in the actual evolution of the mind's life, or as a self-consciously recognized norm or presupposition of the concrete activities of that life. But it may also be considered as having a reference to forces and beings in the world of the really Existent. On the one hand, its genesis and development admit of study as a process capable of scientific verification. On the other hand, the questions respecting its *extra*-mental reference, and place in the universe of interconnected reality, remain for philosophy to undertake. They *remain*, even after we have endeavored to exclude them. They recur, even after — in the name of exact science — we have dogmatically given to them the agnostic, the sceptical, or the materialistic explanation.

In view of facts like these, Wundt feels justified in holding that the relation of philosophy to all the sciences is such as to give to every important subject-matter two aspects, or rather, a place in two systems, — the system of science, and the system of philosophical unity. But so close and peculiar is the relation of psychology, in particular, to philosophy that the partition of sovereignty between the two is an abstract scheme which, in the presence of actuality, always appears unsatisfactory.[1]

The general truth just stated might be illustrated by the example of every important psychological problem.

The problem of sense-perception, the cognition of things by the senses, is primarily a psychological problem; but it involves various philosophical questions over which the different schools of philosophy have divided. As pursued by the so-called "old psychology," its solution was understood to be chiefly a matter of the classification of psychical activities under the heads of "faculty," "intuition," etc. As pursued by the new

[1] System der Philosophie, pp. 5 and 21 f.

psychology, it is rather an inquiry into the genesis and evolution of related psychical processes in dependence upon excited states of the nervous mechanism. The scientific solution of the problem of perception by the senses requires, therefore, an analysis of a complex process into its simplest discernible factors, and a precise statement of the conditions under which perceptions arise and develop in consciousness. We are thus led to examine not only the different sorts of sensations in themselves considered, but also, and chiefly, the laws of their dependence, as respects quality, quantity, time-rate, etc., upon the kind, amount, order, etc., of the stimuli, and upon the structure and locality of the nervous mass to which the stimuli are applied. We are also led to consider the laws according to which the sensations are combined, the sensation-complexes grow in intricacy and are localized and objectively projected, so as to become possessed of those relations which belong to every so-called "Thing," with other things, in the world of space and time.

But is our analysis of "things" ultimate when we have reduced them to localized and objectively projected sensation-complexes? Is there not somewhat over and above, or underneath, all that is reached by the analysis, necessary to the cognition of things, — somewhat corresponding to what we mean, or think we mean, when we affirm of every "Thing" a *Reality* that is not exhausted by the description of concrete psychical processes? Whence, too, comes this form of Space, in which all things are given as existent? What, if anything, that is itself really existent, do we mean by the word "space"? How, moreover, shall we explain Time, in which things appear to have their sequence, as itself arising in our minds, or in reality, from the sequence of experienced things?

With questions such as these the empirical science of modern psychology struggles manfully. In the effort to answer them it employs a keener analysis and a more elaborate experimentation for the discovery and description of the genesis and evolution of the requisite psychical processes. It investigates the rise and growth of those refinements of conceptions involved in all the matured sensation-complexes, such as have already been referred to under the names Reality, Space, and Time. But the mind, roused by the discipline of empirical psychology to scepticism even concerning its own instinctive metaphysics, is not fully satisfied with the answer which the most elaborate forms of this science provide. It demands something more, if it be possible, than a description of the order in which, and the circumstances under which, arose its own mental images of Reality, Space, and Time. It inquires into the *extra*-mental validity and significance of these conceptions; it demands a further reflective analysis in order to absolve them from some of the difficulties and contradictions that seem attached to them, and perhaps reduce them to the unity of some higher Idea. This inquiry and demand give rise to philosophy.

Nor does it seem easy theoretically to draw the line, exact and rigid, about the domain within which the purely scientific consideration of the problem of sense-perception must confine itself. To be *scientific*, in any worthy sense of the word, it would seem that we must make our analysis of the phenomena, and our description and explanation of their uniform relations, as complete as possible. In the very effort, then, to be completely scientific, we cannot avoid starting various latent metaphysical questionings. On reflection a "Thing" always appears to us as involving somewhat more than is fully described in the narrative of our experience with the related psychical processes. There is always in the "Thing" an additional unknown quantity, a *plus x*, as it were, which seems to refuse to be classified or explained in company with all concrete processes. And unless we are willing, with an unsophisticated cheerfulness of superficiality which is no less unscientific than unphilosophical, either to overlook this $+ x$ altogether, or to deceive ourselves with the thought that we have explained it when we have called it by another name (*e. g.*, substance, *substratum*, permanent subject — *Träger* — of states), we seem forced by our problem to enter the deep shadows of metaphysics. When we look back from the land of these shadows, we find it difficult to say at just what point we abandoned the certainties of empirical science.

Schools of philosophy have divided over the problem of perception by the senses. The "empiricists" and "nativists" cannot even keep their strife out of experimental psychology. But this strife within the so-called "scientific" domain is only anticipatory of the larger and profounder contention which issues in the domain of philosophy. Here the manner of regarding and solving the problem of our cognition of things is found to involve considerations determinative of our entire system of speculative thinking. Out of this problem there seem necessarily to arise questions concerning the relation of the brain and the sentient life in man, of "matter" and "mind" in the universe at large, and of the ultimate nature and reality of those existent beings which we mean to designate by the latter two abstract terms. Hence arise, in no small degree, the differences discussed between philosophical agnosticism and scepticism on the one hand, and realism, idealism, dualism, or monism, on the other.

As this general problem of sense-perception is specialized by the particular natural and physical sciences, it is seen to furnish yet more definite material for philosophy. The cognition of "Things," as they are known by these sciences, is said to be based on exact and comprehensive observation. But, in truth, the psychological theory of this so-called "observation" will go but a little way toward the justification of the scientific character of the cognition. Every plain man is, in his practice, a wonderful metaphysician. He uncritically and instinctively makes the world of his immediate experience to be all underlain and interpenetrated with a world of postulated real existences. Psychology shows us not only in what concrete forms ordinary experience proceeds to organize itself into the living development of mind, but also in accordance with what primitive norms, and upon the basis of what necessary postulates, this organization takes place. But the "unseen world" of the physical and natural sciences is much more wonderful than that of ordinary experience. The student of these sciences — scorner of metaphysics though he may be — is a most masterful metaphysician. The world in the midst of which he lives — the world, primarily, of his own psychical processes of imagination and inference, founded upon unusual means for perception by the senses, and stimulated by the rivalry of critics and colleagues — is far removed from, and vastly unlike, the world of immediate experience and first intention. And here we do not need to repeat what has been said in discussing the relation of philosophy to the positive sciences of the external world. We only insist that the treatment of the principles, presupposed and ascertained by these sciences, is difficult satisfactorily to apportion between the science of psychology and the philosophy of nature and mind. Where, for example, does the psychological discussion of such conceptions as Force, Matter, Law, Causation, etc., end, and their philosophical discussion begin?

No less difficulty is experienced when the attempt is made to secure a strict and mechanical separation between the psychological and the philosophical treatment of the problem of self-consciousness. The interest which the human mind necessarily takes in the knowledge of itself is undoubtedly a most potent and indestructible source of philosophy. So true is this that metaphysical answers to the questions, What am I? and How and whence do I, self-conscious and rational being, come to be? long preceded the beginnings of empirical and scientific psychology. To this science, as now understood, it belongs to trace the genesis and evolution of those states which we call "self-conscious," of the concept of that *self* to which all states of consciousness are referred, and of that peculiar form of activity in which the reference consists, — the so-called activity of "self-consciousness." This general problem modern psychology therefore attacks in several ways. It describes the physical and psychical conditions under which, so far as can be ascertained, we become self-conscious. It traces the stages of the development of self-consciousness, in dependence upon these conditions. It strives by analysis to discover the factors and laws which enter into this development.

But again, in the consideration of the problem of self-consciousness, empirical psychology starts a variety of questionings which it cannot answer, or even consider, without an appeal to philosophy. Of the other particular sciences we may say that their attitude is uncritical toward the different ways of answering such questions. But the very business of psychology requires the determination of the most exact and comprehensive answer possible to these inquiries. And as this science presses forward with its attempts at explanation, it becomes increasingly difficult to tell precisely when it crosses the line that bounds it, as science, from the larger domain of philosophy.

The problem of the cognition of things and the problem of the cognition of self are both connected inseparably with the general problem of all cognition. In these two forms of the problem both the objects and the method of cognition appear to be very different. The object in one case is "things;" in the other case it is that "self" which makes no other distinction so clearly and persistently as the distinction between itself and things. The method, in one case, is called by psychology "perception" through the senses; in the other case it is called "self-consciousness." But both processes must be, in some sort, fundamentally alike; otherwise they could not both be called by the common term "cognition." And both objects, — things and self, — it would seem, must be held to have some real likeness underlying or conjoined with that difference which is recognized in the seemingly fundamental distinction made by consciousness, since they are both alike objects for the cognition of the same subject. Here, then, is another problem, requiring discussion from both the psychological and the philosophical points of view. Here, also, is another problem in the consideration of which psychology and philosophy find it necessary to enter into their own peculiar form of partnership. In this case, too, the partnership is unlimited as respects time, and difficult of exact limitation as respects each partner's share of responsibility.

"Logic" is the name given for many centuries after Aristotle to a science which aimed (either as pure or applied) to tell men how they do and must think, as well as how they ought to think. Far be it from our purpose to depreciate the achievements of this science, whether as it was left by its great founder in what was long esteemed a finished form, or as it is now modified under the influences of modern psychology and philosophy. But if the truth must be spoken, there can be no science of logic as independent of psychology and the philosophical theory of cognition. To psychology rightfully belongs the description and explanation of the genesis and organization of experience through thought; the forms and laws of thought are therefore peculiarly its own material. If logical forms and laws are regarded as primarily other than forms and laws of living psychical processes, they are wrongly regarded. Moreover, psychology, in the broad modern way of its study, has reference to thought-processes and thought-products, not simply as made known to introspection in the consciousness of the individual, but also as made known to historico-genetic researches in the evolution of the thought of the race. Therefore, that form of logic which deals with the correct method of discovery and verification, in the particular sciences, is but an apartment of applied psychology. But if logic raises the ultimate inquiries respecting the power of man to know reality, to represent in forms of his thought the forms of the being and action of the really Existent, then it becomes philosophical. Such "logical" inquiries belong to that branch of philosophy which is called the theory of knowledge.

In the discussion of the problem of knowledge, therefore, it is peculiarly difficult to tell where a line shall be drawn between those sciences, on the one hand, which we call logic or psychology, and the domain, on the other hand, of philosophy as the general doctrine of cognition.

Ethics, considered as an empirical science, like logic, cannot be given a place among the sciences as distinct from psychology. Indeed, the practical outcome of the attempt to separate ethics and psychology has been highly injurious to both. This attempt has resulted not only in confining the discussion of psychological problems, among English writers, too closely to the phenomena of cognition, but also in vitiating the interpretation of these phenomena by excluding from it the light thrown by the scientific study of the phenomena of desire, feeling, and willing. It has, moreover, resulted in much *un*psychological discussion of ethical problems. Few of the English treatises on "ethics" so called have been based upon that thorough knowledge of modern psychological conclusions, or that consistent use of psychological analysis, which are indispensable to the highest success. Indeed, under this title we ordinarily expect to find either a work on moral philosophy or one on ethical praxis (*i. e.*, the art of behaving one's self properly in society as at present constituted, especially in English-speaking countries).

In Germany, on the contrary, treatises corresponding to the English books on ethics are comparatively rare. And, indeed, the occasion for the composition of such works has scarcely been felt. For in Germany every writer on psychology, however unimportant, thinks it necessary to touch upon those forms of psychical life that are called "ethical," — and this from the point of view of a scientific psychology. Psychological treatises on the different ethical problems, such as those of feeling, habit, volition, etc., therefore abound. But this does not prevent a rich development of writings concerned with the metaphysics of ethics, the philosophy of rights, and of the State; and with the special classes and forms of ethical principles such as are treated under the head of "theological ethics" (Rothe), Christian ethics, biblical ethics, etc.

Ethics, then, cannot be considered an independent science. What is properly called by this term is either a phase or department rather than a distinct branch of psychology; or else it is moral philosophy. The relation in which the science of ethics stands to philosophical discipline is to be determined as part of the more general question, What is the relation of psychological science to philosophy? When, then, Dr. Stuckenberg considers psychology as propædeutic to philosophy, rather than a branch of philosophy, but at the same time separates ethics from its complete dependence, as a science, upon psychological analysis and upon general psychological principles, he seems to us precisely to reverse the right relations.[1] In the treatment of those problems which are called "ethical" it is no easy matter, however, to distinguish, either theoretically or in practice, between the point of view held by the science of psychology and that taken by ethical philosophy.

Psychological ethics investigates those psychical processes — whether called processes of cognition, feeling, desire, or volition — which enter into what we call conduct and character, as distinguished from mere action and habit. Among such cognitive processes it discovers the genesis and maturing of certain ideas of a peculiar kind. By analysis and generalization of these processes it arrives at the existence of a norm of all ethical ideation, called "the idea of the right," or "the morally good." By the same method of scientific psychological analysis, it arrives at the existence of an altogether peculiar norm of feeling; for this it appropriates the term "feeling of the ought," or feeling of moral obligation. It also traces the genesis and development of those peculiar emotions which are experienced in the contemplation of character or conduct that appears in relations of conformity or opposition to the idea of

[1] Introduction to the Study of Philosophy, chapters iv., v., and ix.

the right, of the morally good. These are the emotions of moral approbation and disapprobation, of ethical good- and ill-desert. Furthermore, it investigates the evolution of so-called "free-will." It traces, that is, the rise and growth of the mind's power to conform character and conduct to certain ideals of reason. In all this, psychology is in the exercise of its legitimate scientific function, — not the less truly because the psychical processes which it classifies and endeavors to explain appear of a somewhat peculiar nature.

The further demand of reason for light upon the problems of psychological ethics has been seen to be one of the main sources of philosophy. The relation of the science of psychology to philosophy is, accordingly, not different with respect to these problems from that which maintains itself with respect to all problems that are common to both branches of knowledge. But the department of philosophy with which psychological ethics stands in such peculiar relations is of a special kind. This department is not metaphysics, in the more limited sense in which we shall employ that word. It is rather the philosophy of one of the Ideals of Reason, — the Ideal of Conduct. When we inquire into the origin, the ground, and validity of those ideation processes in which the Right, the Ought, the Morally Well-deserving or Ill-deserving are given to self-consciousness, we find the resulting problems related to the general postulate of a unity of Ultimate Reality in another than the strictly metaphysical way. The conceptions answering to these terms ("the Right," etc.) do not represent particular real entities or modes of the being of such entities as do the conceptions of Matter, Force, Atom, Mind, Thought, etc. They rather stimulate and guide the feeling and volition in that comprehensive and indefinite way which belongs to a rational Ideal.

Philosophy receives from psychological ethics the problems already prepared for it by the first steps of reflective analysis. Its one greatest and final inquiry concerns the relation in which the ethical ideals stand to that Unity of all ultimate

Reality which it is compelled to postulate. Ethical philosophy thus leads the mind forward to the question whether these and all other ideals, as well as all forms of concrete reality, must not be considered as having their ground in one Being (an Ideal-Real, or really existent, supreme Idea). But this question belongs rather to the philosophy of religion, which is the supreme department of philosophy, — the highest rational synthesis of metaphysics, the theory of knowledge, and the philosophy of the Ideal.

The remarks just made concerning ethics apply as well to æsthetics, which also may be treated either as a branch of psychological science, or as a department of the philosophy of the Ideal.

Abundant reasons, then, exist not only in the past history of philosophy, but also in the nature of the case, for affirming that the relation of philosophy to empirical psychology is peculiarly intimate. Neither in theory nor in practice is it possible to make a mechanical division, as it were, between the two. And if objection be made to the word "mechanical," as not correctly expressing the nature of the division to be made between even the physical sciences and philosophy, we are ready to discard the term. It is not so much as possible to propound and understand the problems of philosophy without the propædeutic of scientific psychology. Every important philosophical inquiry is primarily psychological; not one such inquiry would ever be raised, much less intelligently shaped, by the physical and natural sciences alone. Moreover, the psychological discussion of the problems of mind cannot escape the influence of philosophy. It should never strive to make this escape. And yet a plain distinction between psychology and philosophy, even in the consideration of the same problems, may be made theoretically; and in practice the distinction may be carried out with a measure of success.

Several recent writers have drawn the distinction between psychology and philosophy with more than customary clearness and intelligence. Mr. Shadworth Hodgson, for example, holds, in apparent opposition to most of his own countrymen, that this distinction can be scientifically defined and consistently carried out.[1] He keenly and correctly shows the failure of Sir William Hamilton, John Stuart Mill, and Herbert Spencer to make and observe this distinction. "Psychology," says Mr. Hodgson, "has all states of consciousness for its object-matter; and so far it has precisely the same object-matter as that here attributed to philosophy." And yet by simply "adding psychology to the list of the other sciences," we do not perform the same service as we should do "by superposing philosophy on the other sciences, as something generically different from them." Psychology, indeed, is led, in its search for the conditions *existendi* of the states of consciousness, to the laws and nature of the objects, of substances so called. It "envisages the particular relations of dependence which particular portions of the subjective aspect have to particular portions of the objective. And it is therefore not permitted, like philosophy, to abstract from the substrate, or agent which has the states of consciousness." Moreover, "the analysis of states of consciousness as given in philosophy takes those states in connection with their objective aspects,—these objective aspects it is which give us the states to be analyzed; but in psychology it is in reference to their conditions in the organism or other substratum that they come under analytic dissection." The method and assumption of the two are, accordingly, diametrically opposed. In philosophy, we take the ultimate truths of the sciences and inquire what are their subjective aspects; in psychology we take supposed ultimate subjective aspects and ask what their objective aspects, what their corresponding existences, must be. Philosophy is therefore distinguished from psychology by its elevation of Reflection into a method.

Philosophy is not, however.—we are at once told,—limited

[1] Philosophy of Reflection, i. 50 ff.

to the analytic branch of ultimate subjective science; the constructive branch of philosophy is also necessary and legitimate. The constructive branch must be pursued in connection with the analytic. But the elements given by the different analyses may be hypothetically constructed and reconstructed in various ways. There cannot be anything beyond existence that is not existence. But there may be existences or existent worlds very different from that given in our consciousness. "This whole hypothetical group of phenomenal worlds would constitute the field of the constructive branch of philosophy. It is this right of making hypotheses in explanation of our own world which connects philosophy with science. Here again, however, philosophy differs from the particular sciences, including psychology, in the application of method common to them both. All these sciences use reflection, and by this use are connected with each other and with philosophy. "But philosophy elevates this common thread of reflection into a *method;* and it is its method, founded on reflection, that at once distinguishes philosophy from the sciences and gives it a larger field." The constructive branch of philosophy, when constituted by the method of the most ultimate reflection, is, however, says Mr. Hodgson, "to be regarded as a philosophized psychology, or the return of Metaphysic upon psychology." It is "hypothetical psychology, psychology carried up into more general regions." "Its aim is to put the objective aspect, a new hypothetical world, to the hypothetical subjective aspect with which it begins."

More particularly still,[1] we have psychology described by Mr. Hodgson as dealing with the conditions or causes of states of consciousness in a scientific way. But philosophy considers "*aspects.*" "*Aspect,* as a philosophical term, means a character co-extensive with and peculiar to the thing of which it is an aspect." The two ultimate and necessary aspects in philosophy are the subjective and the objective. "The high and abstract region in which this distinction arises is the watershed of

[1] Philosophy of Reflection, ii. 20 ff.

philosophical systems." The limits and relations between a genuine philosophy and a scientific psychology can be defined only by the removal of causation from consciousness, as such. Now, since the only known causation is material, if you retain causation in philosophy, as respects the ultimate aspects with which it deals, you materialize philosophy. If you do not hold fast by it in psychology, you render psychology unscientific and illusory, since "causation by consciousness is incalculable."[1] In this connection, and it would seem as a result of the effort to distinguish psychology and philosophy, Mr. Hodgson avows his conversion to completely materialistic psychology.

The distinction drawn by Professor Seth[2] between psychology and philosophy differs from the foregoing in several important particulars. Whereas Mr. Hodgson emphasizes especially the ultimate nature of the analysis which philosophy employs, "it is with the ultimate synthesis," says Professor Seth, "that philosophy concerns itself; it has to show that the subject-matter with which we are dealing in detail really *is* a whole, consisting of articulated members." Psychology, on the other hand, belongs with the group of the sciences; although a special relation has always existed between it and systematic philosophy, and the closeness of the connection is characteristic of modern, and especially of English, thought. The explanation of this connection is that in the scientific study of mind "we have, so far, in our hands the fact (the fact of intelligence) to which all other facts are relative." But mind, and its facts of knowing, willing, etc., may be looked at in two different ways. "It may be regarded simply as fact, in which case the evolutions of mind may be traced and reduced to laws in the same way as the phenomena treated by the other sciences (psychology, *sans phrase*)." It is mind in its ulterior aspect, as grounding inferences beyond itself. Now "the last abstraction which it becomes the duty of philosophy

[1] Philosophy of Reflection, ii. 65.

[2] Article on Philosophy in the Encyclopædia Britannica (9th edition).

to remove is the abstraction from the knowing subject which is made by all the sciences, including the science of psychology."

Subject-object, knowledge with its implicates — this unity in duality is the ultimate aspect which reality presents. Philosophy may then be said to be the explication of what is involved in this relation, or a theory of its possibility. Two problems may be discriminated as entering necessarily into this general problem of the explication of what is involved in the relation of subject-object; these are a problem of knowledge and a problem of being. "It is evident, then, that philosophy as theory of knowledge must have for its complement philosophy as metaphysics or ontology." Logic, æsthetics, and ethics are rightly considered by Professor Seth to be sciences affording subject-matter which requires both psychological and philosophical treatment.[1]

A nearer approximation to the correct statement of the relation of psychology to general philosophical discipline is, in at least some respects, that made by Dr. Stuckenberg.[2] This writer objects, indeed, to placing psychology in the same category with the natural sciences. It appears, however, that his

[1] It will be helpful in this connection to quote, from two other writers on this subject, passages which are brought forward with approval in the article of Professor Seth.

"We may view knowledge," says Professor Croom Robertson, "as mere subjective function; but it has its full meaning only as it is taken to represent what we may call objective fact, or is such as is named (in different circumstances) real, valid, true. As mere subjective function, which it is to the psychologist, it is best spoken of by an unambiguous name, and for this there seems none better than Intellection. We may then say that psychology is occupied with the natural function of *Intellection*, seeking to discover its laws and distinguishing its various modes. . . . Philosophy, on the other hand, is theory of *Knowledge* (as that which is known)." — *Psychology and Philosophy* (*Mind*, 1883, p. 15 f.).

"Comparing psychology and epistemology," says Dr. Ward, "we may say that the former is essentially genetic in its method, and might, if we had the power to revise our existing terminology, be called biology; the latter, on the other hand, is essentially devoid of everything historical, and treats, *sub specie æternitatis*, as Spinoza might have said, of human knowledge, conceived as the possession of mind in general." — *Psychological Principles* (*Mind*, 1883, pp. 166 ff.).

[2] Chapter on Philosophy and Psychology, in his Introduction to the Study of Philosophy, New York, 1888.

objection obtains against reducing the science of mind to the rank of a department of physics and chemistry, rather than against giving to the psychical processes a treatment by strictly scientific method. "To make a theory of the essence of the soul, the principle for the explanation of its processes is," says this writer, "both unphilosophical and unscientific." And yet "if the natural sciences may postulate matter, there is no reason why psychology may not postulate mind, as a peculiar entity. It must, however, be treated as a mere postulate, and the supposed essence must not dominate the entire investigation, as if its nature were established." Psychology, then, cannot take the place of philosophy, which is "the rational system of fundamental principles." But while every serious study may be a preparation for philosophy, psychology is peculiarly its propædeutic. In carrying out this distinction, however, Dr. Stuckenberg makes no provision for the philosophical treatment of the principles of the natural sciences; nor does he sufficiently discriminate the scientific from the philosophical treatment of the subjects usually included under the heads of logic, ethics, and æsthetics, as well as psychology. The results of this failure render his divisions of philosophy peculiarly unsatisfactory.

We believe that the previous definition of philosophy, and the fixing of its relations to science in general, furnish the means for indicating more clearly and comprehensively than do any of the foregoing views, its peculiar relations of agreement and difference toward psychology.

The peculiar domain of empirical psychology is the description and explanation of the phenomena of individual human consciousness, as such. Every so-called "state of consciousness" may be said to furnish a number of problems which provoke reflective analysis and scientific research. This research is made more difficult, because self-consciousness, in the form in which psychological science begins to make use of it, implies an organization of experience that has already reached an advanced stage. The science of psychology is by no means satisfied with the mere description and classification of the "states" given in developed self-consciousness. Especially as studied in the modern spirit and by the modern methods, it recognizes the demand made upon it to "explain" these states. This explanation it undertakes to make scientific, especially in two directions. It analyzes the exceedingly complex states, as they are given to developed self-consciousness, into their most primitive and nearly simple factors; and it discovers the laws and conditions of their synthesis. It also traces the evolution of the same states as they succeed each other, with dependence upon preceding states and with a growing complexity, in the life of the soul. In other words, psychology strives to be scientific by being thoroughly analytic and historico-genetic in its study of mental phenomena. It is not, however, as Mr. Hodgson claims, limited in its attempts at exact explanation to the "causal" action of the body (objective aspect, or organism) on the mind (subjective aspect, or conscious state).

But psychology cannot be long and thoroughly pursued as a science without becoming aware of the presence of problems which it seems beyond the power of experimental or introspective analysis and synthesis fully to solve. When scientific study is begun, it finds the distinction between subjective and objective already established. It makes unquestioning use, at first, of this distinction to explain the genesis of states of consciousness from the effect of external influences upon the peripheral or central nervous system. It finds the subject of all the psychical states already self-constituted, as it were, and insisting on its right of referring to itself the states as all its own. It makes use of this reference to explain the present states as arising from previous states, under a theory of the association of ideas or of the influence of desire upon volition, etc. It finds certain collective images, and so-called abstract concepts and intuitions, already set into an habitual mode of procedure, in the uniform development of the mental life. It helps out its *science* by employing these images and concepts. It tells how states of consciousness are "caused" by pre-existing or co-existing states of the brain; or how the body and mind "influence" each other; or how "quantity" and "quality" of psychical states "depend" upon amount and kind of physical stimuli; or how the states, although they seem to "belong" to the mind, do "really" belong to the brain, etc.

As a matter of course, then, the scientific student of mental phenomena raises the question as to the genesis of these very distinctions and presuppositions in which he finds his own attempts at explanation invariably and inextricably involved. He is forced to come to some conclusion, at least a provisional and hypothetical one, regarding the nature and form of development of that (the life of the so-called Mind or Soul) which he is engaged in studying. But he cannot accept any conclusion on such a matter — in however cautious and merely tentative a manner — without appearing to adopt a philosophical tenet. Moreover, he finds that some theory as to the nature of the subject called "myself," and of the objects known as "things" of my experience, and as to the relations existing between this subject and these objects, and as to the validity of the self-reference of all states to the one subject of them all, etc., is helpful in explanation. His case is here somewhat analogous to that of the working physicist, who holds provisionally the molecular theory of the constitution of matter.

The psychologist who aims to keep his pursuit within strictly scientific lines can proceed little or no farther than the point described above. His attitude toward philosophical discipline is that of a giver and a borrower as well. He contributes to philosophy, as transformed by the first stages of reflective analysis and synthesis, the problems which constitute its subject-matter, and over the treatment of which its schools are divided. He gives to these problems the correct shaping which they may receive as presuppositions and discovered principles of that science which is the peculiar propædeutic of philosophy. He borrows from philosophy, as working hypotheses to be tested in an experimental way, its conclusions concerning the nature and validity, in the world of reality, of the principles which his science implicates.

But philosophy is somewhat more than a higher stage of psychology. Its aim is the rational system of the principles presupposed and ascertained by *all* the particular sciences, — in the relation which these principles sustain to ultimate Reality. Its analysis is then more ultimate and objective than that of psychology. Its problems all have, indeed, a subjective origin and aspect; for they are all most intelligently and consistently started in the effort of reason to understand itself. Psychological analysis, as a special propædeutic of philosophy, disengages and prepares these problems. But the same human reason which, with introspective or experimental analysis, seeks to know itself by a scientific psychology, constructs all the other particular sciences. Without it, and except as under its forth-puttings and laws, none of the sciences exist. Its ultimate analysis will, therefore, take them all into the account. It will extricate the presuppositions, and seize upon and appropriate the discovered principles, of them all. This implies more than what Mr. Hodgson calls "the removal of causation from consciousness, as such."

And in its synthesis philosophy will transcend the psychological theory which, after accepting the primary analysis, simply puts together again the two great groups of psychical phenomena, and grounds them in hypothetical realities called "souls" and "things," that it may the better explain the unfolding of psychical development. For, in its synthesis, philosophy will consider all the phenomena, and all the particular things which are regarded by the positive sciences as their subjects, — all happenings and all realities, — in relation to one supreme Reality. This Reality comprehends in itself the ground of all psychical life, even of the ideals of reason itself. It is a unity of ideal Reality, a supreme realized Idea.

CHAPTER V.

THE SPIRIT AND THE METHOD OF PHILOSOPHY.

HOW to arrive at philosophical truth, is a question the consideration of which, whether from the theoretical or the practical point of view, is encompassed by no small difficulties. Even in the pursuit of science the question of method has always been a vexed one; indeed, from its very nature, it does not seem to admit of a definite and final answer. We may, of course, set forth, as laws of so-called "pure logic," or rules of "logical praxis," the compound results of psychological analysis and observation of the means actually employed to secure the growth of the particular sciences. Thus the principles which have come to be established for the discovery and verification of truth in respect to physical phenomena have been the subject of lengthy and learned treatises. These treatises have an undoubted value, whether they are more or less dominated by metaphysical considerations; whether they are styled "Novum Organum," "Philosophy of the Inductive Sciences," or "Empirical Logic" and "Symbolic Logic." Yet the actual ascertainment and verifying of scientific truth proceeds with far less immediate dependence upon the theory of scientific method than we are accustomed to suppose. This remark is justified, even if we exclude the enormous influence from flashes of wit and flights of speculative genius, and from fortunate accident, — things, the occurrence and effect of which it is difficult, if not impossible, to bring under verifiable law.

The method of each one of the particular sciences is itself a matter of development. The actual growth of each of these sciences is dependent indeed upon the right use of the method peculiar to it; but the question as to what method *is* right, is a question which can only be progressively settled by the development of the whole body of the science. The last half-century has scarcely made a greater change in the system of conclusions which constitute the substance of the physical and natural sciences — of physics and chemistry, of physiology and biology, and even of geology and astronomy — than it has accomplished in the means employed by them for ascertaining and testing their conclusions. In that particular science, for example, called "general nerve-physiology," the improved use of microscopy and micrometrical measurement, the new methods of electrical stimulation, of the staining and tracing of nerve-tracts by Wallerian or other degeneration, or by photographing successive cross-sections cut by the microtome, and of the study of reaction-time by the pendulum-myograph or other similar contrivance, etc., are both products and indispensable conditions of scientific advance. What is true of this subdivision of one of the natural sciences is true of them all.

But suppose that we submit, as indeed we are compelled to do, our attempts to form a science of method to those general principles of procedure which hold true of all the inductive sciences. Suppose, that is to say, we by the general inductive method strive to arrive at a true science of the inductive method itself. We are then at once brought face to face with the same fact from another and somewhat different point of view. The history of these particular sciences shows, as has already been remarked, that the particular methods which they severally employ are subject to great and sometimes rapid changes. Moreover, the more highly developed as a specialty any of these sciences is found to be, the more complicated, and the less adapted to general use in scientific discovery, is its peculiar method. We can, to be sure, make a somewhat brave show of generalizing laws, or rather rules, of procedure for all the physical and natural sciences, by an inductive survey of the entire field. But the wider our generalizations, and the more valuable as a psychological or logical study of the behavior of mind as it faces the universe of material reality, the less appropriate and valuable are the same generalizations as indicative of an effective method for any one of the particular sciences. And if our generalizations for a universal science of method seem complete, they perhaps form a basis for only such practical exhortations as follow: "Observe, inquire, test, read, and think; be patient, humble, but bold; be docile, diligent, and yet free."

Psychology — and with it, as a matter of course, all the psychological sciences — has been held to have a method essentially and peculiarly its own. This is the method of introspection, or internal observation, or reflective consciousness. Its motto is, "Know thyself," — that written over the portal at Delphi. The possibility of this method is involved in that fundamental fact which psychological analysis discovers, — the fact of self-consciousness; it is also the fact which, having been discerned to be fundamental by psychological analysis, is given to philosophy as its fundamental problem, — the problem, namely, of the subject-object in the unity of self-consciousness.

The method of introspection, although it was satisfactory to the "old psychology," has been recently subjected to a most searching criticism, largely on account of the growing influence of the physical sciences. It has not simply been complained of for its unscientific and indefinite character; it has even been summarily dismissed as absurd and impossible. Nor has the complaint or sentence of dismissal come from the devotees of rival pursuits alone. In all this decrying of introspection as an effective or possible method of psychological science the professional psychologists have themselves been most prominent.

It must be admitted that the method of introspection alone cannot construct an adequate science of the psychical phenomena. For the work of psychological investigation, like every work of genuine and thorough science, is not satisfied with mere description and classification; it requires explanation. But explanation necessitates above all the genetic method. Lipps[1] may be correct when he maintains, in accordance with the practice and claims of the "old psychology," that the means of knowledge in this science is that observation which is known as internal, — this because its objects are to be observed in that way only. In self-consciousness the Ego envisages those objects, the so-called states of consciousness, which contain in complex and involved forms the problems of psychological science. This truth will forever distinctly separate psychology from all forms of physical and natural science, not only as respects the nature of its objects and problems, but also as respects the method of the solution of the problems.

But the view of Lipps is only half the truth. Volkmann von Volkmar[2] is also right, — not, indeed, when he speaks rather too disparagingly of both the inductive and the deductive method in psychology, but when he unites the essential features of both in what he calls the "genetic" method. In order that the student of psychology may establish a valid claim for his pursuit to a position among the sciences, he must be able to *explain* how the phenomena called "states of consciousness" arise, out of their elements, in accordance with the most general laws of that development which we are entitled to call the "life of the mind." The genesis of these states is not wholly, it is only very partially, if at all, *in* consciousness; it cannot therefore be made the subject of introspection.

To envisage the object already existent, and to envisage it as at once my object and my state, is not sufficient to explain the genesis of the object. The explanation (so far as it can be given by psychological science) of the genesis of any particular state must be found, in part, in the bodily conditions, under the laws investigated by pyscho-physics and physiological psychology. It must also be found in the character of pre-exis-

1 Grundtatsachen des Seelenlebens, Bonn, 1883, p. 7 f.

2 Lehrbuch der Psychologie, 1884, i. 6 f.

ting mental states — conscious or unconscious — under the laws of so-called "association of ideas." The explanation of all states, regarding their purposive and organic development, is to be found in the existence and evolution of a living being (the mind, or soul), with a nature and acquired habits peculiarly its own.

The method of psychological science is, therefore, peculiarly introspective and analytic of the envisaged phenomena called states of consciousness. But it is far broader and more effective than it could be if it were merely introspective. It pushes its analysis of the genesis of the phenomena as far back as possible, by the use of experimental methods and methods of external observation applied to the whole process of mental evolution (study of infants, of primitive man, and of the lower animals, — evolutionary and comparative psychology). It interprets the psychical life of the individual mind in the light of knowledge gathered concerning the psychical development of the race (the psychological study of literature, society, art, religion, etc.). It lays peculiar emphasis upon abnormal and pathological phenomena of the nervous and mental life (psychiatry, hypnotism, phenomena of insanity and of the criminal classes, etc.). It takes account of the rise and fall of particular forms of psychological theory (the history of psychology). It strives to transcend experience by the positing of hypothetical principles of explanation. But in the employment of all these methods this science differs in no important respect from the sciences which deal wholly with physical phenomena. It is only the use of introspection for the possession and, to some extent at least, for the analysis of its objects, which makes psychology, as respects its method, different from the other sciences.

Far too much of mystery, and of the awe which is bred of the sense of mystery, has often surrounded the acquirement, use, and imparting of the secrets of scientific method. But especially esoteric does the subject of method at times appear in the pursuit and communication of philosophical discipline.

The sarcasm of Lotze, although directed against a particular attempt at scientific method in philosophy (the founding of metaphysics on a psychological analysis of our cognition), seems at times to apply equally well to all attempts at method in this domain. "The numerous dissertations directed to this end may be compared to the tuning of instruments before a concert, only that they are not so necessary or useful." "The constant whetting of the knife is tedious, if it is not proposed to cut anything with it." Method, indeed! we may be inclined to exclaim when weary of reading criticisms and defences of the Hegelian Dialectic; let but Hegel, or any one of his critics or supporters, introduce us to some new and vital truth in philosophy, and we will excuse him from any detailed explanation of the method by which he attains it.

A remark like the foregoing, however petulantly or thoughtlessly uttered, may call our attention more closely to the somewhat peculiar relation in which the spirit and method of philosophy stand to the discovery and verification of its truths. The relation of philosophy to the particular sciences is such that it necessarily shares in the triumphs of their special methods; while its own method is, in some respects, an advance beyond them in the same direction with that which they have marked out. Since philosophy is not a physical science, it does not employ any one of the special methods of such science. It has no microscope, telescope, scales, crucible, or other physical apparatus of its own. Neither does it deal, in a primary and independent way, with meteorological, financial, sociological, or other statistics. And yet it considers none of these things, nothing that is human, foreign to itself. It allows to each particular science the way of discovering and verifying its facts and laws which is peculiar to it. In the triumphs of each science, through whatever means, philosophy rejoices sympathetically; for it feels itself thereby enriched.

For the reception of the principles of the positive sciences, as distinguished from their discovery and proof, philosophy does not need to be expert in the use of special scientific methods. But in the most general scientific method, and in that spirit — called the "scientific spirit" — which characterizes the modern pursuit of knowledge, philosophy needs to have a large share. In this broad and somewhat indefinite meaning of the words, its spirit and its method are distinctly scientific. Indeed, since its subject-matter is not confined to any one of these sciences, but embraces them all, and since its generalizations reach beyond those of any particular science and cover the field of experience possessed by all, philosophy must be, in some sort, more scientific than any positive science can be. It must carry the spirit and general method of scientific research into the regions of the most subtile and yet complex analysis, and of the loftiest and most comprehensive synthesis. For it is of the very essence of philosophy to be the highest and purest activity of reason itself.

The special relations of philosophy to psychology are such as require in the pursuit of the former the extension of that method of reflective analysis which is peculiar to the latter. Each of the sciences of nature furnishes, as material for further treatment by philosophy, certain presuppositions upon which, as upon fundamental postulates, all its positive results are obtained. The collection of these presuppositions and the attempt, in an external way, to arrange them into a well-articulated system, is only the beginning of the work of philosophy. All these very presuppositions are, not simply working hypotheses of the particular sciences, but modes of the behavior, and so principles of the constitution and development, of human reason. As soon as this truth is once apprehended with regard to them, the method of their consideration ceases to be purely historical and founded on external observation. The world of "Things" is properly treated by the physical and natural sciences by the method of external observation. And — to use, with a somewhat different meaning, the language of Kant[1] —

[1] Critique of Pure Reason, Transcendental Dialectic, Consideration on the whole of Pure Psychology, etc. Max Müller's Translation, p. 334.

"so long as we connect (internal and external) phenomena with each other, as mere representations in our experience, there is nothing irrational." We may even "hypostasize the external phenomena, looking upon them as no longer representations, but *as things existing by themselves and outside us, with the same quality in which they exist inside us;*" and this without vitiating the results of scientific observation and analysis. But as soon as we raise the inquiry as to the ultimate grounds and validity of such connection and hypostasis, we require the use of the critical method. But the critical method (in the philosophical meaning of the word "critical") is not the method of the physical sciences. It is an extension of the psychological method; it is the method of ultimate reflective analysis. This method philosophy is compelled to employ, because it regards all the principles postulated by the positive sciences as "moments" and modes of the being and behavior of reason itself.

The analytic part of philosophical discipline concerns chiefly the collection and critical sifting of its material. This material comes from the particular sciences; it consists of the principles presupposed or ascertained by them all. The material, as considered by philosophy, is all of the rational order; for it is *reason's world*, both internal and external, which the material constitutes. But without the use of synthesis the material cannot be considered as forming part of a rational system; it cannot without speculative construction be shown to constitute a *cosmos*, — an orderly and beautiful whole. Now, in the case of the particular sciences it is the rational presuppositions, which are accepted but not critically explored by these sciences, that serve as the ground of their unity. The principles of material Reality, called "atoms," being Existent in Space and Time, having Quantity, Quality, and Relation by way of "attraction" and "repulsion," and, though themselves permanent Subject of states, undergoing Change under Law, give Unity to the otherwise diverse phenomena of the science of molecular physics. These principles make the disconnected sequences of our experiences with "Things" into a *science*.

Attention has of late been frequently called to the fact that all the sciences of nature — biology included — are becoming more and more branches or departments of the one inclusive science of molecular physics. In our judgment, there is a long and weary road yet to travel before the goal to which this tendency points the way can be definitely attained. But of the existence of the tendency, and of its marked beneficial effect upon the methods of the particular sciences, there can be no doubt. We now refer to this tendency in order to show that the syntheses of experience for which these sciences stand are made possible only through those postulated principles which it is the business of analytical philosophy to discover and criticise.

Empirical psychology has been shown to have its collection of postulates and empirical laws, with the further treatment of which philosophy is concerned. The postulates of psychological science are, in part, those of the general science of physics; but more particularly they are those of the science of human physiology. They are also, in part, certain postulates of the existence of so-called mind, with a nature (unity, identity, attributes, and accidents) and a development of a peculiar kind. They include also potential and actual relations of the different beings, thus existent, to one another, to the beings called atoms, and to certain other potentially or actually existent beings. These presuppositions are indispensable to give unity to that science which deals with psychical processes. Without them the postulated beings called minds would be supposed out of all relation — were that indeed even conceivable — with that work with which the physical sciences deal.

Now, these most general principles of all the particular sciences, both physical and psychological, are the points from which the synthesis of philosophy takes, as it were, its flight. Supposing them all to have been subjected to the most searching critical analysis, the attempt must then be made to unite them into a rational system. This attempt must of course proceed by use of the synthetic method. It is an attempt at the highest and most complete synthesis of principles, based upon the most thorough and exhaustive reflective analysis.

But can this attempt at supreme synthesis, which it is of the very nature of philosophy to make, itself be made without use of any presuppositions whatsoever? The answer to this question has already been indicated in the discussion of the definition of philosophy and of its relation to the particular sciences. More light will be thrown upon it as we consider the spirit of philosophy, and the principal attitudes of mind (dogmatism, scepticism, criticism) which are possible toward the ultimate problems of philosophy. It is enough at present to say that philosophical thinking, in its analysis and attempted synthesis into rational system of all the principles of the particular sciences, is itself compelled to carry with it two postulates. One of these is the ground of that confidence which reason persistently has in itself. Philosophy — in the language of Lotze [1] — postulates "the existence in the world at large of a 'truth,' which affords a sure object for cognition." Agnosticism, in so far as it is *agnosticism*, can therefore never be a philosophy. Nor can philosophy ever remain satisfied with an agnostic system, — if, indeed, the very words "system of agnostic philosophy" be not in themselves self-contradictory. And, furthermore, the scepticism "without *motif*" which aims to thrust forth and hold in position permanently the inquiry, whether, after all, reason may not be compelled, after its best and supreme efforts, to be self-deceived through and through, is inconsistent with that postulated self-confidence of reason, out of which philosophy springs.

The other presupposition which necessarily enters into every effort of philosophy, of a synthetic and constructive kind, concerns a unity, of some sort, of ultimate Reality. A unifying principle, or group of interconnected principles, is of

[1] Outlines of Logic and of the Encyc. of Philosophy, Translation, p. 147.

necessity the postulate upon which the synthesis of philosophy proceeds. Its further task, as constituting a rational system, is the discovery and verifying of the nature of such principle. *What* the principle is, philosophy may find itself unable fully to comprehend, or — it is at least conceivable — unable even to conjecture in any definitive and defensible way. But *that* the principle is, it persistently presupposes, and must presuppose until it is ready to relinquish all claim to rightful existence for itself as even a rational striving for truth. That the unifying principle is some really Existent, is also an inseparable part of this fundamental postulate of all philosophical discipline. *What* this really Existent is, and whether we may define it or not, are questions to which the different schools of philosophy give different responses. But *that* one really Existent is the philosophical ground and explanation of that unity in manifestation of the world, which the particular sciences both discover and presuppose, is a postulate wrought into the very nature of philosophy. It is a postulate springing from the very being of reason itself.

The technical method of philosophy cannot, however, be separated from the spirit of philosophy, which imparts to it life, guidance, and vigor. On this account it is, in part, that philosophy is less technical in method than are any of the particular sciences; indeed, so far as it can be said to have a technical method at all, the spirit controls the method much more than can be the case with pure science, as such, or with the entire body of the inductive sciences.

The spirit of philosophy is essentially freedom, — the exercise of reason absolutely untrammelled by extraneous bonds or obligations. As Chalybäus has said,[1] that free critical movement which prevails in all the sciences is essentially philosophical. In this regard modern philosophy, of its very nature, surpasses modern science in what is common and essential to

[1] Fundamentalphilosophie, ein Versuch das System der Philosophie auf ein Realprincip zu gründen, p. 1 f.

both. How this freedom may be not only compatible with, but conducive to, the acceptance of the truths of revelation, and the docile reception and performance of many merely conventional duties and practices, need not concern us at the present time. But if the mind of man is even to make the attempt to subject to an ultimate analysis, and to construct into a systematic whole by a supreme synthesis, the principles presupposed or ascertained by the particular sciences, it must possess this absolute philosophical freedom.

The freedom of philosophy includes the power and the obligation to examine critically all the presuppositions of every particular form of human knowledge. It includes also the right of reason to question searchingly, and with the utmost possible candor, its own structure and processes, — their nature and their validity. This right extends even to those postulates of all reason on which philosophy is itself founded; namely, the confidence of reason in itself as able to attain to truth, and its metaphysical faith in that unity of objective Reality whose nature and relations to experience philosophy investigates. To be sure, in the exercise of its freedom to the fullest extent for the investigation, not only of the principles of all the particular sciences, but also of its own being and life, reason finds itself necessarily limited by the laws of its own being and life. As thinking subject, reason is one with itself as object of its own thought. The freedom of philosophy does not then imply the possession by reason of the power to be more or less than reason. We do not wait to call the grayhound free (to borrow a figure of speech) until he has attained the power to outstrip his own shadow.

The history of philosophy shows that none of the particular systems of philosophy have realized to the fullest possible extent this inherent freedom of the philosophical movement of reason. The free spirit is, however, especially characteristic of modern philosophy. During the Middle Ages — it is customary to say — the principle of authority (a distinctively unphilosophical spirit) was regnant in both theology and philosophy. But the method of Descartes emphasizes the freedom of philosophy, although the philosophy of Descartes secured but few of the choicest results of this freedom. In the first of his "Meditations" this thinker exercises, to the fullest extent, the freedom of philosophic doubt. All things may be doubted except the fact that I doubt (*dubito*); or, since doubting is a species of thinking, except the fact that I think (*cogito*). Like Archimedes, says Descartes in his second Meditation, if I may find one fixed point, one absolutely indubitable proposition, I may indulge in great hopes of moving the whole world of thought. Such a proposition the celebrated Cartesian maxim is supposed by its author to be (*Cogito, ergo sum*). From this point of standing, in the subsequent books of his work on Philosophy, the so-called founder of the modern era of philosophical thinking seeks to demonstrate the existence of God and the existence of the soul as an entity separable from the body. From this root, that itself sprung out of the spirit of philosophic freedom, there developed a hardened stalk of philosophical dogma, — rational cosmology, rational psychology, rational theology, — which the critical philosophy was destined to dissolve.

The appearance of Kant's "Critique of Pure Reason" marks another era in the development of the spirit of philosophical freedom. As *critique* it summons pure reason, in its dogmatic use, to appear before the critical eye of a higher and judicial reason; it proposes anew to exercise the rights of the philosophical freedom of doubt; it begins and proceeds with a universal mistrust of all the synthetic propositions of the existing metaphysics, — the very systems which had developed from the Cartesian philosophy. But the still more modern exercise of the same freedom in analysis which Kant himself employed and provoked in all his successors, to the end of time, discovers many unanalyzed and doubtful presuppositions in his critical philosophy. For Kant himself, as Herbart and others have pointed out, assumed in a quite uncritical way almost the entire

Aristotelian and Wolffian theory of the mind. The existence of a body of synthetic truths *a priori*, in physics as well as in mathematics, is another Kantian presupposition, which apparently was taken in a wholly uncritical way. This presupposition has not improperly been called "the πρῶτον ψεῦδος from which, with great consistency, the whole system of 'Criticism' grew up."[1] The critical freedom of philosophy must still insist, in the name of Kant, upon its right to doubt and to analyze, in a more ultimate manner, all the presuppositions of the pure and applied physical sciences. Before this critical spirit the axioms of the Euclidean geometry and of the higher mathematics of modern times, as well as all the recent attempts to erect the late and often hasty generalizations of physics (*e. g.*, the so-called law of the conservation and correlation of energy) into the place of rational and unchanging principles of all reality, must appear and be judged. Such principles may in time become so established for the particular sciences as that these sciences do not feel free to question them. But it is of the very essence and life of philosophy to make them perpetually, so often as occasion requires, the subjects of the freest sceptical and critical examination. For the freedom of philosophy is a freedom from all unquestioned presuppositions whatsoever.

The spirit of philosophy is also absolute devotion to the truth. "It is truth alone I seek," says Locke. This is the attitude of mind toward its problems, and toward all attempts at the treatment of those problems, which is essential to philosophy. The character of the truth which philosophy seeks, with an absolute devotion to truth, is such as to render its method different from that of the particular sciences. Since it is not technically correct statement of matters of fact which constitutes philosophic truth, it is not technical correctness of method in ascertaining the truth, upon which philosophy chiefly insists. The student of the sciences of nature or of mind must indeed have a supreme devotion to truth, otherwise his method of seeking truth

[1] Comp. Ueberweg, A History of Philosophy, ii. 161, note.

will not be most thoroughly scientific. This is so, even if the subject of investigation be, for example, the effect of repeated acts of stimulation upon the nuclei of the ganglionic cells of a frog, or the nature of the connection between those cells and the ultimate elements of the nerve-fibres running thereto. The observer in astronomy strives, in the interests of truth, to recognize and eliminate the errors arising from his "personal equation." But in all the particular sciences the problems are likely to be so technical, and the methods of examination and solution so technically fixed, that the conscious love and devotion to truth alone is comparatively inconspicuous. With philosophy this is not so, or at least it is not so to the same degree. Its problems concern the highest verities; such are the nature in reality and the significance of the system of physical things, the nature and significance of finite mind, the ground and unconditioned value of the good and the beautiful, the being and predicates of the Absolute, and the fundamental rational relations existent among all these forms of reality. For the solution of these problems its one instrument is Thought, — or rather (may we not say?), the most comprehensive and harmonious activity and development of self-conscious rational life. The use of this instrument, the method of philosophy, is reflective analysis, followed by the highest synthesis of the elements discovered by analysis. Devotion to the truth is, then, pre-eminently a self-conscious impulse and guide, an intelligent spirit controlling a somewhat indefinite and untechnical method, in all philosophical discipline.

That this spirit of freedom and self-conscious devotion to truth alone has been exclusively, or even pre-eminently, characteristic of philosophy, it is not our intention to claim. Doubtless there is ground for the complaint, emphasized with such vehemence and bitterness by Schopenhauer, that the professional teachers of philosophy (the *Fachprofessoren*, the teachers of a *Kathederphilosophie*) have not infrequently had an eye on their own fame and advancement, or on the security of their tenure of office, and their standing with the appointing power, rather than both eyes, with a single heart, solely on the truth. It is a fact that many of its most renowned and loyal students, from Descartes to Hartmann, have not been in the "profession" of philosophy. But both the complaint and the fact only serve to make clearer the truth touching that spirit which philosophy pre-eminently requires. And if we consider that philosophy, like theology, and unlike most of the work concerned in the advancement of the empirical sciences, affects with its conclusions the profoundest and most cherished convictions of the individual and of society, and seems to support or to jeopard what men generally hold most important and most dear; and that it therefore places both the thinker and his audience under the most severe conditions for the testing of character, — an historical claim may be established, we think, for the actual superiority, and the vast superiority, of philosophy to either science or theology in its simple, unswerving loyalty to truth, and to truth alone.

The spirit of philosophy is humility and teachableness mingled with independence. In this spirit also the student of the physical sciences and the student of philosophy are called to friendly rivalry by the very nature of their pursuits. The attitude of the great discoverers in physics and biology has fitly been that of the docile mind. This attitude has placed them in awe and expectancy before the problems whose solution would increase our knowledge of that mysterious totality which science calls "Nature," but philosophy calls the "Absolute," and faith calls God. For, indeed, the truly *great* discoverers in physical science have been possessed by the philosophical spirit, and skilled in the use of the philosophical method. The investigation, by technical means, of minute subdivisions of physical science, makes relatively little demand upon the investigator for the docile and humble mind. The botanist may count the stamens and pistils of some newly found plant, may mark its leaves as oblate or spatulate, may classify it by these and other tokens, and trace its genesis as related to other most closely allied forms,—all this, with small regard for the spirit which controls his procedure. But when he uses this particular plant as an example by which to rise to the higher generalizations of his science, and even to link that science with the science of all life, or perhaps to throw a ray of light toward the problem of the "nature" of that Reality in which all living things exist, he needs the inspiration of the philosophic spirit.

The humility and teachableness of philosophy are of use in two principal directions. The very business of him who pursues its studies is with the highest ultimate mysteries. The seemingly simplest thing, the most ordinary occurrence, is in his sight a factor or moment in these mysteries. The "meanest flower that blows" may excite the scientific botanist only to new efforts at classification; but philosophically considered, it may open up all the "seven riddles of the world," and suggest the reconstruction of æsthetics and theology. The student of philosophy lives constantly in the presence of the sublime and awful mystery of Reality. The humble and docile spirit toward this presence alone befits the character of his pursuit.

But in these days philosophy especially requires for its cultivation the spirit of humility and teachableness before the discoveries of the particular sciences. Its pride has been to *construct* the world, too often in more or less nearly complete disregard of the most comprehensive and verifiable knowledge touching the actual mode and laws of its constitution. But its true and final aim, as Lotze said, is not to "construct" the world, but to "explain" it. This business it shares with the particular sciences. Only philosophy, however, seeks the most ultimate possible explanation of the whole world, while the sciences strive to explain, as interrelated under uniform sequences, particular groups of its phenomena. As science then is humble and docile toward the facts of nature upon which it depends for the generalizations which constitute its empirical truths, so does it become philosophy to be humble and docile toward those scientific truths upon which it is dependent for its higher truth. The truth of philosophy lies involved in the truths of science. Without the teachable mind toward these latter truths it has no means of acquiring material upon which to build, as upon a verifiable basis, its structure of supreme and rational truth. And, conversely, Haeckel's complaint of "the lack of philosophical culture which characterizes most of the physicists of the day," who "cherish the strange illusion that they can construct the edifice of natural science from *facts* without a *philosophical connection* of the same," is but a fulfilment of the prophecy of Herbart: "It cannot be otherwise than that the neglect of philosophy should result in a frivolous or perverted treatment of the fundamental principles of all the sciences." This relation of reciprocal dependence between philosophy and the particular sciences it is especially necessary for the former to incorporate into the spirit and method of its pursuit.

But, on the other hand, the spirit of philosophy partakes of a critical independence toward the particular sciences. It does not even receive the material upon which its existence depends in an uncritical and credulous way. When physics claims for its laws an *a priori* origin and an unconditioned validity, philosophy is competent to examine these claims. When biology attempts to lift the principle of evolution from the rank of a working hypothesis and give it the place of an ultimate generalization envisaging the nature of all Reality, philosophy claims the rights of a judge and arbiter in this domain. It knows, as empirical physics and biology cannot, what is necessary to so-called *a priori* origin, to unconditioned validity, and to the right to act as interpreter of the nature of ultimate Reality.

The spirit, which is humility and boldness combined, is at present especially necessary in the philosophical treatment of recent empirical generalizations in biology and psychology. The next great synthesis in philosophy will undoubtedly rest largely upon the basis of these generalizations. Already the speculation of Hartmann has made itself captivating to many by its obviously extensive use of the inductive method, in a spirit of deference to these sciences. We believe both the method and the conclusions of this writer to be defective, as judged by the most approved scientific standards. But who that is intelligently interested does not hear with desire and hope the Macedonian cry made to "synthetic philosophy" by modern biology and modern psychology? What wonderful new systems of speculative thinking may not arise in answer to this cry? The doings of bioplasm, the laws of the genesis and growth of plant and animal organisms, the relations of specific and generic forms and functions, the origin and evolution of the psychical processes of the lower animals, "unconscious cerebration" and "double consciousness," the phenomena of hypnotism, trance, and insanity, the principles of heredity, suggestion, and spontaneity, in art, in therapeutics, and in religious and social construction, — all these and many other strange, new manifestations of the presence and power of that universal *anima mundi*, that One in whose life and being all living beings are, await the more mature and strenuous efforts of constructive philosophy.

The spirit of philosophy is also infinite patience, both in the collection of material and in that analytic and synthetic thinking which constructs the material into a rational system. And surely the student of philosophy has need of patience in the collection of material. As a writer[1] on this subject has said: "It is the activity of the polymathist, one might almost say of the panmathist, which is required as preliminary." But the patience of philosophy, in the collection and preparation of its material, does not lead to the use of the same method as that employed by particular sciences to this end. For the material of philosophy does not primarily consist in facts; nor is its method directed to the discovery and verification of bare relations, in

[1] Schaarschmidt, in Philos. Monatsh., 1877, p. 5.

fact, among the different groups of phenomena. Its material consists rather of those principles that are presupposed in or ascertained by the use of the methods belonging to all the sciences. The student of philosophy needs, therefore, such knowledge of these sciences as will give him the power to state and comprehend the meaning of these principles. It is only as related to this need that he must also have an acquaintance with the details of scientific fact and scientific method.

Patience in analytic and synthetic thinking is also indispensable to the method of philosophy. As the writer just quoted goes on to declare: "And yet the positive, so-called exact knowledge is the least of the things required; for it is not knowledge which constitutes the philosopher, but thinking, concentrated, thorough, and methodically trained. To this the sum-total of scientific attainment is but a premise with which it starts in its search for the last abstractions and highest ideas."

For reasons like the foregoing the dependence of philosophy upon the moral and spiritual characteristics of the philosophical thinker is especially close. Theory and history alike emphasize this truth. Here, far more than in any other form of rational endeavor, the method is the spirit of the man. To pursue any of the particular sciences (even empirical psychology) in their modern form without knowledge of technical method and use of instruments technically developed, would be difficult indeed. But it is the man himself, as a rational, self-conscious life, which, in philosophy, chiefly determines the right and successful use of method. Acquaintance with the science of the sensible may awaken an interest, but rational self-consciousness must also be aroused, and confidence in the Supersensible must be systematically unfolded and defended, in order that philosophical truth may result.[1] The completed system of philosophy is an ideal which will never be realized; but the contribution

[1] Comp. Lichtenfels, Lehrbuch zur Einleitung in die Philosophie, p. 5.

toward it which every workman can make depends in no small degree upon his wealth of experience, maturing into character.

One other factor in the very nature of philosophy is influential in fixing the method of its pursuit. It is defined as a *progressive* rational system. To repeat words already cited from Kuno Fischer, — it is the progressive self-knowledge of the human mind. The bearing of this truth upon the question of philosophic method is at once obvious. The method of philosophy implies for its successful employment a knowledge of the past and present developments of philosophy. It has even been said of late that "philosophy *is* the history of philosophy." Seriously and literally taken, this statement is inexact and inadequate. But it emphasizes with scarcely exaggerated strength an important truth touching the true method of its pursuit. It sounds a much-needed call to a community of intelligent efforts in the consideration of philosophical problems. For here, as in so many other matters, it is true, when rightly understood, that the history of the race and the history of the individual follow the same type. A process involving the construction, criticism, and disintegration and subsequent improved reconstruction of the results of reflective thinking has gone on in the evolution of the human mind. This process is the world-wide historical method of man's progressive rational knowledge. No individual inquirer now undertakes for the first time the ultimate analysis of the fundamental elements of philosophy, or the supreme synthesis of them into a rational system. Every individual thinker lives in and of the thought of his race.

The study of the history of philosophy is, however, a necessary propædeutic of philosophy rather than a necessary characteristic of the philosophical method as such. Eclecticism is not a method in philosophy; neither is the historical method peculiar to or distinctive of philosophy. The choice of the materials which are to enter into any philosophical system, as well as the choice of the principle of their combination, requires guidance from conceptions which rule over all historical systems. The right shaping of these conceptions cannot be gained in a merely historical way; it requires special skill in reflective analysis and in that higher speculative synthesis which is of the very nature of philosophical system.

The history of philosophy is an indispensable help to the modern student of philosophical discipline in the definition of his problems. It shows him what great and permanent forms of questioning have occupied the self-conscious reason of man. These are the same problems as those which are immediately presented to him by scientific psychology, as pursued in the most comprehensive and critical way. Moreover, the answers which have been given to these problems by the successive great masters and more prominent schools of philosophy serve us as stimulus, warning, and guide. The survey of them excites the laudable ambition to become one of that band of workmen who have assumed the burden of the effort to solve — or at least to lighten — "those riddles by which the mind of man is oppressed in life, and about which we are all compelled to hold some view or other, in order to be able to live at all." History also warns each new explorer against making the old mistakes in their old form; and it points out new by-paths or modes of following in the better beaten tracks that may possibly lead into a region of clearer light. The study of the formation, criticism, disintegration, and reconstruction of philosophical systems, and the comprehensive and sympathetic acquaintance with the whole course of speculative thought, is therefore a constant and necessary accompaniment, a perpetual and indispensable propædeutic, of philosophical discipline.

But the history of philosophy is not philosophy, — if by this it be meant that to know this history, however comprehensively and minutely, is sufficient for the student of philosophy; or that the history will organize itself into a system of consistent and verifiable philosophical truths. Nor is the study of history the sole method of philosophical study. It is probably not even the chief preparatory discipline. Were we called upon to choose between it and that other propædeutic which consists in the comprehensive scientific investigation of the phenomena of mind, we should probably (though regretfully) prefer the latter.

Still further, and strictly speaking, historical study is not an integral part of the technical method of philosophy; although by it the material which consists in past results of philosophizing is gathered and displayed. But it still remains material needing treatment by renewed rational effort of each advancing age. The method of such treatment is the method of philosophy; it is not itself historical, but the combination of analysis and synthesis in a peculiar way.

By help of the foregoing considerations we may define more precisely the technical method of philosophy. It is, first of all, the method of reflective analysis directed upon the principles presupposed or ascertained by the particular sciences. This is, so far as the presuppositions of these sciences are concerned, an extension of the modified psychological method. In the pursuit of psychological science we reach a point where the historical description of the genesis and development of psychical processes is seen to imply and depend upon certain presuppositions that have not as yet themselves been subjected to critical examination. The psychological method aims, therefore, at a more complete and fundamental analysis; it passes over, that is, into the philosophy of mind. When this analysis has been made, so far as the material of psychology is concerned, it is discovered that all the other particular sciences also imply and depend upon presuppositions. These presuppositions also are to be subjected to the method of reflective analysis. They are thus seen to be essentially the same as those to which we have already been introduced in the philosophical study of mind. They appear, therefore, as those universal modes of the behavior of reason (whether it be engaged with the subject-object called "Self," or with the object-object called a world of "Things,") which analytical philosophy aims to discover, criticise, display, and defend.

Philosophy, however, does not undertake to build its supreme synthesis upon presuppositions alone. It finds, in surveying the fields of the particular sciences wherein its material lies, a great number of principles which are the results of the widest inductions during centuries of the race's experience. It can in no wise vindicate its claim to the title "science of the sciences," or "universal science," without taking these principles also into the account. Only in this way can it be sufficiently comprehensive; only in this way can it remain in touch with a living and developing knowledge of all Reality. Only in this way, too, can it avoid the complaint and answer the demands of the students of the particular sciences.[1] But it surely cannot receive these principles, inductively ascertained by the appropriate scientific instrumentalities, without subjecting them to its own peculiar method of reflective analysis. They, too, are regarded by it as preliminary results of the activity of that reason whose highest self-knowledge it claims to represent. The inductive principles of astronomy, physics, biology, and psychology must be interpreted by its thinking, to see what higher significance and value in reality they may implicate and represent. These, too, it is the business of analytical philosophy to receive from the particular sciences; but also to criticise, unfold, interpret, and defend, — before the tribunal of reason in its highest jurisdiction.

It is the feeling that this humble, patient, candid work of analytical philosophy should precede and justify all constructive and speculative attempts, which has called forth the demand that philosophy in general be "scientific" and "inductive." It can never be scientific in the sense of using the technical instruments and forms of experimentation belonging to the methods of the particular sciences. It must, however, be

[1] Compare, for example, Riehl, Philosophischer Kriticismus, iii. 84 f and 101 f.

scientific in the sense of obtaining by research from the sciences, as its own material, the general truths they have established. It must also vindicate its claim to the same title by what Schleiermacher called "scientific thinking." It must submit all its conclusions to that testing which follows a perpetually enlarging acquaintance with the generalizations of the particular sciences. Its peculiar method of thus being scientific is the method of reflective analysis.

Nor can philosophy be inductive, if by this be understood the generalization of laws from observed facts and their verification by prediction and experimentation. This inductive growth of the knowledge of Reality it intrusts with confidence to the particular sciences. But it does not venture to proceed with its system-making in a voluntary or indolent disregard, either total or partial, of any principles inductively established. It is inductive in the sense of being eager to learn these generalizations of the particular sciences, that it may — having received them with candor — subject them to its own method of a more ultimate analysis. This is the truth in the captivating plea of Hartmann and others to establish, in a superior manner, a so-called inductive philosophy.[1] But much of the benefit claimed for this method is lost by its advocates (notably so by Hartmann) because the boasted induction is concluded without sufficient thoroughness in the use of both the scientific and the philosophical methods. The philosophical treatment of the phenomena of reflex-action, of so-called instinct in man and the lower animals, of conscious or unconscious psychical processes, normal and abnormal, does indeed demand the "inductive" method. But the philosopher who makes his own hasty generalizations of laws directly from the phenomena may be injuring rather than helping the cause of philosophy, by the use of what he is pleased to call the inductive method.

[1] See Philosophie des Unbewussten, 7th ed., Berlin, 1876, i. 5 f., and English Translation, Philosophy of the Unconscious, i. 6 f.

Let it be repeated, then: The application of thorough reflective analysis to the principles of the particular sciences *is* the so-called inductive and scientific method in philosophy. Only by understanding this can we give to both science and philosophy their respective rights, and so maintain their intercourse in relations of mutual dependence and helpfulness. This view includes all that is true, and excludes all that is erroneous, in the attempt to set up the method called "scientific," "inductive," or "cosmological," in philosophical study.

But analytical philosophy is not the sum-total of philosophy; indeed, it cannot, from the very nature of the case, be a *sum-total* at all. The impulses of reason, out of which philosophy springs, are toward a unifying of knowledge, or rather, of all experience. Philosophy requires, therefore, the freest and highest use of the method of synthesis. It is theoretically and speculatively constructive, of natural right and as in duty bound. And in truth there is no department of scientific knowledge also where analysis alone can supply the demands for satisfactory interpretation of the facts. Reason works synthetically in the organization of ordinary experience and in the construction of scientific system. It postulates for the savage and the boor some sort of unity in reality — a *me* and other "things," and the two related — as the basis of the otherwise disconnected phenomena. Science broadens and defines this postulate, in the many different modifications of it with which its particular departments are concerned. But philosophy listens to the profoundest intimations of reason, and endeavors to conceive and explicate all that which, concerning the being and life of this Unity of Reality, both ordinary experience and the particular sciences imply. Its method is, therefore, synthetical, in the supreme and most comprehensive way.

Now, it is to the legitimate and inalienable rights of this method that the existence and value of all the great philosophical systems called "absolute" must be ascribed. The deductive method in philosophy, so far as it is legitimate and valuable, must be vindicated in the light of the same truth. For every system of philosophical truths, every "synthetic philosophy," is at once called upon to approve itself in two directions. These directions are indicated in two questions. Can you show that your synthesis contradicts none of the principles of science as subjected to reflective analysis; but that, on the contrary, it comprehends and takes due account of them all? Can you use the synthesis itself deductively for the interpretation, in the light of the Unity of Reality, of those principles of the particular sciences upon which it claims to be based?

Fichte desired to make his supreme synthesis in the interests of the interpretation and completion of the Kantian analysis. Schelling found this synthesis of Fichte one-sided, and endeavored to supplement it by the addition of the neglected aspects of Reality, — thus the better to understand the riddles of the world of matter and mind. Hegel complained that the principle of Schelling's synthesis was, as it were, "shot out of a gun;" by the dialectical method he would himself expose in its completeness the nature of that Reality in which Being and Thought are one. We find fault with none of these great thinkers because they have used the method of all constructive philosophy. But by the accuracy and comprehensiveness of the analysis upon which their synthesis was based, and by the power which the supreme principles, reached by the synthesis, have deductively to interpret the particular principles discovered by the analysis, their speculative systems must stand or fall.

Since the great synthetic movement of the Hegelian school reached its highest development and declined, the analytical study of particular problems and the researches of history have mainly occupied the attention of students of philosophy. Signs of new great attempts at system-making are in the air. Indeed, Schopenhauer, Hartmann, and Herbert Spencer, if not also Lotze and Wundt, have undertaken to base a synthetic philosophy upon the consideration of principles derived from the particular sciences.

Fault is not to be found with Schopenhauer because he "posited" a supreme principle, — namely, Will, — and attempted to treat by deductive procedure from it all the different departments of philosophical discipline. But we consider the synthesis founded on a lame and incomplete analysis, and lamentably defective as respects its power of interpreting the world of reality made known by science. Its crude postulating of a *principium individuationis*, and of Platonic ideas that are out of all comprehensible relation in reality with the One Will, and its consequent patent failure to explain what it sets out to explain, rather than the fact that it employs the method of synthesis, furnish grounds for its rejection. For it is not the deductive, or speculative, or synthetic method, as such, which we deprecate in philosophy; it is its unsuccessful result in any case which we decline to approve.

It must not be understood, however, that the progress of philosophy is conditioned upon the consistent and complete employment of this double method of procedure by any one individual or any one age. Every individual thinker, as indeed every particular age, may be more successful in either analysis or synthesis, at the relative and temporary expense of the other. Every individual or age may apply either branch of the one method more strictly and successfully than otherwise to some one or more of the great problems of reflective thinking; for no individual and no age furnishes the complete and final philosophy.

Every individual and every age contributes something to the great whole, which is the self-development of reason in its understanding of the problem of the universe, and the adjustment and interpretation of its own life as part of that problem. But the method of philosophy remains essentially the same with every individual and every age. That method it is which we have endeavored to describe.

CHAPTER VI.

DOGMATISM, SCEPTICISM, AND CRITICISM.

THREE attitudes of mind toward philosophical truth have always characterized the development in reflection of the individual thinker and of the race. These three are dogmatism, scepticism, and criticism; and the order of their actual predominance may be said to correspond to that in which their names are here placed. The dogmatic, sceptical, or critical mental attitude is not peculiar to any particular school or method of philosophy. Either one of these attitudes is perhaps equally compatible with each of the great philosophical schools or systems; no one of them can be held to be incompatible with the use of the correct method of philosophizing. On the contrary, the most fruitful and effective development of the tenets of every school can be gained only through the employment of reason upon these tenets with each one of these mental attitudes. And if the method of analytical philosophy seems to be most closely allied to scepticism and to criticism, and the method of synthetical philosophy to dogmatism, this only shows that the true method, which holds both analysis and synthesis in a living and progressive union, requires for its working all three.

Agnosticism and eclecticism, although not infrequently classed with dogmatism, scepticism, and criticism, have absolutely no claim to recognition as distinct mental temperaments or attitudes toward philosophical truth. Indeed, the term "agnosticism" does not properly serve to define a philosophical system, a philosophical method, or even — as has just been said — a distinct attitude of mind toward truth. This apparently paradoxical proposition might be amply justified in its application to the tenets of the most prominent leader, in England and this country at least, of philosophical agnosticism. We refer, of course, to Mr. Herbert Spencer. As respects his conclusions, this thinker is to be classed among the realists in philosophy; his system is to be defined, not as agnosticism, but — to use his own term — as "Transfigured Realism." It is true that, in his earlier and cruder writings, under the influence of a laudable ambition once for all time to reconcile the ancient strife between science and religion, he stated his discovery of the supreme Principle in terms of agnostic dogmatism. The "deepest, widest, and most certain of all facts," said he, is this, — "that the Power which the Universe manifests to us is utterly inscrutable."[1] But a careful examination of the context of this statement shows us that this Power cannot, in the deeper judgment of Mr. Spencer, be called "utterly inscrutable;" for he himself speaks of it as a Unit-Being, having Permanency, and manifesting itself in the world of phenomena; it is Ultimate Existence, Ultimate Cause; it has an "established order," is responsible for "actions" and even for ethical "influence" upon personal agencies; and it "forms the basis of intelligence." No wonder, then, that in his more mature pronouncements, as "Synthetic Philosophy," he changes the more agnostic to the more positive form. Thus what was originally a provisional assumption becomes a verified truth.[2] Accordingly, we are now told: "Behind all manifestations, inner and outer, there is a Power manifested." "The one thing permanent is the Unknowable Reality hidden under all these changing forms."

What is true of Spencerian agnosticism so-called is necessarily true of all philosophical agnosticism. So far as it transcends that pause before the positing of affirmative or negative

[1] First Principles, New York, 1872, p. 46.
[2] Principles of Psychology, New York, 1876, ii. 503.

statements touching the knowledge and being of the truly Existent, which the sceptical and critical attitudes demand, it can assume, of necessity, only some form of dogmatism. Philosophical scepticism is the genuine and necessary doubt with which the freedom of inquiring reason envisages all the positive content of scientific and philosophical truth. Philosophical criticism is the activity of reason, disciplined and informed, in the use of the most searching analysis of its own processes and of their products. But both scepticism and criticism necessarily issue in the discrimination of those ultimate and verifiable principles — whatever and how many so ever they may be — which demand and support the positive and synthetic construction of philosophy. There is therefore no such thing possible as an "agnostic" *philosophy* as distinguished from the exercise of those rights of scepticism and criticism which belong to all philosophy.

What is true of the conclusions of Spencerian agnosticism is true of its method also. Agnosticism has no special method superior or unknown to all the systems of more positive kind. Indeed, an examination of the customary method of its devotees — largely if not especially, of Mr. Spencer himself — discloses a certain defectiveness in respect of that very scientific and critical quality of which it is accustomed to boast. All attempts hitherto made at a completely sceptical or agnostic philosophy sadly lack consistency and method. From the very nature of the case this must be so. For uncritical scepticism issuing in agnosticism, as Kant long ago pointed out, is essentially dogmatic. A completely agnostic issue to a sceptical and critical survey of the problem of knowledge is self-destructive. But arbitrarily to limit reason in its power to discern not only the existence (*that* there is a "Power manifested," a "Reality hidden under all the changing forms"), but also the nature (*what* is the Power, and therefore that it is not "*utterly* inscrutable") of the ultimate principle, is to throw one's self again into the arms of dogmatism. However, if the limitation be made as the result of the most penetrating criticism, it involves in the making a large positive content of philosophy. It is therefore reflective analysis, and constructive synthesis of the principles selected through analysis, which constitute the method of even so-called agnostic philosophy. In the use of this method every form of dogmatism must pass by the paths of scepticism and criticism to the possession of its right to its conclusions, whether they be affirmations or denials. There is no royal road to professional and systematic philosophical nescience.

It is then perfectly legitimate for the disciples of Spencerian or other forms of agnosticism to adopt a consistent system of affirmative and negative propositions touching man's power to know the Ultimate Reality and touching the Being and Nature of that Reality. But this system they must arrive at as the result of a well-disciplined and thorough critical thinking. Nor do their negations of knowledge, its possibility and its actuality, stand on peculiarly sacred ground. When it is shown that they themselves affirm or deny more than they can maintain successfully in view of ultimate principles of all knowing and being, — albeit their excess of knowledge concerns chiefly the exact limits beyond which reason *cannot* pass, — they must be ready cheerfully to enter anew upon the pursuit of philosophy by its only true method. If they praise Mr. Spencer because he pronounces "utterly inscrutable" that Reality whose existence, nevertheless, he maintains to be the most indubitable of all truths, about whose attributes he has himself pronounced so freely, and the law of whose life and manifestation he describes in terms of evolution, — they cannot well blame some other thinker (for example, Hegel) *simply* because he attempts to show that this Reality is Reason itself, and the law of its being the dialectical movement (an evolution) from *An-sich-sein* through *Anders-sein* to *Für-sich-sein.*

The remarks just made apply, in part, to the plan of Mr. Lewes for getting rid of what he is pleased to call the "metempirical" elements and problems of philosophy.[1] His modified agnosticism or positivism is another of the many attempts, without a thorough and consistent critical analysis, to maintain a system of speculative statements in which somewhat dogmatic negations have too prominent a place. "Whenever," says this writer,[2] "a question is couched in terms that ignore experience, reject known truths, and invoke inaccessible data, — *i. e.*, data inaccessible through our present means, or through any conceivable extension of those means, — it is metempirical, and philosophy can have nothing to do with it." Now it is safe to say, with only a fairly strict interpretation of Mr. Lewes's language, that no such question could ever be raised, or couched in any terms whatever, by the human mind. Do ghosts exist? Is there a well-founded art of palmistry? Are the claims of telepathy true? Is electricity, like light, a mode of motion, or is it a peculiar entity, the bearer of energy but devoid of mass? These are questions in which the particular sciences of physics, physiology, and psychology are interested. We may be ignorant of their answer, but we cannot exclude them from consideration by the human mind simply by calling them "metempirical." And of course Mr. Lewes's philosophical agnosticism does not extend to questions couched in such terms as these.

Questions relating to "things *per se*," their nature and their properties, are, however, metempirical; and by things *per se*, their nature and their properties, Mr. Lewes seems to wish to cover all that we regard as having reality, in distinction from the merely phenomenal. But the problem of how, and why, and with what warrant, men come to imagine (to use Mr. Lewes's term) "Things as they *are*, and underlying the Things which *appear*, — a world behind phenomena, incapable of being sensibly grasped, but supposed to have a more perfect reality than the phenomenal world," — belongs within the distinctive

[1] For a detailed criticism of Mr. Lewes, see Shadworth Hodgson's Philosophy of Reflection, two vols., London, 1878.

[2] Problems of Life and Mind, vol. * p. 30.

domain of philosophy. Just so far as he refuses to consider this problem he declines the pursuit of philosophy, as a theory of knowledge by the legitimate method of reflective analysis and speculative synthesis, and remains in the negative and inert condition of dogmatic agnosticism.

But, like every other professional positivist, Mr. Lewes is not lacking in confidence in the ability of his own reason to accomplish — off-hand, as it were — certain very difficult feats in metaphysical philosophy. The method of his procedure he describes as follows: "To disengage the metempirical elements, and proceed to treat the empirical elements with the view of deducing from them the unknown elements, if that be practicable; or if the deduction be impracticable, of registering the unknown elements as transcendental." But what is implied in the very attempt which is here proposed? Is it not implied that metempirical elements exist in human thinking, and that the very nature of these elements is such as further to implicate the existence of a world of reality such as Mr. Lewes calls transcendental? And is it not also implied that this individual thinker is competent, not only to disengage these metempirical elements and make deductions from the known to the unknown, but also to register in the behalf of the race, the material which is "transcendental"? Now what, we might further inquire in the interest of reason's progressive self-knowledge, is to be done with this collection of "transcendental" refuse material? Is it to be at once and forever consumed in the fire of agnostic metaphysics? Or is it to be doomed to perpetual imprisonment in a cell over which the inscription is written — not to "the great Unknown," but to "the eternally Unknowable"? Or is it to be kept for future analysis, in the hope of further reducing its quantity?

Scepticism and criticism are indispensable to the progress of philosophical thinking. They are attitudes of reason before its eternal problems, as it advances, by the method of reflective analysis, from an incomplete synthesis to one relatively more perfect and comprehensive. But as distinguished from these mental attitudes and the method of advance in the knowledge of its problems which philosophy employs, agnosticism and positivism have no philosophical standing. They serve only to recall the saying of Lessing: "For the vast majority the goal of their reflection is the spot where they grow tired of reflection."

That so-called eclecticism is neither a philosophy nor a method of philosophy follows — as we have already seen — from the nature of philosophy and its method. Nor is eclecticism to be classed with the three forms of mental attitude toward philosophical truth which we have called the dogmatic, the sceptical, and the critical. So far as it differs from that spirit of critical freedom with which the student of philosophy conducts his survey of history, it is an inept way of expressing one of the two fundamental postulates which all philosophical discipline implies. This postulate is that of "the existence in the world at large of a 'truth' which affords a sure object for cognition." The world in which eclecticism expects to find this truth is the world of speculative thinking. But to convert this indefinite postulate of a "soul of truth" to be discovered in the different related systems of philosophical thinking into the definite knowledge of what that truth is, requires the use of philosophical method. And if the material for treatment is gained from historical study rather than from a study of the present conclusions of the particular sciences, it no less demands that we should regard it sceptically and critically before we accept it as material for a positive synthesis.

Dogmatism, scepticism, criticism; and then a new positive construction of those results that have stood the test of critical analysis, which in its turn comes to be regarded by scepticism as unverifiably dogmatic, — it is through these changes of mental attitude that philosophical inquiry is compelled to pass. This is the order of the different phases necessary to the growth of the organism of rational knowledge. The proposition might be illustrated by the experience of every individual thinker and by that of the race. This order applies to the consideration of every particular problem of philosophy ; it applies also to the development of systems and schools. But in every individual and in the race, whether the formation of views touching some particular problem or the development of an entire system is concerned, these different phases are not distinctly separated. Every thinker is likely to be positively confident, or dogmatic, respecting his own answer to certain problems of philosophy ; sceptical and agnostic with regard to any answer to other problems ; and more or less thoroughly critical toward certain answers to still other problems. Similar, in this regard, to the mental attitude of each individual thinker is that of the multitude in any given age.

At present, for example, the *Zeitgeist* is inclined to be confidingly dogmatic toward metaphysical postulates put forth in the name of physical science, but intensely sceptical toward those upon which repose the traditional views on subjects of morals and religion. An hypothesis like the conservation or correlation of energy, or like Darwinian evolution, gains a comparatively easy credence from otherwise sceptical minds. It may even put forth the virtual claim adequately to represent the ultimate principles of the life of all that is really Existent. But the dogma of Theism, that this really Existent is One self-conscious and rational Person, can with difficulty obtain a fair hearing even when it appears in the shape of a modest petitioner for the place of an hypothesis.

Philosophy began among the Greeks in the form of a dogmatic solution offered to the problem of cosmology. The three most ancient schools posited, without any adequate sceptical and critical examination, certain assumed substantial causes of the Being of Things. Heracleitus and his successors in the same line of inquiry (Empedocles, Leucippus, and Anaxagoras) dealt in similar dogmatic fashion with the problem of Change and Motion. The dogmatism of all this period touching the problems of morals and religion was expressed in unquestioned custom, ceremony, law, and popular belief, rather than in definite attempts at a system of philosophical tenets. It was chiefly with reference to this dogmatism that the scepticism of the Sophists found its field of action. They have fitly been called by Zeller "the exponents and agents in the Greek illumination (*Aufklärung*) of the fifth century B. C.;" like all such would-be philosophers, their scepticism was dogmatic and uncritical. They readily leaped to the conclusion: "Objectively true science is impossible, and our knowledge cannot pass beyond subjective phenomena." The Sophists thus exhibit the typical issue of uncritical dogmatism in dogmatic agnosticism.

The germ and spirit of criticism belong to the maieutic of Socrates. This new form of scientific life was designed to separate between the rational and the irrational in that experience over all of which an uncritical scepticism had thrown the shadow of doubt. Toward the speculations of the philosophy of nature, as conducted in his time, Socrates remained a complete sceptic; but in respect of ethical matters he maintained and defended a theory of cognition which holds that real truth is attainable by the method of dialectic. By this method our notions may be brought to a strict harmony with what is in itself true and just. While the other disciples of Socrates, and the schools which they founded, showed little or no power to use his method of reflective analysis, and upon it to erect a relatively consistent system of synthetic philosophy, it was not so with Plato. This great thinker developed the maieutic of Socrates into something resembling a scientific methodology. He extended the results of analysis so as to include many subjects hitherto treated by the philosophy of morals only very imperfectly; and upon these results he founded, as a vast expansion of the Socratic doctrine of concepts, "a grand system of an idealistic nature, the central point of which lies on the one side in the intuition of ideas, on the other in inquiries about the nature and duties of man." He thus gave to the world the first body of positive propositions arrived at by the method of philosophical reflection, — this reflection being conducted through the stages of scepticism and criticism to a stage of reconstructed dogmatism. Platonism has therefore a permanent and absolute value in the evolution of speculative thinking.

Among the immediate disciples of Plato, only Aristotle is of any significance for the development of philosophy or for the study of the method of its advance. But judged by the standard of his age, Aristotle comprehended in his system more of the complete content of philosophical truth, as he made a more thorough and consistent use of the complete method for ascertaining and verifying such truth, than any other thinker of antiquity, and perhaps of all time. His attitude toward Platonism was sceptical and critical upon many points of minor importance, and especially upon the central point of the doctrine of ideas. But notwithstanding this, he gave both to the conclusions and to the method of the Platonic philosophy an incalculably great and positive expansion and reconstruction. More especially, Aristotle founded several of the particular sciences on which corresponding departments of philosophy are dependent; and he labored with amazing skill and success to create a philosophical terminology and to place his synthetic philosophy upon a basis of comprehensive empirical knowledge. Aristotelianism is therefore the second great system which has a permanent and absolute value in the evolution of speculative thought.

The post-Aristotelian schools were founded in the attempt, without any consistent and thorough process of criticism, to formulate certain problems of philosophy — pertaining, for the most part, to the life of sensitivity and conduct — so as to satisfy in a practical way the immediate needs of the individual. They therefore involve a crude mingling of the sceptical and the dogmatic positions with a disuse of the true method of philosophy. These "schools" are therefore, — including the so-called "sceptical," — in the main, all dogmatic. The Peripatetics, who were the immediate successors of Aristotle, busied themselves with certain minor points in his system; they did not attempt by a change of method, or by a more thorough use of the established dialectic and the investigation of nature, to solve any of the greater philosophical problems. The Stoics and Epicureans, in respect of the philosophy of nature and the theory of Being and Knowledge, retrograded from the points reached by Plato and Aristotle. In respect of ethics, upon which they concentrated their attention, their positions, although of no great scientific value, were distinctly critical; and the positive conclusions they reached have a certain amount of permanent value in the development of philosophy. They mark the outcome of the Greek mind in its efforts to deal, by use of philosophical method, with the phenomena and the ideals of ethical life. So, too, does the later Greek scepticism show that placid agnosticism which "accepts the impossibility of knowledge as a natural destiny," — a thing difficult, if not impossible, for minds that, like ours, have inherited the mental peculiarities of centuries of Christian belief and opinion.

Neo-Platonism, as well as its precursors and comrades in philosophy, shows the results of new attempts at constructing a system of thinking in one chief department of philosophy. These attempts are all critical of the ancient dogmatic conclusions on which they are founded, but only in a partial way. They introduce us, however, to phases of the philosophy of religion with the recurrence of which, under changes of garb and presentation, the history of philosophy is familiar. They exhibit that strong tendency to some form of Monism which belongs of necessity to all philosophical inquiry when it is pushed to the consideration of those supreme problems in which the reason of man as a religious being is interested. From all the earlier forms of Monism a sceptical reaction, to be followed by efforts at a new critical reconstruction, arose as the result of the demands of a scientific psychology, especially in the department of *ethics*.

The relation of dogmatism, scepticism, and criticism as the

three perpetually recurring attitudes of mind toward philosophical truth, might be further illustrated by an appeal to the entire mediæval period. The illustrations would be comparatively scanty, however, on account of the comparatively stationary character of philosophy during that period. The theology of the period was, nevertheless,—in spite of any claims to a special source in revelation either through the inspired writings or the inspired judgment of the Christian Church,—a form of the philosophy of religion. It was, that is to say, the result of rational activity in reflective analysis and speculative synthesis, excited by the great facts of the Christian faith and life. Among the earlier Church Fathers (notably Origen and Augustine) there was exhibited no little power of free thought in the use of genuine philosophical method. Some of the conclusions of these thinkers are parts of the permanent positive results of the philosophy of religion. Without these we cannot establish an organic evolution of speculative thought from the Greeks down to modern times.

And even in the so-called "dark" ages, when the principle of authority was recognized as unquestioned, and is often supposed to have reigned supreme, there was considerable room still left for sceptical and critical attitudes from which to regard the prevalent dogmatism. Scepticism and criticism were of course theoretically possible only in the case of dogmas upon which the Church had not pronounced. But in fact there were not wanting serious attempts to treat matters sceptically and critically which fell under the content of established dogmas. Doubt might at least be expressed as to the way of understanding what the Church Fathers or the ecclesiastical councils had held; criticism also might be applied to different prevalent ways of expressing that about the substantial truth of which there was general agreement. The monk Gaunilo, for example, might in a measure anticipate the critical freedom of Kant, in his examination of the Anselmic ontological argument. Nor was the great debate between the positions of Platonism and those of Aristotelianism ever quite settled by Churchly dogmatism. The strife of Realism and Nominalism, although the agnostic rationalism of the latter seemed to threaten the reality of the Trinity itself, resulted in the establishment of a modified positive view containing elements from both, rather than in the complete suppression within the Church of the sceptical and critical movement.

With Descartes the necessity of the sceptical attitude toward all conclusions of philosophical dogmatism, and the intelligent use of reflective analysis as an instrument for the discovery of philosophical truth, become emphasized. But this thinker, who in this regard gave its characteristics to the modern era, was also the founder in direct line of certain great dogmatic systems which were broken into fragments by the sceptical and critical method of Kant. Spinozism is intensely and consistently dogmatic from beginning to close. Its value in the evolution of thought consists in three things; by its failure it demonstrates the inapplicability of the strictly deductive and mathematical method to the problems of philosophy. At the same time it shows by use of this deductive method how much can be done to explain the world, as known by the particular sciences, with reference to the conception of a bare Unity of Substance; and it affords a system of dogmatic propositions from which sceptical and critical analysis may take its start in estimating every new system of abstract modal and monistic Pantheism.

In Leibnitz we find the same fertile and skilful use of criticism upon the existing content of philosophy, combined with the introduction from the particular sciences of new material, and the same free spring from this basis upward to a higher level of synthesis, which characterized the work of Aristotle. But the speculative results of this thinker soon united with other elements to form the system of reigning dogmatism which awaited the criticism of Kant.

The half-use of the sceptical and critical attitude, and the corresponding development of philosophical method, which were characteristic of Locke's philosophy, bore abundant fruit in two different directions. In the one direction this movement resulted in that mixture of dogmatic scepticism and equally dogmatic sensationalism which established itself in England, and especially in France. In another direction it developed, through the critical but extreme idealism of Berkeley, into the relatively consistent and critical scepticism of Hume. [We cannot agree wholly with Kant in placing this thinker among the ranks of dogmatic scepticism.] It was the scepticism of Hume which made possible the modern attempts at a critical reconstruction of the theory of knowledge.

The modern era of deliberate, intelligent employment of reflective analysis, in the maintenance of the candid and free critical attitude, begins with the "Critique of Pure Reason." Yet its author, as we have already remarked, always remained in the dogmatic attitude toward several of the most important of those problems whose consideration, and even whose statement, is involved in the problem he undertook to solve. This made necessary a subsequent application of the Kantian criticism to Kant's own dogmatic views respecting the nature of the mind and its faculties, and to his dogmatic presuppositions respecting the *a priori* synthetic character of the body of truth taught by mathematics and physics. The work of critical analysis and reconstruction from the Kantian point of view is by no means as yet completed. Meanwhile, a vast accumulation of truths and conjectures, due to the modern advance of the particular sciences, — especially of physics, biology, and psychology, — is making a demand for recognition and treatment at the hands of philosophy. Toward this accumulation the attitude of philosophy is for the most part receptive and positive; but it must also be in part critical, if not sceptical.

Since Kant the philosophical spirit has been strongly imbued with the critical principle. No attempt at the construction of a new synthetic philosophy can now gain attention without appearing, at least, to stand toward all previous schools and thinkers in the position of a free sceptic and critic. And yet it is since Kant that the most stupendous systems of philosophical dogma have arisen — though chiefly upon German soil — which the world has ever known. Fichte, Schelling, Hegel, and all the earlier luminaries shining largely by light borrowed from them and from Kant, and now later Schopenhauer, Von Hartmann, and Herbert Spencer have built up great synthetic structures with extreme scepticism toward the results of previous thinking, and with equally extreme confidence in their own power to attain something approaching a final philosophy. Each thinker has perhaps contributed something permanent toward that completer system of associated principles of all Being and Knowledge which constitutes philosophy. But each system seems destined in turn to have many of its positive conclusions regarded as unwarrantably dogmatic, and subjected to a new process of sceptical analysis and critical reconstruction.

The rapid rise and fall of great systems of synthetic philosophy has been characteristic of the century since Kant. It is one proof of the extraordinary mental activity of the age, of the wonderful new growths of the particular sciences regarded as critics and purveyors of philosophy, and of the unabated influence of the spirit of the Kantian criticism. It is not strange that the result has been to create a widespread distrust in the value of all attempts at philosophical system. The fact is also noteworthy that many of the most acute and ardent students of the subject have devoted themselves to the critical and historical consideration of particular problems, and have abandoned all attempts at proposing new solutions for those problems. The last half of the century since Kant has seen a multitude of workers who emphatically deny that they seek a system of their own, or will follow the system of any other; and who even express despair of the possibility of framing again a philosophical whole that shall command an intelligent and enthusiastic, if only a temporary, adherence. But unless the method and attitude which render progressive the self-knowledge of reason have met with some secret constitutional change, an era of new great syntheses in philosophy awaits us in the future.

The naturalness of those changes of mental attitude which lead from dogmatism, through scepticism and critical inquiry, back to a positive reconstruction, is seen in the consideration of each particular problem of philosophy. The tenets of the schools, with which each of these problems is answered, illustrate the truth still further.

The first important problem which scientific psychology — just at the point where it touches metaphysics — hands over to philosophy for a more nearly ultimate solution, is the problem of Perception by the senses. *Naïve* unreflecting consciousness is frankly dogmatic as respects the solution of this problem. To it, indeed, a problem can scarcely be said to exist; for it has never been sceptical toward the native presupposition which takes all "Things" really to be as they seem. But experience quickly forces a measure of the sceptical attitude. That the senses cannot always be trusted, is soon learned; and that the light and color, smell, taste, sound, and feeling (so far at least as heat and cold are concerned) of things are not objectively as they are to us, the modern school-boy knows enough of physics to assert. At this stage of analysis certain systems of philosophy have attempted to call a halt to the progress of scepticism and criticism. But the conclusions of these systems cannot bear for a moment the more searching inquiry into the nature of the object immediately known by the senses, or into the nature of the process of cognition.

Another stand against scepticism and critical inquiry is made when the whole science of modern physics is summoned positively to solve the problem concerning the nature of that which is known in sense-perception as a really existent "Thing." Science is cited in proof of philosophical dogmatism. Then, indeed, a wonderful new world of Reality is disclosed to us as the result (though only very indirectly) of cognition by the senses. The real world which physics knows and propounds as a final barrier to philosophical scepticism, is a world of atoms, — colorless, silent, without smell or taste, discrete and without continuity of extension, restlessly mobile, inherently possessors of occult energies, and blindly obedient to countless numbers of laws.

But the philosophical inquirer declines to stay the march of scepticism and criticism at this point. For the authority of scientific dogmatism is no more terrifying to him than the authority of cloddy "common-sense." What sort of a Reality have we here? he asks. Is this so-called "real" world any other than a system of well-ordered conceptions, introduced in the name of physical science, to account for the world which must always remain more real to every man, because it is the world *he* "immediately" knows? And what is the essence of a world of conceptions if it be not a mental world? Moreover, what one tie, or ties many, can be known to bind into a Unity in Reality this restless multitude of discrete atomic beings? For forces and laws are but names derived from the modes of being and action of what really is.

When, then, scepticism dissolves the dogmatic syntheses of a scientific physical realism, and hands the problem over again to philosophy for further critical inquiry, the issue of this final attempt at analysis and reconstruction may be manifold. Agnosticism denies that the Being which "Things" have can ever be known; perhaps, also, that we can ever know whether things have any real being or not. Scepticism becomes dogmatic, and positively affirms that Things have no reality. Idealism, which has approached and followed the same problem along somewhat different lines, agrees with scepticism in this negation of reality to the object of sense-perception. Positively, it adopts the principle of *esse est percipi;* and, in some form of reconstructed dogmatism, identifies the reality of things with the reality of the subject acting to construct its objects, according to its own mental laws. Realism, again, "transfigured" in some worthy way by the process of criticism, speculatively discusses the nature of this extra-mental existence, in whose being all things have such reality as they possess. And, finally, critical philosophy, in its supreme effort, discerns the possibility of reconciling the valid claims of both idealism and realism by a synthesis which shall establish such a Unity of Subject and Object in Ultimate Reality as shall best explain all the groups of phenomena to which the different conclusions appeal.

The problem of Self-consciousness, like the problem of sense-perception, illustrates the naturalness of reason's progress by the three attitudes of dogmatism, scepticism, and criticism. For *naïve* unreflecting consciousness this problem also has no existence. For it the conviction that I really am, and that I know what I really am, seems neither to need explanation nor to admit of debate. This easy-going common-sense realism is attacked and overthrown by philosophical doubt. That I think (*cogito*), may not indeed admit of settled and serious doubt; and that I am, in some sort, when I think (*Cogito, ergo sum*), may be considered a proposition equally beyond all the successful assaults of scepticism. But *am I* when I do not think, when I swoon or deeply sleep? And do we by the Cartesian phrase — seeming, as it does to all reflecting minds, to skim the surface of that depth of being which we long to explore — tell all, or even the most and best, of what I really am? Now that the phenomena of trance, hypnotism, insanity, and other abnormal conditions of conscious or unconscious (?) ideation and volition are being brought into the clear light of science, will the old answers satisfy the demands of proof for the traditional tenets of rational psychology? What shall we say of the apparent existence of layer beneath layer of consciousness in the sub-conscious being of that which, in reflective self-consciousness, I call "myself"? What shall we say of the partial or total loss of the sense of personal identity; of that complete becoming other than one's self which takes place in hypnotic and insane conditions; of double consciousness, recurring intermittently or periodically? What are we to think of those wonderful phenomena of genius — akin indeed to madness and to inspiration, from certain points of view — that seem to give token of the presence, in the one whom we call our *Ego*, of another One, a mysterious, all-comprehending Life?

When the sceptical and critical examination of the older dogmatic positions respecting the answer to the problem of self-consciousness has been reinforced by considerations like the foregoing, it is not strange that difficulty is found in reconstructing the synthetic philosophy of mind. As respects this problem, too, agnosticism may dogmatically proclaim the impossibility of any knowledge of that reality which souls have; scepticism and materialism may deny that *souls*, in sooth! can have any reality; idealism may affirm that their only reality is the activity of self-conscious ideation itself; and realism may speculate as to what *extra*-mental being can be affirmed of that sort of existences whose very nature appears to itself to be purely mental. But genuine philosophy, with a wise moderation of scepticism and a patient use of critical analysis, will review and modify its syntheses in this department as the progress of psychology and psycho-physics affords the required means.

The more abstract consideration of both the two problems already mentioned constitutes the sphere of metaphysics. This branch of philosophical discipline considers the nature of that Being which we attribute to all — both Things and Minds — that we call "real." In its original dogmatic form it consists of those crude and unreflecting presuppositions which, for the ordinary man, bind his experience into the unity of reality which it seems to its possessor to have. To natural, unreflecting consciousness things are as they appear to minds; and minds are as each mind appears to itself to be. A host of relations also exists, above, around, and between minds and things, and these relations compel each being to govern its own behavior in view of the behavior of other beings. It is not necessary to trace the steps by which sceptical doubt and critical inquiry enforce the reconstruction of conceptions like these. The changing attitudes of mind toward this more complex problem of general metaphysics, and toward the different principal answers proposed for this problem, are essentially the same as those already described.

The earliest dogmatism of the mind toward the problem of Cognition in general is even more unquestioning and pronounced than that toward the problem of Being. To doubt whether I truthfully represent some particular form of reality, whether of matter or of mind, is far easier than to doubt whether I can know reality at all. It is indeed of the very nature of reason and of philosophical inquiry that it should be so. For the confidence of reason in itself, which is the same thing as the confidence that knowable truth exists for it, is a primary postulate of all reflective thinking. In the criticism of all other presuppositions this one remains as a kind of fixed point of standing; from which, if only it can be maintained, reason expects, with a never-tiring cheerfulness, to lift upward the whole world of thought. But even this postulate may be made the object of sceptical attack; it must, in the interests of synthetic philosophy itself, be made the subject of critical inquiry. And even if it were not to be doubted at all *that* I may know the really Existent, the various dogmatic statements as to *how* I may know this Existent, and *how much* of it I may know, require to be subjected to a sceptical and critical inquiry. The theory of cognition thus passes in order, and again and yet again, by the path of dogmatism, scepticism, and criticism, to the form of a higher and newly re-constructed synthesis.

The application of considerations like the foregoing to the

Ideals of Reason need not detain us long. The fact of application is readily made apparent. To the unreflecting ethical or æsthetical feeling the current dogmatism of assertion as to what is morally good or truly beautiful passes unquestioned. This dogmatism, in the solution of these great problems, is practical rather than speculative. To it the existing maxims, customs, laws, precepts, and modes of conduct present and sufficiently define what is morally right and good. The surrounding forms of nature, or — more probably — the traditional rules and products of personal adornment and other art, present and define the æsthetically good, — "the beautiful," so called. But doubt disturbs the repose of this attitude of unquestioning acceptance. Sceptical doubt must be operative in this way if a science, and then a philosophy, of the good and the beautiful, are to arise. But scepticism never produces of itself any improvements in science, any new and better solutions of philosophical problems.

The positive sciences of ethics and æsthetics represent a next higher stage of achievement in synthesis. They show what men in general, in various ages and by progressive approaches, have agreed upon as the rules, maxims, or laws of the beautiful and the morally good. But philosophy seeks the rational and the universal. It aims so to know the essence of these ideals of its own as to connect them with each other (since they are both its own ideals), and with that Unity of Ultimate Reality which reason, of necessity, postulates. It then proceeds by a sceptical and critical examination of the principles alleged by a scientific ethics and æsthetics, which it regards as too dogmatic for the supreme uses of philosophy, with its attempts at a higher synthesis. These attempts too, like all those made by philosophy to solve its problems, constitute the progressive self-knowledge of reason and its progressively higher knowledge of the world. Every new effort rises upon the preceding by leaping from the truth left undissolved by the severer critical analysis to a grander and more comprehensive synthesis.

In the Philosophy of Religion, the highest department of all philosophical discipline and the essentially synthetic branch of philosophical system, the same truth holds. How shall we solve the problem of that Supreme and Ultimate Unity in which the presuppositions and ideals of reason, and all the principles of the sciences, both of nature and of mind, may find their ground? To this problem all the other problems of philosophy point the way. In its complete solution would be found involved the solution of all the others. Therefore the stages by which they severally advance are effective in giving conditions to the advance of this supreme problem. If the problem of knowledge, for example, receive the answer of agnosticism or scepticism, then we must deny that, or doubt whether, man can know God. If the problems considered by the philosophy of nature and the philosophy of mind receive the solution proposed by materialism, then the ultimate Reality cannot be known as the personal Absolute "whom faith may call God." If the problem of the Ideals of Reason — the problem touching the ultimate nature and ground of the beautiful and the good — are to be answered after the manner of a certain kind of idealism, then the Absolute One cannot be the realization of the perfectly beautiful and the perfectly good.

Scepticism and criticism are then as necessary for the best progress of the philosophy of religion as for the advance of any other department of philosophy. Only thus does reason rise on the assured results of its previous efforts at this supreme synthesis to a result more comprehensive and satisfying to its deepest needs. Only thus can all the accumulating knowledge and wisdom of the sciences of nature, life, and conduct contribute to the higher and broader knowledge of God.

When, however, the attitude of scepticism toward philosophical truth is praised for its own sake, or maintained as though in this way alone progress in philosophical knowledge were secured, its relation toward the true method and aim of philosophy is totally misconceived. When criticism is ceaselessly carried on, without any assured and positive result becoming apparent, and when philosophizing issues in no philosophy beyond a system of negations and warnings, then the well-deserved reproach of all merely critical efforts is brought to mind. Then we hear men remarking how wearisome and profitless it is to be always whetting the knife, with no hope of carving anything; to be always tuning the instruments, with no prospect that the concert will ever begin. But all such procedures may remind us that the true method of philosophy is one of positive advance by reflective analysis and synthetic reconstruction of its material; although the employment of this method, in the case of finite minds, involves a passing through the stages of unsatisfactory dogmatism, sceptical doubt, renewed criticism, and higher attainment of truth.

CHAPTER VII.

THE DIVISIONS OF PHILOSOPHY.

THE proper method of dividing the entire domain of philosophy has occasioned almost as much discussion as the proper definition of this domain. Indeed the two subjects of discussion are almost unavoidably connected. For the conception which is held as to the nature of this rational pursuit, and of the whole circle of problems which it involves, cannot fail to influence the distribution of the individual problems among its different so called departments or divisions. No objection can therefore be raised to the legitimate result of this very natural connection. But since the result itself is one of such unfortunate disagreement, the temptation is strong to deny the legitimacy, or even the possible advantage, of paying any attention to the connection. To this temptation Lotze has, in our judgment, yielded somewhat unwarrantably when he claims that each one of the different groups of philosophical problems "appears to be self-coherent and to require an investigation of a specific kind." "We attribute," he goes on to say, "little value to the reciprocal arrangement of these single groups under each other."[1] From this somewhat extreme distrust of all systematic attempts to derive the divisions of philosophy from our conception of its nature, the same author seems to depart, in a measure, when he agrees with Herbart in holding that there are as many independent sections (of Metaphysic) as there are different distinct problems to serve

[1] Grundzüge der Logik und Encyclopädie der Philosophie, ed. 1883, §§ 92 f., and Translation of edition of 1885, Boston, 1887, p. 152 f.

as separate causes of our philosophizing at all. For the number and nature of the ultimate philosophical problems which we recognize certainly depends upon the conception we hold of philosophy.

The reconciliation of such an apparent conflict between the interests of logical consistency and the interests of convenience or of regard for real truth, is not difficult. The main cause of the prevalent divergence of views respecting the divisions of philosophy is, of course, a divergence of views respecting the definition of philosophy. But it has already been shown that all these conceptions, however different, agree in their principal factors. The different ways of stating these views arise chiefly from the wish of each thinker to identify philosophy as such with his own system of philosophical tenets. In other words, the statements too often tell not what philosophy is, but what in the judgment of their authors philosophy ought to be. It is to be expected, then, that those divisions of philosophy which are derived from the different conceptions of what philosophy ought to be, will themselves differ. This general fact may now be illustrated by a number of historical examples.

It is not necessary to repeat what has already been said (see page 15 f.) to show that Kant's division of philosophy was determined by his peculiar views touching the nature and the results of philosophizing. These views do not admit of more than two legitimate and really serious departments of philosophy. These are theoretical and practical, — the former being absorbed in Noëtics, or the theory of knowledge, and the latter being the doctrine of the categorical imperative as the *a priori* ground of conduct. In the case of Fichte such a thing as a consistent attempt to divide philosophy was not possible. In his view the only philosophy is *Wissenschaftslehre*, science of science itself. With Hegel the two fundamental principles — namely, the principle of the identity of Reason and Being, and the principle of the dialectic — lead, of necessity, to the well-known threefold division of philosophy. "The division of the

Hegelian system is, in consequence of the course which thought pursues in it (and we might add, in consequence of its assumption that this course of thought is the course of the self-unfolding of Reality), threefold." Logic, or the philosophy of Being-in-itself, the Philosophy of Nature, and the Philosophy of Spirit, are its necessary three main divisions. By application of the same principles the process of dividing and subdividing, in the same threefold manner, everywhere with a dull monotony characterizes the Hegelian system.

Herbart, too, though not as an uncritical follower of Hegel, adopts the threefold division of philosophy. With Herbart this division follows from his peculiar conception of the nature of philosophy. This he defines as "the elaboration of conceptions." The first stage of elaboration clarifies, distinguishes, and relates the conceptions in the form of valid judgments and conclusions. Hence results Logic, the first branch of philosophy. The second stage eliminates those conflicting elements in the conceptions which appear when we endeavor to combine them into an harmonious view of the world; this occasions the need of Metaphysics. Æsthetics, the third division of philosophy, arises when, to the conceptions, we add ideas of *value*, — conceptions that "occasion an increment of consciousness in the form of a judgment expressing assent or dissent." [1]

A host of later and less celebrated writers on philosophical discipline illustrate the same truth. Each finds a larger or smaller number of divisions necessary or convenient, according to the system of philosophical tenets which he wishes to advocate, or according, at least, to his dominating conception of what philosophy ought to be. One writer, who considers that philosophy is but the science and critique of cognition, would divide it into (1) a general Theory of Science, and (2) a Theory of Conduct.[2] This, of course, reminds us at once of Kant. Another writer, in the spirit of Hegel, maintains that there *must* be

[1] Lehrbuch zur Einleitung in die Philosophie, ed. Leipzig, 1850, p. 47 f.

[2] Riehl, Philosophischer Kriticismus, Band II., Theil ii., p. 1 ff.

three main divisions of philosophy, since the one totality distinguishes itself into two fundamental and essential parts, and then unites itself into a higher Unity. Accordingly, we are to divide the whole field into (1) Philosophy of Nature, (2) Philosophy of Spirit, and (3) Philosophy of Life.[1] Yet another, who believes that the aim of philosophy is to give us both a view of the world at large and a theory of life, would have us distinguish — (1) a general World-schematism; and this naturally breaks up into (2) the doctrine of the Principles of Nature, and (3) the doctrine of the Kingdom of Man.[2]

But that view of philosophy which aims to unite in one system the principles of all Being and all Knowledge naturally finds something like the following divisions necessary: (I.) Philosophy of Cognition, which subdivides into (1) Doctrine of Ideation and (2) Doctrine of Knowledge; and (II.) Philosophy of the Existent, comprehending (1) the philosophy of the bodily-existent, or Philosophy of Nature, (2) philosophy of the spiritually existent, or Psychology, and (3) Philosophy of Human Conduct. The last subdivision comprises Ethics, Æsthetics, and the Philosophy of Religion.[3] The division proposed by Professor Ferrier in his "Institutes of Metaphysic"[4] is obviously based upon the same conception as that of the writer last cited. Ferrier makes *Epistemology*, or the answer to the question, What is Knowledge? and *Ontology*, or the answer to the question, What is true Being? the "two main divisions of philosophy." Strangely enough, — and somewhat inconsistently with the conception underlying this main division, since the question, What is the limit of knowledge? is epistemological, — he introduces a third, "intermediate section of philosophy," which he calls *Agnoiology*. This is the theory of true ignorance (λόγος τῆς ἄγνοιας).

[1] Biedermann, Philosophie als Begriffswissenschaft, Theil i., Vorrede.

[2] Dühring, Cursus der Philosophie als streng wissenschaftlicher Weltanschauung und Lebensgestaltung, p. 10 f.

[3] For this elaborate and in many respects satisfactory scheme of philosophical discipline, see J. H. von Kirchmann, Katechismus der Philosophie.

[4] See p. 47 f.

Another class of writers make the division of philosophy subordinate to their conception of the relations it sustains to religious belief or to the life of conduct. Thus one author,[1] who holds that philosophy is the science of what is supreme and most important for human welfare, and has for its business to guide our choices in accordance with ideas of "value," or worth, divides the entire field into four distinct parts. These four are theology, metaphysics, cosmology, and the theory of conduct. Another writer takes his point of starting from the proposition that philosophy deals only with the supersensible Real, and presupposes as its subject man as a spirit in the image of God, the Absolute Spirit. Philosophy of Nature is then a contradiction. The main divisions of philosophy are, accordingly, given as: (1) Philosophy of Religion, (2) of Morals, (3) of Rights, (4) of Art, or the Supersensible in Nature.[2]

The most recent important work aiming at a system of philosophy is by Professor W. Wundt. As might be expected from its author, this treatise on synthetic philosophy is everywhere conceived and executed in a spirit of fidelity to the method and results of the particular sciences. We have already seen that Wundt regards philosophy as a universal science, having for its problem to unite the cognitions of the particular sciences into a consistent system. On account of the relation in which it stands to these sciences, its divisions must be based on the division of the sciences. Two main problems are therefore given to philosophy in its effort to treat synthetically all the particular sciences. The first of these problems relates to knowing in a process of becoming; the second, to knowing already become (*Wissen, Werdende* and *Gewordene*). Hence the two main divisions of philosophy are (1) Science of Cognition, (2) Science of Principles. These two divisions are then developed into a scheme, which may be tabulated as below:[3] —

[1] F. A. von Hartsen, Grundriss der Philosophie, p. 6 f.

[2] Lichtenfels, Lehrbuch zur Einleitung in die Philosophie, p. 10 f., 17.

[3] System der Philosophie, Leipzig, 1889, p. 33 f.

Division of Scientific Philosophy.

- I. Science of Knowledge.
  - 1. Formal (Formal Logic).
  - 2. Real.
    - A. History of Knowledge.
    - B. Theory of Knowledge, which, in connection with formal logic, constitutes Logic in the wider meaning of the word, is then further subdivided into —
      - *a.* General Theory of Knowledge.
      - *b.* Theory of Special Methods as applied to scientific investigation.
- II. Science of Principles.
  - 1. General, or Metaphysic.
    - The systematic exposition of the fundamental conceptions and fundamental laws of all science.
  - 2. Special.
    - A. Philosophy of Nature, which is subdivided into —
      - *a.* General Cosmology.
      - *b.* General Biology.
    - B. Philosophy of Spirit, which has three subdivisions —
      - *a.* Ethics.
      - *b.* Æsthetics.
      - *c.* Philosophy of Religion.

On the foundation of the three divisions of the Philosophy of Spirit, and with the help of a comprehensive survey of human development, stands the Philosophy of History. Its aim is to give a picture of the whole external and internal life of man.

Without detracting from the value of any of the foregoing attempts to divide the domain of philosophical discipline, none of them seems to us quite satisfactory. They all either include too much that is not philosophy, or else exclude some one of the important branches of philosophy. These faults of redundance or deficiency arise in each case from the fact that the division follows from an inadequate or redundant conception of the thing to be divided. It is noteworthy that, in the various schemes for dividing philosophy which we have examined, each of the four principal conceptions of philosophy has found expression. But these conceptions were found either to include factors that do not belong to philosophy, or else to neglect certain of its important elements. The scheme of Wundt, for example, provides for much under the general cover of the term philosophy which belongs to the particular sciences, — especially to the sciences of logic, psychology, and ethics. This is pretty nearly inevitable, unless we start our effort at division with a conception of philosophy which distinguishes it more clearly than does Wundt from a mere systematic sum-total of the particular sciences. On the other hand, those schemes of division which confine the domain of philosophical discipline to special metaphysics (ontology) or to the theory of knowledge, and those which over-emphasize the treatment of the ethical and religious ideals, omit to mention certain important departments of philosophy.

It is not necessary, in classifying the departments of philosophy, to commit the error of following one's philosophical tenets to either of two extremes. On the one hand, it is unsafe to derive this classification, with the show of necessity belonging only to mathematical demonstration, from one's peculiar and personal conception touching what philosophy ought to be and to hold for true. But, on the other hand, it is unnecessary to carry our protest against the systems called "absolute," and the deductive method they aim to employ, so far as to deny the possibility of any logical division of the different philosophical problems. In such a matter as this the middle path is safer. The divisions of philosophy are naturally, if not with a strict logical necessity, related to the true and comprehensive conception of the nature of philosophy. But this conception itself should be formed by a study of the history of philosophy combined with such an analysis of the work of reason as is adapted to show the relation in which its strictly philosophical results stand to those of the particular sciences. If a conception of the whole domain of philosophical discipline has been formed in this way, the separation of its departments or branches is easy and safe.

There are, then, as many divisions of philosophy as there are distinct problems proposed by the particular sciences to reason for its more ultimate consideration. These problems all concern aspects of the one great problem of philosophy, — questions subordinate to its supreme question. This one supreme problem is the formation of a rational system of the principles presupposed or ascertained by the particular forms of human cognition, under the conception of an ultimate Unity of Reality. The particular branches of philosophy are as many as the particular forms taken by the inquiries subordinate to the main inquiry. So peculiar, however, is the relation in which psychology stands to the special discipline called philosophical that all the problems of the latter are virtually proposed to it only when raised and presented in form already elaborated by the psychological method.

Can man *know* reality? and, *What* is the nature of the reality known to man? These are twin questions, born of the movement of rational life. They are so related, both as respects the character of the inquiries they raise, and also as respects the method of their pursuit and the influence they exert upon each other, that they must forever stand side by side in philosophy. The consideration of either of these questions cannot dispense with the consideration of the other. Neither question can be answered before the other, once for all time; neither has such logical priority as to admit of treatment without borrowing certain assumed conclusions from the other. Both must receive their elaboration and development in reciprocal dependence.

On the one side, then, we may be compelled to admit that no scientific ontology, no metaphysical system of principles pertaining to real Being as known, can be constructed unless we have first made sure that reason can attain the knowledge of real Being. Who, that has not faithfully listened to the cry of the Kantian critique, shall confidently proceed with a synthetic ontological philosophy? But, on the other side, it may be claimed, in an equally irrefutable way, that it is absurd to ask reason to approbate by reasoning its own fundamental postulates, or to proceed without a movement that is inspired and guided by the same principles which it is engaged in critically examining. Such a demand has fitly been compared to the demand that one shall learn to swim without going near the water, or that the hound shall run fast enough to outstrip his own shadow. Whose reason is it which summons reason to answer for itself? Surely, it is no other than the same reason with that which is summoned. What instrument of rational critique is to be employed in vindicating the ultimate truthfulness of reason, or in convicting it of untrustworthiness? Plainly, the same instrument as that which is being critically inspected. Will the knife cut? Shall the knife settle the question of its own ability by a perpetual examination of its own keen edge, or by undergoing a ceaseless process of sharpening? Shall it not rather try the issue and wait the result?

Further remarks upon the relation in which the two problems just proposed stand to each other will fitly be made in other connections. It is enough at present to call attention to their reciprocal dependence. The consideration of the first of these problems gives rise to the department of philosophy called "Theory of Knowledge" (or Noëtics, or Epistemology). In the erection of this department of philosophy it is implied that the science of descriptive psychology, with its introspective or historical method, does not directly furnish the complete answer to the problem of knowledge. This science simply tells the story in what forms and under what circumstances the related states of consciousness arise and pass away. But in telling this story, it is obliged to make note of a remarkable fact. The psychical states are not all regarded by the mind as alike related to an extra-mental reality of Being. Convictions of truth or of falsehood attach themselves to the conceptions of this reality. Sceptical doubt assails, and critical analysis patiently examines and expounds, the meaning and value of these conceptions and their accompanying convictions. And hence arises a department of philosophy.

The inquiry, *What* is Reality? gives rise to the second division of this first principal department of philosophy. More precisely, the main inquiry of this department may be stated thus: What is the content of our complete and most rational knowledge of the really Existent? This division of philosophy is Metaphysics in the narrower sense of the word, or Ontology in its widest defensible meaning. It proposes a general investigation of the essential Being that all real existences have.

The inquiry, What is Reality? — according to that twofold differentiation of its objects which reason inevitably develops — naturally divides itself into two inquiries. General Metaphysics has, therefore, two subordinate departments. The problems of ontology require a more special and detailed consideration of the necessary conceptions and presuppositions belonging to the two main classes of being. We inquire, then, What is the real Being of the Object known as *Not-me?* More precisely, one division of metaphysics occupies itself with considering the essential nature, connection in reality, and relation to the Unity of all Being, which the system of "Things" has. The other division of metaphysics raises the inquiry as to the real nature of the knowing Subject which is also Object known to itself as *Me.* It investigates the essential nature, connections in reality, and relations to the Unity of all Being which Minds have. General Metaphysics has, therefore, two subordinate branches; these are the Philosophy of Nature and the Philosophy of Mind (speculative or rational Psychology).

Theory of Knowledge and Metaphysics (in the narrower meaning of the word) are the two divisions of the Philosophy of the Real. This main department of philosophy, inasmuch as both its divisions have to do with the really Existent, —

with the possibility, certainty, and limits of the knowledge of it, and the systematic exposition of the content of what is said *really to be,*—may have the name of Metaphysics, in the wider meaning of the word. It is chiefly in this meaning that Metaphysics is not infrequently identified with philosophy.

But the entire domain of philosophical research and philosophical system is by no means covered by the conception of known Reality, whether it be of Things or of Minds. The more penetrating analysis of the constitution of reason discloses the presence and influence of certain rational Ideals. The problem of the essential nature and ground of these Ideals in this world of Reality is one of those problems in the solution of which psychological science acts as the propædeutic of philosophy. The task of philosophy with this problem also is one of further analysis, elaboration, and synthetic reconstruction. The material thus prepared for philosophical handling is gathered from many sources and from over an exceedingly wide area. Its preparation requires not only a study of the developing psychical life of the individual, but also of the developing life of the race. The latter expresses itself in manners and morals, in laws and political association, in the growth of every form of artistic production, and of the appreciation of whatever is called beautiful, in the actual world of physical and psychical existences.

But a department of *philosophy* begins to be founded only when these phenomena and the generalizations which they sustain are considered from the philosophical point of view, and are treated with the method of analysis and synthesis peculiar to all philosophical investigations. These presuppositions and discovered principles of all those sciences which deal with groups of phenomena called ethical or æsthetical, constitute the problem of the Philosophy of the Ideal. The analysis of the factors of this problem shows the relation of the Ideal in General to the constitution of human reason. The effort of philosophy, in its synthetic and constructive function, is to found this ideal and rational world upon the world of recognized reality. Hence, we derive the second main division of philosophical discipline, for which the word "Idealology" (or rational Teleology) seems to offer a fitting expression.

The Ideals of Reason, to which the second main division of philosophy has reference, are two, — the Ideal of Conduct, and the Ideal of Art. This principal division is, therefore, subdivided into Ethics and Æsthetics, — both the titles being understood to apply to the philosophical, as distinguished from the merely scientific, pursuit of these subjects (Metaphysics of Ethics, and philosophical—as distinguished from physiological, or technical — Æsthetics). Philosophical ethics moves in the sphere of that unique conception which we designate by such phrases as "the ought," the morally "obligatory," the ethically "right." The uniqueness and importance of this conception, and of the problems which it suggests and determines, constitute the valid reason for devoting to it an entire department of philosophy. In this department philosophy touches life in its innermost and highly sensitive centres. It aims to show how the grounds and issues of conduct take hold on the world of Reality; and how its ideals spring from that world as constitutive and regulative norms of all reason. It establishes and explicates the rational, and therefore the universal and eternal, character of these ideals. But if it is faithful to the law of its dependence upon the particular sciences, it so accomplishes its task as not to warp and violate, but to unfold the rational significance and to establish on real grounds, the testimony of ethical phenomena.

Something similar philosophy essays to do with the conception of "the beautiful," in the department of Æsthetics. This conception, too, — however much it be a matter of evolution as respects the particular forms of those objects which are esteemed beautiful, — is a unique conception. Its character as an Ideal of Reason, and its relations to the world of reality, philosophy attempts to explicate and to set in place in a system of all philosophical truth. No doubt the sphere of this department of philosophy is especially indefinite as to its limit. The content of admitted philosophical truth, which previous investigations have won in this field, has been particularly meagre. The reasons for these defects are not difficult to assign; but they do not concern us at present. That under the term "Æsthetics" we may fitly describe one of the two subdivisions of the Philosophy of the Ideal, there can be no reasonable doubt.

The suggestion of Lotze[1] that "for these two investigations a third, common to both, may be conceived,—namely, an investigation concerning the nature of all determinations of value (corresponding to Metaphysic),"—does not seem practicable, for the further division of philosophy. Indeed, he himself admits that the suggestion has hitherto never been carried out. The problem of determining the nature of the general conception of "*value*," apart from the problem of determining the nature of the ethically and æsthetically good, is scarcely of the sort to serve as the foundation for a division of philosophy.

The foregoing two main divisions of philosophical discipline, and all the subdivisions of both, lead up to the supreme synthetic effort of philosophy. This effort is to establish and explicate the conception of an ideal Reality, a realized Ideal of Reason, in the light of whose Unity *all* the principles of the particular sciences, and therefore all the other departments of philosophy, may be systematized and explained.

May the world of Reality be known, and What is the content of this real world, as knowable and known? What is the nature of that which we call "morally right," and of that which we call "beautiful;" and What the relation in which these Ideals of Reason stand to the world of Reality? These are the problems whose attempted solution divides the domain of philosophy, and also determines the classification of its schools and

[1] Encyclopædia of Philosophy, p. 154.

systems. But under the influence of strong practical necessities and desires, as well as of the never-ceasing intent of reason to unify and idealize, all these problems point the way toward and help onward the consideration of a final and supreme problem. Is this Unity of Reality, in which all things and all minds have their being, to be regarded as also the ultimate ground and the supreme realization of the ideals of conduct and of art? Is the All-Being the alone supremely beautiful and the alone supremely good? May we know such a Being; and How shall we mentally represent the content of such a Being? The answer, so far as answer there be, to the first of these questions, carries us back to the department called "theory of knowledge." The attempt to answer the second question introduces us to the highest and final problem of philosophy. The department which specifically deals with this problem we call the Philosophy of Religion. The answer to this problem is the crowning, but at the same time the most complicated and profound, of the achievements of philosophy.

The departments of philosophical discipline we divide according to the character and interrelation of the great problems proposed to it by the particular sciences, in the manner shown by the following tabulated scheme:—

<table>
<tr><td rowspan="3">I. Philosophy of the Real (Metaphysics, in the wider meaning of the word).</td><td colspan="2">1. Theory of Knowledge (Noëtics, or Epistemology).</td></tr>
<tr><td rowspan="2">2. Metaphysics (Ontology, in the wider meaning of the word).</td><td>A. Philosophy of Nature.</td></tr>
<tr><td>B. Philosophy of Mind.</td></tr>
<tr><td rowspan="2">II. Philosophy of the Ideal (Idealology, or Rational Teleology).</td><td colspan="2">1. Ethics (which considers the Ideal of Conduct,—Metaphysics of Ethics, Moral Philosophy, or Practical Philosophy).</td></tr>
<tr><td colspan="2">2. Æsthetics (which considers the Ideal of Art).</td></tr>
<tr><td colspan="3">III. The Supreme Ideal-Real (The Philosophy of Religion).</td></tr>
</table>

The other great branches of research, although conducted in the philosophical spirit and with philosophical ends in view, — such as the philosophy of history, the philosophy of the state, etc., — are not distinct departments of philosophy. They are rather complex discussions, drawing their material and method from several sciences and from the results of the investigation of several of the subordinate philosophical problems.

CHAPTER VIII.

THE THEORY OF KNOWLEDGE.

THE second edition of the "Critique of Pure Reason" is undoubtedly more apologetic, both in its tone and in its conclusions, than is the first edition. It is in this second edition that we read declarations, touching the need and nature of a philosophical theory of knowledge, like the following: "Philosophy requires a science, to determine *a priori* the possibility, the principles, and the extent of all cognitions."[1] Elsewhere we are told: "Our 'Critique,' by limiting speculative reason to its proper sphere, is no doubt *negative*, but . . . it is in reality of *positive*, and of very important use, if only we are convinced that there is an absolutely necessary practical use of pure reason (the moral use), in which reason must inevitably go beyond the limits of sensibility," etc. Further on Kant declares: "All speculative knowledge of reason is limited to objects of *experience;* but it should be carefully borne in mind that this leaves it perfectly open to us to *think* the same objects as things by themselves, though we cannot *know* them." And again: "I had therefore to remove *knowledge*, in order to make room for *belief.* For the dogmatism of metaphysic — that is, the presumption that it is possible to achieve anything in metaphysic without a previous criticism of pure reason — is the source of all that unbelief, which is always very dogmatical, and wars against all morality."[2]

[1] Table of Contents, Introduction, III.

[2] Preface of the second edition (1787).

It is sentences such as the foregoing which disclose to us the essential method, spirit, and content, of the Kantian critical philosophy. This philosophy is a critique of all those alleged necessary truths of reason which the so-called science of metaphysics is accustomed to systematize. This critique is conducted by reason itself in the use of the analytical and dialectical method, with intent to promote the interests of a rational belief in the principles of right conduct. Kant designed to begin with the sceptical attitude toward metaphysics, to continue in the critical method, and to end with the final refutation of dogmatic unbelief and the establishment of rational faith.

The procedure and conclusions of the Critical Philosophy were themselves acutely criticised by the greatest thinker among the immediate successors of Kant. "A very important step," says Hegel,[1] "was undoubtedly made when the terms of the old metaphysic were subjected to scrutiny. . . . The old metaphysicians accepted their categories as they were, as a sort of *a priori* datum not yet investigated by reflection. The critical philosophy reversed this. Kant demands a criticism of the faculty of cognition as preliminary to its exercise. That is a fair demand, if it mean that the forms of thought must be made an object of knowledge. Unfortunately there soon creeps in the misconception of seeking knowledge before you know. . . . True, indeed, the forms of thought should be subjected to a scrutiny before they are used: yet what is this scrutiny but *ipso facto* a cognition? So that, what we want is a combination in our process of knowledge of the action of the forms of thought with a criticism of them. The forms of thought must be treated on their own merits, apart from all other conditions; they are at once the object of research and the action of that

[1] Encyclopädie der philosophischen Wissenschaften im Grundrisse, Heidelberg, 1827 (or sixth vol. Collected Works) §§ 40 ff., and notes taken in lecture by Henning, Hotho, and Michelet; Translation, The Logic of Hegel, by Wallace, 1874, p. 69 f.

object. Hence they must examine themselves, determine the limits and show the defects attaching to their very nature." Thus much from Hegel, upon the Kantian view of the relation existing between the critical theory of knowledge and a synthetic philosophy.

As to the conclusions of Kant respecting the possibility and the limits of knowledge, Hegel — of course — takes many exceptions. "Thoughts, according to Kant," says he, "although universal and necessary categories, are only *our* thoughts, — separated by an impassable gulf from the thing, as it exists apart from our knowledge. But a truly objective thought, far from being merely ours, must at the same time be what we have to discover in things, and in every object of perception. . . . Though the categories, such as unity, or cause and effect, are strictly within the province of thought, it by no means follows that they must be ours merely, and not also characteristic of the objects. Kant, however, confines them to the subject mind, and his philosophy may be styled subjective idealism." "A general remark may still be offered," says Hegel, farther on, "concerning the result at which the critical philosophy arrived as to the nature of knowledge, — a result which has grown one of the axiomatic beliefs of the day. In every dualistic system, and especially in that of Kant, the fundamental defect makes itself visible in the inconsistency of unifying at one moment, what a moment before had been explained to be independent and incapable of unification. And then, when unification has been alleged to be the right state, we suddenly come upon the doctrine that the two elements (*i. e.*, Being and Knowledge), which had been denuded of all independent subsistence in their true status of unification, are only true and actual in their state of separation. . . . In the Critical doctrine, thought — or, as it is there called, Reason — is divested of every specific form, and thus bereft of all authority. The main effect of the Kantian philosophy has been to revive the consciousness of Reason, or the absolute inwardness of thought. . . . Henceforth, the principle of the independence of Reason, or of its absolute self-subsistence, will be a general maxim of philosophy, as well as a current dogma of the time."

The views of Kant and Hegel, as indicated by the foregoing quotations and as fully to be understood by a critical study of their writings, represent the two opposed positions of modern philosophy touching the problems raised in the attempt to form a theory of knowledge. Indeed, these views cover nearly all that is essential which can ever be said upon the subject of Noëtics. For this department of philosophy, from its very nature, can scarcely hope to derive important new material from the growth of the particular sciences. Its business is the critical and synthetic treatment of the presuppositions of all knowledge, with a view to determine the nature, extent, and certification of knowledge itself.

It is true that we may speculatively hold before the mind the representation of an evolution of reason which shall affect fundamentally its own essential nature as reason. But out of the bare possibility of such an act of imagination we can derive nothing for the purposes of a scientific and philosophical theory of knowledge. If the process of evolution is thought of as involving an essential change in the fundamental forms of reason itself, then all possibility of establishing the reality of an evolutionary process, and of thinking its nature and laws, is at an end. That we may have mistaken the unessential for the essential, the changing and developing for the eternal principles of all change and development, is indeed thinkable. But to trust reason for the discovery and validating of a universal law of evolution, which is to be so conceived of as to annul the validity of the universal elements of all law, is certainly impossible. So also is it thinkable that the progress of psychological science should disclose important new principles as regards the avenues, sources, and expansion of human knowledge. But even the attempt to think of these avenues and sources, and of this expansion, as validating what is contradictory of, or foreign to, the constitutional function of reason, ends in absurdity.

As regarded in one aspect, then, we find that the profoundest and most difficult problems of philosophy belong to the department of Noëtics. This is true if we measure their depth and difficulty by the acuteness and comprehensiveness of reflective analysis necessary to explicate them. They are profound because they lie buried in all concrete experience, — buried and concealed in such manner that ordinary analysis does not serve even correctly to state or clearly to raise these problems. They rise into reflective self-consciousness with a scientific shaping, late in the history of the individual and of the race. They are difficult, because no method of apparent solution prevents their being brought up anew, and yet in substantially the same form, for further consideration. They are like ghosts, with which it is hard to grapple, and even yet harder to lay so that they will not make again a troublesome apparition. Every age and every thinker may ask the question: Is then, after all, the truth attainable? Is not all the labor and acquisition of reason itself illusory?

But, in another aspect, the only possible, or best feasible, solution of the problems of Noëtics lies not far below the surface. The problems are comparatively easy of solution, if we apply the measure of specific research and technical information necessarily involved in the attempt. The philosophy of nature and the philosophy of mind, philosophical ethics and æsthetics, and the philosophy of religion, may always expect an indefinite expanse of their horizon, as the result of the development of the particular sciences on which they depend. But the theory of knowledge will, so far as we can anticipate, require only that the inquirer should move over the same narrow circle of analytical reflection, to the end of time. Lengthy and learned treatises upon the main questions of Noëtics will scarcely seem to bring their authors, or the rest of mankind, much nearer to the final truth. The strength of conviction which attaches itself to the affirmative answer to the inquiry, Is there in the entire content of self-consciousness any certification possible of the truth of reality? cannot be made to correspond to the wealth in details of the arguments adduced to support the conviction.[1] The whetting of the knife is necessary, but need not occupy us long. The tuning of the instruments is also necessary, and may profitably be done before the audience; but it should only last until we feel confident that they are capable of producing a harmony. And even this confidence we shall never attain, until more or less of harmony has actually been produced by playing them when already in fair tune.

This somewhat peculiar mixture of embarrassments and advantages which belongs to the discussion of the theory of knowledge should not be lost out of mind. It may serve to make us the more satisfied for the present with the brief remarks which the limits of this chapter permit. These remarks will keep in view the excellences and the defects of both the Kantian and the Hegelian positions toward the problems of Noëtics.

First of all, something should be added to what has already been said (page 170 f.) concerning the logical relation in which this department stands to the other departments of philosophy. It is not mere excess of arbitrary scepticism which has caused the great multitude of modern thinkers since Locke, and especially since Kant, to insist upon a thorough and satisfactory criticism of man's power to know as a logical *prius* of any metaphysical system. The scepticism involved in this demand, and the critical examination necessary even provisionally to satisfy the demand, are of the very essence of that method which must be employed in philosophy. But the scepticism, just so far as it scientifically establishes limits to knowledge, limits

[1] This statement might be confirmed by calling attention to the fact that Kant's Critique of Pure Reason and Hegel's Logic are both, at the same time, the most important and suggestive, and the most diffuse and repetitious, of philosophical treatises.

itself; it is self-limiting. The critique of reason, the more thorough it becomes, explicates the more thoroughly the grounds and nature of the self-confidence of reason. It demands for its own procedure this same self-confidence; for it is, essentially considered, the self-criticism of rational mind.

A theory of knowledge can, therefore, never legitimately end in scepticism; to bring it to this issue is to terminate the process of reflective analysis in absurdity or in the dogmatic refusal to think at all. The beast when driven till tired may refuse to stir; or maddened by goading, may leap the barriers and run blindly amuck. But either form of behavior in man is an obvious abandonment of rational method. If we were *gods*, commissioned to examine and test the fidelity of human thought and knowledge, in its highest forms, to extra-mental reality, it is thinkable that we should find grounds for a favorable or an unfavorable report. But if we *were* gods, and were as such stimulated by curiosity to examine critically the grounds of our own divine knowledge, it is unthinkable that the final result of this examination should be in principle any more reassuring than that attainable by us as rational men. Divine knowledge is still knowledge, though it be divine; as knowledge it must in some form bear within itself the grounds and evidence of its correlation with reality.

No theory of knowledge, however far the critical process employed in its construction be pushed, can discover other grounds for the certification of knowledge than those which lie in the content of knowledge itself. No point of view outside of reason, as it were, from which to criticise reason, is possible of attainment. If this be a disadvantage, it is a disadvantage not peculiar to *our* knowledge and *our* truth, but to knowledge and truth as such.[1] Whenever we even attempt to think of a knowledge that takes the knowing subject out of and beyond the fundamental forms of his own knowledge, and that

[1] Comp. Lotze, System of Philosophy, Part I., Logic, Bosanquet's Translation, 1884, pp. 414 ff.

envisages him with a truth of reality which is something more than truth known as universally valid to this subject, we land ourselves at once in absurdity. This limitation of the grounds and the certification of knowledge to the content of knowledge, need not, however, be regarded as a deprivation peculiar to man. On the contrary, we certainly have the choice — and there are grounds on which it is wise to make it — of regarding this power of reason to raise and press the critical inquiry, even to the very foundations on which it itself reposes, and to make its own self-limitation and self-consistency the goal of all this inquiry, as a chief possession and pride of reason.

It follows, therefore, that no possible or thinkable way exists of certifying the truth of what is known, except the way of subjecting the content of knowledge to a critical analysis, with a view to determine what, when most thoroughly and consistently envisaged and explicated, it actually is. So far as Kant and his followers insist upon this truth, their conclusions are beyond all possibility of successful assault. Furthermore, no psychological doctrine of a faith-faculty, or of a form of rational activity called "belief," no hypothesis of an intellectual intuition or transcendental dialectic, no claim for exceptions in behalf of certain species of truth called ethical or religious, can possibly withstand this critical conclusion. Strangely enough, — so it would seem to any one who does not keep constantly in mind the historical fact that the Critique of Pure Reason was in its author's purpose subsidiary to the Critique of Practical Reason, — few writers on philosophy have appeared to be greater sinners in this respect than Kant himself. In the passages already quoted, as all through his critical philosophy, he would limit speculative "knowledge" of reason to objects of experience. Objects that are really existent, like God, the Soul, and Free Will, we may "think," but cannot "know." The thinking may, indeed, be with belief, but cannot be called knowledge. "I had therefore," says he, "to remove *knowledge*, in order to make room for *belief*."

But the Kantian language, and all the argument of which it is the expression and outcome, most unfortunately reverses the real distinction between thinking and knowledge as dependent upon a connection with belief. Belief is not a rational act opposed to or contrasted with knowledge; but to convert thinking into knowledge, the thinking must be not only rationally consistent and rationally grounded, but suffused and supported by conviction or rational belief.[1] That which we may simply think, we cannot be said to believe any more than to know. Knowledge requires conviction as truly as it requires thought; and in knowledge both thought and conviction imply a reference to reality. All truth known is truth both rationally thought and rationally believed in. The thought and the belief, if they belong to knowledge (as distinguished from opinion, from the mere passive having or active forth-putting of states), implicate — their very nature is such — a correlated reality.

The Kantian theory of knowledge also, of necessity, breaks down when it virtually tries to vindicate for the metaphysics of ethics and the practical reason what it had denied as forever impossible in the functioning of the pure speculative reason. We say "virtually," for its author obviously foresaw that both scepticism and dogmatism would, from their respective points of view, attack his transcendental ethical system; and he strove hard to defend it against the charge of inconsistency. Kant will not call the practical reason "pure," because he wishes not to assume a pure practical reason, in order rather to show that it exists. But its existence being shown, he considers that it stands in no need of a critique to hinder it from transcending its limits; for it proves its own reality and the reality of its conceptions by an argument of fact. We may *know* the fundamental law of the practical reason; it bears the form of a

[1] Comp. Wundt, System der Philosophie, p. 90. "Alles Erkennen ist somit ein Denken, mit welchem sich die Ueberzeugung von der Realität solcher Objecte und objectiver Beziehungen verbindet, die dem Vorstellungsinhalte der Gedanken entsprechen."

command, — a categorical imperative: "Act so that the principle of thy will can at the same time be accepted as the principle of a universal legislation." Whatever principles are, as necessary convictions, attached to this principle, are postulates of the pure practical reason. Hence we find Freedom, Immortality, and God restored from the spaces swept empty by the critique of speculative reason.

But Kant's categorical imperative is itself only an imperfect and faulty generalization from empirical data of ethical feeling, judgments, and conduct. It is not even an exact summary of the testimony, in reality, of human moral consciousness. Were it a true generalization, however, and therefore worthy to be itself called a knowledge, it could be shown to be dependent for its validity upon many subordinate conceptions and convictions which must also have the validity of known truths. Otherwise, the categorical imperative itself is condemned as a vague and illusory dream of the individual consciousness. Metaphysical postulates, other than the three acknowledged postulates of the pure practical reason, with that inseparably adhering conviction which makes them principles of all knowledge as well as of all thought, enter into the very substance of this categorical imperative. *Beings*, with *powers* called "wills," rationally answering to *ends* that involve *other beings not themselves* but *like* constituted, and who may be expected to *act* as *bound* with their fellows *in a system* of moral order, — all this, and much more, is involved in the main principle of the practical reason. But what an infinity of knowledge, made *knowledge* by the suffusion of rational thinking with rational conviction, and, in some sort, placing the mind of the individual face to face with a world of reality, is here! Some of these are the very things of which we have been told, as the result of the critical process applied to speculative reason, that they may not be spoken of as "known," but may only be permitted to thought, without hope of finding content for the empty form, no matter how much we extend the bounds of experience. If these postulated entities and relations are not *real*, then the categorical imperative and all it implicates is but a dream, — nay, it is only the dream of a dream. Must we not then, in consistency, either include all — and especially the categorical imperative with its accessory postulates — under the condemnation uttered by consistent scepticism, or else retrace the steps passed over in the criticism of speculative reason, and discover grounds for a larger "knowledge," with its eternal accompaniment of rational faith?

The same fate must await all those theories of knowledge which end in scepticism, as the result of critical processes. Nor is the fate much better of those theories which endeavor to save from scepticism certain portions of the content of human knowledge, while denying in general the possibility of validating knowledge as such. The principle of self-consistency is of the last importance to reason. It is, in fact, only one form of stating the undying self-confidence of reason. The practical exhortation of experience in noëtical philosophy is then: Let us by all means maintain a rational consistency.

The maxim of maintaining a rational consistency is violated by those theologians who decry speculation and have no confidence in metaphysics, while at the same time they assume for themselves a knowledge of God, or even a rational faith in him. It is violated by those students of physics who remain agnostic toward all possibility of establishing a rational knowledge of those objects with which theology and philosophy are concerned; while at the same time they assert a valid and indubitable knowledge of physical entities and forces, and of the laws of the behavior of these assumed realities. We cannot play fast and loose with agnosticism, in our forming and holding of a theory of knowledge. The only legitimate outcome of applying the sceptical and critical process to man's power of knowledge is the more consistent reconstruction of the system which the content of knowledge involves. This is possible only through that faith in the work of reason which is its inalienable possession and right.

To sum up the case, then a sceptical view of the possibility of knowledge is self-limiting, its inevitable issue is the recognition of the absurdity and self-destructive character of unlimited doubt. A critical view of the actual process and content of knowledge is necessary to indicate what knowledge is, and what are its limits. For the principles of knowledge, its nature and limitations, are to be discovered only as they are implicated in the act and product of knowledge itself. They are not extraneous to it; they cannot be regarded as imposed upon it from without. The certification of knowledge also can be found only by the method of reflective analysis applied to the actual content of knowledge. No certainty derived from outside of or beyond this content of knowledge itself can ever be gained; no such form of certification is even thinkable. To expect more, to claim more, even to try to conceive of more, ends in irrational absurdity. It is like the effort to think *how* a being would know who had no formal laws or actual content of knowledge. If reality is to be known, the attempt to establish by a critique of reason a tenable theory of knowledge assures us that the reality must be envisaged or implicated in the content of knowledge.

Such a positive, intelligent, and intelligible theory of knowledge, as can alone claim all the valid and advantageous results of both scepticism and criticism, can do nothing more than to exhibit the consistent system of all those principles—laws, presuppositions, and concomitant convictions—which it finds involved in the actual process and products of knowledge. And when we say process *and* products, we are only testifying to the power of reflective analysis to envisage and regard knowledge in two related aspects. These are the aspect of the formative activity, the knowing subject; and the aspect of the formed material of knowledge, the object known. In the actual life and growth of knowledge the two aspects exist in indissoluble union; subject is subject in reference to object, and object is object in reference to subject.

But the question may be asked, — it is a fair and important one, — What if no amount of philosophical thought, however penetrating, comprehensive, and candid, succeeds in producing a "consistent system" of the principles of all knowledge? Must we not then resort to a dogmatic scepticism or to agnosticism in this department of philosophy? Or if we shrink back, on ethical or æsthetic grounds, from being thoroughly consistent in denying the possibility of all knowledge, may we not save the reality of certain special objects of religious cognition by introducing them through some scheme of faith, or of revelation, to the human soul? The affirmative answer to petitions like the foregoing has been given, by no means infrequently, in the history of human thought. But it has always ended in failure, shame, and distress for both those who have given and those who have received it. In saying this, we do not deny the value and rational nature of faith; on the contrary, we are engaged in maintaining views of philosophy which support the claims of rational conviction. Nor do we deny the possibility of revelation, or of the conveyance of truth concerning non-sensuous reality through other means than sense-perception and ratiocination. We cannot admit conclusions, however, which involve the contradiction of reason's confidence in the existence of rational truth, and in the possibility that this truth may be known by activity of reason.

Positively, however, the theory of knowledge should take into account the application of the definition of all philosophy to its own case. Philosophy is progressive rational system. The self-knowledge of reason in the formation of a theory of knowledge is therefore progressive. The lesson to be learned from failure to construct the principles of knowledge into a consistent, and so into an acceptable and defensible system, is not, therefore, a lesson of utter scepticism or of despairing agnosticism. It is rather an invitation to do over again the work of thinking in its application to knowledge. It is a call to a better acquaintance with the actual processes of knowledge, in perception and self-consciousness, as made known by empirical psychology. It is a call to better acquaintance with the laws and processes of thought, as modern logic, after centuries of slumbering in the nursing arms of the giant Aristotle, has awakened to investigate and describe them. It is a call to a more profound metaphysics, to a more thorough analytical and synthetic reconstruction of those principles which we ascribe to all that is really existent. In brief, it is a demand for doing over again and more thoroughly the hitherto only partially successful work of this branch of philosophy.

General considerations like the foregoing must maintain themselves in the discussion of the subordinate problems of the philosophical theory of knowledge. These problems may be presented in the following three questions: What is knowledge? What are the limits of knowledge? How comes, and what is, the certainty of knowledge? The internal relations among these questions are such that the answer of each involves the answer of the other two; the answer of all three depends, in turn, on the view we take of the one problem with which this department of philosophy deals.

Strictly speaking, the answer to the question, *What is knowledge?* cannot be derived by either deduction from some more general principle, or by induction from particular experiences of knowledge. Strictly speaking, then, knowledge cannot be defined. It can, however, be so described as to render it possible of recognition from among other psychical processes and states; its content can by reflective analysis be so explicated as to make the factors, presuppositions, and laws of all knowledge clear. To recognize the impossibility of defining knowledge, we have only to consider that definition itself implies a complex and elaborated knowledge; this is more rather than less true when the definition is of a subject so involved in all concrete experiences as is the nature of knowledge itself. The true and perfect definition of knowledge would therefore be a highly developed and complicated instance of that which in its simplicity we seek to define.

But the psychological investigation of the origin of knowledge does not of itself serve even to *describe* — in accordance with the demands of the noëtical problem — the nature of knowledge. Nor is the question as to the origin of knowledge, properly speaking, a question of the philosophical theory of knowledge. If philosophy were speculatively to discuss the origin of knowledge at all, such discussion would belong to another of its departments; namely, to the philosophy of the mind. But what the sciences of psychology, anthropology, and (we add, with a deferential protest) biology have ascertained touching their peculiar problems, does but serve to make more definite and clear the nature and limits of the genuinely noëtical problem. Knowledge is what it is, in spite of all agreement or dispute over the questions which are raised in the legitimate attempt accurately to describe how it came to be. Whether knowledge, as a potentiality of the race, be a direct gift from heaven, bestowed at once with ungrudging hand when God made man in his own image; or whether it be the result of evolution from some bioplasmic stuff quite incapable of knowledge, although presumably a psychic centre of the lowest forms of sensation-complexes, — at any rate, the factors, presuppositions, and laws of its present constitution remain unchanged. A descriptive science of its origin — were it possible to make such a science indubitable at every point and complete — would not furnish the solution of the problem which the philosophical theory of knowledge seeks.

It is true, however, that the light which science can throw upon the processes and products of knowledge, as respects the order of their succession and their dependence upon cognate or inferior psychical phenomena, is needed to guide the investigator in the field of Noëtics. Here the light from psychology, the science of the individual human mind, is far clearer, and therefore more helpful, than that which can be bestowed by anthropological or biological theories of the evolution of knowledge in the race. We would not deny all value and cogency to the latter, however; on the contrary, we would use them to confirm or to invite to re-examination the conclusions of human and comparative psychology.

Among the considerations, which the psychological study of the rise of knowledge offers to the philosophical theory of knowledge, the following may properly be emphasized. Knowledge must always be distinguished from the mere having of psychical states. This proposition remains unshaken, however highly complex or valuable, from the ethical and æsthetical points of view, the psychical states in themselves considered may be conceived to be. That there should be psychical existences whose experience consists solely of a succession of enjoyable states of sensation or of feeling, without reference of the states to reality, may perhaps be thinkable. Such beings, however, would be without "knowledge." For all states of knowledge imply reference to somewhat beyond themselves regarded as mere psychical states, — however true it may be that this somewhat and the reference to it must be given to knowledge as implicated in the states.

Knowledge is therefore chronologically a later and logically at once a higher and more fundamental activity of the mind. Even in its earlier and more elementary stages of the perception of Things and the consciousness of Self, knowledge emerges only as preceded by a process of evolution. The psychical existence, called man, does not *know* anything, at first and for a considerable time after birth. He *has states*, — presumably of various kinds. These states may be tentatively described as sensation-complexes, feeling-complexes, memory-images, volitions, or motor activities with their accompaniments of peripherally or centrally originated feelings of effort, etc. But knowledge has not yet dawned within the mind. How knowledge can arise out of these states, — if by the inquiry we mean to ask for anything more than a narrative of the successive stages by which perception and self-consciousness emerge and clarify themselves, — descriptive and explanatory science of mind cannot say. Such science reminds us, however, of the important truth that knowledge, in the case of every individual man, comes as the result of a development. The development is conditioned upon factors and processes of which we gain information only as an acquisition of complicated and indirect scientific research.

It follows, therefore, that knowledge implies memory and thought. This is as true of those objects called "Things," as known in immediate perception by the senses, and of that object called "Self," as known in self-consciousness, as it is of those objects whose existence is inferred by the most complex and circuitous processes of scientific investigation.

At this point not a little embarrassment may be occasioned to the conclusions of analytical reflection by the customary theories and terminology of empirical psychology. This science is accustomed to reduce all forms of consciousness to three, of which knowledge is a distinct and separable one. Memory and thought are then regarded as subordinate forms of knowledge, consequent upon perception and self-consciousness. We do, indeed, need a term to distinguish the general knowledge-element in all psychical states, — the element or aspect of intellection, as distinguished from the elements or aspects of feeling and volition. On the other hand, knowledge, as the philosophical department of Noëtics discusses its problem, implies memory and thought. These processes cannot, then, be considered as stages of knowledge, subsequent in time, or logically, to knowledge by perception and by consciousness of self. They are words expressive of psychical facts and processes on which knowledge by perception and self-consciousness is dependent.

But memory and thought do not, of themselves, constitute knowledge, although they condition its attainment. Memory-images might rise and fall in consciousness forever; but unless the reference of them to a world of reality were consciously made, no knowledge would be implied or would result. And thought might elaborate the psychical states as such in an endless concatenation; but unless, beyond the reference which thought implies to related states of ideation, there were implicated the reference which all knowledge makes to a world of reality, our psychical existence would fall short of the solidity of a consistent dream. Thinking, as such, is not real life.

But perception (*Wahrnehmung*) *is* taking hold on the truly real, the really true; and so is also that knowledge of self which is called sometimes "internal perception," or self-consciousness. For there is no reality, which is knowable in immediate knowledge, except the object *known* (not simply imaged or thought) in perception or self-consciousness. Empirical psychology, with its scientific description and explanation of related psychical states, can trace the stages which mark the birth and development of knowledge. It shows that comparison, analysis, and synthesis — whether consciously or unconsciously [1] performed — are pre-conditions of all knowledge, whether of things or of one's self. But it also shows that the full meaning and complete content of knowledge cannot lie in the application of this relating activity of the mind to the elaboration of its own states. It shows that reality is envisaged in every mental act which belongs under those categories needed to describe an act of knowledge. This reality is not "pure being," or "being as such;" it is the concrete object given to consciousness as implicated in that complex form of living which we call by the term "knowledge."

The "Being" of which the Hegelian dialectic treats may be regarded by the critics of Hegel as but a systematic ordering of abstract conceptions. But the Being that is known by the most unthinking mind, in every act of perception or self-consciousness, is concrete, indubitable reality. The friendly student of Hegel, moreover, cannot fail to see that this most abstract

[1] Compare Wundt, Grundzüge der physiologischen Psychologie, vol. ii., sections on Psychologische Entwicklung der Gesichtsvorstellung, Bedingunger und Grenzen des Bewustseins, etc.; Hartmann, Philosophy of the Unconscious, vol. i. chapter on The Unconscious in the Origin of Sense-perception; Ladd, Elements of Physiological Psychology, part ii., chapters vi. and vii.

(with the exception perhaps of Fichte) of all philosophers everywhere manifests a wholesome dislike of mere abstractions. This apparent (and in a measure real) inconsistency of Hegel is largely due to his exaltation of *thought,* not only to a supreme, but even to an exclusive, position in the realm of rational life. Thought serves, indeed, to condition and to explicate the content of knowledge. It is therefore necessary both to the earliest forms of immediate knowledge and to the extension of knowledge by scientific and philosophical method. [We here use the terms "scientific" and "philosophical" in their most general meaning, as expressive of all the further and logically higher elaboration of immediate knowledge.] In knowledge, however, reality is implicitly given, as concrete object envisaged by the subject in the unity of a self-conscious life. It is the business of science and philosophy to explicate the content and to interpret the meaning of these acts of knowledge. But behind or above the concrete acts neither science nor philosophy can place itself, either to criticise or to explain. This inability — if one please so to call it — is of the very nature of knowledge. Yet this fact is not significant of the inability of knowledge to give us reality; it is rather significant of the inability of thought, as a ratiocinative process, to comprehend or explain either the origin or the nature of knowledge. In so far as there is knowledge, there is reality known; in so far as there is real knowledge, there is power to know. This is the secret of the weakness of Hegel and his followers, that they identify reality solely with a dialectical process, instead of showing that in all complex rational life, and in all scientific and philosophical elaboration of the content of this life, the presence of reality is involved. "Objective thought" — to use Hegel's term — is the object known as real, because realizing itself, in all self-conscious rational life.

It is also as accompanied with and suffused by conviction that knowledge distinguishes itself from the mere having of psychical states. That which is known is necessarily believed in as real. To distinguish knowledge and faith as separate avenues of receiving truth, and then to exalt one over the other as critic and judge, involves a *πρῶτον ψεῦδος*, a primal and fatal heresy, toward reason itself. It is true enough that most men to a wide extent, and all men to a certain extent, believe firmly and passionately in what they cannot be said to know. It is also true that the grounds of much of this so-called faith are to be found in a too easy acceptance of current views, in prejudices arising from the emotional activities of the soul. Much of so-called faith is, indeed, of yet lower origin; it is born of base sloth or of selfishness; it is unintellectual, unspiritual, visceral. But similar things may be said of much, indeed of most, which passes current for knowledge. Science itself is only just learning, but is far indeed from having fully learned, how to free itself from such so-called knowledge.

The foregoing facts militate no more against the possibility of knowledge than against the rational power of that conviction which inseparably belongs to knowledge. Indeed, the same process and attitude of mind toward truth may be called either belief or knowledge. No one can be said to know an object or a relation in the reality of which he does not believe; neither can he be said to believe in the reality of that which he does not seem to himself to know. The words "seem to himself," however, mark the fact that all our language, as descriptive of our experience, recognizes in knowledge a factor of intellection and a factor of feeling as well. The mistaken identification of the former factor with the sum-total of that concrete and living experience which is fitly called knowledge, results in separating in thinking what is never separated in life. No knowledge is without belief; it is this inseparable factor which constitutes one of its chief constituents.

At this point psychological science might be summoned to the instruction and support of Noëtics. This science shows us that, although it has been customary to speak of perception and self-consciousness as forms of knowledge only, in distinction from feeling and volition, perception and self-consciousness as knowledge actually involve ever present feeling and volition. The theory of perception by the senses doubtless needs reconstruction from this point of view. As reconstructed it shows that knowledge of "Things" does not come, and could not come, by pure intellection. The series of sensation-complexes, by synthesis and localization and projection of which the perception of external objects takes place, is as truly defined and combined by its "pleasure-pain" quality as by its merely intellectual distinctiveness. An ever-present activity of volition is also, we believe, the necessary condition of that externality which things must have, — or else they are not *Things*. How a being which did not feel and will, as well as have, compare, and combine sensations, could know a world of material objects, it is impossible even to conceive. The activity in which the "Thing" is envisaged as a reality is one, indivisible fact of knowledge; but the description of this activity recognizes feeling and willing, as well as intellection, among its necessary factors. And the same truth holds with respect to that form of immediate knowledge which is called self-consciousness.

It belongs to the detailed theory of knowledge to describe more fully the nature of the conviction which belongs to all knowledge, whether of things or of self. The same department of philosophical disquisition is called upon to defend this conviction against the assaults of scepticism. Such defence can be successfully conducted only by allowing scepticism, under the control of critical analysis, to run its course to the inevitable issue of showing itself absurd. What we may learn as to the meaning, grounds, and limitations of that conviction which is an inseparable factor of all knowledge, the theory of knowledge must itself undertake to disclose. In general it may be said that the readjustment of belief, as respects the particular objects or relations to which it attaches itself, and as respects the subjective intensity with which — so to speak — the attachment is formed, is a dependent part of the evolution of knowledge itself, in the individual and in the race. *What* to hold for true, as certainly known and because known, cannot be determined once for all by processes of ratiocination. The progressive development, as respects comprehensiveness and consistency, of the system of knowledge is the only cure for false belief as it is for false knowledge. "False" knowledge! We feel a strong repugnance to the use of such a phrase; and with good reason, for it calls out all the protest latent in the indestructible self-confidence of reason itself. And yet how much that has been called "knowledge," in every field traversed by the knowing mind, has been all too clearly shown to be false! How much more, now not only firmly believed in, but also — if the testimony of the majority be received — most indubitably known, will in the future be shown to be false! Is not this as true of those objects of which we suppose ourselves to have immediate and indisputable knowledge by perception and self-consciousness, as it is of those more remote and occult objects and relations in which modern physical science so firmly believes? Our reply to questions like this must be an affirmative.

But on the other hand, the philosophical theory of knowledge endeavors to show how, rightly explicated and interpreted, all these primal beliefs, which enter into the essence of knowledge, may be allowed to stand. The growth of knowledge by successive purification of false beliefs does not prove these primal beliefs to be guilty of falsehood. And indeed how could they be *proved* guilty of *falsehood?* For in them reposes the mind's attachment to truth in distinction from falsehood; and even its power to discover and appreciate the distinction at all. Ultimately, then, it is positive and progressive rational system, disclosing and harmonizing more and more clearly and completely the content of rational life, which affords the only antidote for philosophical scepticism. Inasmuch as every such rational life, in the very forms of its manifestation, actually though unintelligently partakes of this unchanging universal reason, it has knowledge, with its constituent factor of confidence in itself, as an envisaging of reality. But philosophy, as theory of knowledge, explicates the content of knowledge and the nature of its constituent conviction, and so renders us intelligent as to what is really known and believed in as known.

Further remarks in this line are prohibited for a treatment so brief as ours; and, indeed, to treat of what is really known, belongs to another department of philosophy. This department is Metaphysics, — a department whose problem, with its answer, has been seen to be the twin sister of Noëtics.

The philosophical theory of the nature of knowledge may be further illustrated by special application to the different *Stages or kinds of knowledge.* For this purpose a division may be made into immediate or intuitive knowledge (of perception and self-consciousness), scientific knowledge, and philosophical knowledge. To all these the general remarks just made are applicable, though in different manner and different degrees. What it is to know, as all men have experience of knowledge in the perception of things and in the consciousness of self, has already been for the present sufficiently described.

Scientific knowledge, considered from the philosophical point of view, appears to differ from ordinary knowledge chiefly in the following two respects. Its improved means of perception increase the field of intuitive knowledge; it thus seems to open to view a world of wonders that is more real than that of our customary experience. Its carefully guarded inferences, its verifiable and verified manner of forming conceptions into judgments in a systematic and orderly way, extend the field of ratiocinative knowledge; it thus seems to demonstrate the nature of things and minds as they most really exist. But the reality of things as seen through microscope or telescope is, in the sight of the theory of knowledge, not in the least more unassailable by scepticism; nor is it ethically and æsthetically more valuable than the realities of ordinary vision. If the reality of the world of external perception is not to be known by use of the naked eye, it is not to be known by the use of microscope or telescope. The objects thus seen by the trained observer are not a whit more easy to verify as essentially real than are those which the swineherd daily beholds. If the latter are relative and their reality subject to doubt, so are the former. If the former imply an indubitable conviction of the presence of a known reality, so do the latter. In this sense of the word, all knowledge is relative, — that given in scientific observations as well as that given in the observations of all men. The metaphysics of the two is the same.

But what a world of reality does physical science open to imagination and thought when we follow its modern lofty flights of reasoning, — accomplished, shall we say? with one wing of hypothesis and the other of experimental verification! Occult beings called atoms, with wondrous powers of changing their states and their relations to other atoms, are ceaselessly weaving events and combining themselves into new aggregations in that world which no sense-intuition can ever know, but which is contrasted with the world of sensible things as the alone eternal and real with the fleeting and the illusory. Scientific knowledge is of that which is non-sensible and yet real. The reality of the objects thus scientifically known depends, however, upon classes of postulates too-often forgotten. It depends upon the reality of the objects known through the senses or in self-consciousness; for these objects afford the only data from which the objects known by science can be inferred. It depends upon the validity of the thought-processes, because it is derived by these thought-processes from data of sense-perception and self-consciousness. Only on the presupposition, then, that immediate perception gives knowledge of reality, and that the processes of thought are valid in reality, can the reality of the world which science discloses be vindicated. And, indeed, scientific knowledge, as scientific, is not concerned with reality at all. Its formula of thought is the hypothetical judgment. It reasons, — If this is so, then that is so, or will be so. Its only test is consistency of thinking. Science is satisfied if it becomes a harmonious system of conceptions.

What! — it may be asked, with the air of being startled at the fear of losing so much wealth of reality from our grasp, or of being puzzled at hearing that form of knowledge, which calls itself "science" pre-eminently, so sceptically attacked, — Is it then to be maintained that all this goodly fabric of modern physics is nothing more real than a fairly self-consistent dream? Certainly; *unless* in perception and self-consciousness there is knowledge of reality involved, and *unless* the movement of that elaborative thought which science employs is representative of processes that occur in the really existent. A positive system of metaphysical beliefs, adopted after an intelligent and thorough criticism of human reason, can alone save the modern system of physical science from a final banishment into the "death-kingdom of abstract thought." Without such positive system, so-called scientific evolution is even more abstract and unreal than the monotonous tit-tat-too of the Hegelian logic. But these beliefs *are* of the mind, integral and inseparable constituents — or rather themselves regulative and constitutive — of all those perceptions and conceptions out of which scientific system is made.

It is therefore to a reflective analysis of knowledge itself that science must appeal for its validating. Science necessarily assumes a position of trust toward the fundamental modes of the behavior of mind in thought; otherwise it cannot itself be "science," even in so far as science involves merely the consistent elaboration of mental images. But if science is to be regarded as somewhat more, — namely, as knowledge of a world of really existent things standing in knowable relations, — then it is bound hand and foot to the fate of noëtics and of metaphysics. Its devotees may affect or actually feel indifference, or they may laugh and even sneer; but they will not thus escape their condition of dependency on philosophy.

They certainly will not improve their condition by substituting a mixture of uncritical credulity and dogmatic agnosticism for a well-reasoned theory of knowledge. The ascertained principles of science can be held to extend our knowledge of reality only as we receive in good faith, after critical examination, both the testimony of intuitive perception and the objective validity of the forms and principles of thinking.

The objective validity of the forms and principles of all thought is therefore a postulate of science, if science is to be called knowledge in the meaning we have attached to this word. The term "objective" has been ambiguous in philosophy; it will probably continue to be used ambiguously. It had different meanings in the two great systems of Noëtics with a reference to which this chapter begun. Kant, no less than Hegel, and in his sceptical Critique of Pure Reason as well as in his dogmatic positing of the categorical imperative, affirmed the objectivity of thought. In the Kantian view the categories, or constitutional modes of the functioning of the understanding, give to thought the objectivity it has. These "subjective conditions of the spontaneity of thought" (as Kant himself in writing against Eberhard calls them) are constitutive of this objectivity. They make our ideas to be *objects*, appearances of extra-mental reality (the phenomenally real).

But besides the categories, and as seemingly necessary to give actual content to the otherwise merely empty form of perception and thought, the Kantian theory of knowledge implies the *Ding-an-sich*. This "thing-in-itself," however, can never get into consciousness, can never become known. Every concrete and actually known Thing has its own content, or material, furnished by sensation. But sensations are eminently subjective, and cannot constitute a knowledge of aught beyond themselves. They cannot, then, give knowledge of reality at all. Neither can we regard the existence and nature of this reality as known indirectly by inference to be the *extra*-mental cause of our sensations. For cause is itself one of these purely "subjective conditions of the spontaneity of thought." The same is true of reality. Kant's *Ding-an-sich* can, then, never be an object of knowledge, or even of imagination or of thought. It cannot legitimately be an object of belief. For what we can neither imagine, think, nor know, in that we cannot believe; and vain and illogical are all the efforts of practical reason to find a rational ground in reality for conduct, when knowledge and reality have once and forever parted company.

But with Hegel the objective validity of the forms and principles of all thought means something more and better than was provided for by the Kantian critique. With Hegel it is just these forms and principles, not as dead and barren forms, but as factors ("moments") in a living and eternally true self-evolution of thought, which are the true and only reality.

The satisfactory theory of knowledge accepts the critical method of Kant, but pursues it with more thoroughness and fidelity than its author employed. It therefore does not come to Kant's sceptical and inconsistent outcome. It finds with Hegel, as against Kant, that the purely negative and limiting conception of *Ding-an-sich* represents nothing important or actual in the processes and objects of knowledge or thought. It may therefore be consigned to the dark and chaotic places where mere abstractions wander, as the ghosts conjured up by speculative minds. It also finds that the positive content of the conception, missed by a sceptical analysis, is to be found present in every act of knowledge. That *extra*-mental reality is, all acts of knowledge imply. That it is, they all, as concrete instances, demonstrate. What it is, the growth of knowledge makes progressively clear. This is true of the individual, and it is true of the race. Therefore, the true theory of knowledge also decides against the system of Hegel, who selected a single form of thought, and by a systematic arrangement of abstract conceptions aimed to tell us, once for all, what is the Reality which all knowledge envisages and implies. This true theory turns rather to science for an extension of knowledge as to what the nature of the really Existent is. Physics enriches the content of the now positive conception of the *Ding-an-sich.* Psychology, ethics, æsthetics, sociology, history, and the science of religion contribute to the same end. Philosophy in all these departments, and with use of all these data, builds up its positive system of knowledge concerning this ultimate Unity of Reality.

What are the precise forms of all thinking, upon the postulated validity of which the conclusions of the sciences can be accepted as knowledge, it is the business of logic in particular to consider. It is of these forms — conception, judgment, syllogism, induction, deduction, etc. — that logic treats. But the further reflective analysis which philosophy bestows upon these forms shows that it is in the particular form of judgment that knowledge is expressed. The truth of intuitive knowledge is stated in the so-called primary or psychological judgments; the truth of science is stated in judgments that refer to other judgments as grounds. For validating in reality these forms of scientific observation and inference, and so for enriching and expanding by scientific progress our knowledge of reality, Noëtics has no other method than the one of reflective analysis and successive syntheses. Here, as elsewhere, it can only clear away, as much as possible, the obscurities and apparent contradictions which attach themselves to the knowledge of knowledge, as to every kind and form of knowledge. It can then the more intelligently reaffirm the confidence of reason in its own modes of self-conscious life.

The so-called principles of all thinking (as distinguished from the logical forms of all thought) the philosophical theory of knowledge examines with especial care. These it tends, especially since the days of Leibnitz, to reduce to two: they are, of course, the principle of Identity, and the so-called principle of Sufficient Reason. In the statement and explication of these principles — especially of the latter — the development of the theory of knowledge finds one of its most important and fruitful themes.

The *principle of identity* — in its obverse form called the principle of non-contradiction — is reason's law, binding it inexorably to consistency. This principle does not warrant the affirmation that any unchanging beings, whether things or minds, must be assumed to exist; much less that reason is compelled to accept the self-contradictory task of telling what sort of Being such things and minds could have. It does not mean that some rigid and permanent core of a substance, or *Ding-an-sich*, must be possessed by all things and all minds, on peril of their losing, otherwise, all claim to be called "real." The principle of identity conveys no knowledge whatever as to the essence of any particular reality, or as to the unchanging modes of the behavior of aught that is real. It simply states two ultimate facts pertaining to all thought, — two facts united in one principle. The truth of knowledge elaborated by thought is necessarily expressed in the categorical judgment; and in the categorical judgment the constituent factors of the judgment must remain self-same. But it may be asked: What is "self-sameness" but identity; and does not the law compelling self-sameness apply to all factors of all judgments and to all constituents of all things? Does it not, moreover, hold true of every real being, whether it be a thing or a soul, that it must be always identical with itself?

The full reply to questions like the foregoing would take us into details concerning the nature of conception and judgment, and concerning the meanings attached to words such as "Thing" or "Soul," which it is beyond our present limits to follow. Two or three suggestions as to the character of some of these details must suffice. In reality the psychical occurrences which we represent under the terms of logic — conception, judgment, reasoning — are never, as actual occurrences, stationary conditions of mind. Thought is a never-ceasing movement of ideating mind; and the movement is at every step suffused with factors of rational conviction and controlled by law. A logical theory which can appeal to psychical facts will then be morphological, evolutionary. The general fact that the states of self-conscious ideation called comparison, abstraction, generalization, etc., unfold themselves into each other in an orderly way, is the general fact which underlies the theory of conception, judgment, and the other logical forms. But every actual conception, or rather process of so-called conceiving, and every act of judgment, or rather process of judging, is necessarily a growth. This growth is not in violation of the principle of identity; were it so, no conception could actually take place.

All conceptions of all objects are susceptible of change under the principle of identity. So, too, actual judgments are not stationary combinations established, by the sign of equality, between ready-made entities called concepts. They too spring into existence as successive self-evolving states of conscious ideation. Regarded, however, as forms of thought, both conception and judgment may always be referred to intuitive knowledge, in order to see, as it were, whether they will form themselves anew with their customary content unchanged. The form of conceiving or judging which stands this test, so often as repeated, is called "*true*;" it represents in thought the reality of immediate knowledge. And where (as is generally the case) the mind, on inquiring what conception or judgment to frame, cannot settle its inquiry by immediate knowledge, it reasons its way to the affirmation it seeks. That is, it connects the required judgment (determines the direction and end to which the process of related states of ideation shall grow) with other judgments, in which the former shall find its grounds. But knowledge is not reached by thought, nor is truth of thought affirmed, until the mental action takes the form expressed by the categorical judgment. *S is P*, is then the universal formula for positing the knowledge of truth elaborated by thought. To this formula all the knowledge which thought affords may, for its legitimate expression, be reduced.

But neither *S* nor *P* can, in knowledge elaborated by thought, represent a simple "moment" or single factor of self-conscious life. Both *S* and *P* must stand for a composite of such factors. *What* composite we call *S*, and what *P*, or that we shall always signify the same potential or actual combination by this word, the principle of identity does not provide. We may change our conception of the nature of any particular *S*, and of the nature of any particular *P;* and as well of the relation maintaining itself between them. But if we are going to tell "the truth" in pronouncing the judgment *S is P*, the principle of identity binds us inexorably to rational consistency. The same elements of ideation, combined in the self-same way, must be represented by *S;* the same by *P;* and the same by the copula expressing the relation between *S* and *P*. Otherwise, *S is P* cannot be tolerated as a judgment expressive of the truth.

The customary formula of logic for the principle of identity in its positive aspect is $A = A$; in its negative aspect *A is not = non-A*, or *A* is not $= B$. But all forms of statement imply the principle itself. For if the principle of identity do not apply to the *A* which is in the place of *S*, to the *A* which is in the place of *P*, and to the relation signified by the sign of equality, then the formula itself cannot stand. Yet every attempt to apply this principle to each of these three constituents of the judgment must itself take the form of a categorical judgment falling in its turn under the principle of identity. All expression of this principle therefore implicates it, as, from the beginning, controlling the expression itself.

The principle of identity cannot, of course, be proved, in any sense of the word "proof," or in any of the many degrees of probability attaching themselves to the proof of all kinds of existences and occurrences. All proof, as all attempts to think at all, imply the working of this principle with a strictness that admits of no degrees. Moreover, no particular existence or conception of the existent can be substituted in the formula $A = A$, which shall receive merely by its substitution the sanction of the principle. Physics cannot substitute for *A* one of its elementary realities called atoms; and so maintain, in the name of the principle of all thinking, that — for example — the nature of the oxygen or hydrogen atom is forever self-same. Psychology cannot substitute for $A = A$ a categorical judgment affirming that in reality the soul remains, through all changes of states, identical. Not even philosophy can follow Fichte in his subtle but fallacious transmutation of the formula $A = A$ into the formula *Ego = Ego*. Physics may show grounds in experience for believing that the nature of the atoms does not change. Psychology, after pointing out what can properly be meant by personal identity, may defend the proposition, even by appealing to an invincible belief, in the case of the soul. But of atom and *Ego* alike, — and yet no more than of our mental representation of the meanest and most trivial occurrence, — if we have knowledge elaborated by thought at all, this knowledge must be expressed by the categorical judgment under the principle of identity.

No other subject in Noëtics has been treated with so wide-spreading and mischievous laxity of thought and speech as the so-called "principle of sufficient reason" (*Principium rationis sufficientis: Satz des Grundes*). In the name of this principle, physical science has often, almost with the same breath, decried all metaphysics and *a priori* constructions of reality, and maintained the rational necessity and universality of some one or more of its most recent conceptions of force and law. In the name of the same principle science has joined hands with philosophy in the denial of the being of that "personal Absolute whom faith calls God;" and, as well, in the denial of the freedom of the human mind. In its name, as an ultimate rational necessity, the claims of scientific *knowledge* have been so extended as to reduce all the problems concerning the world, man, and God, to the terms of molecular physics. Thus in the name of reason certain highest and most valued ideals of reason — freedom, God, and immortality — are made to confess their inability to find for themselves a ground in reality.

That gifted and suggestive but perverse thinker, Schopenhauer, has nowhere else done better service for philosophy than in his treatment of the principle of sufficient reason. This service took the two directions of analysis of the principle, and exposition of certain fallacies connected with its use. In his work on the "Fourfold Root of the Principle of Sufficient Reason," Schopenhauer discusses the principle with a view to discover both the common elements of all the forms it takes (the "Root"), and also its division into cognate but distinguishable modes of application (for the root is "fourfold"). Frequently in his philosophical writings he exposes with ridicule the attempts of physical science to understand everything under its own peculiar ways of applying this principle, without resort to metaphysical explanations; while at the same time it introduces clandestinely a whole host of unexplained and uncritical *causæ occultæ.* Without accepting the accuracy and sufficiency of Schopenhauer's treatment, we refer to it as a legitimate warning against supposing that physical science can dispense with metaphysical causes, and yet maintain a claim to explain the world of reality.

The statement of the principle of sufficient reason is of the greatest importance for a theory of knowledge. And yet it is doubtful whether scientific precision can be given to any attempt at its statement. The reason for difficulty here is not precisely the same as that which has been noted with regard to the principle of identity. In the case of the latter we observe its simplicity and absolutely fundamental character, apart from all consideration of the nature of particular experiences. In the case of the principle of sufficient reason, the difficulty of discussing it arises rather from its manifoldness of formal application and the way in which it enters into the conditions of different kinds of experience. Ethical and æsthetical considerations also appear to militate strongly against certain forms of conceiving and stating this principle. That we cannot say, "Every being must have a cause," is clear from the fact that even all scientific explanation, under the law of physical causation, postulates uncaused beings as the very ground of its explanation. Physics explains all physical events, and the genesis and changes of all physical beings, out of the postulated and unexplained being of the atoms. The philosophy of religion, too, finds in the Unity of the Absolute its ground for that interrelation of the phenomena which — so science considers — demands the affirmation of universal force and universal law. Neither can we say, "Every event must have a cause;" unless we are ready to modify our conception of cause so as to include under it the relation of motive to volition, and of the being that acts to his own particular action, — however mysterious the nature of such being and the spontaneity of certain forms of its behavior may be.

To us it seems that the so-called principle of sufficient reason may best be described in something like the following way. If the description appears loose and indefinite, it may on that account the better fit all the different classes of phenomena which fall under the principle.

Psychological science shows us that knowledge is elaborated by relating different ideation-states in uniform ways. In all knowledge indirectly attained through processes of reasoning, besides the mere fact of the association of the states, the consciousness of the relation must be recognized. Knowledge elaborated by thought implicates therefore the being aware of an orderly and rational procedure. But knowledge also involves conviction which has reference to reality; for knowledge is not of ideation-states, as such, but of objects, — of things or minds. Indirect or mediate knowledge implies, then, the consciousness of fixed relations, interconnected modes of being and action, belonging to the objects. In and by this rational procedure all experience becomes articulated, as it were; and as far as knowledge seems to go, so far goes the belief in the reality of the related objects, and of the relations of the objects. This every rational mind, developed to self-consciousness, necessarily has. This, too, is the basis, in the normal and necessary procedure of the mind, upon which rest those extensions of the limits of ordinary knowledge which science aims to make. But science, or — in particular — physical science, has no prescriptive right upon this principle; it has no claim to define or limit it, as a principle of all thought, so as to shut out from its legitimate use the unscientific multitude or the little group of thinkers who, in spite of physics, claim to have a rational faith in Freedom, God, and Immortality.

It would almost seem that the essence of the principle of sufficient reason as employed by the sciences can be best stated in a practical maxim: Always try to explain. But scientific explanation consists in relating the changes of one being to those of another being, under the form of fixed and uniform sequences. It might also be said that another maxim, as a warning, must be added: Remember that all scientific explanation postulates the presence of the unexplained. For as reflective analysis shows, and as science when it comes to rational self-consciousness admits, scientific *explanations* tell only the story of the uniform modes of behavior of those beings whose existence and natures science postulates as the ground of all explanation, but can never explain.

The philosophical theory of knowledge defends the fundamental principles of all thinking against a sceptical issue to their critical examination. It thus validates that extension of knowledge which science proclaims. The further examination of these principles, and of the conceptions and presuppositions implied in their use, belongs to Metaphysics, — in its main division under this name, and in its two subdivisions as Philosophy of Nature and Philosophy of Mind. Without this positive outcome to Noëtics, however, neither of the two branches of Metaphysics can claim to do anything more than to represent a consistent schematizing of states of consciousness. But then without this outcome science itself is nothing more.

Knowledge as extended by thought is, in its latest and

highest stage, philosophical knowledge. This knowledge has often been called *a priori* or intuitive. But as customarily employed, both these terms are likely to mislead those who use them. By *a priori* we can mean, in this connection, nothing more than the universal and necessary modes of the behavior of rational mind. The term "universal" we cannot understand so as to deny that the multitude of men do not self-consciously recognize the so-called categories, while philosophy itself has not yet succeeded to the satisfaction of all in either explicating or cataloguing them; but also that their employment as formal principles by the individual requires psychical development. If the categories are forms of being, they are so because they are the necessary forms of psychical becoming. By the term "intuitive" we cannot mean that it is possible to envisage these modes of the behavior of rational mind, as it were, in their naked and abstract essential character. We can mean only that, while their explication is a matter of reflective analysis and discursive thinking, such mental effort infallibly finds them implicated in all knowledge by thought; as well as, also, that to doubt that the experience which implicates them is knowledge, or that the knowledge is of reality, is impossible in consistency with the nature of reason itself.

We cannot, then, claim with Fichte that knowledge of knowledge, philosophical knowledge, is alone worthy to be called science. But we can claim that the objects of philosophical knowledge are capable of being, not merely imagined or thought, but also known.

Little need be added concerning the application of the general principles of a theory of knowledge to the remaining two of its subordinate inquiries. The true and safe answer to the question, What are the Limits of Knowledge? follows easily upon reflection from the very nature of these principles. The limits of knowledge cannot be dogmatically fixed, whether the dogmatism which attempts this impossible task call itself by its right name, or take the title of scepticism or of agnosticism.

The formal principles which, in a certain sense, exist as limitations of knowledge, are those fundamental modes of the functioning of mind which philosophical criticism distinguishes as implied in all knowledge. Using a figure of speech that is perhaps legitimate, but represents only the shadowy outlines of the dark region of so-called negative thinking, the fundamental forms and laws of every kind of knowledge may be represented as barriers beyond which the mind cannot pass. Some of the current impressions of being "limited" or "bound" in knowledge are the result of an uncritical and sentimental refusal to undergo the labor of accurate observation and persistent thinking. The impression is increased through a confusion of the different stages and modes of knowledge, with a resulting attempt to apply terms and conceptions, which belong appropriately only to one stage or mode, to other stages and modes where they do not belong. How many a one, for example, has tried, with mourning over the "limitations" of his knowledge, to fancy how an atom of oxygen would look and feel, if only one were organically constructed so as to see and touch it!

Elaborate doctrines and systems of nescience have been founded on inquiries no more discriminating than the one just suggested. We venture to assert that the entire system of Kantian antinomies may be largely resolved into the mistaken attempt to apply the terms of sensuous perception and imagination to subjects that admit only of a philosophical knowledge. Spencerian agnosticism, and those vagaries of Hamilton and Mansel on which this agnosticism as proclaimed in the "First Principles" is based, have scarcely so good a right as the Kantian antinomies to represent the *limits* of human cognition. That one cannot sensuously picture how the boundaries of a space would look in which there is nothing to see and no eye to see with; or finds it impossible to "conceive" as a member of the causal *nexus* a Being that is *ex hypothesi* the Ground of all that interrelated action which science both assumes and discovers; or declines, in the name of reason, to make the effort to jumble together innumerable contradictory so-called attributes and call the compound by a sounding title (be it God, the Absolute, or the Unknowable), — all this, and much more of the same sort, is not enough to establish insuperable formal limitations to all our knowledge.

That psychological and philosophical analysis, when pushed to its final outcome, discloses facts and laws of rational life which must be accepted as they are given, and cannot be explained, is undoubted. This is the legitimate result of the analysis; and until its outcome can be regarded as, in this direction, final, the self-criticism of reason cannot be satisfied. Such facts and laws may be said to represent the formal limits of the mind's action. The possibility of a different set of facts and laws, under different *extra*-mental conditions, or in the case of other psychical existences, *as a bare possibility*, is indeed tolerable to the imagination. But the very effort to question certain of these facts and laws, involves the mind in an intolerable inconsistency. One may ask, for example, How do things seem to an animal with scores of eyes, or with a single peripheral area sensitive to light but unorganized into an optical instrument? or, How do things appear to angels or to fairies? But one cannot ask, How do *things seem* to beings that are devoid of all sense-perception? without either taking all intelligible meaning out of the phrase — "things seem" — or else landing one's self in irrational consequences. So also may one indulge in the pleasing fancy, and even call it a science of mental evolution, precisely how it is that oysters and jelly-fish and amœbas, or even undifferentiated drops of vegetable bioplasm and blood-corpuscles, are conscious. But the inquiry after a Being which is to be mentally represented under terms like "Will," "Final Purpose," "Thought," "Unity," "Reason," "The Idea," and at the same time as foreign to all the actual self-conscious life of human reason, must indeed end in bringing upon itself insuperable limitations.

How absurd it is to try to think what thought would be, if the "barriers" of the principles of identity and of sufficient reason were removed, scarcely any one needs, it would seem, to be reminded.

As to material limitations of knowledge, or the fixing of definite barriers to the content of what may be known, the theory of knowledge has nothing whatever to propose. That can be known which is known; and in the progress of knowledge experience is constantly widening the realm of the known. As to what we may know, the empirical conditions belonging to each kind, stage, and condition of knowledge, practically determine. Here science is powerful to assert or to deny; but both its assertions and its denials are, so far as they preserve the forms of strict science, merely hypothetical. It may say, for example: If the conditions of perception by the senses remain the same, then the limit of such perception is to be fixed approximately at such a fraction of an inch; or at a distance travelling from which light would have too small intensity to excite sensations of sight, etc. But science is becoming in all its branches more cautious about arbitrarily fixing the permanent limits of its own positive domain. Possibly we may soon have it proclaimed as a necessary corollary of evolution that man will at some time in the future pass the present barriers of nescience in matters of rational psychology and the philosophy of religion. Then the race will have developed the knowledge of God, the Soul, Freedom, and Immortality, and will have become as certain of these truths and existences — that they are, and what they are — as of the real grounds for the theory of evolution itself.

As to the Certification of Knowledge — how it comes, and what it is — we shall content ourselves for the present with pointing back to the remarks made in the earlier part of this chapter. In effect they may be summed up in the following declarations. Verification of the processes of knowledge, as valid in reality, that is external to the actual life of the knowing mind, can never be attained. Even the proposal to search for such verification is intrinsically absurd. Only by that knowledge of knowledge which reflective analysis bestows, can a well-founded certainty of knowledge be gained. The theory of knowledge is itself, touching the problem of certifying knowledge, only the explication of that which is implicated in all acts of knowledge. To know, is to be certain; knowledge validates itself. But precisely *what* it is that knowledge validates, — this is an inquiry with which Noëtics can deal only by way of handing it over to Metaphysics. The latter critically examines the content of what is really known.

Moreover, to reach reality otherwise than as implicated in knowledge, is impossible. Thought elaborates the content of what is known; but mere thinking never certifies the reality of what is thought. On the other hand, all knowledge is of reality; and to know, is to be certain that somewhat really is. What, in its immediate reality, and what in its larger significance and relation to the ideals of reason, is the somewhat known as certainly existent, — this it belongs to the succeeding branches of philosophy to explore and describe.

CHAPTER IX.

METAPHYSICS.

THE present attitude of many thoughtful minds toward that branch of philosophy which is technically called Metaphysics is an interesting psychological phenomenon. This attitude is sometimes one of strange vacillation between shame-faced interest and expressed distrust. It is sometimes also a confession of a previous philosophical movement which, within the minds of those who maintain the attitude, either through the exhaustion of ineffective exertion or inherent lassitude or traditional confusion, has sunk below the horizon of a clear self-consciousness. Thus it often implies a preference for unscientific and incomplete metaphysical analysis to that which, at least, aims at being thorough and scientific. And so we hear preachers and even theologians uttering their scorn for metaphysics while confidently discoursing the most stupendous ontological generalizations touching supreme realities. Students of the particular sciences there are — both of the physical and of the psychological — who with unwavering confidence claim theoretically to construct the universe in precise conformity to what is really Existent, and yet have small respect for a critical discussion of those concepts of Reality, Space, Time, Matter, Motion, Cause, etc., which they are themselves so constantly employing.

There has been much in the history of speculative thinking, even since the establishment of the Kantian criticism, to give occasion for a weariness of metaphysics. And yet this feeling is itself, both in its origin and its form of manifestation, a proof that it is vain to hope for the final exclusion of metaphysical inquiry from human minds. The cure for the weariness is not a scornful or an indifferent attitude toward further effort of a similar kind. Its cure is rather (perhaps after a period of rest — if the need of rest be felt by the individual or by the spirit of the age) to be found in the cheerful acceptance of the task of achieving a better metaphysics. "Jacobi, Fichte, and Schelling all belong," says Herbart,[1] "to the age when people were singing, —

> "Da die Metaphysik vor Kurzem unbeerbt abging,
> Werden die Dinge an sich jetzo *sub hasta* verkauft," —

a summons which may be rendered into the following elegant couplet: —

> "Hear ye ! Things-in-themselves will be sold under the hammer !
> Since Metaphysics lately deceased without leaving an heir."

However, as Herbart at once proceeds to remark, we now know this age pretty well; and there are good grounds for the supposition that, in the case of its authors also, Metaphysics simply assumed other names, and under cover of them continued its existence, — essentially the same as before. This latter interesting historical fact Mr. Shadworth Hodgson[2] has embodied in two lines of his own composition. They are a reply to all would-be auctioneers of the effects of a deceased metaphysics, and run as follows: —

> "What though Things-in-themselves have been dispersed by an auction,
> Who was the auctioneer? Why, Metaphysic herself."

The warning from experience and history, that thinking man cannot safely, and indeed cannot long at all, neglect a serious inquiry into the nature of Reality, might be illustrated and enforced at indefinite length. Further argument of the case does not fall within the limits of a brief treatise like ours. Moreover, nothing new could be said in direct answer to that

[1] Allgemeine Metaphysik, vol. i. § 94.
[2] Philosophy of Reflection, i. 162.

sceptical inquiry which would invalidate everything that the most careful analysis and constructive thinking can do in dealing with ontological subjects. This inquiry will now be considered to have been met in the noëtical department of philosophy. Accordingly, we raise the question, What is that which is known as really existent? after having shown that all knowledge erects, as of its very nature, a barrier to the sceptical questioning of man's power to know the really existent. Not that sceptical inquiry can be regarded as at once and forever settled by any theory of knowledge. We only claim the undoubted right to proceed to Metaphysics with the self-confidence of reason in the principles of its own life as those principles are re-affirmed by a positive attitude toward the problem of Noëtics.

The inquiry, *What is Reality?* gives rise to that division of philosophy which we call Metaphysics, in the more specific meaning of the word. More precisely, the metaphysical problem may be stated thus: What is the content of our knowledge of the really Existent? Bearing in mind, then, the method of all philosophical inquiry, we may define this branch of philosophy as follows: Metaphysics is the critical and systematic exposition of those necessary conceptions and presuppositions which enter into our cognition of that which we call *real.*

But the metaphysical problem perpetually recurs in each one of the principal divisions of philosophy. This is the necessary result of that conception of philosophy which sees in it the search for a rational system of the principles of all the particular sciences in their relation to an ultimate Reality. Indeed, the actual organization of human experience compels speculative thinking to consider its problems with reference to Nature, to Mind, and to the Absolute. Even for its own ideals of the beautiful and the morally good, reason strives to find ground in that which really exists. We have, then, to undertake the philosophical treatment, first of those most general conceptions and presuppositions which constitute the essence of all which we call "Real" (whether Things, Minds, or God); second, of the more particular conceptions and presuppositions determining the nature of the two classes of realities into which we find our experience of reality divided. The resulting departments of philosophy are: Metaphysics (in the narrower sense, or Ontology), Philosophy of Nature, and Philosophy of Mind. The conclusions reached in these departments will necessarily influence those to be reached in the subsequent treatment of Ethics, Æsthetics, and especially Philosophy of Religion.

Metaphysics therefore requires the most careful analysis of the meaning of a conception which has hitherto been employed in a vague and indefinite way. This conception has been presented under the terms "Reality," or "the really Existent," etc. But what do we *mean* by these terms; or rather — since metaphysical inquiry is not concerned with the meaning of terms any further than is necessary to the clearness and completeness of its analysis — What is it really to be? In its ability to answer this question metaphysical analysis takes its chief interest and finds the most important test of the value of its conclusions. We must not, however, expect that the analysis will result in explaining, descriptively or syllogistically, the ultimate elements which it discovers in the answer to this question. Just because the elements it seeks are *ultimate*, they do not admit of such explanation. There are indeed no more general or specific terms in which to envisage, think, or express them; otherwise the analysis would be condemned as incomplete. Nor do the fundamental "conceptions" of so-called Ontology admit of being established by processes of induction or deduction; they are themselves those *momenta*, or terminal factors of mental representation and belief, which enter into all knowledge, and so condition and make possible the processes of induction and deduction. Neither are they explicable by analysis resolving them into what are more fundamental forms of knowledge or of objects known; they are explicated by analysis as given (*data*), as implicated in all forms of knowing all objects that are known. It is only with this understanding of the nature of its subject-matter and of the words used in speaking of them that metaphysics can proceed.

The primary and most inclusive category which it belongs to metaphysics to discuss is therefore that of "Reality," or "the really Existent." The terms "pure Being," "Nothing," "Becoming," and propositions such as "pure Being = Nothing," or "Becoming = Unity of Being and Nothing" have no place in metaphysics. Indeed, the discussion of such propositions is absolutely without value in any department of philosophy. In proof of this statement might be adduced the fact that the Dialectic of Hegel moves wholly in the sphere of empty abstractions (abstractions, that is, that not simply disregard certain forms of our knowledge of reality, but all forms of all knowledge) and of negative thinking, until it plants itself upon the category of Reality. This fact in part explains the wearisome repetitiousness of the Hegelian Logic. Plainly, all the categories are here made to do duty several times over, — either as mere forms of thinking without content, or as forms of knowledge with a real content introduced we know not whence, or as forms of being, assumed without sufficient appeal to actual experience.

The view of Hegel is opposed by Lotze when explaining his own conception of the sphere of metaphysics. This sphere the latter limits — and, as we think, rightly — to the real or the actual. "Real (*wirklich*)," says Lotze, "is a term which we apply to things that are, in opposition to those that are not; to events that happen, in distinction from those that do not happen; to actually existing relations, in contrast with those that do not exist."[1] This language is unfortunate, and does

[1] Quoted from Bosanquet's Translation of the Metaphysic, book i., Introduction. The translation of the passage is perhaps not altogether a happy one, the German being as follows: "Wirklich nennen wir die Dinge, welche sind, im Gegensatze zu denen, welche nicht sind; wirklich die Ereignisse, die geschehen, im Unterschiede von denen die nicht geschehen; wirklich auch die Verhältnisse, welche bestehen, im Vergleich mit denen, welche nicht bestehen."

not bring out the desired contrast. For things "that are not," are not *things* at all; events "that do not happen," are not *events* at all; and relations that do not "actually exist," are not *relations* at all. The contrast which is implied but not well expressed in this statement is a contrast between mere states of ideation regarded as representing unknown things, events, or relations, and things, events, or relations as objects of knowledge. But even the representative states are known to the subject of them directly, and to other minds indirectly, as actual events implying real relations (of a psychical kind). Moreover, if we use the somewhat uncouth and inappropriate word "Things" to indicate all concrete knowable realities, we must say that the representative states are themselves actual events in real being, — that is, actual states of things.

We repeat then our declaration that the most primary and comprehensive question of Metaphysics is this: What is it really to be? or, in other words, What content must the object known have in order that it may be known as really existent?

In attempting an answer to the foregoing inquiry our analysis soon discloses the fact, that that to which the act of knowledge, with its corresponding conviction, attaches itself as having reality, is never a simple factor. Reality is never a simple being, existing in no particular state or as pure being; it is never a simple indivisible state, that may be considered as state of no being, or as state unrelated to any other state; it is never a simple relation, that may be envisaged or felt as a relation without implying beings that are related in respect of their states. Being, state, and relation — all these and perhaps much more — must be implicated, in order that reality may exist to knowledge; in order that there may be Things known, Minds known, God known, — in any manner or degree whatever.

The correlate of the foregoing conclusion in metaphysics is the fact of psychology, that knowledge (which, as distinguished from any form of mere mental representation or of mere thinking, is the only psychical state that implicates and guarantees reality) is a relatively complex and late development of mind. Nay, more; it is an unceasing and never-to-be-perfected growth, which, as it expands, embraces more and more of reality. In nothing of the nature of psychical activity which falls short of knowledge is reality implicated, with any content whatever; but in the simplest act of knowledge the unchanging principles of reality are all implicated. In the development of knowledge by sense-perception and self-consciousness, by scientific investigation, and by philosophical reflection, the system of real beings — their natures, relations, and laws of being — becomes the object of knowledge.

The primary and indubitable reality, back of which or above which or underneath which it is impossible to go, is the fact of knowledge itself. This fact is not only an actuality that can neither be explained nor doubted, but it is itself the type, the source, the guarantee of all that is actual. That which is first of all, really and indubitably existent, is this fact of knowledge. It is here that modern metaphysics plants itself, if it is to make a final and secure stand against the scepticism which would invade and reduce under the misrule of fancy or of despair the entire domain of reality. It is to this fact, with all which is implied in it, that the Cartesian maxim applies. If by *cogito, ergo sum*, or *cogito* as equal to *cogitans sum*, we mean only to assert the primary and indubitable reality of this fact, we cannot be gainsaid or disputed. Self-conscious cognition is: it is an actual *datum;* and the very attempt to be sceptical thereupon does but lead to confirmation by repetition, of this fact of reality. For even the *dubito* = *dubitans sum* = *dubito, ergo sum.* But the *ergo* is not expressive of a conclusion drawn in the region of mere thinking; it is rather expressive of that rational conviction respecting an envisaged reality which all knowledge involves.

Objections will undoubtedly be brought against the position just taken, by some on the ground of its being too narrow, and by others on the ground of its being too comprehensive. Objectors on the former ground would maintain that mere consciousness and real existence, necessarily implicated, are the true correlates. We are therefore told that "consciousness and existence are mutually limited and limiting," and that non-objective existence and non-real consciousness are terms without meaning. "It is the lasting service," says Mr. Shadworth Hodgson, "of the post-Kantian philosophers, Fichte, Schelling, and Hegel, each in his degree, to have established the doctrine of the perfect coextensiveness and mutuality of existence and consciousness."[1] This same writer even goes so far as to declare: "The absolute, the infinite, the *Ding-an-sich*, like all other objects, can exist only in consciousness; the only questions are, what is their nature and analysis, and what is their origin." This view appears to identify, both positively and negatively, not only the knowledge of reality, but the really existent itself, with the sum-total of concrete psychical states; and this without distinction as to the nature of the states, or admission of the possibility that fundamental beliefs of the mind can ever avail to give evidence of the existence of aught besides their own occurrence as states of consciousness of that peculiar kind which we call "belief."

On the other hand stands that doctrine which depreciates all knowledge by the senses and immediate self-consciousness as incapable of defining what is real; and thinks by processes of ratiocination, or by impacts of a faith-faculty superadded to knowledge, to attain reality, as it were, in a roundabout way. To such theories it is by "pure thinking," or by "intellectual intuition," or by "faith," which is the superior of knowledge, that the question must be answered: What is it really to be? By such doctrine it is deemed possible gradually to break down or overleap at once the barriers erected by the fundamental forms of all knowledge of the concrete and real. "Things" and "souls" are then resolved into abstractions; and the problem

[1] Time and Space, p. 26.

of *knowing* the actual content, however partially, of that most concrete, real, and "*content-full*" of all existences, the life of the rational and personal Being whom we call God, becomes a matter of passing judgments of relation between concepts that have no correlates among objects known.

In opposition to all views like the foregoing we desire to maintain the identity of *knowledge* and of *being* as known. It is not every state of consciousness that, as such, is identical with the really existent; neither is the knowledge of this real confined to psychical states that have attained the heights where the thin air of "pure thinking," "intellectual intuition," or rational "faith," prevails, or where the high-climbers alone can get breath and keep their feet. The state of consciousness, in order to be co-extensive with a reality, must be known as a state of some being, either immediately through self-consciousness by the being whose state it is, or through perception by some other being. If it be indirectly known by science, its data must be mentally represented as knowable in one of these ways. That is to say, it is in terms of knowledge, of the known and the knowable, and not in the general form of consciousness and state of consciousness, that reality is implicated. The meanest, most thoughtless being that knows, that is conscious of Self or perceives a Thing, is in that very knowledge certain of real existence. But without such knowledge, or unsupported by such knowledge, pure thought and intellectual intuition and faith have nothing to do with reality.

Against this truth the psychological fact does not militate that even we, self-conscious and rational as we esteem ourselves to be, often evince our real existence by states of consciousness that cannot be called states of knowledge. Let it be granted that one often wakes up, as it were, simultaneously to the knowledge of self and to the memory of having passed through a series of psychical states which, as remembered, seem to bear not a trace of having been, while occurring, actually referred to any real subject,—not even to the self whose states they really were. Some such psychical states are undoubtedly of a highly complex order; as, for example, those passed through by one sunk in deep revery, or absorbed in listening to music, or in viewing a spectacle. They may even consist of highly complicated trains of ideation supported upon a basis of complex unuttered language; such as are the trains of ideation through which the mathematician goes when intent upon solving some problem. To psychological research must be left the question whether such states ever *actually* occur without implying a reference to the real subject whose states they are; that is, whether as states they occur in mental form resembling that in which we recall them when we mentally represent their occurrence by an act of memory so-called. But if they were not, in their occurrence, actual states of knowledge, then no real existence was implied in them. Yet even mentally to represent them, after their occurrence, as having occurred, it is necessary to endow them with the features common to all states of knowledge. This is the same thing as to make them knowable, and, as such, real by implication.

In other words, all states of consciousness imply reality only in as much as, and in so far as, they are *states of knowledge;* only as states of knowledge have they anything to yield in answer to the question: What is it really to be? States of mind (occurrences referable to the psychical subject) and states of things (occurrences referable to the subject that is not me), not as such, but as known and knowable, involve real existence.

Implicated, of necessity, in this primary reality of the fact of knowledge, metaphysical analysis discovers the four so-called categories of Substantiality, Quality, Causality, and Relation. These four are implied as belonging to reality, — concretely given, and co-existent. No one of the four can be resolved into any of the others. Each of the four implies all of the others; and each is to be explicated (not to say *explained,* since, strictly speaking, this is not possible) with constant reference to all of the others. [Indeed, this dim light, or faint shadow, which the different categories throw over each other — serving, as it does, less to make any one of them stand out in clear and bold relief than to keep them all in a phantasmagorial shifting under the attempts of analysis to limit their shapes — is one of the most interesting and yet embarrassing of the results which attend the consideration of metaphysical problems.]

Substantiality cannot be resolved into really existing quality; but quality cannot be known as really existing without reference to substantial, or real, subject of such quality. Quality is always *of* some subject; and the latter, if known as real, may be called a "substance," to distinguish it from a merely grammatical or logical subject. Causality, as a category, is not to be resolved into mere relation; but as predicated of the subject in reference to the quality it appears under the terms, as it were, of a fundamental relation. On the other hand, relation, in order to have reality as distinguished from mere appearance of relation, implies causality as existent on the part of the substantial subject with reference to its quality. To this subject all qualities may be said to be related under the category of causality.

The conceptions to which these four terms correspond, and the propositions in which the descriptions of metaphysics express the nature of the terms, are all derived by processes of reflection from the individual facts of knowledge. As actually experienced, they are concrete *momenta* implicated in all the facts of knowledge. Every fact, or actual occurrence, of knowledge has then a manifold and concrete content which involves these four categories. This manifoldness of the concrete content of every actual state of knowledge may be described in terms somewhat like the following: Every fact of knowledge implies a subject knowing as determined by its relation to an object known more or less definitely as such and no other object. But in every act of knowledge through self-consciousness the subject knowing is regarded as having become the object of knowledge to itself. The very essence of the knowledge called *self*-consciousness consists in this, that the subject knowing as it is determined by relation to an object, and the object known, is one and the self-same being. Out of this fact of knowledge, which is called self-consciousness, we may (perhaps rightfully) refuse to derive any theory as to the real unity, or permanent identity in reality, of the mind. We may be unable psychologically to explain the fact of self-consciousness. In the interests of this inability we may try to adopt and defend an atomic view of the nature of all consciousness; we may represent the case as though the mind could never so far catch up with itself as not to be at least one step behind the act of self-realization in the unity of self-consciousness. But neither in these ways nor in any other way can we invalidate the primary fact of knowledge, with all the conviction of being really existent which it involves. Indeed, without invalidating this primary fact, we may make a variety of sceptical admissions.

We may doubt whether the being that now knows is the same being as that which knew a moment since; I have only the authority, as we say, of memory for that. But that the being, which, as subject, knows in the self-conscious act, is really one and the same with the being known, as object in the selfsame act, — this is a known reality which it is impossible to doubt. Subject and state — the latter known as belonging to the former — are, then, terms expressive of what is in reality involved in every fact of self-consciousness. It is from this ultimate psychical reality that metaphysics derives the categories of substantiality and quality.

In every fact of knowledge there is also implicated an object known more or less definitely as this particular object, and no other. If the knowledge be by perception through the senses (by mental states that involve somewhat more than the having of localized sensation-complexes, states that have, as it were, matured into *knowledge*), then the object is known as a

"Thing" having determinate states, and as related to other things co-existing in time and space. If the knowledge be through self-consciousness, then the object is known as the "Self" in such or such determinate state, and related to co-existing realities. That is to say, the *object* of every act of knowledge is known as a subject of states, existing when known in some determinate one of these states.

But in the case of those objects which are known as things, the relation of the object known as real to the subject really knowing is one of non-identity. No object is known as a "Thing" unless it is known as *not*-me. In the case of those objects which are known as self, the relation of subject and object is, as has already been said, one of identity in reality. In both classes of cases, however, the relation of subject to its own states is implied as belonging to the object of knowledge. The object of perception cannot be known as a "thing," as involving anything beyond the subjective occurrence of mere sensation-complexes, without mental recognition in it of that peculiar relation which exists between every real subject and its actually occurring states. Nor can the object of self-consciousness be known as "Self," that is, be an object of *self*-consciousness at all, except upon the same terms. For these reasons it is that all knowledge involves the mental affirmation of actually existing states as belonging to those real subjects which we call either things or minds.

When we come to inquire into the peculiarity of that relation which is known to exist (or, should any one wish to emphasize the conviction which belongs to all knowledge, he may say, *believed* to exist) between a real subject and its states, we find its very indescribable essence to be what metaphysics denominates a "real cause." All states are *of* their subjects; they are not self-produced. For the term "self" designates the subject whose the states are, rather than the states, which are actual only as they are states of some really existing subject. Hence it is from the ultimate psychical reality, the fact of knowledge, as implicated in it, that metaphysics derives the category of causality.

The foregoing analysis of the fact of knowledge need not be repeated in order to discover that the reality of relations, as known, is implied in this fact over and over again. Indeed, it is this which gives its truth to those definitions of knowledge which tell us, "To know is to relate;" or to those definitions of being which advocate the formula, "To be is to be related." The modern doctrine of the relativity of knowledge is, so far as it is true, well grounded in this ultimate truth of all experience. The Logic of Hegel affirms it, even at its beginning, when it exclaims: Let Thought and Reality in their Identity now be! For its first product is a proposition positing under the relation of equality Pure Being and Nothing. That the primary fact of knowledge implicates the reality of the category of relation, if it implicate any reality whatever, there can be found no one to doubt.

The detailed discussion of the so-called "categories" is the work of metaphysical system. The discussion must be critical and reflective, but must also keep itself constantly in touch with the concrete realities of experience. It must avoid the pretence of profundity which explains those forms and presuppositions of all knowledge that, of course, are the basis and authority of every attempt at explanation; it must also shun that frivolous or *naïve* self-confidence which is satisfied with insufficient analysis, or else with the refusal to analyze at all. Neither scepticism, nor positivism, nor faith (so-called intellectual or so-called religious), nor easy-going "common-sense," nor off-hand appeal to the opinions of boors and charlatans, will worthily fill the place in reason of a thorough and patiently elaborated but progressive metaphysical inquiry. Our brief sketch of the nature of Metaphysics as one branch of philosophy must content itself with the barest outline of the field to be thoroughly covered by every metaphysical system.

Substantiality is, then, the category which covers our knowledge, and its conviction, respecting a "real subject" of those states that are known to be actual states, of Things or Minds.

This real subject is the so-called "substance" whose existence and nature have been the cause of endless metaphysical debate. Critical philosophy must first of all strip this category of those misleading figurative conceptions which have come to surround and even to penetrate it. By substance we cannot fitly mean to designate some undifferentiated material or spiritual "stuff" out of which (by the addition of "form" or the process of differentiation) the concrete realities of experience are produced. "Atoms," if known to be really existent at all, are (each one) concrete individual substances in possession, as it were, of a full complement of qualities. And by so-called "mind-stuff" nothing that is known or knowable can be designated except the mental abstraction which the thinker chooses this uncouth term to represent. There is no known or conceivable substance (real subject of states) in general; there really is only the known or knowable individual subjects of actual states.

We may indeed speak intelligibly of a so-called "universal substance." But, if so, we must mean to designate by this term that concrete reality which may be, or must be, regarded as the subject of all states. It is scarcely necessary to say that the popular impression, which tends to picture some core of reality as contained in all things, or as underlying and supporting them all, results from the natural mythology of the knowing mind. It is the inevitable product of the attempt to represent in terms of sensation that which is known as indeed implicated in sense-perception, but is not to be given to thought in terms of sensation. Human knowledge is the knowledge of being that is both sensuous and metaphysical. The very word "subject" is itself this embodied figure of speech.

Nor is critical philosophy satisfied to substitute for the term "substance," as giving all it implies respecting reality, such phrases as that of John Stuart Mill, so celebrated in English philosophy; namely, "permanent possibility of sensation."[1] This celebrated phrase, if by it we understand nothing more than the declaration that with every mental representation of a thing we may also experience the expectation of a possible repetition of a certain series or group of sensation-complexes, may be taken for what it is worth in the region of descriptive psychology. As a specimen of reflective analysis in metaphysics, the dictum can scarcely be called successful. For so far as it attempts to explicate the notion of substance at all, it only somewhat vaguely repeats this notion. That "substance" is indeed "the permanent," in contrast with changing states, is a statement sufficiently familiar to Metaphysics. That substance is to be regarded as the potentiality of states, is a declaration involving not only the category of substantiality, but also that of causality. That it is the "permanent possibility of sensation," is a decided under-statement of the legitimate conclusions from all our experience; for it limits the real being and causal action of the subject of the states to the potential production of a limited kind of changes in us (and these of the purely subjective order called "sensation"). But the question recurs: What *is* permanent and potential of future states? Certainly not the sensations themselves, and not the expectations of a possible recurrence; for both of these are fleeting, and impotent to produce, in reality, any changes at all. It is to this "subject" of the states that we attribute the permanence, and also the potentiality, of all present and future states.

Further and still negatively, we never envisage or otherwise know, in its naked simplicity as it were, this "permanent potentiality," this subject of the states, the so-called substance, whether physical or psychical. It can only be said to be known as necessarily implicated to reason, present and actually existent in every object known. It is envisaged only as an object known to be in some particular state. Neither can it be said

[1] An Examination of Sir William Hamilton's Philosophy, chap. xi.

to be known as the result of reasoning alone. It is true that thought is implied in all knowledge of the really existent; and that all such knowledge comes to the individual as the result of a development. Knowledge of the really existent follows upon processes of psychical analysis and synthesis which we may feel obliged to describe as involving instinctive inference. But it is also true that knowledge is the basis and guarantee of all that we more properly call "thought," *so far as it implicates reality*. No knowledge of the really existent is possible that is not rooted in the immediate cognitions and convictions of self-consciousness and sense-perception.

On the other hand, it would seem that for this primary knowledge, in both of its two forms, the category of substance is expressive only of a vague (and, we may even say, "blind") yet inevitable belief that *there is* the really existent. This belief, as yet undefined and inexplicable as to its origin and significance, enters into all perception and into all self-consciousness. It so characterizes these processes that they are processes of knowledge, and that it is impossible to consider them as mere successive acts of mental representation. It clings to all the further elaboration of knowledge by science and philosophy. It binds the workman in these fields to the persuasion that the object of his labors is not mere seeming (*Schein*). It reappears under a variety of terms, from the *Ding-an-sich* of Kant — which, even if we regard it as the result of merely negative thinking, is no less prized and cherished in positive conviction — to Mill's "permanent possibility" of sensation. It may seem an exceedingly slender thread, so far as content goes, but it appears strong and important enough when we make it serve to connect us with the world of reality, — with those subjects of states which we called "Things," and "Souls," and "God."

But why not, it may be asked, consign this category of substantiality, once and forever, to its appropriate place in the "death-kingdom" of abstract and negative thoughts? To this question we may reply, first, we could not if we would. It refuses to be banished; it refuses to die. Metaphysics must at least recognize it as a persistent and invincible, if blind, belief; and also as a belief which so enters into all knowledge as to make knowledge, in distinction from mere mental representation, a possible thing. But we may reply, second: We would not if we could. For further elaboration of the category of substantiality, as conjoined with the other categories, and so making possible and valid the scientific and philosophical extensions of knowledge, shows it to have an incomparable significance and value. Even in general metaphysics we shall be obliged again to refer to what, of an ideal character, is implied in this category.

Quality (or attribute) is a term which we apply to a generalization from repeatedly recurring similar states of a subject conceived of as the same. The truth implicated in the primary fact of knowledge is this, that the act of knowing and the object known are always mutually defined in the one fact of knowledge. The act of knowing is a knowing of this rather than some other object; the object known — to declare the same truth from another point of view — is known as this rather than some other object. The psychological account of the genesis and nature of knowledge must, at this point, again call attention to the truth that all knowing involves memory and the so-called relating faculty. Metaphysics marks the fundamental and essential form of knowledge as implicating being, by its doctrine of the category of quality.

In reality, however, there are no qualities or attributes; in reality there are only the present concrete and definite states of the subjects called *Things* or *Minds*. In reality also — as will be further explained later — by the "states" we can understand only the concrete and definite "modes of the behavior" (to employ a term of Lotze's, which, though figurative, as all terms for the categories must be, is nevertheless expressive of the truth) of the real subjects themselves. The repeated recurrence of similar modes of behavior progressively defines to knowledge *what* is the object known. Quality is the "what-sort-ness" of the object as known. But by that instinctive metaphysics which enters into all knowledge, the recurring modes of the behavior of the object are ascribed to the potential nature of the object regarded as a "Thing." The real subject of the states is not simply posited with an indefinite faith in its bare existence, but as definitively known by its own modes of behavior. It is known as really having qualities or attributes which define it as related to other more or less similarly constituted things. Obviously, in this metaphysical realization of states and subjects of states, the categories of causality and relation are again involved.

Causality is the category under which metaphysics brings all application of the principle of sufficient reason to the world of reality. We have already seen that this principle, as necessarily employed in the elaboration of knowledge by processes of conscious reasoning, guarantees only the consistency of the system of mental representations. What we call "pure science," and indeed all science regarded as cut loose from either *naïve* or intelligent metaphysics, goes no farther than this. What we call pure science is then only a systematic and logical arrangement of abstract conceptions; the *purer* it becomes, the farther does it remove from reality, which is always concretely manifold, beyond the power of all the combined sciences adequately to describe it. Furthermore, the claims of the purest science to be *science* at all, depend upon its valid application of this principle of causality, as a principle of thinking, to the ultimate facts of knowledge. It is this which distinguishes science from consistent and logical dream-life, if such there be. Therefore, when we examine the grounds on which all science reposes its claim to extend the realm of knowledge, we find this category involved in them.

All the talk of science touching "forces" (or modes and degrees of energy), "causes," "action," "influence," "laws," etc., is symbolical. The symbols do not clearly express the true findings of the reflective analysis of facts of knowledge. It belongs to that branch of philosophical discipline which we call the Philosophy of Nature, more specifically to point this out. There, too, if anywhere, must we expect to find stated the true significance of these terms. None of them, however, can claim to give the essential meaning of the primary fact of knowledge. In this fact the reality of causality is found implicated as a persuasion that the states of the self-knowing subject and of the object known — that all states, indeed — have their origin in the reality of the subject of the states. States can never be known or conceived of as passing over from one subject to another. Neither is any real transaction defined or expressed by declarations concerning the "influence" of one thing upon another, or of one mind upon another, — beyond the further limitation of that causal relation in which every real subject stands to its own states. To be sure, we are obliged here to introduce a possibly indefinite expansion of our application of the category of causality in our knowledge of reality.

Suppose (as is indeed true, and were it not true, experience and especially science would be impossible) that we observe everywhere evidences that certain changes of states of different so-called real beings (*e. g.*, X and Y) occur together in a fixed order. Accordingly, we say that the being X depends, for its passing through the succession of its states a, b, c, d, e, etc., upon the being Y passing through the states α, β, γ, δ, ϵ, etc.; or the latter is the *cause* of the former. By "cause," in this use of the word, we mean to state something more than the observed general fact that the changes occur in a fixed order; we mean to state that the changes in one being determine the changes in another being. But here again that which determines — the ground of the related changes — is not to be found in the changes themselves, nor in aught of the nature of "influence" or "force" so called, that passes between them. *In reality* there is the fact of the changes of one being, and the fact of the changes of the other being; in each case the word "causality," as representative of a *real* relation, applies primarily to the subject of the changes and its changing states.

When then we endeavor to apply the conception of causality in reality to an entire system of changes, regarded as reciprocally determining, a wonderful kind of postulate with reference to the real nature of the subject of these changes seems to become necessary. It seems to become necessary to regard them all as changes of one real subject, whose states they are. Only in this way does it appear possible to realize, as it were, the mystery of the general fact of all knowledge; of the fact, namely, that the changes of states of one thing or mind determine the changes of states of another thing or mind. To the examination and criticism of such an apparently justifiable postulate as this a large measure of metaphysical philosophy may fitly be devoted. For the postulate has an important bearing on other of the categories customarily named. It is also seen on further consideration to lie at the base of that "Unity of Nature" of which we hear so much (that is, if this unity is a unity that has reality and is more than a transitory unifying *actus* of the imagination of the individual mind); and it certainly forms the very core of the supreme Unity of Reality which the philosophy of religion seeks to explicate. We shall therefore have further occasion to refer to this category of causality.

Relation is a term which covers, in the most absolutely universal manner, all knowledge of reality. We may indeed find fault with Lotze for insisting that "to be" = "to stand in relations." For if by "being" we mean "being in reality," then it is indeed true that all real beings are actually related; but it is not a true, because an insufficient, description of the content of our notion of real being, to say that it is equivalent to the one category of relation. But if by "being" we do not mean to designate reality, then we may as well say with Hegel that it equals "Nothing," as to say with Lotze that it equals "to stand in relations." With Lotze, however, as against Hegel and Herbart alike, we must insist upon the truth, that the content of real being is not = "to be unrelated" (whether called "pure being" or "simple position"); but on the contrary, unrelated real being is a contradiction in terms.

As a category, relation can neither be defined nor simplified by reduction to more primary terms. The analysis of the most primary fact of knowledge finds the category always implied as belonging to the really existent. In knowledge itself, regarded as a psychical act or process, there is involved the relation of subject and object. In the subject of knowledge and its changing states, there is involved that peculiar relation which we have called real cause, or ground. But, on the other hand, causality cannot be reduced to *mere* relation. Between the states there are always implied relations of similarity or dissimilarity, of sequence, etc. So true is it that "to know is to relate;" and that the very essential content of that being, which all that is really existent has, involves the actuality of relations.

Other more complicated and yet irreducible forms of knowledge, that are also forms of being as given in each most primary fact of knowledge, are discovered by the analysis which metaphysics undertakes. Two of these are the categories of *Change* and *Number*. Every being that we know, or conceive of, as really existent is a "substance," a ground of states, in relation to other reality. This implies that every being is known as the real subject of actual change, and as a unity of discrete manifoldness; that is, as having number. Substantiality, quality, causality, relation, are categories that imply, but are not, the categories of change and number. As the subject of its own states, and as related to other subjects of states, every real existence is capable of change; so, and only so, is every real existence a unity implying manifoldness, a being falling under the category of number.

Change belongs to reality; this declaration follows from an analysis of the primary fact of knowledge. In so far as it is possible to regard those objects of perception which we call "Things" as without *extra*-mental being, and thus as owing the reality they have to the fact that our expectation of the "permanent possibility of sensation" accompanies and fuses with the actual processes of sensation, it is possible also to regard all changes called "physical phenomena" as not *extra*-mental, as unreal. It is also possible to hold that all changes in external nature so-called are but the expressions *in us* of the action of beings who are not themselves the subjects of like change. It is even possible to resolve the entire ground in reality of the apparent changes of external nature into the changes of position in space of physical beings whose interior states remain unchanged. Something like this modern physics attempts when it tries to account for all physical phenomena, as due to the motions of atoms that have unchanging natures and undergo no changes of interior states. But all such theories at most, as says Lotze,[1] "can only suffice to eliminate from *external* nature any change in reality itself, and to reduce it to mere variation in relations (to us as percipient minds); no less, on the contrary, but the more inevitably, must an actual *interior* changeableness find a place for itself in that real being for which, as for the perceiving subject, the above-mentioned appearance of an objective change is assumed to originate."

We may fitly go much beyond the theories just mentioned, however, in claiming an indubitable knowledge of the reality of change. This category is *known* to apply to the entire world of things. The truth of the statement is implied in the fact of the knowledge of things. For to be a "Thing" is to be the subject, not of one state, but of various states; that is, to be the subject of change. In so far, then, as perception is the knowledge of things, it is the knowledge of a substance changing its states. This confidence, which belongs to the earlier condition of the ordinary knowledge of nature, attends the whole

[1] Grundzüge der Metaphysic, § 32.

theory of modern physics as to the constitution of the world of things. Physics, to be sure, affirms that the real subjects of all the changes in this world of things are the so-called "atoms." But the atoms themselves are said to have unchangeable natures, because they are found unchangeably (that is uniformly, so far as experience reaches) to behave, under similar circumstances, in similar ways. The one kind of change in these elements of material reality which physical theory recognizes is motion. To unfold the content of this conception, in its application to reality, belongs to the philosophy of nature.

Yet again, the validity of that view of nature to which all the scientific knowledge of the modern age stands most completely pledged, and upon which it has (however rashly) risked its claim to confidence with the multitudes for a century to come, depends upon the reality of change. We refer of course to the theory of evolution. What a vast amount of metaphysics — much of it crude and over-confident enough surely — is involved in this scientific theory! As a scientific theory, philosophy cannot assume the place of a judge over its claims. As involving a philosophy of nature, however, the theory must enter the lists with other contestants for the place of supremacy, asking and giving no favors, but relying upon the careful application of philosophical method to whatever of well-founded scientific generalizations it can produce. But a metaphysics of evolution is impossible without admitting the reality of change in external nature. Indeed, the theory of evolution is nothing, if not a descriptive history of change. Is this history simply a history of the growth of human knowledge; or is it a history of an evolution of nature, — of the really existent object of knowledge? If the principle of "Becoming" had, since the days of Heraclitus, and until lately, fallen at all from its supreme position among the eternal ideas, it has surely been reinstated by the modern theory of evolution.

Modern psychology, making use of experiment and the genetic

method of study, looks upon each so-called state of consciousness, as well as upon the entire history of every soul, in the light of development. A *state* that is statical, merely state, does not exist. Psychical reality would seem to be conceived of as existing in a rigid form, if we judge the case by much of the language which lingers in works on logic and psychology. But in reality no "rigid" state of consciousness actually exists, or can exist, — not even in the minds of the writers of the works who discourse upon it. Neither is the conscious life of mind to be symbolized as a constantly flowing stream, so thin as to admit of not more than a drop or two of water side by side within its banks. The rather is it like a kaleidoscope kept turning, now more slowly, and now more swiftly, sometimes with a steady, and sometimes with an unsteady hand; sometimes, too, the field is in obscurity amounting to quite total darkness, and sometimes in wonderfully brilliant light. But however we account for the varying rate or scope of consciousness, and however we figuratively represent its facts, the one fact of knowledge at all involves the reality of change. To say "I think" is equivalent to saying that the movement, which belongs to all psychical life, is realizing itself. Not to change in reality is not to think at all. The mental picture of an unchanging being, could we frame such a picture, would be the equivalent of no real being; it would not even be equal to the seeming to be (*Schein*); it would be equal only to nothing, to no being at all (*Nichts*).

From the days of the Eleatics to those of Hegel's subtle dialectic, plentiful oppositions, contradictions, and dilemmas have been discovered by metaphysics in the conception of reality as the subject of change. But the oppositions, contradictions, or dilemmas are specious rather than real; and the solution of them belongs to logic rather than to metaphysics. They consist in thinking obscurely; they do not belong to the knowledge of reality. The reasons for their origin and persistence are chiefly twofold, — the same reasons which have given origin and persistence to the old-time puzzles of Achilles and the tortoise, of the arrow always flying and yet at each moment at rest, and to similar logical curiosities. One of these reasons is found in the attempt to bring the category of substantiality under the terms of sensuous imagination, or of — what Hegel called — "figurate conception." The other is the paralogism so frequent in "pure" science, which consists in forming by generalizations from experience a highly abstract conception, elaborating it by processes of thinking, and then covertly introducing into its alleged application the very factors drawn from reality, which the process of abstraction had agreed to disregard. Instead then of dwelling upon the cheap logical puzzles connected with the inquiry, for example, how real and pure being can remain self-identical and yet pass over into other being, etc., metaphysics notes the factor ("*moment*") of change as essentially belonging to all real being. Every thing and every mind which answers the question, What is it really to be? does so in the actuality of a living and interrelated movement, does so not as statical and pure being, or as being with unchanging relations and states, but as a succession of changes realized.

A real unity of the actually manifold is also implied in every primary fact of knowledge. Hence the so-called category of *Number*, as implying oneness and manifoldness belonging actually to all that really exists. This primary fact of knowledge, in its subjective aspect, implies a dividing and a unifying *actus* as entering essentially into every act of knowing. It is customary to point out that knowledge implies analysis and synthesis. Rightly understood, the statement is true. But such analysis and synthesis as belong essentially to all knowing cannot be identified with those conscious and voluntary processes which we call by these terms. A description of the psychical processes themselves serves to show how it is that we number things and build up abstract systems of knowledge in the discussion of that conception of "discrete manifoldness" with which mathematics deals. Such an elaboration of knowledge is made possible, however, only by the nature of the primary fact of knowledge. In this fact the reality of change is shown to belong to the very life, so to speak, of the subject of change. It implies the act of separating and uniting as an integral factor in that process of self-realization which the act of knowledge is.

In its objective aspect, as the being known, the fact of knowledge involves the same category. Every object of knowledge is necessarily one and yet manifold, — a being exhibiting its qualities, as it were, in changing relations to other beings and in a succession of changing states. As substantial and real cause, every being is necessarily regarded as a unity; as having changing states and entering into changed relations, it is necessarily regarded as manifold. It is, then, a unity of the manifold. If not the former, then it cannot be regarded as real; and if not the latter, then it cannot be regarded as this being rather than some other being, and is reduced to the condition of an abstract being, of a "pure" being = nothing.

The system of thinking ascribed to Pythagoras, which found in number the one formal principle of all that really is, seems fanciful enough to modern thought. But like the Eleatic philosophy, and the philosophy of Heraclitus, it seized upon one of the categories and, misunderstanding its nature, elevated it to the place of supreme and absolute sovereignty. That its principle was a *principle* indeed, and so entitled to a place in the system of metaphysics, because implicated in all knowledge of reality, does not admit of doubt. All that is known as real, whether of "Things" or of "Minds," whether in the intuition of perception and self-consciousness, or by the elaborations of science, is both one and manifold. There is no unity in reality, no one real being, that is not also manifold in respect of its changing relations and states. There is no actual manifoldness of relations and states that does not implicate a unity of some real being; there is no multiplicity of real beings that does not involve a unity in reality of the world of such beings.

In the discussion of the two foregoing categories, it is impossible to avoid the confession that the vague character of the category of substantiality exercises upon us a constant influence. Change is real; and the real is always manifold, and yet one. But change without limit is never known as real; indeed the very attempt to conceive of absolutely limitless change in that which is really existent ends in the irrational and the absurd. Neither can the unlimitedly manifold realize itself as one.

What, then, is it that limits change, — what but the subject of the changes? What is it that, as it were, connects into a unity the otherwise wholly discrete manifold, but the one "Ground" of the many connected elements? We may call this cause of the limitation by the terms "nature," or "character," or "essence," or by some other similar term. We may speak of the nature of each particular thing or species of things; of the nature even of the atoms, — those hypothetical elements of material reality out of which scientific thinking aims to build up the unities that particular things are, as well as the Unity of the universe of things. We may also ascribe a nature or character to souls, whether of men or of the lower animals; we may even carry this important fiction over into the phenomena of the life of plants. But by all these terms we simply introduce, in disguised form, an amplification of essentially the same factor of all knowledge to which the name of "substance" has been given. "Nature" and "character," — this signifies the sum-total of the unchanging norms or modes of the behavior of the subject of the changing relations and states.

It may be, however, that we try, in the interests of scientific clearness and accuracy, to describe our knowledge of reality by a more popular and attractive phrase. It is the fashion in these days to talk much of "law," or of "uniformity of nature," as a general expression for the presence everywhere of the so-called "reign of law." This conception is thus made a category; nay, it is hypostasized and even deified. Law is everywhere; law reigns, controls, compels, forbids, produces; it sits "over" or "between" or "underneath" the real beings, and compels them unceasingly to feel and to acknowledge its potent sway. But nothing exactly corresponding to this word "law" belongs to the realm of real existences as a something related to them, with an existence of its own. We have here to deal with a convenient figure of speech somewhat similar to that which we employ in speaking of qualities or attributes as though they were actual existences attached to every so-called "Thing." In its subjective aspect, "law" is the formula prescribed to the movement of the life of mind. The prescription is as follows: You may, or you must, think the changes of X and the changes of Y as reciprocally dependent in the following more or less definite way. In its subjective aspect, then, every law is realized only as the actual movement of a knowing mind. What then becomes of the "laws of nature" and of that general deference to a fixed order, — amounting, in the estimate of modern physical science, to an unswerving obedience, — which is called the "uniformity of nature"? Have we valid reasons for affirming that the conformity to law actually belongs to the external object of knowledge? In what terms, furthermore, are we to describe that content of the really Existent which fixes limits to the changes of every so-called "Thing," as well as of the world of physical reality at large?

This foregoing problem may be proposed in a somewhat different way. Anything, — called, for example, X, — in order really to be a "Thing" at all, must be the subject of only such changes of states and relations as belong under a series X^a, X^b, X^c, etc. The thing called Y, in order also really to be, must be the subject of another series, Y^a, Y^b, Y^c, etc. Moreover, all things, taken together in their ceaselessly changing states and relations to each other, must, as subjects of these states and relations, observe some principles of reciprocal limitation, in order that the world as an orderly and beautiful totality may really exist. To say this is to claim that the causes of the limitations of the changes are to be found in the subjects of the particular series of changes; and, since the series unite in higher series, the claim extends itself so as to take in a total unity, in that one subject which we call "Nature" or "the World." But how can these particular subjects of change maintain their relative unity, and how can the one subject of all the changes maintain its absolute unity, except by conformity to law?

It must be admitted that the analysis of general metaphysics leaves much which is obscure clinging to this conception of a real subject of the changing states. How can each particular subject be self-limiting as respects its own changes, and yet related to other real subjects, in the unity of one "Nature"? But it must also be admitted, it seems to us, that the analysis discloses the presence of another category which is needed in order to give the complete essence, so to speak, of that conception of substantiality to which we found a sort of blind but inevitable attachment in every fact of knowledge. We inquire, then, after a suitable expression for this additional factor discovered by the analysis. We will attempt such an expression by laying down the following proposition: Every real existence is known as a "realized idea." But no one using such a phrase as this could regard it as marking the stage of clearest and most nearly ultimate analysis of that strange presupposition respecting the real subject of changing states and relations which the fact of knowledge undoubtedly implies. Let us then confess it: the phrase is figurative. But what of conception or belief that is not merely "figurate" does this phrase express? In order really to be, every subject of states must be self-limiting of its own states. This self-limitation does not have respect merely to the number of the states actual or possible. The manifold states must also be *so* realized as accords with the unity of an idea. What is true of every grouping or series of states is true of all the more manifold groups and series of the relations existing in the reality of one World. The world is known to be real only as the universal subject of all the states and relations is known under similar terms, — the terms, namely, which correspond to the phrase, a "realized Idea." To be known as real is to be known as the ground of the occurrence of the states and relations, *in conformity to an idea.*

In this meaning of the words, therefore, metaphysical analysis discloses the category of "*Finality*" (or end) as necessarily involved in the answer to the question: What is it really to be? The judgment which states the belief corresponding to this category is not: Every event must have a final purpose; or, everything must be constructed according to some (extraneous) idea; or, the whole world depends on final purpose, or shows evidence of its existence everywhere. These propositions may be true, but the proof of them is not categorical; it is not given or implicated in the fact of knowledge as determining the content of the object really known. Neither can it be claimed that every primary fact of knowledge seems to involve the cognition and belief corresponding to the term "finality." The knowledge which involves this category seems, in some sort, to imply a larger growth of experience and a deepening of the reflective insight of the mind. But certainly our larger knowledge of a World of Things — unities of the manifold standing in a regular way related to other like unities — implies finality. And this is true whether the so-called world be that of the most primitive savage or that of the most scientific and philosophical minds. Knowledge of the real is interpretation; and interpretation of the real implies the actualization of the ideal. But the further unfolding of this truth belongs to subsequent departments of philosophy.

Two other categories, or norms of knowledge determinative of the content of what is really existent, remain to be mentioned. They are Time and Space. It is customary to distinguish these from categories like the foregoing by calling them "formal," or by introducing the discussion of them (so Lotze) in the cosmological rather than the ontological division of metaphysics. The distinction thus emphasized undoubtedly exists. It is not, however, in our judgment a sufficient reason for following the common custom. To be a subject of changing states and changing relations, whose manifoldness is realized in the unity of an idea, — this it is to be, as all real existences are. But *to be* "time," or *to be* "space;" or even *to be the subject* of time or space, — such phrases as these do not represent fitly what is implied in our knowledge of that which we call real.

Our experience follows norms which compel us to drop the preposition "of" and make use of the preposition "in," when speaking of the relation of real existences to the conceptions of time and space. Those real subjects which we call things are said to be known as existing *in* space; those which we call minds, as well as those which we call things, are said to be known as existing *in* time. It would seem then that the reality of these two categories, and the nature of the relation in which all real existences stand to them, as well as the manner in which the fact of knowledge may be said to implicate them, are of a somewhat special kind.

Metaphysics does not need to show that *Space* is no *extra-mental* existence, infinitely spread out as a medium in which ready-made particular existences called things can be conveniently set. The sciences of psychology and of physics have now effectually disposed of theories built upon any remnant of conceptions so crude as these terms imply. The elaboration of knowledge by modern physical science has (it claims) shown that the real correlate of that which is perceived as statical, extended, and continuous, is an indefinite manifoldness of discrete and moving beings, that are not only imperceptible, but are also unrepresentable in terms of the sensuous imagination. When then we inquire, How would atoms look or feel as extended in space? we appear to be asking: How would that look or feel which, *ex hypothesi*, can never be seen or felt; or how would that seem as extended to sight and touch to which these senses have no conceivable applicability whatever? On the other hand, the modern psychology, especially by following the methods of experimental analysis and speculative construction, has led to similar conclusions. It has rejected the old-time distinction of the attributes of matter into primary and secondary, as not implying a fundamental difference in genesis and validity; and it has presented something like an uninterrupted history of the conditions on which, and the processes by which, the perception of extended things is gained. Nay, more; it has tried, with some success, to sketch the development of the conceptions of the spatial attributes and relations of things. Psychology cannot, indeed, be said to have explained the genesis of the idea of space. In all its attempts at explanation it comes upon the necessity of admitting either that the space-idea as a formative principle is present and unaccounted for; or else, that it is necessary at some particular point in the evolution of sense-perception, to introduce it, without being able to say why it should be introduced at just that point, rather than some other, or indeed why it should be introduced at all.

For these reasons the metaphysical analysis of the content of the object known as real leads to the recognition of space as a formative principle of the perceiving mind. Space is the universal and necessary mode of the perception of things by the senses. The so-called objects of sense are not "Things" until, or unless, they are perceived in this form. But necessary forms of perception by the senses are also necessary forms of representation in all sensuous imagination, and in all "figurate" conception. We say, then: all things are necessarily in space. This category then gives the content of the real, because it is the universal and necessary mode of the actual process of the mind in knowing all physical beings by the senses.

But is this all that is signified by so much as there is of categorical character and significance belonging to space? The cognitions and beliefs implied in knowledge seem to compel us to a negative answer. The subject of those changing states and relations which we know as "not-ourselves" maintains itself as, in some way, the *extra*-mental ground for the space-principle of the perceiving mind. We find ourselves compelled to believe and say, — not simply all things are perceived, or are mentally representable, only as *in* space, but all things *are* in space. And these two declarations can never be made the exact equivalents of each other.

So often, therefore, as the conclusion of idealism affirms, on what appear the best of grounds, the subjectivity of space, so often does the blind instinctive realism which lurks in every fact of knowledge through the senses, affirm some sort of *extra*-mental reality for space. What mode of their real being "in space," considered as distinct from being mentally represented, the subjects of physical changes and relations can possibly have, this realism cannot say. So often as it proposes a definite description, the idealistic theory convicts it of the folly of trying to tell us how things would look and feel, if nobody saw or felt them; how they would appear extended, in case they appeared to nobody at all. The theory of the subjectivity of space is, therefore, always right in denying all such reality to the so-called "intuitions" of spatial properties and relations as implies that these intuitions are *copies* of somewhat existing, that is not-mental, and yet really exists, as it is copied off by the mental process itself. On the other hand, the apparent demonstration that space is *merely* mental, that it has no ground in what is other than the mind "intuiting" it, can never satisfy our minds. If any answer to the inquiry, What that is not grounded in the perceiving mind is the reality of space? is ever to be discovered, it must come through the extension of knowledge by science and philosophy. If we know, even partially, what the reality called "matter" is, we may discover in it the answer, at least in part, to our inquiry after the nature of the reality we assign to space. If we knew fully what matter is, we should have the complete answer to this inquiry.

The general metaphysical discussion of the category *Time* corresponds to that of space. The similarity is such, however, as to permit of several important differences. The likenesses and unlikenesses of the two categories in their relations to reality are most easily brought to view in a symbolical way. But to psychology does it chiefly belong to discuss the "line of time" and the "line of space." The important metaphysical difference between the two conceptions — time and space — is that which leads us to apply the former both to things and to minds; while it requires various modifications of our meanings if we attempt to apply the latter to minds at all. Connected with this important difference is another. It may be stated in the form of a question: Do we not so know things in perception, and especially the mind by self-consciousness, as to affirm that they and it must be in time, in order really to be at all?

It is plain also that the relation of time to the other categories differs, in an important way, from that of space. We find nothing in our knowledge as implying substantiality, quality, causality, relation, or change and number, that makes these conceptions dependent, as it were, for their realization on the *extra*-mental reality of space. In other words, reflective analysis appears to give us no ground for affirming that space is necessary to the reality of the subject of changes and relations, or to the actuality of the changes and relations. But the case is not the same with the category of time. The subject to be the real ground of its states must be conceived of as permanent in time. The reality of change, in states and relations, requires the reality of time. The primary fact of knowledge, then, whether as perception or as self-consciousness, and all the elaboration of knowledge by science and philosophy, implicates the reality of time. What further can be meant by such reality, and how it is implied by the sciences of nature and of mind, it belongs to the two subdivisions of general metaphysics to discuss.

CHAPTER X.

PHILOSOPHY OF NATURE AND PHILOSOPHY OF MIND.

FOR purposes of further and more detailed investigation the general inquiry, What is the content of that object which is known really to be? divides itself into two branches. One of these relates to the system of things which we call "Nature," in the narrower sense of the word; the other relates to those objects which we call "souls" or "minds." This twofold division of the problems of being arises, of necessity, in the very development of knowledge itself; the experience on which it is based can scarcely be said to be divided by scientific research or by philosophical reflection. It is rather appropriate to employ the phrase just given; and to say, the sum-total of knowledge "divides itself," as a primary condition of knowledge, in this twofold manner.

As to the possibility of uniting in one system the two halves of reality known, whether by some higher intellectual intuition, or in the final outcome of that synthesis which philosophy aims to accomplish, this is not the place to remark at length. It has already been assumed that the reality of the knowing subject as object to itself, and the reality of the object known by the subject as not-itself, are both implicated in the fact of knowledge. This fact then is itself a demonstration of the possibility, — nay, of the actuality, — of some sort of unity between the two. The process of knowledge is such a unifying *actus*. At the same time the duality of the two kinds of objects, and the incomparability of their qualities and changes of states, is also part of the content of knowledge.

Indeed, that things and minds are *not* the same realities is a truth which enters into our ordinary, and even into our scientific convictions, far more deeply and comprehensively than any conviction of either a more primary or a higher unity. Developed intelligence does not confuse things with ourselves, — not even when we have as yet no conception of the self as separable from the sentient organism. Even the errors of localization and projection with which experimental psychology is familiar depend, for their existence as errors simply, upon the "diremption" of our experience. To every self-conscious mind all else is known as a "Thing," set over against — as we are wont to say — the existence of the "Self." Physical science is distinguished from psychological in that both its objects and its methods are markedly different, with a constant dependence upon this act of "diremption." The thorough discussion of the philosophy of nature and of the philosophy of mind, as distinct branches of metaphysical inquiry, must then always precede the final synthesis of philosophy. And any attempt at such synthesis which omits or relatively depreciates either of these two branches is thereby doomed to failure.

In prosecuting these two more special branches of metaphysics, the method of reflective analysis as used for the explication of the categories will no longer suffice. The general forms of all being are indeed implicated in all knowledge. But the satisfactory answer to the questions, What is the real being of the system of Things? and What is the real nature, and relations in reality to the World, to its fellows, and to God, of the human Mind? implies a vast accumulation of positive scientific knowledge. Accordingly, the validity and completeness of any answer to these questions — and this is the same thing as the truth and comprehensiveness of our philosophy of nature and of mind — depend upon its attainments in scientific knowledge, and upon its ability to give a philosophical treatment to such knowledge. For philosophy employs for its material, not only the principles presupposed in all knowledge, but also the principles ascertained by the particular sciences. It does not aim to construct the world of physical and psychical existences as a system of pure thoughts, or even to know it as such a system. It aims rather to know what these existences really are, in accordance with the growth of knowledge derived from all the particular sciences.

The philosophy of nature and the philosophy of mind are therefore subjects for the most detailed and comprehensive scientific examination. This examination, however, in so far as it is strictly scientific, is preliminary to philosophy rather than part of it. The appropriate particular sciences hand over their principles to philosophy for its subsequent handling. This handling consists in subjecting the principles to further criticism by reflective analysis, and to the interpretation of their categorical or metaphysical intent; it consists also in illumining them all by the light of philosophy's supreme synthesis, while employing them all in the perfecting of this synthesis.

It is, of course, impossible for us even fully to sketch the two great departments of philosophical discipline whose titles stand at the head of this chapter. The bare mention of some of the principal subjects which they cover, with an occasional suggestion or explanatory remark, must suffice. But undoubtedly a very brilliant future for them both is near at hand. How indeed can it be otherwise, since the interests of philosophy are perennial, and the modern sciences of physics, biology, and psychology are raising and illumining so many philosophical problems?

That a philosophy of nature is possible, we do not deem it necessary to argue. It is true that Newton bade physics "beware of metaphysics." But it is also true that Schelling summoned men to "come to physics and behold the eternal." If we understand the warning as simply directed against all attempts unduly to influence physical theories from points of view taken in a system of pure thinking so-called, it must certainly stand. It is as important for the philosopher as for the physicist. Let the former learn from the latter what is known, by those processes of elaborating knowledge which science understands so well how to employ, concerning the principles of things. But if the Newtonian warning involves the exhortation not to attempt to take philosophical account of physical principles, not to consider each of them in the light of every other, and all of them in the light of the supreme syntheses of philosophy, — why, then, the warning was neither observed by its author, nor should it be observed by any thoughtful man. Schelling's exhortation, too, must be heard. But it does not fitly woo us to those beautiful dreams, supposed to be representative of the real life of nature, which the systems of philosophical Absolutism devised. It encourages us rather to attempt the philosophical understanding of nature's life, as it is actually presented in the accumulations of physical principles that have stood the test of experiment, criticism, and continued research.

The modern science of that system of things we call "the World" may be said, so far as its discovered principles are necessary to a Philosophy of Nature, to have two main divisions. The first of these is physics, including astronomy and mechanics as dependent upon the physical theory of masses at rest or in motion, and chemistry, thermics, magnetism, etc., and all the special forms of atomic and molecular combinations and motions. The second of these is biology, which on the one hand is reaching downward to find its basis in molecular physics, and on the other hand is reaching upward to make its application, if possible, to the life of souls, or minds. [In making this twofold division we should not forget, but rather affirm, the statement of the late Clerk Maxwell:[1] "Chemistry is extending . . . into regions where the dynamics of the present day must put her hand upon her mouth." A similar remark is appropriate on considering the utter inability of biology as a merely physical theory to follow the extensions of modern experimental and speculative psychology.]

[1] Encyclopædia Britannica (ninth ed.), xix. 3.

The unobserved real subject of all physical changes is called "Matter." What matter is in reality, we are accustomed to be told cannot be known. But such a statement rests upon the same misconception of the nature of knowledge and its implication of reality known, as that with which the theory of knowledge made us familiar. Undoubtedly the term "matter" may be used to cover a bare abstract conception of one or more so-called physical qualities, — a conception insufficiently generalized from a few only of the many modes of behavior exhibited by the known physical objects. In this sense, of course, there is no real matter corresponding to the conception of matter. There is indeed no matter, in general. But there is also no mind, in general; no quality, in general; no cause, in general; no motion, in general; no energy or force, in general. That which is in general merely is not real. The "pure" being called matter is the equivalent of a pure material nothing; that is to say, it is no "Thing," and has no real existence.

But matter as known is the subject of every change of physical state, of every motion, of every so-called physical quality; it is, therefore, the real cause of all changes in the world of physical beings and events. What, more precisely, matter is, it is the very business of the sciences of nature to tell us; for they are *sciences* only as they are knowledge of those objects which we call material. Such knowledge comes through the intuitions of sense-perception, and through the elaboration of scientific research and philosophical reflection. The more we gain in knowledge of the manifoldness of the life of that one subject, to whose existence all discourse of matter and the physical universe refers, the more are the certainty and comprehensiveness of the physical sciences secured. It is he that imperfectly generalizes respecting the whole from some one or more of the infinite modes of the life of this subject, and then considers his own meagre generalization as adequate to describe the concrete wealth of reality, who is most inclined to deny to others all knowledge of this reality.

The pride of a superior wisdom, a startling discovery of some so-called law, is the forerunner of a fall into the most abject depths of agnosticism.

Matter as known by the senses is an external and extended object, having properties which are as many as those perpetually recurring modes of experience through the different senses which define the immediate knowledge of this object. Of these extension itself is the most primary and essential. Without extension no object of sense-perception exists. The object perceived is necessarily extended; its extension is of its very essence as object. Of its externality the same statements may be made. Without externality no object of the senses exists. The object perceived is necessarily external; its externality is of its very essence as object.

But the analysis of psychology, helped to its conclusions by philosophical reflection, shows us that we are warranted in attributing these qualities of extension and externality only to the object which is immediately known as having them. This is the object perceived — by the senses of the skin and of the eye. Such analysis, in connection with a more or less speculative theory of the evolution of sense-perception, attributes to the mind the action constructing the perceived object. It shows that the laws of this evolution, so far as we know them, are chiefly laws of the mind. While then it affirms that, if we mean by "matter" *simply* that which is given to us as object in every process of sense-perception, we may say it is all necessarily extended and external, we cannot say this of matter as possibly known or knowable in other ways than by immediate perception.

Somewhat similar courses of discussion belong to that attribute of impenetrability which we ascribe to matter. In this case, however, our knowledge of the quality ascribed to the object is apparently less immediate and direct. We seem to ourselves to become gradually aware of the impenetrability of objects as we have increasing experience of the difficulty of making them cover the same places in space, — whether in the field of sight as gathered from different points of view, or, more particularly, in the field of touch and muscular sensation. But we never become by the senses persuaded of the impenetrability of matter in such manner that we can deny *a priori* the possibility that two *atoms* may coincide. All attribution of extension, externality, and impenetrability, to matter must then be limited to matter as object known by the senses, or as imaged by that sensuous imagination which necessarily follows the forms of sense-perception. But that matter as further known to physics or to philosophy, as considered irrespective of its being an object of sense-perception, must have these qualities, neither so-called "common-sense" nor "physical realism" has any right to affirm. As said Clerk Maxwell,[1] "many persons cannot get rid of the opinion that all matter is extended in length, breadth, and thickness. This is a prejudice . . . arising from our experience of bodies consisting of immense multitudes of atoms."

What may be (though it usually is, only with some difficulty) seen to be true of the qualities of extension, externality, and impenetrability, is more readily admitted with reference to all the other qualities of matter. Such are its heaviness or lightness, its hardness and softness, its roughness and smoothness, its toughness and pliability, or its friable character; such are all the other modes of the behavior of external objects as given chiefly by use of the muscles, tendons, joints, and skin. Such are its size and shape as known chiefly by sight. All our experience, as embodied in our language, explains itself upon the theory that the color, smell, taste, and sound of things are to be regarded as known events in us, referred for their cause to that which is object perceived as extended and external by the senses of the eye and the skin.

But it has already been remarked that all the discoveries of the relative character of that object of sense-perception which we call matter do not in the least affect the persuasion that in

[1] Encyclopædia Britannica (ninth ed.), iii. 37.

knowing this object we have the certification of its reality. It is known as a real subject of changing states and relations, that is not-ourselves, but that possesses an independent and manifold life in the unity of its own "Ground." We affirm, then, with so-called "common-sense," the reality of the object known by the senses; and we turn to the special sciences of nature with our further inquiry as to what is the real nature of this object thus known.

That real subject of physical changes which we call matter is known to modern physics as having *Mass.* If we take for the moment no account of the hypothesis that electricity is a physical entity which has, however, no mass, we may say that the declaration, — all matter has mass, — is equivalent to affirming this quality as universally and necessarily characteristic of this real subject. Indeed, the proof that the mass of any portion of matter is unalterable, and the inference that the entire mass of the physical world is unalterable, have been declared to be the most convincing ground we have for believing that matter is real. Mass is the absolute and unchanging *quantum* of any portion of matter considered by itself, and of the entire system of material entities considered as a unity. It is the business of philosophy to inquire what is involved in this accepted principle of all physical science. It is its business to show in detail how the permanence of a real subject, conceived of as a ground or real cause of changing states and relation, with a fixed adherence to an end, as it were, is involved in the conception which physics has of mass. Thus the categories of substantiality, causality, relation, change, and number, are all implied when we ascribe this quality to matter. This is, however, because the quality of mass cannot be considered as the only quality of matter. For change and causality do not belong to matter as *merely* having mass. The material universe considered as a collection of mere masses of matter would be statical; there would be in it no provision for motion, or life, or any form of change.

Another universal predicate of matter is *Energy,*—the conception which physical science strives carefully to define and then to substitute for the popular and unscientific conception of force. The latter conception,—we are told,—since it is "suggested by the muscular sense," is too vague and anthropomorphic to serve the highest scientific interests. The suggested change of terms is doubtless worth the making; but it does not escape the difficulty experienced when we try to tell what, that is real in the material universe, is meant by either term. Modern physics sometimes claims to consider energy as an objective reality in the physical universe, "because it is conserved in the same sense as matter is conserved." Strictly speaking, such a declaration can have no real significance. Strictly speaking, what is meant by the declaration is this, that, on similar grounds to those on which we assume the unalterableness of mass, we assume that the quantity of energy is unalterable. Both are principles established on purely empirical grounds, albeit so firmly as to serve as postulates of all reasoning in general physics. With respect to the conception of energy also, philosophy has to consider how far it represents the real nature of that subject called matter to which it is given as a predicate by physical science. For philosophy is satisfied neither with that "figurate conception," which regards forces as inherent in matter, or as passing from one portion of matter to another, etc.; nor can it tolerate that dodging of the metaphysical question to which physics resorts, when it tries to reduce the essence of energy to changes in amounts and directions of motion.

When, then, we learn from Newton that "force is whatever changes a body's state," etc., and hear that the phrase, "or tends to change," has been added to the Newtonian definition; and when we are told that energy is "the power of doing work," or "the capacity for operating, or for producing an effect" (namely, motion), the shifting of phrases should not deceive us. We are not to suppose that physics has thus escaped the use of metaphysics, or the need of a more accurate metaphysical analysis.

For every one of these so-called scientific definitions fairly bristles with the old-time presuppositions and beliefs. A Being of matter, which makes it an agent, a cause of changes, the possessor of potentialities and powers, is certainly implied as known in all this.

The science of physics strengthens our conviction by its division of energy into "potential" and "kinetic," and by its discourse of "tendencies," "strains," "tensions," etc.; as well as by its statement of laws such as affirm that "to every action there is always an equal and contrary reaction," or that "every action between two bodies" is a stress. For every material body, the real subject of its energy potential and kinetic is the same portion of matter; and for the world at large it is the same unchanging *quantum* of universal matter. Every material body may then be regarded as a "system," more or less imperfectly complete in itself; but the entire *quantum* of matter is the universal material system. The energy which every system possesses, in virtue of the relative motions of its parts, is called "kinetic;" the energy which every system possesses, in virtue of the relative positions of its parts, is called "potential."

For every system, large or small, whether comprising one body or many bodies, the principle of the conservation of energy holds true. But in every system both forms of energy must be conceived of as co-existing in reality. The evidence of the kinetic energy is the direct or indirect knowledge of actual motion, for energy *is* "whatever changes the state of rest or uniform motion of a body." But such a thing as a state of rest is never actual; on the contrary, now and from the beginning every really existent material system must be known, and thought of, as ceaselessly in motion. Therefore by potential energy also we mean the real cause of motion. For we are told, "the word 'potential' does not imply that this energy is not real and exists only in potentiality; it *is* energy, and has as much claim to the title as it has in any other form in which it may appear." And, of course, in order that the sum of the two forms of energy may remain in any system the same, if the two co-exist in reality, they must be interchangeable. In reality, then, potential and kinetic energy are only two forms of manifesting the presence of that one cause of all motion, possible or actual, which we call matter.

The modern theory of dynamics affords to the philosophy of nature the materials for reflective analysis from which to know the character and laws of that unity of reality which accounts for the existence of manifold physical changes. These changes are all conceived of as related to each other, and as measurable quantities of mass and energy. Motion is the one form of real change to which this theory reduces all the other perceived physical changes. Motion implies the applicability of the categories of time and space to matter, not only as object immediately perceived, but also as reality scientifically known. But the motion of which we have immediate knowledge by the senses is a perceived change of place. The reality of the motion, as a change in the real subject, is no more certified as a *copy* of the change perceived, than is the reality of its extension by the extension of the object perceived.

Moreover, we have just heard of "tensions," and "tendencies" to move, and potential energies, that are not conceivable in any terms as actual correlates of motions perceived. And yet the entire possible round of changes, which can take place in the subject called matter, would seem to be expressible only in terms of motion. Are space and time then necessary as extended actualities *in* which real masses may actually come and go as do the perceived objects of the senses? Surely here are difficulties and apparent contradictions in the very core of physical science. Shall we say that the more "pure" and demonstrable it becomes, by reduction of all its formulæ to mathematical relations in the amounts and directions of motions, the more sensuous and philosophically indefensible do its conclusions seem?

The property of mass, considered as a constant united with certain variables, gives rise to two other properties of matter: these are *Weight* and *Inertia*. If two bodies having mass are placed at a given distance from each other in space, and are unhindered, they at once develop motion toward each other; or if in any way hindered, they develop some pressure or strain indicative of a so-called tendency to motion. As capable of doing this they are said to have weight: and since this capacity is measurable, all matter, as ponderable, falls under the category of number. But since that which produces, or tends to produce, motion is called "force," it is found necessary to assume a specific cause of the weight of all bodies that have mass; this cause is called the "force of gravity." The uniform modes of the variation in quantity of this force are then called the "laws of gravity;" and the force of gravity is said to vary directly as the mass and inversely as the square of the distance of the bodies displaying this property.

So also do we find that bodies having mass, when at rest, never begin to move, and when already moving never change the velocity or the direction of their motion, without having regard, as it were, to the amounts of the mass, and the velocities and directions of the motion, of other bodies. All matter is therefore said to tend to remain in its present state, — of rest, if it be at rest, and of motion with a given direction and velocity, if it be in motion. This tendency too is measurable; and the general capacity of matter to develop this tendency is called "inertia." The amount of the unwillingness, in any one body, to change without taking regard of other bodies, is considered to have its cause in the amount of potential and kinetic energy possessed by such body. Thus is the property of inertia made to imply a unity of causality to account for the changes of position in space which the different masses of matter undergo.

The manner in which the student of physics works out and expresses in numerical terms the changing relations of mass, weight, inertia, and force kinetic or potential, should be instructive and stimulating to the student of philosophy. Here a *circulus in concipiendo* as well as *in arguendo* is everywhere apparent. Even with these comparatively few and simple factors to take into account, the explanation of reality by the science of physics is far from being complete. But all attempt at complete explanation is made more difficult by the apparent necessity of admitting the presence, in the unity of the physical universe and as essential constituents of it, of other entities than those to which the foregoing properties apply. Such an entity, apparently, is the so-called ether; another such — unless the two shall be found to be really one — is electricity. Undoubtedly, the inclination to follow to the utmost the love of simplifying by analogical and symbolic reasoning will incline us to affirm that these entities must have, at least to some extent, the above-mentioned properties of other matter. But keeping within the strict limits of ascertained scientific truth, we have little right, at present, to claim that this is so. The energetic and skilful efforts of a Sir William Thomson have not as yet developed any satisfactory theory of the unknown medium of the waves of light which will serve to liken it to so-called "ordinary" matter. And the trend of discovery in electricity is perhaps in a direction to remove this entity farther away from the possibility of applying to it the laws of those bodies that have mass. Yet these entities are, as has been said, factors in the unity of the material universe.

We should have no hesitation then in enlarging our use of the terms "matter" and "mass." Entities like ether or electricity are also kinds of matter; and since they are measurable they may be said to have mass, although no signs of their being ponderable can be discovered. Weight and inertia are therefore not essential properties of the subject of physical changes. Indeed, no valid *a priori* reason can be discovered why there should not be as many kinds of matter "in mass" as there are admitted kinds of atoms, or elements of material reality. Neither can we ever establish, on other than grounds of probability by extension of experience, the propositions relating to the inertia of all matter, and to the conservation of mass and of energy. For even these few and simple factors,— properties, forces, laws,—already introduced, indicate that the unity of material reality is such as to imply a manifoldness of life and being too great to express in terms of physics. The manifoldness, however, all falls under the principle of *finality;* and so *the unity is a realized idea.*

The known *physical constitution* of bodies, or mode in which sensible quantities of matter are aggregated to form a mass having observed properties, increases the complexity of the problems which a general theory of physics is required to solve. If we divide all bodies, as respects their physical constitution, by the differences in changes of their dimensions resulting from internal stress, two great classes must be distinguished. These are solids and fluids,—the latter being subdivided into gases and liquids. But every mass, whatever its physical constitution, tends to resist changes of its bulk and shape; or—what is the same thing—it "requires force to change its bulk or shape, and requires a continued application of the force to maintain the change, and springs back when the force is removed." This property of matter is called "elasticity." Of this property, as respects their bulk, all bodies are said to have some, and all fluid bodies to possess it to perfection. Solids possess some degree of elasticity of shape; fluids no degree of this property. The theory of the limits, kinds, and degrees of this property is very complicated. It gives evidence of a variety of internal relations between the parts of a material mass, under the action of so-called forces of cohesion and repulsion, which it is beyond the power of the imagination to depict. As modifications of this general property of elasticity, many other "properties" arise. Such are the viscosity of liquids, the "molecular friction" (also sometimes called viscosity) of solids, certain qualities of bodies like crystals, resiliency, pliability, torsional rigidity, etc.

And yet, with all this manifold equipment of occult properties, the unity of the physical universe is somehow maintained.

But all this variety of the physical constitution of bodies is as nothing compared with that which modern chemistry brings to view. The coarser changes that result in the redistribution of mass and energy suggest changes that consist in the redistribution of the elements belonging to the mass and of the energies belonging to each element. This suggestion is converted by chemistry into a demonstration. And, behold! a world of wonders is made obvious to the eye of reason, such as can never be made obvious to the eye of sense.

Modern chemistry postulates nearly seventy kinds of elementary material existences, each having a most complex nature of its own. Not one of these beings ever does anything without reference to the behavior of other beings with which it is allied. Yet not one of them ever does anything that does not strictly comport with its own unchanging laws of behavior. Acting together, they form the constitution of all existing material bodies, and by their changing relations account for the varying properties of these bodies. The general fact of their interrelated action, according to the kinds to which they belong and the circumstances under which they are placed, is set forth by ascribing to them the property of "affinity." The word is a symbol of the presence of the most stupendous mysteries. Strictly speaking, the sets of properties are as many as are the so-called kinds of these atoms; and the number of properties belonging to each set is as many as are the different modes of the behavior of each kind under all possible relations. And, since the motion or tendency to motion of the atom, requires a postulated cause in some force, each atom may be said to be the happy possessor of as many forces as are these modes of behavior. The principal feature peculiar to these chemical forces of the atom is the extremely minute distances over which the forces act.

A distinguished astronomer has said that, at each instant,

every body in the solar system is conducting itself as though it knew precisely how it ought to behave in consistency with its own nature and with the behavior of every other body in the same system. But no planet considered as a physical mass is at all so richly endowed as is every atom. The atom must know precisely how to behave, under an almost infinite variety of relations to an almost infinite variety (quantitative and qualitative) of aggregations of other atoms. From the beginning of that everlasting time which science is fond of postulating, it has threaded its way securely amidst its fellows down to the present hour. It has danced countless millions of miles, with countless millions of different partners, many of which required an important modification of its mode of motion, without ever departing from the correct step or the right time. Surely the most fanciful mythology of physics in which philosophy has ever indulged, from the "love" and "hate" ascribed to the elements by the ancients, to that "mirroring" of the world which Leibnitz ascribed to every monad, cannot surpass in magical import the "laws" of chemistry concerning the "affinities" of atoms.

This indefinitely great variety in the natures and changes belonging to the elements of material reality the science of chemistry is endeavoring to reduce to a few general terms. The number of elements known to it is, however, on the whole increasing rather than diminishing. And since the majority of them are comparatively or extremely rare, while the number of those combined in the masses of which the earth and its plants and animals are mainly composed is exceedingly small, the secret reasons for precisely such manifoldness in unity are still far removed from human knowledge. The great principles of combination by weight and volume, and the form of the atomic theory which aims to account for these principles, are in the process of elucidation. Through these principles a gleam, or at least a glimmer, from the category of finality is always seen to appear. A chemical notation is possible; the elements have "valency," and admit of being arranged as monads, dyads, triads, according to their apparent maximum valencies. "Rational formulæ" are devised in attempting to account for the behavior of the atoms.

For the more satisfactory discussion of the principles of chemistry the philosophy of nature will doubtless have to await many years of scientific exploration. But enough is already known to warrant certain favorite affirmations. The very elements of all known material reality, the very beings whose unchanging natures are assumed as the basis of all change, proclaim the truth of metaphysics. They are permanent subjects of all physical events. They must be regarded as the real causes of the changes in states and relations of all material bodies; but they always act as self-limiting natures that are united, under an ideal system, into an orderly and beautiful whole. They *are*, only as they are in and of that supreme Unity of Reality, whose essential nature and ideal significance philosophy ever strives more clearly to define.

The more complicated inorganic forms which, like the crystal, tax the "ideal" nature of the atoms for a large contribution from their wealth of occult energies, enhance, at the same time, the difficulties of physical science and the claims to a hearing for philosophy. Meantime, the diverse play of the so-called "energy" of masses and atoms goes on. Having admitted a mode of energy called "gravity," and another called "heat," and another indefinitely large group of modes called "affinity," it is difficult to see just where we can stop multiplying *modes*, and yet maintain our consistency. Magnets are facts; crystals are facts, — as truly as are planets and pulleys and levers. They are facts, however, to account for which the law of the conservation and correlation of energy finds itself inadequate. They stand, in the inorganic world, as a rebuke to the prevalent unphilosophical identification of this law with the principle of sufficient reason or with the category of causality.

But when we pass from the realm of the inorganic into the realm of living beings, we practically leave behind the equipment with which physics and chemistry can supply philosophy for an understanding of the world of material reality. We have the word of Professor Huxley[1] for it: "The biological sciences are sharply marked off from the abiological . . . in so far as the properties of living matter distinguish it absolutely from all other kinds of things, and as the present state of knowledge furnishes us with no link between the living and the non-living." He will readily credit this statement who has thoughtfully watched the amœba under the microscope, or the muscle-nerve machine under all varieties, degrees, and circumstances of irritation. Philosophy has no need to postulate a new metaphysical entity called "vital force." It is enough to know that the phenomena called "life" ascribe to the subject, whose changes the phenomena are, an altogether new set of predicates and potencies. If we confine ourselves to physical phenomena there is no philosophical objection (except that arising from its vagueness) to ascribing, with Mr. Tyndall, to matter (as the "mysterious something by which all this has been accomplished") the "promise and potency of every form of life."

The word "life" represents an abstract conception. The rather does the philosophy of nature require of biological science some description of those properties which belong to all actually existing beings said to be alive. The question philosophy asks is herein only a modification of its more general question. It wants to know from biology what it is really to be as all living beings are. This question a recent writer has attempted to answer, from the scientific point of view, in such terms as follows: "A living being is a being composed of elements, in incessant chemical renewal and reacting upon one another in a way to maintain the form and functions [of the being] in a determined cycle of evolution, similar to the cycle traversed by other living beings from which the one under

[1] Encyclopædia Britannica (ninth ed.), iii. 679.

consideration comes forth or to which it is bound by community of origin."[1]

A living being requires, then, a correlated action of an immense number of those elements which chemistry describes. And yet the life of the community, as it were, does not bind the same atoms to enter into and remain within it; for incessant renewal and growth are taking place. But the category of finality must also be satisfied; for an ideal is followed, both as respects the morphology and the physiology of the combination. The form and the functions are maintained; though the same elementary beings, which follow the ideal, are not necessarily permanently retained. Moreover, a "cycle of evolution," a recurrent conformity to the ideal in consistency with series of changes in form and function, takes place. Nor is this cycle independent of cycles followed by other beings in like manner said to be, or to have been, alive. On the contrary, it is similar, not indeed to all the other cycles in all respects, but to certain definite kinds of cycles, to those, namely, from which, specifically, it "comes forth, or to which it is bound by connection of origin."

But how is this similarity, specific and determined, and yet admitting of so much individual variability, really secured? And what is it that really binds with the bond called "community of origin"? In other words, to what in the nature of the really existent shall we ascribe this new and most marvellous form of a unity of the manifold? Philosophy insists on asking such questions as these. And scientific biology, solely by enlarging and refining its description of the correlated phenomena, is unable to answer them. It is early in the development of the comparatively new science of biology to expect successful attempts to subject its principles to a philosophical treatment. But as the biologist is fond of predicting wonderful triumphs for his science in the near future, so may the philosopher indulge the

[1] Fernand Lataste, in the Comptes rendus de la Société de Biologie, séance du 5 Jan., 1889.

cheering expectation that his system of conclusions will be correspondingly enriched.

This is the place to mention the necessity and the promise which lie before philosophy as an offering from biological science. Especially urgent does the necessity appear, and especially attractive the promise, when we consider the efforts which biology and psychology are making to clasp hands over that barrier which has hitherto separated them. Those phenomena to which Von Hartmann has appealed in proof of his principle of "the Unconscious" are rapidly being multiplied. They are, with great difficulty but with promise of an accelerating rate of movement in the near future, being reduced to generalized statement of fact. Some of them provoke philosophy the more because they so completely baffle science. Such are the phenomena of reflex action; the phenomena ascribed to "instinct" (that pack-horse of explanations that do not explain) and to unconscious cerebration; the phenomena of genius (or of that inborn quality of mind which, without the training of conscious processes performs feats of intelligence and skill ordinarily demanding this training); and the phenomena of unconscious inference (if such there be), and of hypnotic and other similar conditions.

As problems for philosophy, there exist in the same borderland of biology and psychology many other kinds of interesting phenomena. Both these sciences are uniting their forces to investigate the states of trance, clairvoyance, ecstasy, etc., and the cases of hypersensitive beings (for example, as alleged by Reichenbach and modern experimenters in hypnotism), the alleged phenomena of thought-transference, telepathy, etc. The philosophy of mind is deeply interested in the light which such researches throw upon the questions of human personality and of the reality of mind. But the philosophy of nature is interested in any light which they may throw upon the nature of so-called "Nature," of that subject called matter to which some investigators would assign all these changes, both physical and psychical.

No fear need be entertained that the common researches of biology and psychology will ever succeed in diminishing the incomparability of physical and psychical phenomena. The atoms may be found to move, in deference to other atoms, in ways that now seem absolutely unimaginable; and psychical phenomena may become correlated with the motions of the atoms, with a strictness far beyond what we are now willing to admit as likely or even possible. But the simplest fact of consciousness will remain as unlike the most complicated combination and motion of the atoms as ever.

Philosophy will doubtless be greatly influenced by biology, psycho-physics, and experimental psychology, as respects the construction which it gives to the content of its notion of the real subject of all physical change. We leave the further elucidation of this content to another branch of philosophical discipline. We only gather some of the results of this meagre sketch of the work belonging to the philosophy of nature into the following sentence: All the different substances, forces, and laws, known to the physical sciences as belonging to the most general conception of "Matter," are to be regarded as the related modes of the behavior of one subject,—really existent, the self-limiting cause of all material change, in accordance with immanent ends.

The Philosophy of Mind encounters in some quarters a special opposition because the reality of its subject is denied. Sometimes this denial assumes the character of an *a priori* necessity, or at least of a conclusion derived from such a necessity. At other times it is based upon alleged grounds of observation and experiment. The primary definition and discussion of this problem belongs to psychology. The descriptive branch of this science furnishes the analysis of psychical states into their simplest elements, gives the history of the genesis of the most complex from the most simple states, and defines those uniform relations which are found actually to exist among the different states.

As experimental, biological, and psycho-physical, psychology also endeavors to establish correlations between the phenomena of consciousness and the structure and functions of the nervous mechanism. Comparative psychology aims to explain the psychical processes — whether of different kinds of psychical beings, or of different races of men and eras of human history — under principles which belong to all forms of the general theory of evolution. In whatever way the science of psychology is prosecuted, since it necessarily involves the preliminary assumption of a subject of the psychical states (the so-called *Ego*, or the generalized conception called the "self"), it introduces the problem of the reality of mind.

Psychology as pursued from the biological, experimental, and psycho-physical points of view, is particularly fond of claiming its ability to succeed "without a soul." Such ability may be conceded, in so far as it is satisfied to remain a science without power to explain actual events, by really acting forces, in accordance with laws that are valid in reality. But the advocates of "psychology without a soul" are often inconsistent in their pursuit and practice as regards their favorite principle. For the postulate of a single real subject of the phenomena (the Mind) they are found substituting some other, less appropriate and equally meagre postulate. Thus they make a particular congeries of material molecules with a peculiarly rich equipment of potencies, to be the *real* subject of all the psychical states and processes. That is to say, matter, assumed to be known as an indubitable reality, is the one real subject which somehow has acquired the power to develop a phenomenal being (the so-called "soul"), in whose activity alone it is itself known as real through the means of the phenomenon of a metaphysical postulate. This may well seem even to its most ardent advocates a somewhat extraordinary potency to ascribe to matter.

The final syntheses of philosophical system must undoubtedly recognize that Unity in Reality which the known universe of material *and* psychical beings certainly implies.

So far forth it must certainly be a monistic system. But in order to be a true system it must be, not only consistent in elaborating the content of all known physical and psychical facts, but also in fundamental accord with the primary fact of knowledge. This primary fact of knowledge has been seen to implicate the duality in reality of the subject of knowing, which is the object known in self-consciousness, and the object known as the subject of physical changes. Indeed, it is upon this primary fact of knowledge, with what it implicates, that the distinction between "Things" and "Souls" is based. Upon the same basis rests the distinction between the physical sciences and the psychological sciences, and the distinction between the "Philosophy of Nature" and the "Philosophy of Mind."

But the reality of the Mind is implicated in the primary fact of knowledge in a peculiarly convincing and impregnable manner. The fact of knowledge itself is the first and fundamental reality. As such it is, in its very nature, the self-realization of the knowing subject. As a fact, it is the realest of all events; it is the very type of all actuality, — the occurrence which is a *datum*, behind which, or beyond which, knowledge cannot go. Whatever is implicated in it *is* real; to attempt to question this is to imply it, and so is the attempt to explain it. Indeed, no agnosticism or materialism can question the reality of the subject of knowledge in so far as it is given in the fact of knowledge; neither of these forms of thinking claims to call it in question. And this reality can as little be explained by rational psychology as it can be questioned by agnosticism or materialism.

It is during the detailed effort to show precisely in what sense we are to understand the reality of mind, that the difficulties of the philosophy of mind emerge. Here the attempt to prove too much is as mischievous to right thinking as the attempt to disprove what is plainly implied. The mind, in the highest and widest flights of self-consciousness, never knows itself by envisaging, as it were, its own simplicity of reality; or by rationally attaching to any particular conception which it forms of itself the unquestionable faith of intuitive self-knowledge. In the light of psychological science and of the principles of general metaphysics, philosophy proceeds to answer in detail, — What it is really to be as all minds are. Its narrative contains as much of truth as it contains of knowledge gained by scientific researches and reflective analysis. The philosophy of mind, like the philosophy of nature, is subject to a progressively improved construction as the psychological sciences advance, and as reflective analysis becomes more searching and complete.

At the same time, it can never be otherwise than true that the living experience of knowledge gives legitimately to the mind a conviction, and a clearness of representation and conception, touching its own reality, which it is quite impossible for it to attain, touching the reality of so-called things. With the irresistible force of this living experience any attempt at metaphysical materialism will always have to deal. And psychology, studied in unprejudiced fashion, never has any difficulty in overthrowing such a form of materialism. So often as we try to postulate *matter* as a reality, out of which both physical and psychical changes are to be explained, we are liable virtually to decide the great question of metaphysics in disregard of the only authority in metaphysics; namely, the philosophical *mind.*

The work of explicating the content of knowledge in answer to the question, What is it really to be a Mind? is, on the whole, then, much easier than the task of forming a philosophy of nature. All the categories seem to lose something of their vague and figurative character when applied to the description of the reality of mental life. Of course, the language employed in conveying the description is necessarily figurative. The terms for the categories are necessarily embodied figures of speech. They are taken from modes of experience that are originally of things. The nature of the development of language, and the order followed in the development of experience, account for this fact. At the same time it is also true that the conceptions stirred within the consciousness by the terms when applied to the mind are not "figurate," in the same way and to the same extent, as when applied to an *extra*-mental reality called matter. For the terms all find their legitimate interpretation only in actual experiences of the self-conscious mind. For example, we have concrete actual experiences with ourselves by which to interpret such words as "permanent subject," "cause," "force," "quality," "change of state," "unity," etc. But it becomes increasingly difficult to tell what these words mean, when we transfer them from the mental realities in which they are born, to realities of which we have no knowledge (such as "atoms," "electricity," "ether," "physical energy," etc.) except by difficult processes of inference.

It accords with the foregoing truth to say that the substantiality and causality of the mind are terms for that which is realized in every act of self-conscious knowledge. Every such act is essentially referable, and is by self-consciousness actually referred, to one subject as its "ground" or real cause. Thus also is every such act an actual change of states, known to take place by the subject of all changing states. Undoubtedly, we find insuperable difficulty involved in every attempt to represent, in terms of the sensuous imagination, any reality corresponding to these terms. This is, however, because the sensuous imagination has no fitness to represent any of the ultimate norms of knowledge, — the so-called categories. But surely no one would think of claiming that the difficulty is peculiar to the case of the psychical states and processes. For who would think of claiming that he can form an adequate picture of what it is to be an atom, and thus to be a subject of immanent potencies and actual changes of states? Or how shall we picture to the eye, or on the skin, or in the muscles, the force of attraction that binds Mars to the Sun, or unites the atoms of oxygen to those of hydrogen in a drop of water? On the other hand, the essential properties of matter, such as its extension, impenetrability, or its mass, weight, inertia, etc., as well as its thermic, electrical, magnetic, and other phenomena, and the measurement of the quantities of these properties and of the relations of the beings possessing them, seem to imply an inescapable reference back to processes of a psychical nature. But whatever being has the actual experience whose formula is *cogito ergo sum*, that being knows so as to need no telling what it is really to be the subject of a state.

The careful analytic treatment of all the principles of psychological science, from the point of view of reflective analysis already adopted in general metaphysics, is the peculiar business of the philosophy of mind. When this business is undertaken by a community of scholars who are skilled alike in the interpretation of modern psychology and in metaphysical theory, a new and improved philosophy of mind will be the result. The deeper mysteries of the soul will never be penetrated by investigators who care for nothing but to add some new fact to the somewhat dreary array already existing in psychometry or electro-physiology. Nor will these mysteries prefer to disclose themselves to him who is satisfied with gazing on the spinal cord of a frog while undergoing stimulation, or with cramming the latest conceits in psycho-physics from the German laboratories. On the other hand, the high and dry metaphysical construction of theory in the philosophy of mind is worse than inadequate.

Of all the predicates to be applied, as involved in the very nature of knowledge, to the reality called "Mind," none is more important or more liable to misrepresentation than its Unity. The older rational psychology endeavored to construct, on a basis of immediate knowledge, a picture of the soul as necessarily simple or uncompounded; therefore indiscerptible; and therefore indestructible or immortal. The picture was copied after that of a hypothetical material reality, — an uncompounded and indissoluble physical monad. The claim for the soul that it *is* such a unity, with all the allied claims as to its indestructibility, was lost in the struggle with criticism and scepticism. But why should the philosophy of mind concern itself about the establishing of such a unity for the subject of psychical changes? For this is a kind of unity which can, in reality, have no existence anywhere, either in the realm of matter or in that of mind. In other words, to be really existent, whether as a "Thing" or as a "Soul," implies a different kind of unity from that which the old psychology ascribed to the mind as its peculiar privilege, its most precious treasure.

The grounds of the mind's claim to be a real unitary being are laid in every act of self-conscious knowledge. In every such act the subject of the act becomes, in the highest sense of the word, really one, and knows itself as one. But to represent this real but psychical unity after the analogy of a rigid and unchanging oneness of being, is to miss the very conditions of its existence at all. There is, in reality, no unity that is not an actual unifying of the manifold. And this the mind is, really, in every actual event of self-conscious knowledge. Of this event we may say that it is, in its nature, a realization of the highest — nay, of the only conceivable — kind of psychical unity.

All that is implicated in this admitted unity of consciousness, as a concrete and actual and indubitable experience, it belongs to the philosophy of mind to set forth. The task is made more important and difficult, as well as interesting, by two classes of scientific considerations. These are, first, such as bear on the doctrine of "faculties" of the mind; and, second, such as have to do with certain abnormal or unusual phenomena, like so-called "double-consciousness," etc. But in the treatment of these and other allied considerations, the futility of all attempts to construct a doctrine of the soul's unity, as involving its indestructibility, upon a basis of so-called intuitions should be conceded. Immortality of mind cannot be envisaged in self-consciousness. Neither can it be intuitively known what it would be to be really one, as every mind is one, if all the peculiarities of the concrete process of self-knowledge were left out of the account. But he who mourns over the loss of power to establish by intuition the soul's indiscerptible simplicity in reality, and its resulting immortality, does his own soul a wrong that is not necessary. It is hard to see what advantage one would have, if one could really be an immortal unit without the actual life of self-conscious knowledge; and equally hard to see what one would lose by the dissolution of this merely mathematical unity, if only one could continue to experience the benefits of actually living the manifold life of self-consciousness.

Modern psychological science, by its modification of the old-time theory of faculties, has done much to improve the philosophy of mind. In this work great credit must be awarded to Herbart and his followers. The credit is all the greater because they have never fallen into the folly of trying to establish a "psychology without a soul." No one making such an attempt can rightly claim to be a disciple of this successor of Kant at Königsberg.[1] The unity of the real subject of all the psychical changes is a postulate from which Herbart does not swerve. The prevalent doctrine of faculties he rejects on the ground of its inconsistency with the true being of the soul, which he regards as a simple, real essence. Like every such essence, it can have only one attribute; for plurality of attributes is inconsistent with real unity of subject. Its sole attribute is its one mode of reaction, of "self-preservation," as it were, on every occasion of its being in "propinquity" or "connection" (*Zusammensein*) with other real beings. The characteristic mode of the soul's reaction in self-preservation is ideation; and as combinations and modifications of ideation-processes all the psychical life is to be explained.

The effort of Herbart to regard every psychical act, and every so-called psychical faculty, as but a mode of the life of the one

[1] Herbart's work is entitled, Psychologie als Wissenschaft, neu gegrüudet auf Erfahrung, *Metaphysik* und Mathematik, Königsberg, 1824.

subject, whose nature unfolds itself in accordance with its immanent idea, is most praiseworthy. But the form which he gave to this effort is needlessly narrow. All attributes or faculties are indeed only modes of the behavior, under changing relations, of the one real subject called Mind. But the unity of this subject is not a punctual unity; neither is it a unity such as forbids it to behave in more than one fundamental mode of reaction. It is, as we have already seen, a unity which implies, the rather, a manifoldness of *momenta* or factors in every actual activity; and, accordingly, a number of predicates (faculties or powers) as shown in the actuality of every act.

But especially is the unity of the mind demonstrated in the character of its evolution. Of no other real being is it true, to the same extent or with the same remarkable significance, that what it *really is* can be known only by what it *actually becomes*. So that if we entertain the fiction of describing all that the mind really is in terms of a single attribute, we may select as this attribute, its "capacity for development." This is substantially what Wundt has done [1] at the conclusion of his psycho-physical examination of the nature of the soul. "By the term 'soul,'" says he, "we mean the inner being of the same unity which, from the external point of view, we regard as the body belonging to it." This irresistibly leads to the postulate that "spiritual being is the actuality of things, and that its most essential property is development." Little of scientific or philosophical value would be gained, however, by making such a declaration respecting the one "essence" of the soul's life. The wonderful variety of powers, or qualities, implied in the actual variety of its changing states, remains as great as before. These are all implied in its development. Nay, more, the fact that its being is a life, which consists in the actual unfolding of these implied powers, in definite relations and according to many laws, but with the unity of a self-realizing idea, enhances our estimate of the number of its predicates. The qualities or faculties of the

[1] Grundzüge der physiologischen Psychologie, ed. 1880, ii. 463 f.

mind can never be fewer in number than those modes of the behavior of all minds which refuse to be reduced to similar terms. The philosophical doctrine of the mind's unity is therefore not dependent upon the number of the mind's faculties which the science of psychology accepts.

The philosophy of mind can scarcely be in like manner indifferent to the scientific description and explanation of phenomena like those of "double consciousness," etc. It cannot easily escape the feeling that some of the views still current as to the soul's real nature may be profoundly modified by the progress of scientific investigation. The same thing is true of the alleged cases of unconscious surrender of the will of one person to another, of attribution to the wrong will, as it were, with self-condemnation and remorse, of the results of conduct, and of other abnormal and pathological phenomena of an ethical order. In general, it must be said of all such material for philosophical consideration that it still needs to undergo a great amount of strictly scientific elaboration. In certain lines, psychology has during the last twenty-five years been among the most enterprising and successful of all the empirical sciences. For that very reason, it has acquired an immense mass of material, partly derived from observation unchecked by experiment, and partly from more or less unsuccessful experiment, which requires further testing. It is quite too soon to assume, on grounds of empirical psychology, the necessity of reconstructing all the categories. On the other hand, that the speculative theory of mind, as well as many an ethical and theological theory, will need to be re-shaped, there can be little doubt. But the study of the history of human thinking is a great quieter of exaggerated alarms at such a necessity. No form of elaborate human knowledge is older, or rests on broader foundations, than the philosophy of the mind. In no form are the changes of important opinion slower; in none are the great centres of accepted truth more secure. The student of the philosophy of mind will therefore welcome, as constituting a basis for his theory of mind, all the principles discovered by psycho-physics, psychiatry, hypnotism, nervous pathology, and criminal statistics; but he will make sure that all alleged principles are *discovered*, in fact, and that they are so stated as to be properly expressed *principles*.

A broad field for philosophical research opens before us whenever we attempt, on a basis of the particular sciences, speculatively to determine the relations of the human mind to matter, to other finite minds, and to God. Here it is impossible to resist the influence of ethical and æsthetical considerations. And as a matter of fact, these relations lie not only in the sphere of what actually is, but also in the sphere of what ought to be. They require, therefore, for their right speculative treatment a thorough equipment in the sciences of ethics and æsthetics. Nor can the phenomena of the religious being of man be left out of the account. Indeed, for the philosophical theory of the relations of mind to other mind, and of all finite minds to God, ethics, æsthetics, and the science of religion are quite indispensable.

The general relations of the mind of man to matter are just now being made the subject of most painstaking scientific research. All such relations, in fact, exist (so far as we have any information as yet scientifically verifiable) in the form of relations between the human mind and the human body. Indeed, the progress of science is more and more in the direction of treating all the more abnormal and astounding phenomena in terms of these relations.

The philosophical importance of studies in psycho-physics and physiological psychology is therefore obvious. These branches of psychology have already made important changes in the philosophical points of view, if not in the tenets of philosophy. The ancient figures of speech, which allow or invite us to speak of the body as the "seat," the "tabernacle," the "organ," of the mind, are rapidly being clothed with a new meaning. Reflective analysis discovers a single great truth as underlying all these figures of speech. The life of the mind is one of development in reciprocal dependence on being that is other than itself. That this life is *its own life,* remains as true to-day as ever before. That the development is a spiritual development, and implies a spiritual nature and spiritual potencies belonging to the subject of the development, psycho-physics can never disprove. But this mind-life begins and continues, a development related under law to the genesis and development of a manifold unity of interacting material molecules. It is quite too much to expect that the physics of masses or of molecules, or that chemistry, or biology, should adequately explain the existence and unfolding of this series of spiritual relations. And we have no adequate reason for affirming that any of the principles of these sciences reign supreme over such relations. Indeed, the most general principles of these sciences — such as the conservation of mass and the conservation and correlation of energy — avowedly cannot be maintained *between* brain-motions and psychical states.

At this point philosophy enters another protest against the current tendency to bring all the force of the principle of sufficient reason to bear in favor of a materialistic theory of mind, and even to make the working postulate of physics co-extensive with the category of causality. Psycho-physics and physiological psychology can never, whatever extension of their discoveries may in the future be made, invalidate the reality and spirituality of the subject of psychical changes. These sciences, at most, can only present the general facts of correlation between psychical changes and changes in the relations of the substance of the brain. Phenomenally considered, the correlations are reciprocal. There is as good and unimpeachable evidence to show that the latter are, in turn, conditioned upon the former, as that the former are conditioned upon the latter. Considered metaphysically, each class of changes requires its own characteristic subject as its cause or "ground." If the regard that mind shows for molecules of matter, and the regard shown by them for it, is an ultimate mystery, we are no worse off (provided we can formulate the terms of this regard, — "the laws" of the correlation) than we are with respect to the real causes of reciprocal physical changes. But it belongs to philosophy in its attempts at a final synthesis of the principles of both Things and Souls, — that is, of all finite reality, — to determine, if possible, the nature of that Unity in which they all have their "Ground."

Both the Philosophy of Nature and the Philosophy of Mind require the thoughtful consideration of one doctrine which is potent in both realms. We refer, of course, to the theory of evolution. The metaphysics of this theory, as it is taught on purely scientific grounds, is often extremely crude and inconsistent. This is largely due to two causes. The scientific advocate cannot elevate his interpretation of certain facts of observation to the place of a supreme principle, without calling freely upon *a priori* considerations to fill in the gaps and enlarge the circumference of his legitimate inferences. Moreover, if the theory of evolution is itself anything more than a passing fancy, it is representative of what has gone on, and still goes on, in the world of reality. Therefore, it is legitimately philosophical in its nature. Therefore, it needs not less metaphysics, and surely not more of poor metaphysics, but, the rather, more of better metaphysics. And, indeed, what can be more inspiring to the student of philosophy than the demand made upon him by the present condition of science in respect of the doctrine of evolution? He is invited to regard the universe, not as a statical affair, a problem in mechanics admitting of an *a priori* or mathematical solution, but as a history of genesis and growth, as one vast and continuous self-unfolding Life. This requirement does not justify the removal of important and eternal distinctions. It is not as though the categories were all invited to a kind of *hara-kiri*. The theory of evolution constitutes a demand for an enlarged philosophical interpretation of the world, as a totality in all space and all time, — the Unity of a progressively self-realizing Idea.

The exclusive or undue emphasis of the considerations peculiar to either of the two departments of metaphysics results in the one-sided tenets of one of the two great rival schools of philosophy. Realism almost invariably starts from the physical, and ends in the philosophical interpretation of all that is, and happens, through natural forces and laws. Idealism starts from the purely psychological interpretation, and ends in affirming the reality of Mind alone.

CHAPTER XI.

ETHICS.

WITH the introduction of distinctively ethical conceptions and laws we enter upon the second main department of philosophical discipline. Permission was taken to call this department the Philosophy of the Ideal (Idealology, or Philosophical Teleology). The division itself implies that the realm of really existing beings, considered simply as respects what they actually are and actually do, does not cover the entire sphere of philosophy. Besides that which really is, reflection must have reference also to that which *ought to be*. Experience does not consist wholly of the monotonous and indifferent cognition of the existence and happenings belonging to matters of fact. Neither is all we know, or long further to know, covered completely by the sciences which strive to systematize, under terms of uniform relation, changes of the states, as such, of things and minds.

That much which actually happens ought not to happen, has been the common belief of mankind in all ages. Nor does that skilful apologizing for the laws of physical and psychical existence, which the scientific spirit affects, succeed in driving this belief from the human mind. On the contrary, so confident do men in general continue, of their ability to distinguish the sphere of actuality from the sphere of the ideal, that they without hesitation pronounce judgment against Nature herself. She seems to them somehow inexcusably deficient in respect of conformity to their ethical and æsthetical ideals. So bad or ugly are some things and some souls that — the feeling seems unavoidable — they certainly ought not to have been, or even to be permitted to be. For the ignorance and prejudice which so frequently accompany this kind of judgment no apology is offered. But its persistence, as deeply rooted in the most fundamental convictions of the mind, is a fact which provokes inquiry. Nor is it at all likely that the painful discrepancy between what is and what ought to be will be in the least diminished by any discoveries of modern science. The "struggle for existence," and "the survival of the fittest" only, with all that these phrases imply, may be clothed by these discoveries in the garb of beauty and benevolence. But the facts to which they appeal appear awful and mysterious; the laws they assert meet with strong repugnance from important elements in the life of the soul. And he must have become particularly insensitive, on both the ethical and the æsthetical side, whose ideals seem to be satisfied by the world of reality.

The ideals themselves, therefore, demand that treatment which philosophy employs. For their presence in striking contrast to the actual being and behavior of things, is a most significant fact. It stimulates reflective analysis to a remarkable degree. Inasmuch as these ideals are given in the actual experience of the human mind; and inasmuch also as the mind strives to bring itself and all the procedure of physical forces and laws to the test of the standards required by the ideals, — synthetic philosophy must take great account of them. Philosophical Ethics and Æsthetics are therefore legitimate and necessary branches of philosophy.

Moreover, it is in this general department that philosophy takes hold upon the principles of *conduct*. Some might — it is possible — dispute with Matthew Arnold over the exact fraction which should be chosen to designate that portion of "life" which "conduct" is. But even if we restrict the term to such action as is performed, with more or less of deliberation and choice, in the intelligent pursuit of ends, a philosophy of conduct is required. Indeed, it is in its approaches to the treatment of ethical principles, and in its consequent influence on the life of duty and of religion, that philosophy comes into closest contact with the interests of men. Were it possible, then, for philosophy to neglect ethics and æsthetics and still aim at completeness in its own domain, such neglect would be impolitic.

All the different schools of philosophy attempt to meet the demand for philosophical analysis and philosophical system made by ethical and æsthetical phenomena. Even agnosticism, which is no philosophy in so far as it remains consistent agnosticism, aims at establishing a theory of ethics. Just at present, as a matter of fact, it has attached itself to a so-called "ethics of evolution." Schopenhauer and Hartmann, also, feel constrained to give especial attention to ethical philosophy. It is indeed an integral part of the philosophical system of both that the so-called "Ground" of all phenomena is necessarily *un*ethical. Yet the pessimistic pantheism which these thinkers advocate aims, in their case, to be especially fruitful in the interpretation of ethical and æsthetical phenomena.

Glimpses of profounder reasons for the need which philosophy has of ethics and æsthetics come to us from the principles already established. Even general metaphysics and the philosophy of nature excited the conviction that what we call "Matter," as the cause of physical events and the ground of physical beings, is not without an ideal character. The unity of being which material things are known to have, seemed to imply the immanence, as it were, in the subject of all these changes of a self-limiting idea. And when the sciences of nature and of mind were seen to be converging upon the problem of determining the most general relations in which "Things" and "Souls" stand to each other, and to the Unity of Reality whose being and action determine the natures and relations of both, the horizon where philosophical knowledge reaches its limit began faintly to appear. For, certainly, the nature of this fundamental Unity of Reality cannot be investigated, if the presence and meaning of our ideals are to be left out of account. Herein must be found the real and the final cause of the arising and growth of these ideals. We are persuaded that much more than this will appear true as regards the relation of "the Good" and "the Beautiful" to that Unity of Reality which philosophy seeks. This very advance of our knowledge philosophy aims to secure by cultivating ethics, æsthetics, and the philosophy of religion as important parts of its discipline.

The Philosophy of the Ideal is, then, a main cognate department of philosophy, in distinction from the department of Metaphysics. It treats of that which men have the idea ought to be, as distinguished from what they know really is. So far forth there is reason in the twofold division adopted, for example, by Dühring,[1] into philosophy of science and philosophy of life. In the latter (which includes Æsthetics and the Philosophy of Religion) we seek for the application of reflective thinking to the ideals of life, — *of life*, in the widest sense of the word. Thus understood, human living includes, as its choicest experiences, the production and joyous appreciation of beauty, the doing and loving approbation of duty, the knowledge, trust, and blessed communion of soul, toward God. As Calybäus[2] has pointed out, the distinction between science and wisdom is one of the oldest and most firmly rooted in the popular mind and in philosophy.

It would be a fatal mistake, however, to suppose that the Ideals, with which this department of philosophy is concerned, stand in no empirical relation to the concrete realities considered by the physical and psychological sciences. That these ideals — the conceptions of the beautiful and of the morally good, and the feelings and dispositions attaching themselves to each — exist in the form of concrete psychical states, is a

[1] Cursus der Philosophie, p. 1 f., 8 f., etc.
[2] Fundamentalphilosophie, p. 22 f.

matter of fact determined by observation of others, and by self-consciousness. Their existence all along the path of human evolution is testified to by many phenomena of human history. But much more than this is indisputably true. The structure of human society, the products of legislation and of art, the constitution of literature, are all complex forms of reality which have their source in these ideals. Indeed, in a limited but not unimportant way the influence of these ideals has been felt in modifying external Nature. Even the surface of the earth and the course of the seasons is not isolated from effects more or less directly due to the conceptions of men respecting the Beautiful and the Good. Nor does our imagination succeed in defining just how much more, with the growth of knowledge, may in time come into the sphere of physical changes that are possible through a wise or a foolish use of means on the part of mankind.

When we consider the influence of the real upon these ideals, our views become more clear and defensible No one acquainted with the modern sciences of ethics and æsthetics can for a moment maintain that the conceptions, feelings, and judgments, which control human conduct, have developed in complete independence of the world of facts. The two spheres — the one, of that which actually is, the other of that which we think ought to be — are not identical; they are rather in some respects exclusive of each other or antagonistic. But they are certainly not wholly independent. We rely chiefly upon an historical and comparative study of the phenomena to show how the forces and laws of material reality have influenced the ideals which men frame of the beautiful and the morally good. But it is not with the descriptive history of the alleged genesis and development of these ideals that philosophy is primarily concerned. It is interested rather in the conclusions to be drawn from this history regarding the real nature of these ideals. It is also especially interested in the effort to throw light on the further definition of that Unity of all Reality which constitutes its final problem in synthesis. Is this One that is the "Ground" of all the manifold life of related action in which things and souls engage, to be conceived of, and believed in, as also the source and actualization of the ethical and æsthetical Ideals?

The relation of philosophical Ethics and Æsthetics to philosophy at large, and to Metaphysics in particular, as well as especially to the final synthesis which the Philosophy of Religion attempts, should now be obvious. We confine the remaining discussion of this chapter to the first of these two sub-divisions of the Philosophy of the Ideal.

The science whose investigations precede the philosophy of morals is also called ethics. It is a branch of psychology, — a psychological science, in the truest meaning of the words. Philosophical ethics treats, by the method and with the spirit peculiar to all philosophical discipline, the presuppositions and discovered principles of scientific ethics. Here, therefore, the relations between science and philosophy are particularly intimate and often perplexing. Ethical phenomena certainly invite scientific treatment. They are certainly also phenomena of a psychical origin and character. They constitute therefore part of the great domain of facts and laws with which the science of psychology, in the widest sense of the word, has to do. But just as certainly they are of a unique character, and therefore in a measure justify the claims of ethics to a somewhat separate existence as a science. But this unique character does not excuse ethical facts and laws from submitting to all the tests of science and philosophy. In spite, then, of the shyness of ethics to enter the arena of scientific psychology and of critical thought, into that arena it must come. There must it contend; and by its ability to stand against all the hardest tests of science and against all the assaults of scepticism, the reality of its conclusions must be judged.

Ethics as a science presents to ethics as moral philosophy certain presuppositions and discovered principles which require critical handling before incorporation into the system of philosophical truths. The presuppositions it is the work of philosophical analysis to explicate and define; they are to be found actually implicated in all the psychological sources and norms of conduct. The discovered principles consist of those generalizations upon the basis of diverse ethical phenomena which the scientific study of man, as capable of conduct and as actually exercising this capacity, has already established. In other words, if there are, besides those fundamental principles (categories), which metaphysics distinguishes as belonging to all the actually existent, others which control all our mental representations of that which ought to be, it is the task of philosophical analysis to point them out. If there are convictions, rooted in the primary facts of the mind's being, that attach themselves to all ethical phenomena, the philosophy of the ideal is concerned with these convictions. In general, the relation of philosophy to the particular sciences is such that philosophical ethics is bound to depend for its conclusions upon "data" furnished by observation and induction.

Scientific ethics has at present two main sources from which to derive its system of so-called ethical laws. These are, first, the observation of all those phenomena of consciousness to which the title "ethical" can properly be attached. It may be said that, since the springs of conduct are laid in entire human nature and involve every possible form of psychical action, descriptive and explanatory psychology must furnish the knowledge of ethical laws. The second main source of the systematic treatment of ethical phenomena is comparative and historical study. This study covers the development of ethnic conceptions and customs regarding matters of moral concern. It may even embrace those actions of different species of the lower animals that are alleged to have an ethical character and significance. Its dominant idea is derived, of course, from the modern theory of evolution.

The observation cultivated by the science of ethics should be as comprehensive and penetrating as possible. It should not follow solely the method of introspection; it should be external as well. The study of human conduct as indicative of the character of its psychological impulses, antecedents, and principles, may profitably include the debased and criminal classes, children, and even idiots and imbeciles. All the verified results of such induction the philosophy of morals will be bound to take into its final account. It will be bound also, however, carefully to weigh each result, and always to remember that in the process of realizing our ideals the significance and character of the true Ideal appears as the *end* of the process. Especially careful will philosophical ethics be of those hasty generalizations, so abundant in these days of laudable ambition to arrive at *exact* science, which are derived from tables of statistics and other similar data. The great value of such data cannot be denied. But even in less complicated sciences than ethics the fruitlessness of merely heaping up tables of facts is sufficiently obvious. No amount of external observation, and no handling of an indefinitely increased amount of statistics, will ever enable the student of morals to dispense with the acquaintance with his own nature as gained by intelligent use of introspection. In this sphere, pre-eminently, the philosopher needs the equipment of personal experience. He needs also, of course, the psychological tact and skill necessary to analyze and interpret that experience. He who has not seen and felt — seen clearly and felt deeply — in his own soul the varied experiences, — the aspirations, struggles, mortifications, triumphs, and defeats, — of moral human nature, is so far forth unfit scientifically and philosophically to portray and interpret it. In saying this we make no exception of the religious elements and experiences of human nature. For in them also we agree with Mr. Spencer in finding a "soul of truth." We give, however, to the facts and arguments by means of which the conclusion is to be established a far different interpretation from that which he proposes.

The scientific study of the phenomena of ethical consciousness results in a view of human nature which includes a number of important unsolved philosophical problems. This study reveals so-called "human nature" as set over against other "Nature" in the most wonderful and sharp contrast. That it marks the inherent, universal, and irresistible tendency of man to regard himself as not classifiable with "things" and as superior to them, the fair and comprehensive student of the phenomena cannot doubt. All efforts made in the interests of so-called "science" to bring the entire being of man into a strict and mechanical connection with the system of things meet with their most determined resistance from ethical feelings and ideas. The average man is disposed to be docile, on being told that he positively must conform to the sovereign sway of physics and chemistry, — that he must, indeed, consider himself a thinking and feeling machine. But when he is told that he must also believe himself to be a *moral* machine, he positively cannot think or feel his way into terms corresponding with the required conception.

The questions which philosophy raises respecting the constitution of human nature as moral, may be divided into two main groups. Of these one contains the problem of so-called moral freedom, or "free will;" the other covers a miscellaneous set of inquiries which may be said to deal with the problem of the nature of "conscience," — in a somewhat loose and indefinite meaning of this term. Both these problems, like all philosophical problems, lead the inquirer quickly into the region of those ultimate facts which are data of all experience, and of those principles which are its unchanging laws or norms.

The problem of moral freedom is generally stated in terms that provoke discussion as to whether we shall say yes, or no, to the question: Is the Will free? Such a form of statement, while not necessarily involving us in error, is certainly liable to grave objections. By such use of the term "Will," a so-called faculty must first be conceived of as virtually separated from the complex life of the Soul; then this faculty must be set over against all the other so-called faculties as on some special terms of reciprocal relation with them; and, finally, the necessity of thinking this relation as falling under the law of causality is either affirmed or denied. The entire treatment of the problem thus becomes alien to the methods of procedure employed elsewhere in psychology and philosophy. Both parties to the controversy over the question, when stated in this way, are apt to do violence to the methods and the conclusions of these branches of human knowledge.

The advocate of moral freedom, whenever he can for a moment pause in his defensive fighting, is tempted to strengthen his position by an untenable theory of "intuitions" and intuitive "beliefs." His view seems to imply that, by an act of self-consciousness, one may envisage the entire content of one's real being, and see, as with an inner eye, a faculty of Will sitting in supreme sovereignty upon the throne of the soul. On the other hand, the determinist ordinarily contends upon the assumption that *he*, at any rate, has all the clear and positive knowledge, all that is worthy to be called science, on his side. But his science is too often found to consist in an utterly unwarrantable application of a physical hypothesis to the case of the human soul. His mechanics and dynamics of the subject of psychical states is the more pronounced, the more doubtful it is. He assumes that ideas and feelings act on so-called will, as masses act on masses, or as atomic entities act on one another, with measurable forces and directions. To self-consciousness he concedes only the power to behold the surface of the psychical machinery. What he claims for himself, in the name of the principle of the conservation of energy, is the power infallibly to tell what the co-efficient of the potential part of the motive force must be assumed to be. The study of psychical phenomena, unprejudiced by the determination to make quasi-physical conceptions and laws apply to these phenomena at all hazards, is quite too tedious a process for him to follow. One great principle, however, he certainly feels compelled to borrow from the equipment of the mind. This is the principle of causality itself. But even this is summoned to enforce the deterministic conclusion, after being subjected to skilful and somewhat unscrupulous manipulation.

It would be impertinent to offer a discussion of the problem of moral freedom in a few words, — so often has the problem already been discussed from the beginning of philosophy until now. A few words must suffice, however, to indicate certain lines along which the discussion may most profitably proceed. At the very beginning it is important to determine the nature of those primary psychological facts in the existence of which the problem of freedom is implicated. These facts may be summarized as the one fact of self-conscious and responsible choice. That no mind *is* free until it *becomes* free, that moral freedom, if possessed at all, is gained only after a certain psychical development is passed through, is an indisputable conclusion from the study of psychology. If, however, the mind ever attains to moral freedom, it does this in the forth-putting of self-conscious and responsible choice. It is not to mere volition that the claim of moral freedom is most intimately attached.

The factors necessary to those psychical activities which are best entitled to be called "acts of free will" are the following five: (*a*) Mental representation of two or more ends to be gained and of the means necessary to their attainment; (*b*) excitement of the sensibility in the form of desire; (*c*) deliberation, or conflict of so-called motives, regulated by the direction of attention; (*d*) decision, — the appropriation to self of one end, and its system of means, to the exclusion of others (that psychical process which corresponds to the words "I will," — *choice*, peculiarly so designated); (*e*) fiat of will (generally, if not always, accompanied by the feeling of effort, and resulting, under psycho-physical laws, in starting the train of means necessary to the attainment of the chosen end). It is evident that, while these factors may be fused, as it were, so as to be almost simultaneous, they constitute, in the order just given, the "moments" of that complex self-conscious process in which ethics has a peculiar interest. It is evident also that the fourth one (*d*) is of distinctive importance and value.

The actual occurrence of psychical processes with the factors just ascribed to deliberate choice admits of no doubt. Just as little doubt can there be that to such processes, pre-eminently, are attached the conviction of freedom and the judgment of responsibility. I cannot indeed say: I know by the immediate knowledge of self-consciousness that, when I thus choose, I am a really free being; but I can say, in the name of this authority, I know that I pass through this psychical process of choice, and that to myself, considered as the subject of this process, I attach the idea and the feeling of being free and responsible.

This unique psychological fact of deliberate choice comes before philosophical ethics for an explanation in accordance with the principles which apply to all real beings and actual events. It is itself an actual experience; about this we need not hesitate. It is a unique experience, and appears in some sort to separate the subject of it from other real beings in the world. Can the conviction of freedom justify itself in the face of all that we know concerning the necessary nature of reality? The conviction has in its favor, not only its own inherent force, but also certain conclusions drawn from that conviction of responsibility to which its relation is so unique. For it is not easy to weaken the force of that argument which ethics has so frequently drawn in these terms,— to be morally responsible, one must be morally free. Or, in other words, the responsibility of the subject who chooses implies his freedom in choosing. How, then, is a place to be made for such convictions in a world known to be real under the principles already disclosed by science to the philosophy of nature and the philosophy of mind?

It is plain that the answer to this question, so far as it can be answered at all, requires the making of several distinctions.

Some of these have already been provided for; others of them are required at this stage in the discussion of philosophical ethics. What is it to be free? What is it to be related under the principle of causality? Are the two, in reality, compatible or incompatible? Can we *explain* otherwise than by the principle of causality? If not, and if there be freedom of mental action in choice, and if freedom and causality be incompatible, how can the fact of such freedom be explained? But if it be inexplicable, may it not still be fact? Or may not the principle of causality and the fact of freedom both be so stated as to seem not incompatible? It is with questions such as these that philosophical ethics has to deal in its inquiry whether the fact of choice, with all that it appears to imply, can be adjusted to its place in the world of actually existent things and minds.

In discussing the foregoing questions, some help may be received from considerations with which metaphysics has already made us familiar. In all explanation of physical changes we found the physical sciences constantly assuming the presence and determinative action of the unexplained. For we found these sciences referring all physical changes, for their ultimate explanation, to certain beings in whose reciprocally related action the changes really consist. These beings all had to be conceived of as endowed with "natures"; they admitted of classification into kinds according to their respective natures. What they do is "*explained*" as due to their fixed and natural modes of behavior. They do what they do, as having these natures, and yet as always acting in view of the action of other beings. But when we seek for an explanation of the "natures" themselves, we find ourselves only talking in circles in the effort to explain. *So* the atoms behave, *because* it is their nature to. *Such* we know their nature to be, *because* so they always behave, That is to say, the explanations of physical science all end in the assumption that the real causes of the changes are the beings whose the changes are.

But since the world is many atoms and yet one world, philosophy propounds the ulterior view. The changes of the different beings are correlated changes, because the subject of all their changes is in reality One. The spontaneity of the action of this one Being, as an ideal Unity of the manifold, is taken, therefore, as the ultimate fact, as the unexplained "Ground," on which the explanation of all the observed changes finally depends.

But when we turned from the philosophy of nature to that of mind we found less difficulty in conceiving how there might take place in reality the necessary unifying of the manifold changes, according to an idea. Every mind is essentially one being, subject and cause of all its psychical states, with a capacity for development after the fashion of an idea. Every occurrence in the development of this being requires, therefore, a reference to the unity of the subject of all the states, as its explanation, real cause or ground. In some sort, it is true, we "explain" psychical states by other states, either physical or psychical; for the states may be known to follow each other in more or less uniform ways. But every such explanation is only relative; it implies the existence of a "nature" of the soul, considered as one subject of all the related states. All psychical processes, however complete our knowledge may be of their antecedent or concomitant processes, must be referred to an unexplained spontaneity of the subject of them all.

It will at once be said, and truly, that this result of metaphysical analysis only secures for minds the same spontaneity that atoms have. The question as to whether the spontaneity of mind can so differ from the spontaneity of atoms as to include in the former a moral freedom denied to the latter, does indeed require a further study of the "natures" of the two. Such study reveals the reasons for defining the spontaneity of mind so as to meet the demands of moral freedom and responsibility.

Everything we know of atoms compels us to consider them

as incapable of freedom. No known phenomena suggest the occurrence in their case of interior processes with factors corresponding to those which enter into self-conscious choice. On the contrary, all the conclusions of the physical sciences depend upon regarding their natures as, from the first, fixed and unchangeable. Those orderly, continuous, and reciprocally determining changes, which evolution delights to describe, depend upon the hypothesis that the "natures" of the atoms remain the same. But we find that we must mean something different from this when we speak of the "nature" of the individual mind. Here the modes of the behavior of the subject of them all *appear* as progressively self-determining. The "nature" of the subject is not only expressed in every choice, but within certain limits it is dependent for its characteristics upon every choice. That this is so, many of the phenomena with which all our science of life is familiar tend to demonstrate. For they confirm those *naïve* convictions of freedom and responsibility in choice, to which reference has already been made. And if other phenomena tend to show that what we call the mind's nature, as already acquired, must be regarded as in part accounting for the character of each choice, this truth is not inconsistent with the spontaneity of freedom. Indeed, it may be claimed that the contrary of this would be incompatible with a true mental development. The spontaneity of mind actually arises and maintains itself as a living process of self-determining development. For that unexplained and inexplicable spontaneity which we call the "nature" of the mind is not, like the nature of the material elements, fixed and unchanging from the beginning to the end of its activity.

And now it may be claimed by the determinist, and objected by the advocate of free-will, that to ascribe the determination of the choice to the unexplained nature of the mind is a complete surrender of the freedom of the choice. For this "nature" of the mind is itself as truly determined by inheritance and environment as is the nature of the atoms. It can therefore be said to be unexplained, only on account of our ignorance of the causes which determine it. Individual choices, too, so far as unexplained by the direction and intensity of so-called motives, when referred to the nature of the person making them, would all be explained if only we perfectly knew the nature in which they originate.

We reply to this claim and to this objection that the very terms of its statement unwarrantably beg the whole question. For what do we mean by "nature," as applied to the mind, but its most uniform modes of behavior? And to say that these *are* from the beginning strictly determined by antecedent and accompanying influences, whether physical or psychical, is to assume to know that the nature of mental reality is incompatible with freedom of choice. The assumption is unwarrantable. For no such knowledge of the laws of heredity, and of the effect of surrounding influences, can be attained as makes it perfectly clear why minds develop as they do; that is, why each one attains a personal character, in a series of choices, no one choice of which can ever be said to be strictly predictable as determined by the pre-existing influences.

When then the determinist finds himself unable to account for the choice as determined by known influences, and therefore refers it to the pre-existing nature of the person choosing, as determined by this nature, and therefore not a free choice, he may be accused of extracting a real cause from a convenient figure of speech. Every man chooses as he does choose, not only because of reasons obvious to others, but also because it is his nature to. But how do we know it is his nature thus to choose; and what do we mean by his nature as determining his choice? Why, thus he has just chosen; and has similarly chosen often enough before. Yet always with the conviction, perhaps, that his choice was free and responsible.

There would seem then to be no positive argument for the freedom of human nature that, as it were, takes us behind the ultimate fact of choice, and the convictions attaching themselves thereto. That is to say, the freedom of the mind in choice cannot be explained. But the fact of such freedom does not appear incapable of finding a place in the world of real beings and of actual transactions, if once we take in earnest the legitimate conclusions of a philosophy of the mind. Choice is an indubitable fact of mind. Like every other form of the behavior of mind, it is conditioned upon, and correlated with, other transactions in a world of reality. Unlike every other form of the behavior of both things and minds, it has the peculiarity of appearing to the mind itself as its own free, self-directing activity. It is the special kind of spontaneity which claims for itself the convictions of moral freedom and of responsibility. Nor is there anything in the principle of causality, as legitimately applied to the mind, which constitutes a basis for denying the validity of this claim. On showing thus much, the philosophy of ethics must apparently cease from further attempts to explain.

On the other hand, to take the positions of determinism in earnest and maintain them with a perfect consistency ends nowhere else than in thorough-going materialism. Its case rests upon the postulate that all the psychical processes must be wholly "explained" on principles similar to those which prevail in physical science. Hence we are to take, not as conveniently vague and figurative, but as true to reality and scientifically exact, the current discourse about the "influence" of motives upon the will, about the choice being "determined" by the greatest apparent good, etc. A complete psychical dynamics — we are virtually told — *must* be true; although all human intercourse and estimates of a truly ethical sort assume that it *is* not true. Nor does such a science of psychical phenomena hesitate to help itself out by resort to metaphysics. Its metaphysics, however, makes light of the reality of the mind's continuous but constantly self-directing evolution; it lays emphasis rather on the "nature" and "energy" of physical masses and of atoms. In its most extreme and monstrous form it adopts the statement of M. Luys,[1] and affirms that all spontaneous effort of the mind is an illusion, for every object of attention or choice is forced on us by that cunning conjurer, the brain; because "the cell-territory where that object resides has been previously set vibrating in the brain." But in this form, determinism is as unintelligible in its metaphysics as it is wild in its psycho-physical hypotheses.

The second important philosophical problem, respecting the nature of man as ethical, is the constitution of so-called "Conscience." In the more vague meaning of this word it includes also all the springs, in sensibility, out of which conduct arises, and by which it is influenced. The problem therefore demands the analysis of moral human nature by psychological science. It is, however, when the inquiry concerns the existence and character in human consciousness of certain ideals of all conduct that the problem peculiar to philosophy begins to emerge.

It is scarcely necessary to enumerate the concessions which must be made to the opponents of all so-called "intuitional" systems of morals. Moral ideals are of course not inborn, in the sense that every one is conscious of them at birth. They unfold themselves, if they exist at all, into greater clearness as the result of a psychical development. Neither do they, any more than those categories which metaphysics recognizes, take such a shape as enables them to be envisaged, in full content of meaning and naked reality, by the self-conscious mind. They are rather found as implicated in those judgments which we call moral; and as needing to have their significance and value explicated by a process of reflective analysis. Moreover, it must be conceded (and to this fact reference will be made again) that the judgments which embody, as it were, the ideals are the products of evolution and the subjects of change, both in the individual and in the race.

What I think is right; and, therefore, What I think I ought to do; and, therefore, What I morally approbate in myself and

[1] The Brain and its Functions, p. 254.

in others, — all this is undoubtedly different in different cases, places, and times. To discover the reasons for the changes in the content of the judgments corresponding to these words is the business of ethical science, chiefly as studied from the evolutionary point of view. But to maintain this view is a very different thing from regarding the ethical ideals themselves as wholly explicable by the effects of intercourse, environment, and education. *That* I have the ideas of the right, of the ought, and of the morally well-deserving; that I attach to these ideas a peculiar value and significance; and that certain unique convictions accompany every self-conscious act of applying the ideas in concrete judgments, — all this is the problem with which philosophical ethics has to deal. In the treatment of this problem, like that of the problem offered by the categories to metaphysics, philosophy may begin by disregarding all the attempts of evolution to account for the primary facts.

The relations of the moral ideals, as dictating the form to all moral judgments, are as peculiar and mysterious in respect of their ultimate and unquestioned validity, as is the relation of the categories to the world of real psychical and physical beings. These relations are found implicated in the primary fact of actual moral judgments. And as thus implicated, they appear original, universal, and necessary, as do the categories themselves. Indeed, they may without great impropriety be called "moral categories," — ultimate and irresolvable norms of all distinctively ethical life. Of this character reflective analysis finds them actually possessed, whether historical and descriptive science can explain, or not, by what stages of evolution they came into this possession.

It is a primary fact of moral self-consciousness that some conduct is pronounced, or *judged* "right," and other conduct wrong. All beings known to have a moral nature actually do, in their judgments, thus discriminate two kinds of conduct to which these two mutually exclusive and contradictory predicates apply. Some men call that conduct right which others call wrong; and every man is liable, at different stages of his moral development, to changes of view as to precisely what conduct he shall call by either one of these two predicates. But no individual being, man or other animal, can be esteemed a subject of truly ethical experience who does not actually make the distinction. To make the distinction at all, whether in accordance with prevalent judgments or not, — this is, in part, what it is to be as all moral beings are. The Right is then one of the universal norms of all moral judgment. And that this idea is not reducible to lower or other terms, may be shown by the fullest appeal to the facts of experience. If by "the Right" we mean to designate any other standard of being or action than that uniquely ethical one (the *morally* right), then we mean something other and less than all men appear to mean, when they actually pronounce a distinctively moral judgment. Nor is it consistent with the facts of the most primary ethical experience to regard the opposite of the right, that which we call "wrong," as merely negative. By the wrong, men do not mean the merely *non*-right. The predicate wrong is, to be sure, the denial of the right; but it is this as a positive violation, and not an ethically indifferent negation, of the ethical ideal.

Universally and necessarily attached to the idea of the right, and like it implicated in the primary fact of moral judgment, is the idea of "the Ought," of the binding obligation upon choice of that which is deemed right. Whatever conduct is judged right, that is also, by virtue of the intrinsic nature of this judgment, also judged obligatory. In conduct, and in all actual existence and action as far as dependent upon conduct, that *ought* to be which is right. To esteem certain conduct right for me, is inevitably to induce the judgment: I ought to choose this conduct. On the other hand, that which is wrong in conduct, or in reality as dependent on conduct, *ought not* to be. And as for me, what I judge wrong for me, I ought not to choose to do. We are unable even to imagine the possibility of the morally right not being morally binding; or of anything but the right being morally binding. Although, then, the idea of the ought is original in the sense that it cannot be derived from any other idea, it has a certain dependence upon the idea of the right. Something similar to this we have already seen as respects the correlation, but not identity, of the categories of substantiality, causality, change, etc.

Universally and necessarily attached to the idea of the right as that which ought to be in conduct, and to the idea of the wrong as that which ought not to be, is the idea of Moral Desert. This idea also is implicated in those judgments which constitute our primary ethical experience. On contemplation of that conduct which is right and therefore ought to be, ethical reason pronounces a judgment of approbation. Such conduct (or rather conduct so regarded) is necessarily approbated. On contemplation of that conduct which is wrong, and ought therefore not to be, a judgment of disapprobation is necessarily pronounced. Such conduct is necessarily disapproved.

Judgments which pronounce moral obligation and moral desert are accompanied by a peculiar tone of feeling. The judgments, "he ought," or "I ought," cannot be made with clearness of ideation and indifference of feeling, at the same time. Here knowledge is necessarily penetrated with some warmth of emotion; and if the element of feeling be totally wanting, the judgment lacks something characteristic of all ethical judgment. In token of this fact we may instance the use of the word "feeling" as applied to the same complex psychical process which is also called a judgment. Indeed, men say "I *feel* that I ought," rather than "I judge that I ought;" and moral approbation or disapprobation is habitually expressed in terms that apply only to emotion. It is even customary to say "I *feel* this or that to be right;" thus bearing witness to the peculiar connection of the two judgments, "It is right for me," and "I ought to do what is right," with the feeling characteristically accompanying the latter form of judgment.

The title "intuitive" — when properly explained — may then be applied to the three ideas of the Right, the Ought, and the morally Well-deserving, and to their three correlate and contradictory ideas. They signify norms of the moral life, implicated in the most primary judgments of every being that has arrived at moral self-consciousness. To put forth judgments conformable to these norms is actually to be a self-conscious ethical mind. But in saying this we afford only a partial solution of the problem of moral self-consciousness. Inquiry must further be made concerning the genesis and character of the concrete judgments themselves. For these moral ideas are never, as such, intuitively known or envisaged, as it were, in immediate self-consciousness. On the contrary, no being and no conduct known by sense-perception or self-consciousness present the picture of a satisfactory actualization of these ideas. For that reason, in part, they have been spoken of as "Ideals" of moral reason. But judgments called moral are actual occurrences in the psychical life of moral beings. Can they also be pronounced "intuitive," in any defensible sense of the word?

In answer to this last question philosophical ethics must defer to the results of psychological and historical research. And in such research the theory of the evolution of moral judgment is entitled to have its voice heard. In fact, most adults — that is to say, moral beings who have become more or less trained experts, as it were, in moral judgment — do actually pronounce, according to what appears to be an unreasoned *dictum* of conscience, some conduct right and other conduct wrong. But in fact also, all persons, even the most expert in moral judgment, often hesitate as to which of these two predicates they shall apply to a given form of conduct. And that the greatest variety of equally honest and intelligent opinions prevails as to the rightness or wrongness of many ethical transactions, is too obvious to need argument. The more careful student one becomes of the psychical facts, the more will one hesitate to say that any of these forms of moral judgment do not result from a development. Indeed, the doubt is warranted whether the word "intuitive" can, in strictness, be applied to the pronouncements of conscience even regarding those dispositions of the mind which all theories of ethics hold to be of the highest and most essential ethical significance. That untrained childish conscience necessarily judges it right to choose to tell the truth, to do justice, and to love one's fellow, no acute observer will find it easy to believe. Indeed, every acute observer will find large multitudes of his fellow-adults choosing, almost habitually, to do none of these things; and yet, apparently with a large measure of "good conscience" so-called, approbating their choices as morally right and obligatory. Who does not know that the vices of lying, injustice, and hatred, as habitual dispositions of mind, are quite too often covered up by the title of a virtuous fidelity to some ecclesiastical, political, or commercial concern?

When the discoveries of ethnic and evolutionary and comparative psychology are brought to bear upon this problem, the intuitional character of the decisions of conscience becomes more difficult to maintain. To lie, particularly if one lies to a stranger or to a foe, and to cheat, particularly if it is largely and successfully accomplished, has undoubtedly been "right" in the sight of multitudes of men in all times. And was it not written by them of old time: "Thou shalt love thy neighbor and hate thy enemy"? Must it not then be admitted that facts are conclusive against the claim which makes intuitive any of the moral judgments that concern particular forms of conduct? Are not even those forms of moral disposition, which (like the disposition to veracity, to justice, and to benevolence) are most indispensable to a rightly constituted moral system, the result of a process of development, in the individual and in the race?

Notwithstanding the facts to which an evolutionary theory of ethics successfully appeals, a certain relatively intuitional character for the judgments of conscience may still be maintained. We have already seen that the hypothetical judgment, "If this is right in conduct, then it ought to be done," is indeed absolute and unconditional. Such a judgment states the unalterable and intuitively discerned relation of the moral ideals. A certain relatively intuitional character for the concrete judgments pronounced under these ideas may also be maintained as a result of those æsthetical and ethical forces and laws which have control of human development. Undoubtedly, the entire constitution of government and society among the civilized peoples of to-day embodies and enforces the current forms of ethical judgment. Ethical progress tends away from special rights and duties toward those which are recognized as universal and necessary. Into this ethical constitution every individual is born, as a member of it. In it and by it he is trained from the very beginning to the end of life. All the experience of the individual impresses upon him the judgment that certain forms of conduct are right, and therefore obligatory, and that certain others are wrong, and therefore forbidden. This general training from the larger constitution of the society in which the individual lives is made more special, concrete, and effective by his immediate education and surroundings. Under the principles of heredity and influence from environment every member of society will, therefore, be predisposed to certain forms of moral judgment and feeling. So strongly will these influences operate that the forms of judgment and disposition they tend to promote will have their paths greatly smoothed for them. In some cases they will operate so strongly as to create from the very dawn of moral experience a special tendency and a tact to judge, and to judge fitly, between the right and the wrong in choice and action. In other cases the birth of power to pronounce and to feel the right and the wrong of even those things upon which the ethics of advanced and Christian civilization is clearest, will be long delayed. In the centres of our civilization at the present hour there are "consciences" that do not judge it wrong to lie, to steal, and to hate.

It might be expected that the time and occasion of arrival at the stage of a "relative" intuition would be different for the different formulas of moral judgment. As a matter of fact this is so. It is also a most interesting truth that, in the ethical development of the individual, and particularly of the race, the first not infrequently becomes the last, and the last first. To love one's neighbor, and especially one's enemy, is the last of the virtues to be deemed indispensable, in places and among peoples of a low condition of moral culture. But in these days, among Christian nations, there are many who still doubt whether it is wrong sometimes to be a coward and sometimes to lie, who would not for a moment admit that one may ever with good conscience hate liars and cowards.

From the point of view now gained we will return to the problem of the moral Ideals. Historical and descriptive science, under the well-known formulas of evolution, aims at telling us how and why men have come to judge and feel thus and so respecting what is right or wrong in disposition and in conduct. The success of science has been only partial. The phenomena to which it points, and the generalizations which it bases upon the phenomena, are sufficient to show, however, that the ethical judgments and feelings of mankind are, in general, subject to development. But here, as in other cases of evolution, science discerns certain tendencies toward fixity of form which reveal the norm followed, and the significance of the process. That the so-called altruistic virtues are to be seen, slowly and by tortuous paths, yet surely, climbing into ascendency, we can scarcely doubt. The supreme principle of love as the fulfilling of the law is plainly destined to be in the future, as it has been in the past, more and more clearly recognized. Yet the virtuous essence of certain right forms of conduct toward self — the so-called "egoistic virtues" — cannot readily be reduced to a common statement with that of the altruistic virtues. The conflict between the considerations urged by ancient Stoicism and those urged by Epicureanism, on the one hand, and by the self-abnegatory side (for it is only one side, albeit the principal side) of Christian Ethics, on the other, cannot be settled by an off-hand formularizing. Even the supremacy of the principle of benevolence is a truth up to which the reason and conscience of the most moral have only partially developed. Nor is it likely that cases of conflict between the disposition to benevolence and the demand to do justice or to speak the truth will ever cease sometimes to perplex the man of a truly *right* mind. These and all other generalizations as to particular duties and obligations, as well as the acceptance by conscience of the supremacy of the principle of love, and the power to apply this principle, are subjects of ethical development. It is for this reason, in part, that the term "Ideals" of moral Reason fitly applies to the moral categories.

The historical and descriptive science of ethics is not competent to explain the existence or the nature of the moral Ideals themselves, by the hypotheses of evolution. To narrate by what stages, and under what changes in environment, mankind have come to judge thus and so concerning *what they ought*, is not the same thing as philosophically to explain the genesis, with its peculiar nature, of the idea of mankind *that they ought* always and unconditionally to do only what is right. The fullest description of the molecular motions which are the antecedents of states of sensation, would not of itself account for the existence and peculiar nature of these psychical states. The most complete story of the arising and combining of sensations and sensation-complexes would not account for the objectivity, for the metaphysical postulate of the reality, which "Things" have. The consonance and dissonance of mere ideas, even if we could approve all the Herbartian mathematics as correctly formulating these psychical processes, would not render intelligible the first self-conscious sensibility of the soul. So the perfectly unique and absolutely incomparable nature of the ideas expressed in the sentence, "This is right for me, and therefore I ought to choose it," is made only more apparent by all the futile attempts at explanation put forth by evolutionary science. Whenever the first self-conscious being — no matter what ape or other animal — had the experience of a single judgment expressible in terms of these ideas, then ethical experience was born upon the earth. Nor can its ancestry be described in terms of other than ethical conceptions and feelings.

The idea of the right as that which ought to be, hovers before the minds of men, an indefinite but grand and absolutely worthy ideal. After it they grope blindly, or reach out with a somewhat intelligent vision. It is ever near at hand, but only in the shape of some judgment pronounced with a more or less definite certainty of conviction that it faithfully corresponds to the ideal. This idea is the guiding star of humanity; but it does not remain subject to telescopic measurements in a fixed position before the eye of conscience. It exists in some souls as a vague stirring of intelligence and conviction respecting the rules of conduct. In some it becomes a burning passion. The heads and hearts of men are bowed before it, though its manifestation is in forms changeful and hard to define. The experience of the entire race — and of the ethically noblest, most clearly — seems to affirm: "However much we strive, and learn, and pray, we only dimly know what is the right; but our faith never wavers that, whatever it is, it and it alone ought, in disposition and conduct, really to be."

In conjunction with the problems just presented, two others require treatment. One of these concerns the content of that which is entitled to be called right. The other problem may be proposed in the question: Why ought the right to be chosen in preference to the wrong? The principal points of philosophical ethics thus evoked can be best discussed by substituting for the term right another term of the same meaning. That which we call right is the same as the "morally Good." To say that a certain disposition or kind of conduct is right, is equivalent to saying that it is morally good. The latter term suggests a view which, in our opinion, it is impossible for any scientific research or philosophical analysis to overthrow. "The Right" is a species or kind of "the Good;" but it is a unique species, for we must at once qualify the general term "good" by an adjective. It is, therefore, not every form of the good which can be identified with the right. But when we say the right is the *morally* good, we are only affirming in another way: The right is such a good as it is; it is a unique and incomparable kind of good.

Two distinct classes of opinions — schools in ethical philosophy — emerge through the attempt to solve the problems just propounded. One of these replies to the question, What is the peculiar content of all that which is to be called right? by regarding the morally good as good only for an end lying outside of itself. The other regards the morally good as absolute good, — good as supreme end in itself. Almost inevitably the first of these answers results in a eudæmonistic system of ethics. For happiness is the only conceivable end which morally right disposition and conduct can serve, if the moral rightness of disposition and conduct be not itself the end.

It is difficult, if not impossible, for us to regard the attainment of mere truth as in itself constituting a supreme end of conduct. Accordingly, we do not find systems of ethics based on the reasonableness of the maxim: Act so that knowledge of what is true may abound, as the ultimate end of conduct. Such a maxim would neither guide the moral judgment, nor satisfy the moral sentiments, nor express the content of the morally good. Neither is it possible to give to the æsthetical ideal, to "the Beautiful," the place of an ultimate end, to serve which the morally good is but a means. Happiness is then the only good which can be a rival of the morally good for the position of the supreme end. The discussion of this problem in ethics has thus necessarily to be carried on between the advocates and the opponents of some eudæmonistic scheme.

The student of mind who approaches either ancient or current ethical controversies with the greatest possible freedom from prejudice must be prepared for many sad departures from psychological truth and from the results of cautious reflective analysis. On the one hand, he will listen to arguments for the supremacy of the morally Good, as an end of all conduct, that seem to assume the possibility of moral being and moral action devoid of necessary connection with any other form of good. Doing right is thus essentially resolved into a dreary and monotonous activity of so-called will, in blind obedience to so-called conscience, — and this without regard for consequences affecting the happiness of one's self or of other sensitive beings. But a being incapable of any form of happiness, and existing out of all relation to other beings capable of happiness, could not be a moral being at all. Action that has no effect upon sensitive being, and that tends to produce no results in modifying some conscious life, is not conduct at all. The sphere of the morally Good cannot be described as lying outside of the sphere of that well-being which consists in states of sentient souls. This is rather the sphere of the non-moral.

On the other hand, the arguments for Eudæmonism have almost habitually been guilty of gross breaches of plain psychological truths. This charge certainly holds good against them so often as they follow the example of their great antagonist Kant, in maintaining that all happiness is qualitatively equivalent, and that different happinesses are to be only quantitatively estimated, as more or less.

The inquiry, What is the content of that which is right? or, What are the essential marks of the morally good? requires a two-fold consideration. We may understand the inquiry to mean, What is that disposition of mind which is right? or,

What are the tendency and significance of those forms of conduct which men call right? The answer to both of these questions involves an immediate appeal to experience, — but to experience as explicated by the process of reflective analysis.

The morally right disposition of mind is the subjective moral Good; from the point of view of conscience, it is not only the supreme good, but it is the only distinctively *moral* good. In the experience of every man this disposition is that which his own conscience approves; it is the disposition, namely, to choose and approve what is pronounced right in his moral judgment. But the moral judgment of men has been seen greatly to vary, to be the subject of a process of development in the individual and in the race. Therefore, the disposition which different men call right is different in different cases and stages and times of ethical development. But never can it be said that conscience is in any case, stage, or time indifferent as to the character of that disposition which it pronounces morally good. On the contrary, there is always required of the "good disposition" a certain direction toward ideal forms of conduct, and a sufficient intensity and persistence to overcome tendencies adverse to such conduct. Judging the real character of this morally good disposition by those norms which the morally best persons have come to recognize as of universal value and obligation, we may say that this disposition is one of affectionate fidelity toward veracity, justice, benevolence, etc. In this way we fix to some extent, although rather indefinitely, the characteristics common to every disposition of mind which can be pronounced morally good.

But truth, justice, benevolence, and every other commonly recognized form of virtuous disposition and conduct, in an ethical community of sentient and rational minds, are necessarily to be regarded as promotive of the well-being of this community. This regard is indeed only partially justified by any estimates or inductions made upon a basis of actual facts. It is in part a moral sentiment; in part, at least with many men, it is a rational or a religious faith. But however the result comes about, the morally good disposition, and the conduct which springs from it, are regarded as promotive of the highest well-being of those in any way affected by such disposition and conduct. May we then say that the essential characteristic of the good disposition (the "good will") is that it is the disposition to promote the highest well-being of all beings affected by it?

Should such a general proposition as the foregoing be adopted, even in a provisional way, it might at once be seized upon by both parties to the conflict. Eudæmonistic ethics identifies the highest "well-being" with happiness. It could then claim that the foregoing statement necessarily admits of no interpretation but the one which makes happiness the ultimate end, and virtuous disposition and conduct good as means toward this end. On the other hand, the opponents of eudæmonistic ethics could try to show that "the disposition to promote the well-being" of others *is* benevolence; and that by making this disposition the essence of subjective moral good we may reduce to its ultimate terms the description of the supreme end of morality. They could also point out with invincible conclusiveness that by identifying unqualifiedly the Good, as happiness, with the end sought by conscientious conduct, we rob the ideas of the Right and the Ought of their peculiar significance. For not all that is good is also right; and it is not every form of good which I ought to seek for myself or for others. The right — they could reiterate — is the *morally* good.

The effort more definitely to fix the characteristics of that disposition which is morally right leads to the discovery of certain perplexing relations between happiness and morality, — respecting one's disposition toward one's self and toward others. The propositions, "I ought to promote my own highest well-being," and, "The disposition to do this is right," would undoubtedly be accepted, if properly qualified, by the most thoughtful moralists. But the proposition, "I ought to promote my own happiness as the only conceivable form of my highest well-being," would undoubtedly be rejected as contrary to sound moral principle. So would also the proposition, "I ought to promote my own happiness irrespective of the well-being of others." On the other hand, the disposition to sacrifice my personal happiness to my own higher well-being and to the well-being of others is not simply admissible as a morally good disposition; it is even demanded as essential to such a disposition. But the disposition to sacrifice the happiness of others to my own well-being, in whatever form, would (although not plainly immoral) be suspected of immorality. The disposition to sacrifice my own happiness except to the end of promoting my own highest well-being, or the well-being (including the happiness) of others, would also be condemned at the bar of enlightened conscience.

In regard to myself, and as well in regard to others, I am obliged to recognize different kinds of happiness attaching themselves as psychical states to different forms of psychical life. Here, too, conscience makes distinctions that, however they may have been arrived at through an ethical development, are now universally recognized by good men as valid and obligatory. The happiness which belongs to the morally good disposition appears to moral judgment and moral sensibility as having a peerless value. It belongs to the morally good disposition to seek and to approbate this happiness. Yet it cannot be said that the essential characteristic of this disposition is the desire to promote even this kind of happiness as such. Above all, the priceless value, the unconditioned worth, of the morally good disposition itself is taken for granted in all moral judgment. From the point of view of conscience, this disposition is the supreme thing in the well-being of all minds.

It would appear, then, that the essential characteristics of the morally good disposition are by no means so few and simple as is often supposed. On the contrary, ethical life is extremely complex and profound. Its foundations implicate, and its end involves, all that enters into the wealth of being attained by a measureless development. If we say that to be good is to have the disposition to promote one's own highest well-being and the highest well-being of others, we do not thus simplify the interpretation of ethical experience as our experience with masses of matter is simplified by the statement of the law of gravitation. For we are immediately obliged to recognize different kinds of well-being, or of "the Good" in general. We have also to note that, measured by its own standard, each of these kinds may be said to be supreme. Yet we cannot in our conceptions follow one of these kinds of the Good without introducing considerations from the others. We cannot divorce the morally good from all other good, and still conceive of it as *good.* But on the other hand, we cannot reduce the morally good to terms of that general good which the Utilitarian chooses to designate as happiness. In this connection, there are few more impressive passages in controversial literature than that in which John Stuart Mill declares his opposition to Mansel's fast-and-loose method in dealing with ethical conceptions. "I will call no being good," says this great advocate of eudæmonistic ethics, "who is not what I mean when I apply that epithet to my fellow-creatures; and if such a being can sentence me to hell for not so calling him, to hell I will go." What an invincible and noble confidence must that be in the supremacy and unconditioned value of the good disposition — even in the very limited form of a disposition to veracity — which could evoke such honest and manly words as these!

In brief, there is evidence in the very nature of the morally good disposition that it is not the following of a fixed formula which constitutes the essence of subjective morality. It is rather the reaching of the soul, always more or less blindly, out after an ideal. The definition of this ideal as it realizes itself in a disposition of mind is made more and more clearly, as moral reason gathers into itself the ripened fruits of all past experience. The good disposition is spiritual life, constantly organizing itself into higher and more intelligible forms of expression. It points for its ultimate and supreme realization to a perfected and systematic ordering of all sentient beings in relations that admit of a union of all forms of that which is good.

The second form of the inquiry, What is the content of that which is entitled to be called the morally good? has already been virtually answered. It was stated (see p. 317) in the following words: What are the tendency and significance of those forms of conduct which men call right? It is in the attempt to answer this question that Utilitarianism deems itself most successful. Its reply is in substance a brief one: Those forms of conduct are right which tend to produce happiness. In the effort to justify this reply it has been obliged greatly to expand and to modify its original claims. This fact does not, of itself, discredit its scientific authority; for such work of expansion and modification belongs to the very nature of advance in all scientific knowledge. Eudæmonistic ethics must be refuted, if refuted at all, in the most subtle and comprehensive of its manifestations.

It must be admitted that there are kinds, as well as amounts of happiness, to be distinguished. It must be admitted that moral conduct which has nothing to do with the happiness of any sentient being is inconceivable. It must be admitted that the morality of many courses of conduct is determined by their relation to the problem of increasing the happiness, or diminishing the misery, of mankind. But after all has been admitted, the analysis of Utilitarianism is not complete; its claims to take into account all the phenomena of an ethical order are unjustifiable.

It is impossible to go further, then, in describing the marks of all right conduct, than to say: It is conduct conformable to the highest attainable conception of the ethical ideals. This is, of course, not a definition of right conduct, if by "definition" we mean the reduction of the adjective "right" to some simpler and more comprehensible term. It is a description, however, of the character of that norm, as it were, to which all conduct must conform in order to be entitled to be called *right*. An ideal condition of society has been found to be the vague but lofty end — a condition which shall realize, in their highest terms, all the forms of the Good — to which the morally good disposition points. Of this ideal condition, the morally good disposition is not only a means, but the prime constituent. It is *the* condition recognized by conscience as the worthy supreme end. And so all conduct which tends toward the realization of this ideal is to be called right. Whatever conduct becomes known to reason as necessarily tending toward this end is absolutely right, as conduct. But, so far as we distinguish conduct from disposition, deeds from character, the rightness of the former is always the rightness of means to an end.

If utilitarian or evolutionary ethical science cannot solve satisfactorily the problems already brought before it by moral philosophy, it certainly cannot be expected to furnish an answer to those still remaining. Why does the judgment of obligation, with feeling of conviction, follow the judgment defining the right? Why *ought* one to do the right, whenever one knows what it is right to do? To this inquiry no answer is possible which does not consist in virtually reaffirming the same essential relation in which moral reason necessarily places the ethical ideals. This connection of the Right and the Ought is not one which can even be conceived of as the result of a process of development. As to what is right, I need to learn. Indeed, on this point I must be ever learning. But that what is right in disposition and conduct is obligatory, — to be persuaded of this, it is only necessary to be a moral being. And the whole essence of morality is gone as soon as a separation appears thinkable between the right and the ought. Indeed, it may be said that no relation between the categories with which metaphysics deals is more immediate and peremptory for the human reason than that existing between these ethical categories.

The philosophy of ethics, finally, combines with the philosophy of nature and the philosophy of mind to prepare material for that supreme synthesis which the philosophy of religion seeks to accomplish. What, it inquires, is the relation of these ethical ideals to the world of reality? In calling them "Ideals," and in discussing them as such, we have already in part defined their relation to the real being of the mind. But is the being of things an ethical constitution? Is the evolution of physical reality susceptible of being judged by ethical standards? And especially with reference to history, which implies such large reciprocal influence of mind and external nature, what meaning can we attach to the attempt to discover in it moral forces and moral laws?

That there are certain tokens of a "power not ourselves" which "makes for righteousness," to be found in external nature and in man, especially when the evolution of man in history is regarded with a due emphasis, we think it possible to maintain. But the few remarks upon the existence and interpretation of these tokens which it is permitted to make must be reserved for another chapter.

CHAPTER XII.

ÆSTHETICS.

IT will add to the effectiveness of the very brief treatment which this department of philosophy can receive, if we compare its subject-matter with that already treated under the head of Ethics. The problems which arise in considering the Ideal called "the Beautiful" are similar to those which arise in considering the ethical ideals. The distinctions involved in the answers to these problems illustrate both the likeness and the unlikeness of the two classes of ideals. The Beautiful is one form of the Good; to be and to enjoy that which is beautiful is to share in the reality of the Good. But, in spite of the close alliance which philosophical thinking establishes between this form of well-being and the morally good,—both by direct comparison and by considering the relations in which the two stand to happiness,—no identification of them is possible.

The relation of the ideal of beauty to the different so-called faculties of the soul and to the psychical states ascribed to these faculties may be compared with that of the ethical ideals. In this way a philosophical theory of the content of the subjectively beautiful may base itself upon the science of psychology. The apprehension and appreciation of the beautiful is inseparable from pleasurable states of sensuous and ideating "intuition." Nothing can be regarded as beautiful—the ideal of beauty can never be realized—except as it is concretely presented to the senses or to the imagination, in pictorial form, for contemplation; and unless on being contemplated, it produces that characteristic form of happiness which we may call æsthetical, within the contemplative mind. The beautiful *must be* actually agreeable, whether its entire essence be held to consist in being agreeable, or not. If we speak of the beautiful as an idea, or an ideal, we must admit the correctness (though not necessarily the completeness) of Hegel's definition of beauty, — "The sensible manifestation of the idea." Whereas, then, the intuitive standard for testing the morally good is by no means the immediate power of giving pleasure belonging to that to which the test is applied, the intuition of beauty can arise in no other way than through the experience of the effect of such power. That which is intuitively discerned or otherwise known as right produces, on contemplating it, a peculiar satisfaction called moral. That is beautiful which, on being intuited, produces a peculiar satisfaction called *æsthetical.*

The immediate connection, in every concrete experience, of the agreeable activity of senses and imagination with the intuition of the beautiful is of great influence upon the principles of all art. It is the aim of art to produce the peculiar pleasure which belongs to the appreciation of beauty. Varying standards of excellence there are in æsthetics as well as in ethics. The principles of true art are tested by an appeal to those natures that carry within themselves the highest standards of judgment. But the appeal made by the beautiful object to those choicest and most artistically cultivated souls seeks to evoke in them, also, a state of pleasurable appreciation. And nothing can, by any stretch of courtesy, be called "beautiful" which does not only aim at, but also succeed in attaining, the production of this state.

In architecture, for example, the main lines which limit the form of the whole, or manifest the related arrangement of the parts, must be capable of being traversed by the eye with pleasurable ease; otherwise they violate the principles of beautiful construction. No part of the structure must be so visibly lacking in support as to evoke the distressing imagination that it may fall. The porch must not be so large as to compel the beholder, from the point of view he is expected to take, to make the difficult effort to fill out the picture of the building it conceals. Colors must not violate the laws of relation recognized by physiological optics; ornamentation must not be suggestive of low and disagreeable associations, so that it can be called "vulgar" and "loud," or of equally disagreeable over-refinement, so that it must be called "finical." Curved lines and straight lines must not be brought into such relations as that the former will distort or disorder the latter, and produce in us a sympathetic pain; etc. All the arts in the same manner, not even excluding poetry, with its relation to the art of music, are compelled to observe similar principles, dependent upon the pleasurable or painful activity of senses and sensuous imagination.

In judging of the beauty of natural objects we find the same direct reference to a standard which measures their power to produce, in the very act of being intuitively contemplated, the æsthetical pleasure. Nor can we except those natural objects and phenomena which, by reason of their awful vastness or their threatening of human interests, fill the beholder with the vague but sweet pain that is characteristic of our appreciation for much that we call grand and sublime. This inseparable relation of the beautiful to the immediate production of a peculiar pleasure in the sensitive soul is implied in the most primary facts of experience. In an indefinite and preliminary way we therefore define "the beautiful" as that which produces in us a peculiar kind of pleasurable feeling. The peculiarity of the pleasurable feeling produced by beautiful objects cannot be defined, but must be known as felt. Nor is this description any more indefinite than that we are obliged to give in speaking of any form of feeling. Those objects are called beautiful which excite this peculiar pleasurable feeling. The pleasurable feeling of beauty is that which arises in connection with the intuition of such objects as we call beautiful. This circle in definition corresponds to the movement of the mind.

But experience enters a protest if we try so to interpret the facts as throughout to identify the agreeable and the beautiful. Nothing, indeed, can be called beautiful which is not, in so far as it is beautiful, æsthetically agreeable. Moreover, the judgments of men differ as to what should be called beautiful even more than they differ concerning the morally good and the sensuously pleasant. But of the beautiful — like the morally good and unlike the agreeable — we affirm a universal and objective value and validity. The agreeable is a state of, or an event in, some sentient mind. Its objective correlate consists in nothing but a certain peculiar arrangement and mode of change of material molecules, both within and without the nervous organism of the sentient being which has the agreeable feeling. This fact is a matter of scientific knowledge, rather than of ideal significance.

The beautiful is distinguished from the agreeable by the possession of two characteristics in which the latter is deficient. These are objective validity, and ideal worth. By use of these terms we designate, in a preliminary way, the most marked differences between the beautiful and the agreeable. That differences corresponding in some sort to these terms do exist, we may confidently appeal to experience to show. We know that, strictly speaking, the agreeable exists only as a state in us. We believe that the beautiful really exists, in nature, in art, in spiritual character and life. Scientific knowledge asserts that the objective correlate or cause of the agreeable feeling in us is not necessarily something agreeable in that which is other than ourselves. On the contrary, æsthetic faith affirms that the objective correlate of the peculiar pleasurable feeling with which we greet the apprehension of the beautiful is itself beautiful.

Moreover, the conviction is invincible that the beautiful has, in some sort, a right to be; and also that it ought to be appreciated. The proof for such statements as these is abundant. The way in which the old-time saying, *De gustibus non dis-*

putandum, must be understood if the interpretation is true to the dictates of æsthetical reason, is in proof here. When, for example, one contends with one's friend that he ought to like olives, or ought not to like onions, the seriousness of one's contention is the measure of one's departure from a truly rational procedure. But it requires a stretch of charity that seems to carry it beyond reason for one not to feel that the failure in one's friend to recognize and admire the beauties of nature or of the choicest art witnesses to a defect in his rational constitution. To differ about the merely agreeable can end only in stating the fact of difference; and, perhaps, the causes (æsthetically indifferent) in the constitution and habits of the organism that explain the fact. But dispute about the beauty of this or that object, implies an appeal to reasons that have an objective and universal application and value.

It must be admitted, however, that it is difficult, if not impossible, to draw a fixed line of separation between the agreeable and the beautiful. This difficulty is partially due to the fact that human nature is so thoroughly æsthetical. Indeed, the suffusing of all pleasures of sense and imagination with the distinctions and estimates of æsthetical reason, must be regarded as a chief characteristic of human nature. It is more than doubtful whether the idea of beauty, and the peculiar and pleasurable approbation which the intuition of the beautiful evokes, belong to any of the lower animals. The phenomena to which evolution points in justifying its use of this principle of natural selection prove either too much or nothing at all. They prove — if anything regarding the characteristic idea of, and feeling for, the beautiful — that relatively brainless birds or even insects have a far higher æsthetical development than belongs to the more cultivated classes of the human species. It is probably, then, the agreeable, and not the beautiful at all, which influences the life of the lower animals. But in man's case, regard for the beautiful may become so predominating an influence as to suffuse all the life of appetite and sense. Hence the indulgence of any of the forms of gratifying human appetites or desires may come to have an æsthetical significance and worth. Man is capable of "eating" rather than "feeding;" of lifting the intercourse of the sexes above the level of a bestial pleasure; of substituting for the animal's instinctive washing and plucking, or licking, of hairs or feathers, that careful self-adornment which approaches the "beauty of holiness."

Moreover, it should never be forgotten that pleasurable feeling itself may become an object of æsthetical appreciation. The song of birds and the hum of insects are not beautiful simply, or chiefly, because as sounds they follow the laws of musical art, and produce in the hearer an appreciation of their æsthetical quality as sounds. They are rather beautiful because they lead the imagination at once to depict the joyous psychical life which calls them forth. These states of pleasure themselves, imagined to be so innocent and free from care and blame, are the beautiful objects. The laughter and carols of children are beautiful for the same reason. Undoubtedly a large part of our appreciation of the beauty of events in nature is due to a similar activity of the imagination. Even our own pleasures of gratified appetite and desire we, on reflection, esteem very differently, if they have been, in the having of them, touched with true æsthetical qualities. Especially true is this of the happiness which actually goes with the morally good disposition and its right choice of fitting forms of conduct. This form of pleasure (ethical approbation) in ourselves or in others, is itself an object of æsthetical appreciation. Morally right states of soul, whether contemplated as actual or only possible, appear beautiful. To æsthetical reason the agreeable, as a condition of the subject of psychical states, may appear as also beautiful.

The relation in which the ideal of beauty stands to the concrete æsthetical judgments of men may also be compared with the relation of the moral ideas to ethical judgments. As to what is beautiful, and as to whether any particular claimant for the name "beautiful" is entitled to receive it or not, there is a well known divergence of current opinions. Probably the uncertain character of æsthetical standards is far greater than that which prevails in the sphere of morals. For this two principal reasons are to be assigned; the two are, however, connected in the evolution of the human race. The influence of unreasoned feeling — of feeling, indeed, for which it is difficult or impossible to assign any reasons — is much greater in determining the standards of æsthetical than of ethical judgment. The majority of men are indeed unable to assign sound reasons for their judgments respecting much which they pronounce right or wrong in morals. Even experts in the application of that one standard, "the tendency to promote happiness," which Utilitarianism proposes, more frequently than otherwise fail strictly to justify all the general rules they propose for the control of conduct. Yet on the whole rules of conduct in ethical matters are far less dependent upon unreasoning feeling for their justification than are rules for judging the beautiful in nature or in art. For, in the next place, the important practical interests of men may be said to have compelled a more forward stage of the race in the formulating of general moral judgments. That the unwarranted use of another's signature, or the cruel abuse of his person, or the slanderous mention of his name, should be promptly and uniformly judged to be wrong, may be said to be a necessary of human social development. That certain combinations of colors and lines should be in like manner condemned as ugly, may be said to belong rather to the luxuries of the race's development.

Indeed, the relation of judgment and feeling in the contemplation of beauty is such as to prevent an early maturity of the former, whether on the part of the individual or of the race. We feel that to be obligatory which we judge to be right. We judge that to be beautiful which evokes a certain feeling in us when we contemplate it. The education of judgment in matters of æsthetics can neither begin nor proceed through the communication of rules for correct judgment. You may tell me that this or that object *is* beautiful, and assure me that I ought to know and feel it to be beautiful; but if I assent, and say, "It is indeed beautiful," when as yet the object has aroused in me no pleasurable appreciation of its æsthetical qualities, I mean nothing of which æsthetics takes account. I mean something different from, and far less than, what you wish me to say. The only recognized right standard of judgment in matters of æsthetics is, therefore, the pleasurable feeling of appreciation in those who have most cultivated this feeling.

Accordingly, we scarcely hesitate to say that the same object, whether in nature or in art, may fitly be pronounced beautiful or not beautiful according as it does, or does not, arouse æsthetical feeling in those who behold it from different points of view. Such an admission of the indeterminate character of beauty cannot be brought under the same category with the uncertainties which belong to the judgments of different persons respecting some particular form of disposition or of conduct. If a careless, false, or malign disposition, or some form of conduct proceeding from such disposition, is judged right by any one, we do not admit that the judgment may possibly be a correct judgment. We do not for a moment think of conceding that to him who judges such disposition and its forth-putting right, and finds complacency in it; to him it is right. To the pathologist, from his professional point of view, we can yield the right to call "beautiful" a preparation of cancerous tissue, or of an organ filled with destructive microbes. But to the surgeon who indulges the morally wrong disposition, and thereby determines his acts in possessing himself of this beautiful object, we make no similar concessions. This distinction, which is clearly enough made in practice, is doubtless largely due to difference in stages in development. It may be possible for philosophical analysis to formulate rules, defensible on grounds of æsthetical reason, for the determination of our appreciation of the beautiful. But apparently it is also true that the rational relation of æsthetical feeling to the judgment regarding what is beautiful is such as to make the latter always dependent upon the former.

The relation of the ideal of æsthetics to disposition and to choice is also of interest to the student of this branch of philosophy. The ethical ideal makes a demand for action upon the practical reason of man. Each one realizes it in himself as best he may by shaping after it his own character and conduct. In respect of this ideal every one is summoned to artistic endeavor. Something of the same thing is indeed true with respect also to the æsthetical ideal. For character and conduct that are conformed to the ideal of the morally good are entitled to the regard of the beholder as examples also of the ideal of beauty. To strive in this manner of artistic endeavor is therefore, indirectly, a matter of moral obligation for every man. Nor can the student of life fail to notice the fact that the shame at being found ugly, in person as well as behavior, is closely akin to a moral feeling. The striving to be, and to produce, that which is beautiful may be said, therefore, to appeal to our voluntary powers on both ethical and æsthetical grounds. Every realization of the ideal of beauty, whether in the form of the pleasurable appreciation of what is beautiful in nature, art, and spiritual experience, or in the form of that which seems plainly fitted to produce such appreciation, is in itself an obvious increase of the well-being of things and of minds. So sure are we of this that we say of the beautiful, as of the morally good, it *ought* in reality to be, and it *ought* to be admired and sought by all rational beings. We feel also a certain sense of being wronged, or of disgust that is closely allied to moral disapprobation, when we contemplate anything which appears ugly and is at the same time regarded as remediable by human conduct. Indeed, we feel competent to pass judgment on Nature and on Deity with reference to the æsthetical character of the objects for which we consider the one or the other responsible.

Nevertheless, it cannot be said that the voice of beauty comes to the soul in the form of a categorical imperative. Indeed, whatever hortatory or mandatory character the æsthetical ideal possesses appears to belong — in part, at least — to the intricate and wonderful relations which it sustains to the ideal of the morally good. "The possession of beauty" is a phrase sometimes employed to describe the end of that impulsive longing which the contemplation of beautiful objects arouses within the sensitive soul. But the phrase is too figurative strictly to define a psychological or philosophical truth. Strictly speaking, beauty is something which cannot be "possessed," or enjoyed as possessed. The æsthetical enjoyment evoked by the contemplation of beautiful objects is, indeed, a state in us; that is, it is *our* state, and so may be said to be a possession of ours. The right or opportunity to use the objects for the purpose of producing this effect may be sought and gained or lost; it is a matter of money, of marriage, of proximity, of friendship, etc. But these are indirect ways of appealing to choice and of influencing conduct. The direct and proper significance of the appeal which beauty makes to the voluntary powers of man is not a command or an exhortation to choose; it is rather a challenge to admire. The answer to the challenge is the feeling of admiration. When we experience or fail to experience the feeling for beauty, and when we in consequence judge the object to be beautiful or to be not beautiful, we know of nothing *to do* in consequence of such feeling and judgment, — except to seek or to avoid the further contemplation of the object.

And yet indirectly the feeling for the beautiful is a very powerful stimulus and guide of human conduct. The attraction of natural beauty is one of the secondary and yet potent facts in the distribution of the race, and in the determination of the times and rates and directions of its development in civilization. The beauty of the morally good disposition, and of those forms of conduct which flow from it (especially in the more heroic and sublime types of character and action), is a not unimportant additional reason for cultivating such a disposition. And true art has its impulse in that vague and indefinite but passionate longing which follows the suggestions derived from contemplation of beautiful objects, and chooses to shape some kind of an artistic product for itself. Thus in the realm of disposition and choice the ideal of beauty and the ideal of the morally good, without losing themselves in each other, combine to allure and ennoble mankind.

It is, however, in its relation to the constructive imagination, as guided more or less by rules derived from observation by the relating faculty, that the æsthetic ideal is most peculiar. This fact has been implied in all that has hitherto been said. It is doubtful, indeed, whether the feeling for beauty can be aroused by an object which does not set the imagination at work in its effort at the synthesis of manifold elements under the unifying control of an idea. All æsthetical feeling, except the vaguest and lowest, implies that the subject of the feeling is actively engaged in constructing the object to which the feeling corresponds. This is the truth of our meaning when we pronounce devoid of "imagination" those in whom the feeling of æsthetical approbation is not aroused by beautiful objects. In all the higher forms of beauty, at least, the imagination of the beholder must *make* beautiful the object which the taste of the beholder feels to be beautiful. He who is incapable of the requisite synthetic activity of imagination, to keep pace with the developing glow of æsthetical emotion, is also incapable of "sensing" and admiring the object presented. *The* object to be admired is not existent for one thus deficient. In saying this we do not deny that single notes or masses of uniform color may awaken a genuine æsthetical feeling. On the contrary, we affirm again that man is æsthetically distinguished by the whole diameter of his being from the other animals by his capacity to give a quality and a value to all his sensuous experiences that are unknown to them. But it must not be forgotten that the single note of common musical speech is really always a "clang," a harmonious whole composed of many psychical elements; and that no color-mass can be perceived as such without the activity of the mind, in the orderly synthesis of otherwise discrete elements, being called into play. If, however, we should admit that the separation of the æsthetical from the sensuously agreeable may be made without the activity of the constructive imagination, at least in the case of certain relatively simple and low forms of beauty, we could not claim the same admission for any of its higher and more complex forms, whether in nature or in art. The simplest landscape, or melody, or picture, that is to appear beautiful, requires this free movement of the constructive imagination.

The peculiar play of the imagination to which beautiful objects appeal is not simply constructive of these objects. It is "projective" of the life of the soul affected with the æsthetical feeling into the life of the object. The beautiful in any high degree, intelligently appreciated, implies a communism of life, a sympathy of being between its life and the life of the soul. Nothing dead, or conceived of as dead, can appear beautiful to the living contemplating mind. Whether the tacit affirmation of the imagination, that it correctly represents to itself the life of that which is an object, a *not*-self, be scientifically and philosophically defensible, or not, is a question to be settled on its own grounds. But as to the meaning of the soul's act in making the affirmation there can be no doubt. For this we go to the experience of the artist, or of the person appreciating the beautiful in nature and in art, for our true account. When Emerson asks, —

> "Is it that my opulent soul
> Was mingled from the generous whole?"

or when Byron exclaims, —

> "Are not the mountains, waves, and skies a part
> Of me and of my soul, as I of them?"

we find in the words of each a testimony to the common and necessary experience of æsthetical human nature. What we cannot, by imagination, project ourselves into as sharing with us a common life, that we cannot regard as beautiful: so essential is sympathetic activity of the imagination.

Considerations like the foregoing are, of course, too vague and indefinite fully to satisfy the demands of æsthetical science or of the philosophy of the beautiful. A certain vagueness must be expected in regions where feeling (ordinarily unanalyzed and in its very nature difficult or impossible of analysis) holds such powerful sway. But even such considerations are not without philosophical interest and importance. It is a most significant fact that, on being brought into the presence of certain objects, human nature responds with a peculiar feeling of pleasurable approbation. It cannot be claimed that the approbation is given to the objects *because* they are useful, — not even if we extend the meaning of the term "useful" to that utility which serves as a means of evoking the pleasurable feeling. The candid testimony of all lovers of beauty is that it is the "beauty" they admire and enjoy; it is not the utility of the object in producing the joyful admiration which they call its beauty. This fact of experience cannot be gainsaid, and should not be distorted or overlooked by associational or evolutionary theories of æsthetics.

On the other hand, *why* we call certain objects rather than others beautiful, and with pleasure approbate them as such, an examination of the æsthetical phenomena does not enable us immediately to tell. When we are assured by some expert in art that we are wrong in our æsthetical judgment, we find great difficulty in alleging satisfactory reasons for the judgment. It appears to be an irrational outcome of a state of feeling, and to express little more than the fact of feeling. More careful psychological analysis of the mental conditions produced by the intuition of the beautiful shows, moreover, that this intuition produces strivings, and tendencies to action, which are akin to the excitement of the soul in the presence of the morally good. But this analysis also shows that a spontaneous constructive activity of the imagination is the natural support of æsthetical feeling. This play of the soul is awakened by the presence of beauty. It is a joyful and beautiful psychical life. And, furthermore, in appreciating all beauty, the mind projects its own life of joyful and worthy activity into the object appreciated as beautiful. If the object be a natural object, the imagination considers the soul-life of nature to be revealed, in some form, in the object. The same thing is true of every beautiful object of artistic production. This sympathetic projection of imagination is then characteristic of the activity of the mind in the presence of those objects which it calls beautiful.

Is then that Unity of Reality in which, if at all, the more perfect realization of the æsthetical as well as of the moral Ideal is to be found, itself a psychical Life? Is every object, called beautiful as the imagined participant in a living community — that is, sympathetically imagined as a partner in a psychical and ideal totality of existence — actually what it is imagined to be? We are not yet ready to attempt, even by way of hypothesis, the completer answer to this question. It is, however, a question which the philosophy of æsthetics makes inevitable. And to raise it in this definite form requires that a further attempt at analyzing the nature of the beautiful should be made.

If æsthetical reason instinctively, as it were, postulates the objectivity or reality of the beautiful, it would seem that we should be able further to determine this ideal by analyzing the nature of those objects which we esteem beautiful. The analysis of the states of consciousness which such objects evoke succeeds, indeed, in only vaguely suggesting certain factors assumed to belong to the beautiful in reality. It thus accounts for and justifies the mysticism which surrounds all artistic endeavor, and which restricts the attempts made by the admirers of nature and art to explain the powerful impressions which they experience. But the objects themselves have an existence not determined by the states of feeling which they call forth. The objects belong to the world of really existent beings and events. By examining their common characteristics, may we not succeed in dispelling, at least partially, this somewhat provoking mysticism? The history of the science of art, and the history of so-called æsthetical philosophy, is full of endeavors to solve the problem of the nature of the beautiful. The rules for producing what *ought* to be appreciated as beautiful, and the principles determined by reflective analysis as belonging to whatever really *is* beautiful, constitute two forms of the attempted solution.

The science belonging to each form of art is, of course, a subject of development. But the different forms of art differ greatly in their apparent susceptibility to those definite statements of law at which all science aims. They also differ in respect to the stage already reached by the science corresponding to them. Thus we may arrange the different arts in the order of their so-called intellectual character, — meaning by this character either the amount of clear conceptions communicable by them, or the amount of agreement already reached as to the principles of judgment which should rule in them. Music, for example, may be called the least intellectual of the arts, because it is capable of embodying and conveying the least amount of clear conception. It originates and moves most effectively in the realm of vague and mystical feeling. It is degraded, as *music*, when it becomes imitative of "things according to their external appearance," or of definite forms of ideation and thought. But for this very reason in part, it is the most "interior" and spiritual of all the arts, the truest representative and artistic stimulus to all degrees and kinds of emotional life.

But judged by the amount of scientific knowledge already attained concerning the laws regulating the nature of the artistic products which ought to be admired, music is the most highly developed and intellectual of all the arts. No other art can more profitably employ the highest culture given to the best talent. At the other end of the scale, as respects the intellectual nature of the product, stand poetry and the dramatic art. Their characteristic mode of expression, in language, compels them to be the medium of more or less definite descriptions of the external forms of nature, or of the thoughts and purposes as well as of the emotions of men. But the science of poetry — considered as a system of defensible rules for the construction and estimate of what is æsthetically good poetry — is scarcely more mature than that of other less "intellectual" arts. Yet this "science" has been diligently and intelligently cultivated for more than two thousand years.

In all forms of art we shall find artists themselves indisposed to regard highly the attempts of science to lay down *rules* for either artistic production or for the estimate of beautiful objects. Even so the artists agree not with one another. But how shall "science" exist, except upon a basis of induction? And upon what shall the science of the arts base its inductions, if it be not upon such existing products of artistic endeavor as do actually produce states of pleasurable æsthetical appreciation in the minds of those contemplating them? How, then, shall material for inductive science be secured except by securing actual agreement in respect to the experience of this appreciation?

In every form of art there are certain examples which by almost universal consent of those regarding them from appropriate points of view are possessed of this power to awaken æsthetical appreciation. These are the acknowledged masterpieces in music, architecture, sculpture, painting, poetry, and the drama. It is to the contemplation of them, and to the analysis of their characteristics, that the teachers of art are accustomed to direct their pupils, — often in decided and intelligent preference to the mere impartation of ready-made rules. Yet here again, when the attempt is made to state the results of this analysis as the reasons why, in their judgment, they are compelled to call these acknowledged masterpieces beautiful, the spirit of the beauty which the masterpieces really possess seems to have departed from them. For the best authorities and most trustworthy judges of what is really beautiful, and therefore ought to awaken the peculiar approbation due to the beautiful, even when they agree in the feeling of approbation, do not agree in their analyses.

If every art had its set of universally accepted rules for the production and estimate of its own form of the beautiful, it would by no means follow that æsthetical science, as established upon an inductive basis, could satisfactorily solve the problem of the nature of the beautiful. Every art would, indeed, have *its own* science. Students of music might then be definitely informed what rules determine the characteristics of the beautiful in their particular art. Students of architecture, sculpture, painting, or poetry might enjoy the same important advantage. The teaching of the science of art might then be compared, for its scientific character, to the teaching of physics, or, at least, of physiology or psychology. But would such a state of development of the science of the arts solve our philosophical problem? Would it tell us what is that in *every form* of artistic beauty, and also in every beautiful natural object, which carries the secret of its beauty. Some music is confessedly beautiful; so also is some architecture, some sculpture, etc.; so also are many objects in nature, and certain conditions of soul. But what is that which is common to them all, by virtue of the possession of which we call them all by the common term "beautiful"? It is in this common characteristic, or common set of characteristics, that we must seek and find (if anywhere) the essence of the æsthetical ideal.

Moreover, an examination of the rules (or so-called science) of every form of art shows that in two other respects they are found unable to suggest the solution of the philosophical problem. They are to a large extent negative only. They tell what combinations of tones, lines, colors, words, etc., must be avoided in order to escape giving offence to cultivated æsthetical taste. The difficulty, the impossibility even, of telling precisely what combinations shall be made in order to secure the approbation of this taste, especially in all the higher forms of art, is too obvious to need argument.

We are far from wishing to underestimate the present attainments of the critics of the beautiful in art or in nature. We would be much more cautious even about speaking disparagingly of what definite science can do toward training, to intelligent judgment and feeling, the practisers, the patrons, and the admirers, of every form of art. Let it be admitted that a complete set of rules, for the due admiration of the natural scenery of any particular region, may at some time be formulated by experts and posted in the neighboring inns and railroad-stations, for the benefit of travellers æsthetically inclined. Let it be admitted that Tyndall is right in supposing his æsthetical pleasure in the Alps to have its roots in the pleasant gambols of his ape-like ancestors; and that Grant Allen has hit the mark with the high-sounding declaration that all æsthetical pleasure is "the subjective concomitant of the normal amount of activity, not directly connected with life-serving function, in the peripheral end-organs of the cerebro-spinal nervous system." With all this admitted, it is hard to see wherein the problem of philosophical æsthetics has been made clearer or easier of solution. This problem inquires: What that is Universal (common to all objects) and Real (actually existent in the objects) constitutes the essence of the Beautiful?

When we consider the treatment which philosophy has actually given to the æsthetical Ideal, we are obliged at once to admit its indefinite and unsatisfying character. The results of reflective analysis attained by none of the so-called systems of æsthetics can be said to be beyond reasonable doubt in respect to important particulars. This is perhaps in part due to the fact that the analysis has been imperfect. But it is also largely due to the very nature of the subject with which the analysis attempts to deal, and to the attempt to explain more than it is right even to hope to explain. .That certain combinations of real elements, in every form representative of life, do produce in the human mind emotions of the peculiar kind and value which we call æsthetical, is an ultimate fact. If philosophy can tell what those elements are, and under what relations they must combine in order in fact to produce this emotion, it has done all that it can expect to do in defining the essence of the beautiful. In perception by the senses we find that when certain syntheses of sensations, differing in quantity and quality, take place, then the knowledge of a real object, not-me and having space-form, arises in the mind. Why the reality and space-qualities of the object are given in the course of development and as the result of certain syntheses of sensations, is a question to which descriptive and explanatory science furnishes no answer. So, too, it may well be that we can never tell why certain combinations of certain factors of real being, when perceived, appear beautiful to the perceiving mind. The ultimate fact is that objects thus constituted *are* beautiful. They are in fact recognized as representative of the peculiar form of well-being which is the æsthetical ideal; and are greeted with the peculiar emotion, to have which belongs to the very constitution of æsthetical reason.

The further task of philosophical æsthetics is set before it in the shape of a more satisfactory analysis of the characteristics of all beautiful objects. A mere sketch of the lines of determination which it seems to us necessary to follow must for the present suffice. The lines mark out those factors, or *momenta,* which enter into the being of every object that is beautiful. The factors cannot, however, be called qualities of the object, in so far as their æsthetical character is concerned. Moreover, the lines must also mark out the characteristic forms, or laws, of combination which the factors have in every beautiful object.

That which is "beautiful" in any object can never be a

single element of its being, or a simple quality or state. The true artist is indeed fond of regarding simplicity as characteristic of all genuine art. But the term "simplicity" must here be understood in a qualified way; it is not the synonym for what is single and unrelated, but the opposite of what is strained, or artificial, or excessively ornate. *Change* is involved as necessary to the characterization of every beautiful object. But since the object which is to appear beautiful must always present itself in some concrete form, this change belongs to the object under the conditions of space and time. The change is then recognized as suggestive or representative of movement. Nothing that is apprehended as incapable of change, of motion in time or space, and so of the successive realization of different moments of physical or psychical being, appears beautiful to the human mind. But not all movement of physical or psychical being is beautiful; the movement which is beautiful must have two characteristics. It must have spontaneity, or a certain semblance of freedom; and it must use this spontaneity, as it were, in self-limitation to an idea.

Most theories of the nature of the Ideal of æsthetics as determined by an analysis of beautiful objects, recognize the above-mentioned factors in some form. Change, under the conditions of space and time, — movement in the ideal framework which supports all perception through the senses and all representative imagery, — is manifestly essential to the beauty of music and of poetry. The same category must be concretely recognized in all the objects deemed beautiful, even by those forms of art that appear to represent rather what is motionless. The beautiful in architecture and sculpture is suggestive of the free spontaneity and ideal self-limitation of life in motion.

The Kantian exhortation for the intuition of the *a priori* character of geometrical forms runs somewhat as follows: Construct them by mental movement, and then you will know their real nature. The exhortation of æsthetics for the intuition of the beauty of architectural forms is similar. They must be swept by the moving eye, actively constituted by synthetic imagination. Only in this way can the outlines of a building, or the arrangement in space of the parts within its outlines, be intuited as beautiful. Moreover (to anticipate another important consideration), its vertical lines are perceived in their beauty as tending "upward" with aspiration, or as resisting with dignity and self-poise the "downward" pull of gravity. Under the moving eye and active imagination, the horizontal lines and portions of the building marshal themselves over against one another, on the right or on the left.

In all sculpture a yet more subtile and highly intellectual use of the category of change is necessary to the beauty of the object. The particular field of movement here represented is that of human or animal life; although the representation of the life of plants is, in an inferior degree, possible for sculpture. In order to appear beautiful the sculptured object must suggest, either the motion that belongs to life, or the dignified resistance of that tendency to motion against the vital interests of which external physical forces are the cause. The beautiful statue, representing an animal form, stands firmly poised and easily resisting gravity; or else it appears as itself full of vital movement in response to some emotion of the soul. The intuition of the beautiful in the forms of natural objects falls under the same principle.

Much that is said of the freedom of art, as applied to the spontaneous play of the artist's feeling and imagination, belongs also to the object produced by his free artistic activity. All natural objects, too, when regarded as beautiful, seem to partake in the same spontaneous and expressive psychical life. The imagination of the beholder must recognize them as, in some sort, free beings, active spontaneously and out of their own resources rather than as compelled by extraneous force. The object which is apprehended as forced by another to change cannot, so far as it is regarded as thus forced, be also regarded as beautiful. It is indeed true that there is beauty in a painful struggle for noble ends. But the very struggle, although suggestive of painful emotion in the object, is also suggestive of strenuous and self-moved resistance to external forces, in the interests of æsthetical or ethical ideals. The form of Laocoön reveals only too clearly the frightful agony of his conflict with the huge serpents that encircle him; and we know that the conflict will be unavailing. But it also shows us a higher, because a human, life contending against a lower life with all its resources of muscular and mental energy, in the behalf of an end that is morally approved. The supreme and ever-adorable examples of the power which such artistic representations have to evoke æsthetical feeling, where exulting joy mingles with sympathetic pain, are the *ecce-homo* pictures of Jesus. Such beauty as they can attain, besides its source in ethical considerations, acknowledges the principle for which we are now arguing. *Spontaneity*, whether in active exertion or in the endurance of suffering with resignation, belongs to every object which is to be intuited as beautiful.

The philosophical æsthetics of Hegel and his school insists upon the presence of some recognizable idea in every beautiful object. Theories of the beautiful in general are accustomed to note the truth that a unity in variety belongs to the nature of the beautiful. If we recur to the results of analysis in the chapter upon Metaphysics, we find that these two forms of statement imply essentially the same experience regarding all reality. The only real unity is obtained by the self-limitation of the subject of change, in respect to the series of changes through which it passes, by some immanent idea. Now, no object, whether a product of artistic effort or a natural product, which is regarded as subject to unregulated change, can be esteemed beautiful. Indeed, strictly speaking, no such object can really exist; no such assumed being could become an object to the human mind. Chaos is not beautiful,— would not be beautiful if it were conceivable. Disorder is not beautiful. The beautiful object may, indeed, appear lacking in perfect symmetry; it may appear the more beautiful on account of this lack. But this is because the lack itself is expressive of a natural and joyous spontaneity of movement; while perfect symmetry is liable to appear artificial and forced. Moreover, we have already seen that every beautiful object must appear capable of varied life; it falls under the category of change. But the change cannot be unlimited change, with no idea or end in view. *Finality*, or the self-limitation of the object according to some idea, appears then to be a necessary factor, or "moment," in every beautiful thing.

A more careful consideration of these characteristics of all beautiful objects seems to show that they are such as can be possessed — at least in that form and fulness which is necessary to awaken æsthetical feeling — only by what has life. Indeed, if we were compelled to sum up in a word those characteristics which entitle certain things rather than others to be called beautiful, we should say: It is their "lifelikeness," their fulness of life. Thus does an analysis of the beautiful object lead us around to a conclusion similar to that suggested by an analysis of the state of feeling for the beautiful. This state of feeling was found to be dependent upon an activity of imagination in projecting psychical life into the object contemplated. We now find that, if any objects are to be regarded as really beautiful, they must in reality possess the characteristics of psychical life. Either, then, the beautiful is merely subjective, is only a state of pleasurable feeling in the mind of the beholder, or else the object contemplated and esteemed beautiful is itself possessed of such characteristics as entitle it to be called a form of life. The sympathetic communion of our life with other life is necessary to the appreciation of the beautiful. If this communion is only a fancy of the mind with respect to the object, and if the object is not in reality possessed of these characteristics, then we cannot speak of the objectively beautiful, whether in nature or in art.

The foregoing considerations serve to indicate the unique nature of the æsthetical Ideal. The feeling for it, and the judgments pronouncing what is entitled to call forth this feeling, are all relative to the ideal. They are states of mind characterized by vague and unsatisfied, yet pleasurable. and noble, striving after something not yet attained. They are one mode of the soul's reaching after a higher and unconditionally worthy (an ideal) form of its own life. But this activity of mind implies its own objective correlate. No particular object, no beautiful work of art, or beautiful natural form, or beautiful state of the self-conscious mind, represents this ideal with a complete satisfaction of the demands of æsthetical feeling. And yet every object is deemed beautiful only on the mind's assumption that it shares, in some worthy degree, the characteristics of its own ideal striving and satisfaction in such striving. Every form of life that appears as a free and self-controlled approximation to its own idea appears, so far forth, to be beautiful. But the degrees of approximation are infinitely various; the life attained is not all alike worthy in the estimate of the contemplating mind. The noblest, fullest life — if we could only perfectly describe it — would correspond to the Ideal. If such life exists in reality, then the perfectly beautiful, the ideally beautiful, exists. But the shadowy outline of such a life hovers above the mind, alluring it. The objects that seem to have more or less of such life appear in their several degrees to be beautiful. The mind that experiences this life responsive to the contemplation of such objects realizes the feeling for the beautiful. And above it and them, as a Somewhat or Some One, that may serve as a goal of all the striving, is placed the Idea of the Beautiful realized,—the Being that experiences, and is, the perfection of all Life.

It is only in some such confessedly vague way that philosophical æsthetics can at present explicate the content of human experience with the beautiful. That æsthetical, like ethical, reason is in a course of progressive realization of its ideal, we have every reason to believe.

The different forms of the beautiful, as ordinarily recognized by the language of art, are connected with the different combinations of those characteristics which are common to all beautiful objects. When we intuit forms of change, in correspondence with some ideal, that are rapid and imply easy adaptation to environment, we have the æsthetical feeling belonging to the graceful in art or nature. When we contemplate what is measureless and vague in outline, in impression of strength, what can be attained only by vast exertion, we are stirred to the feeling for the sublime. The grand, the charming, the stately, the piquant, etc., are forms of beauty, the analysis of which leads to similar results.

The fact that a very large proportion of the objects which appear beautiful owe their beauty to *association* is doubtless of great scientific and practical significance. But it is a fact which enables us neither to find the essence of the feeling for the beautiful in the laws of association, nor to reduce to simpler terms the real characteristics which belong to all beautiful objects. All states of mind fall, as a matter of course, under these laws. Yet the nature of human reason and the reality of things and of minds are not explained by the statement of the regular forms of the recurrence of particular ideas. This is as true in æsthetics as it is in ethics, or even in metaphysics.

An intimate and interesting relation has been found to exist in experience between the ideal of beauty and the ideal of the morally good. The morally good disposition is naturally regarded as beautiful. But we can say this only on the supposition that we do not accept notions current in certain ethical systems as to what the morally good disposition really is. That the beautiful is naturally and necessarily regarded as also morally good, we are forbidden to say. Yet the feeling that all beauty *ought to be* united with moral goodness, is strongly intrenched within the human mind. The contemplation of beautiful objects, with a genuine æsthetical feeling, is also ethically purifying. Important psychological reasons may be given for this fact, among which are the following: Such feeling is opposed to, and exclusive of, the domination of appetite, avarice, and all the lower forms of desire. It is in fact essentially *un*selfish, — the admiration and love of the beautiful being as unlike the seeking and love of self as are the love of truth, of justice, or that love which we call benevolence. It may be said to have the characteristics of altruism, or of "otherworldliness." There was, therefore, important philosophical truth concealed in the phrase peculiar to the Platonic, and indeed to the entire Greek, way of thinking, which united with the copulative the beautiful *and* the good (*τὸ καλὸν κ' ἀγαθόν*). In the present development of morality, and under the present conditions of human living, it will not do so to press this kinship as to annihilate ethical distinctions. In cases of practical conflict between men's notions of what is, æsthetically considered, beautiful and what it is agreed by the great majority to call morally right, the latter must inevitably prevail. The evolution of judgment in ethics is further advanced, and has reached a stage of consistency and rationality that is quite beyond anything which the science of æsthetics can show. Society, with its daily life and conduct, builds itself solidly on a moral code that has been wrung from powers of darkness and superstition by centuries of hardship and strife. But the code of artistic feeling and judgment is yet an airy and somewhat evanescent affair. It has not the toughness of fibre necessary to contend with conceptions and judgments which are so clear and prompt in most men's minds that they seem to merit, and do widely receive, the title of "universal and necessary truths."

If, however, the really beautiful and the really good were found to be incompatible, an important and influential schism in reason would have to be confessed. From the confession we are doubtless permanently safe, when we consider that both the really beautiful and the really good appear, to the mind, in their highest and ultimate form, as Ideals. The confession which the two ideals, when compared, elicit, is not one of their incompatibility in reality. It is rather itself a tendency of the human mind to insist that, somehow and somewhere, the two shall be perfectly realized in one state of being, in one most beautiful and most righteous form of Life. To be sure, every definite and concrete object of which we have experience falls far short of effecting the desired unity. Neither do we find the perfect and ideal happiness of which we have also a mental picture associated with everything — or, indeed, with any one thing — which we call beautiful or morally good. But beauty and the morally good disposition, nevertheless, appear to us forms of well-being that have an absolute significance and value. And from this point of view we turn again to that Unity of Reality in which the philosophy of nature and of mind discover the "Ground" of all things and of all souls, and inquire whether we may not at least cherish the fair and reasonable postulate that it is also the Realization of the ethical and the æsthetical Ideals.

CHAPTER XIII.

PHILOSOPHY OF RELIGION.

NOTHING is more impressive to the thoughtful student of human nature than the existence of certain conceptions, emotions, and beliefs of that peculiar character which we call "religion." The attempt to reduce the religious elements of man's being to a very few elementary forms is, in our judgment, a complete failure. The sources of religion in human nature are both varied and profound. Religion, says Herbart,[1] "is much older than philosophy, and strikes its roots much deeper in the human soul." That philosophy is older and more deeply rooted in human nature than is science, we have also seen to be true. If then we arrange the forms of intellectual striving which result in religion, philosophy, and science, in the order of the support which they receive from the constitutional needs of humanity, we must place science last of the three. But it is religion as a life, with its more or less *naïve* and uncritical conceptions, and with many unjustifiable beliefs, that has outlasted all the changes of opinion to which the philosophy of religion has been subject. No fear need be entertained that it will be unable to survive the modern effort to bring its phenomena under so-called scientific treatment.

The general relation between philosophy and the particular sciences was found to be such as to encourage the expectation that the philosophy of religion might, in a measure, place itself upon a secure scientific foundation. It is doubtful, however, whether a science of religion, in any such form as to serve

[1] Einleitung in die Philosophie, 5th ed., § 155.

philosophy for a teacher and guide, can be said to exist. All efforts hitherto made to subject the nature and growth of the complex life of religion to a descriptive and evolutionary treatment have been sadly lacking in scientific quality. Such efforts are even less hopeful in prospective result than are the attempts at a physiological and evolutionary science of ethics or æsthetics. It is necessary then for philosophy to go straightway — in its own name and with its own authority — to those sources which lie within the facts of human life. Within the sphere of religion there exists no body of principles, established by careful scientific induction, on which philosophy can safely rely. Its reflective analysis and its efforts at synthesis derive little benefit indeed by stopping to consult the modern theories concerning the origin and growth of religious beliefs. The *facts* upon which these theories claim to have established themselves must, of course, enter into its account. But it is only as considered in connection with a great number of other even more important facts (usually quite neglected by the ardent defenders of an inductive and objective science of religion) that their significance for philosophy can be realized.

It is for this reason, in part, that philosophy comes into such very close relations with religion. Within the sphere common to both there is no recognized standard of defensible generalizations to which, in case of conflict between the philosopher and the man of the popular religious faith, an appeal can be taken. A genuine science of religion (corresponding to the science of physics or the science of psychology) does not exist. Did it exist, it would constitute such a recognized standard of appeal.

But it may be said that a science of theology exists, and that this science must be accepted as the arbiter between popular belief and philosophical thought respecting matters of fact and law in religion. Has, then, theology so succeeded in giving scientific form and certification to the phenomena of religious belief and knowledge that it can — as can physics or psychology — require of philosophy to accept at its hands a body of principles, not simply presupposed by it, but also ascertained by its inductive researches? The word "theology" is variously used. Sometimes it signifies little more than the iteration, in more technical and uncouth phrase, of the popular conceptions and beliefs respecting religion. But it cannot retain the claim to a scientific character when, through fear of being accused of rationalism, it does not itself lay hold upon and employ the method of reason, — the method of philosophy. In so far as theology actually employs philosophic method, it becomes a philosophy of religion. And, in fact, by far the greater part of what has been called the science of theology is actually philosophy of religion, though the method of reflective analysis and rational synthesis be used in a vacillating and inconsistent way.

The science of theology has, without doubt, a high place among the forms of systematic and certified human knowledge. As a *science*, and not as a dogmatic restatement of popular beliefs or a fragmentary attempt at the philosophy of religion, theology moves in a narrow and restricted sphere. It is the critical and systematic exposition of the particular tenets held by a sect or branch of believers in some more or less definite form of religious faith and life. It is Calvinistic or Arminian; it is the *Dogmatik* of the Lutheran Church or of the Reformed Churches; it is the theology of the Westminster Confession or of the Thirty-nine Articles; or it is the so-called New England Theology. Each of these forms of scientific theology may furnish the philosophy of religion with new material for its consideration. But by the very nature of that definiteness which they have as partially exclusive systems, none of them is a science of religion fit to be the judge over, or sole guide of, the philosophy of religion. In so far as they involve common elements, they show the wide-spreading character of the conceptions and beliefs with which they attempt to deal. In so far, however, as they subject these conceptions and beliefs to thorough reflective analysis, and build upon the results of this analysis that common supreme synthesis which all religion implies, they share together in a common philosophy of religion.

It may be claimed, however, that the method by which theology arrives at its truths is so peculiar as to place it above philosophy in the position of authority or supreme judge. The "device," *Philosophia est ancilla theologiæ*, prevailed during the Middle Ages; it is still accepted and acted upon by many thinkers in the Roman Catholic Church and in other great branches of religious belief. But it is the characteristic achievement and priceless possession of modern philosophy to have gained freedom from the power signified by this device. Indeed, the device itself is a denial of one of the chief characteristics of all philosophy. It cannot be the "handmaid" of theology; to resume this position would be to surrender the birthright and title of modern philosophy. Neither has theology suffered from losing her handmaid.

If, then, the theologian wishes to enter the fields of philosophy, he is heartily welcome therein; but only on terms consistent with the laws of the domain. If he do not become a philosopher, if he do not diligently and intelligently cultivate the knowledge of mind, the knowledge of knowledge, the knowledge of moral philosophy, and the philosophy of religion, he will scarcely attain the place of a trustworthy theologian. But he cannot change the nature or the methods of philosophy by his bare presence in its field.

The existence of various claimants to the privileged place of revealed systems of religious truth, and the existence of some one form of revelation recognized as special and unique, do not change the nature of the relation between religion and philosophy. All the several claimants must appear before the bar of reason and present the grounds on which their claims rest. And if the alleged truths revealed by each have been previously given the form of theological science, whether in a critical or in an uncritical way, this science can contest conflicting claims before no other arbiter and judge than philosophy itself. Moreover, even when any particular form of revelation has been acknowledged to be true, this does not do away with the necessity of a philosophy of religion, or even greatly abridge the work it has to perform. The existence and the recognition of revelation are themselves religious phenomena, which imply most important truths with regard to the nature and connection of all reality and of the supreme ethical and æsthetical ideals. A revelation which should contradict the truths implicated in all knowledge, and in the particular principles recognized by the sciences of nature and of mind, of ethics and æsthetics, is unthinkable. Of what could it be a revelation? To whom could it be a revelation? What could it reveal? Any intelligible answer to these questions is quite impossible without admitting the right and the duty of philosophy to deal with all the phenomena of religious conceptions and beliefs. It is only a philosophy which takes a shallow view of experience and reality that refuses to consider alleged facts and principles that are too vague and vast for clear definition,— tokens of the feeling of the human heart after remote and ever unattainable ideals. On the other hand, it is only a philosophy which has parted with its crown and birthright that will receive any alleged mysteries of faith when presented in terms that defy and flout at the clearest ideas and choicest convictions of reason.

All rational knowledge is suffused with conviction; and the influence of the ideals of the morally good and the beautiful is known in the awakening of the feelings of aspiration, awe, admiration, and affection. That "faith" and "feeling" should enter into the very essence of the life of religion, need cause no wonder and give no offence. Neither philosophy nor science succeeds in fully satisfying the mind's demand for *explanation*. And some of the mind's most imperative demands are not satisfied by explanation at all. But the faith which religion requires must be of a kind to comport with the knowledge which science and philosophy furnish, although this is a far different thing from saying that science and philosophy must furnish an explanation of the objects to which the faith points, or else deny the rationality of the faith itself. Conviction, that arises we know not how, attaches itself to all the objects of knowledge. The faith which is inseparable from religion is not a blind and arbitrary defining of the object of religion. As far as it approximates this condition, whether in the mind of individuals or in particular systems of theology, it is unreasonable, and cannot abide. As a conviction of the presence and power of the ideal within the real,—in that particular form which is required not only for the life of dutiful and beautiful conduct, but also for the life of religious devotion and blessedness,—faith is not contradictory of, but akin to, the most primary, invincible, and valuable activities of reason itself.

A true philosophy can, therefore, never contravene or mar the life of true religion. Philosophy strives rather, with keen, loving insight to discern, and with tenderness and sympathy to appreciate, the significance and value of this life. It regards religion as a witness to the ultimate Unity of the Real and the Ideal. And if science, falsely so-called, wounds religion, or spurs on philosophy to wound her, the cure of the wounds is no more to be found in irrational religious zeal and belief than in irreligious science and philosophy. The only cure for all such wounds is more of knowledge,—of *knowledge*, with its blending of intuition and inference with primary convictions of truth. As said the great theologian, Julius Müller: "Wounds which have been inflicted on humanity by knowledge, can be healed only by knowledge."

In case of an apparent conflict between the two, religion has great and obvious advantages over philosophy. By that persistent faithfulness in conviction and devotion toward an Ideal, which is her essential characteristic, she can ultimately compel the respectful consideration of philosophy; while her grasp upon life and conduct among the multitudes of mankind, and even with the leaders of reflective thought, is by far the more firm and unmistakable. The facts of experience to which she invites philosophical analysis, and the contributions made to the final synthesis of philosophy by the principles implicated in the experience, are of the most enduring character. Moreover, they make the irresistible appeal which comes from objects that awaken the strongest and profoundest passions and emotions of human nature. For all the roots of our physical and psychical life are bathed in the hopes, aspirations, fears, and yearnings which are fed from the springs of religion.

A recent writer[1] on a branch of this subject raises the question, Which of several tenable but rival theories to account for our actual experiences is to be believed; and then makes answer as follows: "That will be most generally believed which, besides offering us objects able to account satisfactorily for our sensible experience, also offers those which are most interesting, those which appeal most urgently to our æsthetic, emotional, and active needs." No one wise in reflective thinking, and in the history of such thinking, can fail to sympathize with the words of Mr. Shadworth Hodgson:[2] "Religion I saw was like an expansive force which would shatter any man-made system of philosophy, unless that system were a true image of the universe itself. Nothing can be true which does not find a place, in the theory, for that passionate determination of the mind to God, which I do not say is described by, but which breathes from, the writings of men like Coleridge. And the reason is this, that the passionate religious tendency is not a sentiment fluttering round a fancy, but is a feeling rooted deep in the structure and mechanism of consciousness."

Those facts entering into all the life and growth of mind, out of which the life of religion perennially springs and by nourish-

[1] Prof. Wm. James, on the "Psychology of Belief," in Mind, July, 1889, p. 346.

[2] Philosophy of Reflection, vol. i., Preface, p. 20 f.

ment from which it grows, may be mentioned under five heads. These are, —

1. Certain vague but powerful feelings which impel the mind to belief in the presence of the invisible and to the inquiry as to right relations toward this presence. Among these is the feeling of dependence which, as absolute and equivalent to a consciousness of being in relation to God, Schleiermacher considered the source of all religious life. This feeling, under the influence of intelligence, develops from the primitive fear of unknown forces that are beyond man's control, into the rational belief in Providence as "other" Being than the beings we immediately know, which shapes both our ends and theirs. Religious rites and ceremonies, as well as the rational conduct of life, arise from the pressure of this motive to stand right with the invisible "other" Being.

2. The higher and more distinctively ethical feelings and ideas furnish also a principal source of religion. This statement must be accepted as matter of fact, whatever theory may be held as to the possibility of separating the sanctions and rules of ethics from the tenets of religious belief. *In fact*, the feeling and idea of moral obligation, the fear of retribution and the expectation of reward, are experiences of the human mind which impel it to the belief in the object of all religion. The peculiar objectivity, the "otherworldliness," of the so-called "voice of conscience" has been recognized in connection with all degrees of ethical development. Who, or what, that is within me and yet does not appear to be myself, speaks to me and declares, "Thou oughtest," or "Thou oughtest not"? The theological argument which, from the *in*-equity of rewards and punishments as empirically determined, infers the existence of a Being who will right this *in*-equity, may not be acceptable to the mind of the present age. But that the expectations which are actually awakened in the ethical consciousness are most powerful factors in the impulse of human nature toward God, it would argue inaccurate observation of the facts to deny. In

their more intelligent form, these ethical experiences suggest and guide that inquiry after some certified relation of the real world of beings, forces, and events, with the ethical Ideal, which has always been the most painful and burdensome of all philosophical problems. The sense of justice and truth, the feeling that goodness and the well-being it brings ought to exist in reality, the persistent conviction that the kingdom of reality cannot (in spite of all appearances to the contrary) be a region of moral negations, much less a kingdom where evil is supreme, have driven men to faith in God during all the dark ages of the world's history.

3. The higher and more distinctively æsthetical feelings and ideas are also a powerful motive to religion. It is not without reason that the advocates of a world without God strive to diminish the value of æsthetical feeling and the amount of beauty, as distinct from mere utility, to be found in the objects of human experience. In its most vague and primitive form the susceptibility to æsthetical influences is akin to the susceptibility to religion. It has been the "beauty of holiness," quite as much as its utility, which has attracted the minds of men. Without this susceptibility it is difficult to tell what the forms of divine service would have been. Many, perhaps most, of those religious ceremonies which prevail among the lowest peoples are lacking in qualities which appeal to our æsthetical feeling; some of them are positively, and in a high degree, repulsive to a refined taste. The beliefs of religion, too, have been too largely shaped by crude ethical conceptions, to the damage of the æsthetical quality they might otherwise have possessed. It is customary to inveigh loudly against certain religious practices and beliefs, in the name of æsthetics as well as of ethics. But the sympathetic student of human nature will recognize, here as everywhere in religious phenomena, another aspect. He will be ready in the consideration of this subject to give the principle of evolution all its rights. The science that can call the hideousness of a cancer "beautiful,"

surely might enable us to see how the Aztec priest, who lifted the bleeding heart of the victim to his idol's mouth, was still an æsthetical as well as a religious being. In the Roman Catholic Church the beauty which untutored minds have seen speaking from the face and form of the Madonna and her Child, has allured them toward the divine life. And all the growth of devotion to mere fact and law which modern science demands does not serve to quench the rational conviction that what is grandest and most beautiful in ideal must be realized in the Universe as the object of all religion.

4. What we will call "the metaphysical impulse," in even its most instinctive and least rational form, serves in the interests of religion. As the otherwise unknown cause of the perpetually recurrent groupings of experiences this impulse posits a Being actually existent in the world of reality. We may call that which it posits by the name *X*, for ought we know about it to be gathered from such terms as "*substratum*," "substance," etc. But no "Thing" exists without this *X*; and there is no knowledge of any "Thing" until this metaphysical impulse has done its work. Science proceeds to differentiate its experiences under the more or less intelligent rule of this same impulse. The world of psychical states, as instinctively and necessarily organized into its two great classes and assigned to its two kinds of subjects (things and self), science underlays with a world of postulated realities, called "atoms," "forces," "principles," and "laws." Thus it arrives at a comprehensive and defensible conception of the unity of the world. But the man who knows no science is not without some vague conception of a unity in reality to all that of which he has experience. Even in the lowest forms of religion the multiplication of gods many and lords many has not been wholly unlimited. In fetichism and the most debased polytheism there are fewer deities than there are things and men. The divinity serves as some kind of a principle of unification, as a bond in reality of many things and many men. It is this metaphysical impulse in which we find a source

of religion. Were man not metaphysical, he would not be religious. There is no religion without the sense and belief of reality.

5. In its highest form the foregoing impulse becomes a demand, definitely conceived and more or less completely accomplished, for the unifying of all experience in some known or postulated Unity of Reality. But the instinctive impulse must be quickened and broadened by a many-sided experience, as well as guided by the principles of the particular sciences, in order to attain this, its highest form. It is this form of the impulse toward God which conceives the demand for Him as expressive of the most profound, varied, and lofty life of reason itself. The truth which Tolstoï makes one of his characters utter must be so interpreted: "It is not the mind that understands God, it is life that makes us understand Him."

The intimate relation of philosophy and religion is thus seen to have its ground in the very nature of reason itself. Philosophy aims, by reflection upon all the many-sided forms of its own life, to comprehend that which religion accepts as concretely imaged and set before the mind. Religion includes the direction of conduct with reference to the relations in which the object of religious faith is depicted as standing to the individual mind and to the world of things. It regards the laws of conduct as emanating from the will of this object; the mind is therefore regarded as determined to character and conduct by the expression of this will. Religion therefore regards those acts as obedience or disobedience, pleasing or displeasing, to Deity, which ethics regards simply as in accordance with, or in violation of, impersonal laws. It considers the course of events in the physical universe as, in some degree and manner at least, a manifestation of the presence and attributes of the object of its faith, and of its affection or fear. It considers rational souls as capable of existing, and indeed as actually existing, in relations with this object which imply a community of nature and interests between the two.[1]

[1] Comp. Lotze, Outlines of the Philosophy of Religion, 2d ed., § 80.

Philosophy feels the obligation to treat in its own method the phenomena of the life of religion. As it collates and reflectively considers these phenomena, it notes that they bear witness to an origin in the same sources as those in which it finds its own impulse and guiding principles. To the vague feeling of dependence in which, in part, religion originates, it attempts to furnish such grounds in a knowledge of the Nature of all Thought and all Being as shall convert it into a principle of rational life. It shows that it is true, and how it is true, of man, as of all other known or knowable beings, "In Him we . . . have our being." In brief, it justifies to reflective thinking the feeling of absolute dependence which the life of religion instinctively cultivates.

The vague feeling after a unity in reality between the different beings of the physical world, and between us and these beings, with the forces and laws which we primarily know as concerning them, it also makes the subject of reflective thinking. It thus undertakes, in a critical and thorough manner, to construct — as it were — "the metaphysical core" of that conception to which reason is entitled in answer to its own demands. It summons all the sciences which describe the nature of the world and the nature of men, as realities concretely determined in human knowledge, to show that our manifold experience implies, in reality, a Unity of Being.

The philosophy of religion further undertakes to show, in the name of the particular sciences, what is the nature of this ultimate Unity of all real Being, and what are the more definite relations in which this Being stands to the being of man. In attempting this stupendous problem it is obliged to take account of those facts of æsthetical and ethical life with which religion is also in the closest connection. What religion vaguely believes and yet faithfully feels, philosophy strives to make a matter of certified knowledge, with reference to the character of the æsthetical and ethical ideals. The supreme synthesis at which it aims requires that — if it be possible in accordance with all the facts and with the principles ascertained by the particular sciences — these ideals of reason shall be regarded as having their realization also in that same Unity of all Reality, in which the particular beings, called things or minds, have their "Ground."

This brief analysis of the relations which exist between religion and philosophy is the rational justification of the facts of history. In history, philosophy and the life of religion have always been intimately connected. To say that the historical connection of theology and philosophy has always been one of intimate interdependence is scarcely more than to say the same thing in another way. Religion as a faith and life cannot bear to be shown to be irrational. But philosophy too is not thoroughly and consistently rational unless it take — with all the high value which they certainly possess — the facts and principles of religious faith and religious life into its final view of the universe.

The claims of the philosophy of religion are therefore somewhat unique. They are not based simply on the existence of certain persistent and special phenomena, called the beliefs and life of religion. They are also based on the fact that its own existence has its roots largely in the same metaphysical, ethical, and æsthetical demands as those which religion supplies. Religion believes in, and worships, and shapes conduct with reference to, a certain Ideal-Real. The nature of the Ideal of religion is such that, if the existence of a corresponding Reality be even once admitted as an hypothesis, it changes materially our points of view from which to regard all the chief philosophical problems.

The first problem of the philosophy of religion is to determine the reality and predicates of that Being whom, under the imagery derived from its experience with human personality, religion believes in and worships as God. In fidelity to the interests of this problem the so-called "arguments" for the being of God must be handled critically. Will that presuppositionless reflection which philosophy requires justify the claim of these arguments to constitute a *proof?* The answer to this question requires the making of distinctions, some of which are quite too apt to be overlooked. Of *proofs* for the being of God, in the sense of mathematical or other forms of strictly deductive demonstration, we cannot properly speak in this connection. All such demonstration proceeds syllogistically from acknowledged principles to particular applications of principles, either singly or in combination. Its type is the mathematical argument as employed in the Euclidean geometry. But if God is, His being is a matter of fact; and the demonstration of matters of fact can follow only from general statements, or principles, expressive of matters of fact. The only principle from which the particular fact of the reality of any being called God could follow, as a strict logical consequence, is the principle — acknowledged or assumed — of the real existence of God. But this is the very fact or supposition for which we are seeking proof. On the other hand, the result of the philosophical denial that we have any verifiable or defensible knowledge of an absolute and real Being called God is, in logical consistency, the confession that philosophy has no verifiable or defensible knowledge of reality at all.

The essential element in all the arguments for the being of God, as the real "Ground" of all other being, is metaphysical, or ontological, — as Kant long ago pointed out. The several "arguments" are indeed one; they involve the same process of reasoning, based upon all the facts of knowledge, as that by which philosophy reaches its postulate of a Unity of all Reality. The *ontological* argument, customarily so-called, proceeds from the existence in human minds of the conception of a "supreme" or "most perfect" Being to the reality of the existence of such Being. But the existence of the conception is no proof of the existence of the reality, unless we admit that postulated faith in the highest determinations of reason itself, upon which all metaphysics relies.

The *cosmological* argument proceeds from the contingent nature of the world of concrete realities and events to the necessary Being of their Cause or "Ground." In its customary form this argument makes — as Lotze and others have pointed out — a somewhat strange and unwarrantable use of the words "contingent" and "necessary;" and therefore loses much of the cogency which it might otherwise claim, by claiming more than it can maintain. For, strictly speaking, the cosmological idea — that is, the idea of an orderly totality consisting of an indefinite number of things and events bound together under the terms of universal law — excludes "contingency." According to this idea, every thing and every event is regarded as "constantly conditioned by its own adequate reasons;" its real being, if it be entitled to be called really existent at all, gives it a right to the title of "necessary" existence as a real cause or "ground." To such a real being "the smallest, meanest, and most insignificant thing has just as good a claim as the most perfect."

The *teleological* argument reasons, from the fact of experience, that things and events in the world appear conformable to ends, to a single designing and creative reason as the supreme cause of the world. It is of this proof, which he calls "physico-theological," that Kant remarks: It "will always deserve to be treated with respect. It is the oldest, the clearest, and the most in conformity with human reason. It gives life to the study of nature, deriving its own existence from it, and thus constantly acquiring new vigor." It is this argument, however, which has been most stoutly (and to a certain extent, most successfully) resisted by modern physical science. That it involves many gaps, certain inconsistencies, and several subordinate assumptions which, of themselves, need verification, the candid inquirer can scarcely have a doubt. It cannot be said to amount to a demonstration of the conclusion at which it arrives. On the other hand, it is at least equally unfair, as an understatement of the truth, to say that no verifiable knowledge of the "World-Ground" is to be reached by setting forth from the experience which we have of the presence of manifold forms of being, and especially of life, that make upon the mind the irresistible impression of a reciprocal arrangement and operation of elements in the realization of some idea. Indeed, the more widely and profoundly the conception of a universal mechanism is explored, the more widely, profoundly, and intelligently does the presence of *Finality*, of significant ideas, come to be discerned. The expanded conception of mechanism extends, instead of narrowing, the sphere of the ideal interpretation of Nature.

The philosophy of religion begins its attempt to render rational the knowledge and faith that have God for their object by recurring to those fundamental results of philosophical reflection which belong to general metaphysics and to the philosophy of nature and the philosophy of mind. These results show that all developed cognition involves the postulated reality of its object. That loosely and inadequately organized system of knowledge, which is possessed by every mind that has *become* rational, implies some sort of a real unity relating the various things of experience to one another and to the knowing mind. The growth of all science is in the direction of substituting for this imperfectly organized system of knowledge a system that shall be elaborate, exact, universally valid, and complete. Each particular science proceeds upon the hypothesis that it is dealing with one of the world's subordinate unities,— a particular group or class of phenomena,— with a view to reduce to system the cognitions pertaining thereto. Each particular science, therefore, presupposes a sort of fragmentary unity in reality as that portion of Nature with which it is peculiarly concerned. But the growth of none of these particular sciences is possible without introducing considerations that bind it, as a particular science, to others of a common class. One of the most notable assumptions made use of by all intelligent students of nature is the unity of all science,— and so, by immediate inference, of the objective realities in whose cognition as related the science itself consists. The physical sciences are fast binding themselves more closely together by extending over the particular members of the community the conception of universally existent physical entities under universally controlling laws. Nor does the scientific mind easily tolerate the belief that no kind of unity in reality exists between the objects of the physical sciences and the world of minds. Biology and psycho-physics and the theory of knowledge agree in assuming the existence of such a unity.

All the particular sciences are penetrated with confidence in the validity of those principles which are of the very constitution of reason itself. These principles are, indeed, the presuppositions, whether crudely or intelligently made, of all scientific cognition as well as of all the knowledge which belongs to the more ordinary rational activity of man. It is possible to summon these principles before the bar of the critical judgment. It is possible to be sceptical as to the *extra*-mental worth and application, so to speak, of even these most universal and necessary presuppositions. The issue of such scepticism, whether in irrational agnosticism or in its own self-limitation, and the return to reason's inalienable confidence in her own forms of life, the discussion of the theory of knowledge has already set forth.

The philosophy of religion may confidently rely upon all the other departments of philosophy for confirmation of some such statement as the following: *A Unity of real Being is the primal Subject, the ultimate "Ground," of all those related changes which human cognition apprehends as the being and action of the empirical system of minds and things.* The alternative of this statement is not knowledge, but a denial of knowledge. It is such a denial of knowledge as, consistently carried out, converts all human science into the merely subjective and unverifiable play of ideas. All reasoned scepticism in opposition to this positive statement ends in the most complete Solipsism.

On this conclusion of scepticism, however logically drawn, reason reacts and postulates again a world of reality. It is as rational to deny real existence to the minds of others, and to the things and events of the world of our common experience, as to deny the reality of the existence of the one Ground of them all. But all these forms of denial are alike irrational. If then we designate by the convenient but indefinite term, "the Absolute" (or the uncouth but expressive term, "the World-Ground"), this unitary Being which is the alone real subject of all the concrete and individual empirical realities, we are warranted in affirming: The existence of the Absolute (or the "World-Ground") is the most certain of all philosophical truths.

But there is a long way in reflective thinking from this "Absolute" to the Being whom religious faith accepts and worships by the name of God. And it would be uncandid and unwise to affirm that all the steps of that way can be taken with a like confident appeal to the accepted results of philosophical reflection. All attempts to solve the great problem of philosophy, however agnostic, may be shown virtually to admit the necessity of this postulate of the Absolute. The equivalent of the statement we have just propounded in the name of metaphysics is made by the advocates of every manner of philosophical system, — realistic or idealistic, theistic, pantheistic, or even avowedly atheistic. This is as true of "the Unknowable" of Herbert Spencer or "the Unconscious" of Hartmann, as it is of the "Self-same One" of Neo-Platonism or the "I Am" of the ancient Hebrews. It is as true of Spinoza's Infinite Substance or Schopenhauer's "Will" as *Ding-an-sich*, as it is of the Triune God of Christian theology. All these and similar terms imply that ultimate analysis, and that supreme synthesis, which finds the fundamental categories recognized by metaphysics to have their truest application to the Absolute, to the one real Ground of the existence and action of all particular things and minds.

It is at this point, however, that the most profound difficulties belonging to the philosophy of religion emerge. May the personality of the Absolute be affirmed as a proposition valid in synthetic philosophy? and, if so, on what grounds that are recognized by the consensus of philosophical opinion? The "metaphysical core" of the conception of God is, we believe, a principle universally recognized by all serious attempts at philosophical system. But the fact cannot be concealed that when, in the interests of religious faith, the effort is made further to define the Absolute as personal, much tacit dissent and even open and intelligent opposition is encountered. The essence of that personality which Theism desires to secure for the Absolute or World-Ground, is, first of all, self-consciousness. The next inquiry before the philosophy of religion may then be stated in terms somewhat like the following: Does this Unity of Reality, the so-called Absolute, present itself, as objects for itself, with those changes in reality of which it is the ultimate cause; refer them to itself as the one real Subject of them all; and so realize in a mental life of its own the unity which, by the postulate of our reason, it is known to be? Thus much, at least, would seem to be implied in the question: Is the Absolute self-conscious Personality? This is the first great disputed inquiry in the philosophy of religion.

The answer which the philosophy of religion proposes to the question just raised involves three sets of considerations. These are, first, the objections to the self-consciousness of the Absolute; second, the arguments for the self-consciousness of the Absolute as far as they are implied in the essential factors of the concept of the Absolute; third, the affirmative arguments to be derived from the more purely emotional, ethical, and æsthetical impulses of human nature.

The objections to affirming the self-consciousness of the Absolute, of that unitary Being which philosophy recognizes as the "World-Ground," are derived from two principal sources. Of these the first is the very nature of self-consciousness. It is said that to affirm self-consciousness and absoluteness of the same Being is to affirm a contradiction in terms. Since self-consciousness is essentially a limitation and implies a conditioning of one being on another, the Absolute cannot be self-conscious. In considering this objection we take from descriptive psychology the results of its analysis of consciousness and of self-consciousness. This analysis shows that all our consciousness — that is, all immediately known psychical or mental life — is indeed conditioned on other being than that of the being which is itself conscious. This conditionating is twofold. Consciousness as an act implies the stimulus, or occasioning activity, of that which is other than the conscious being; consciousness, as a so-called power displayed in every conscious act, implies a nature (derived or conditioned) of the being that, on occasion of being acted upon by other being, becomes conscious.

As to self-consciousness, too, a scientific analysis of the process shows that it, in fact, occurs only as a reference of some concrete and individual state to the Ego as the subject of all states; and that the states thus referred are generally, if not always, conditioned by the action of being that is recognized as *non*-ego; while the form of the reference is always conditioned upon the derived and conditioned nature of the self-conscious mind.

Admissions like the foregoing do not prove, however, that self-consciousness is, essentially considered, possible only for dependent and conditionated being. They simply assert that all *our* acts of self-consciousness are actually states of such being. In other words, they warrant only the obvious conclusion that *we* are not self-conscious absolute beings. We *are* self-conscious; but we are *not* the kind of being that is entitled to be called the Absolute, the "World-Ground." Self-consciousness *per se* requires simply the conscious reference of those changes in the reality of mental life which we call "states" to a real unity of this mental life, to the so-called "self," as their subject or ground. Psychological analysis finds nothing belonging to the essence of self-consciousness which is incompatible with absoluteness of being. On the contrary, if the Absolute is indeed the real subject and ultimate cause of all those changes which in reality occur, then it may, for that reason, the more "conveniently," — if we may so speak, — and in strict truthfulness, refer them to its self-hood as its own consciously cognized states. So far as self-consciousness constitutes personality, we may even affirm with Lotze: "*Perfect* personality is reconcilable only with the conception of an Infinite Being; for finite beings only an approximation to this is attainable."

The second class of objections to the self-consciousness of the Absolute, although less frequently urged, are more difficult to answer. They arise on ethical grounds. They concern that most difficult of all philosophical inquiries; namely, the true way of mentally representing the relations of the Absolute to all finite and limited personal beings. How shall this be done so as to conserve the essential interests of moral principles? To say that, in one aspect, all material things are but dependent phases of the life of the Absolute, and that all so-called physical forces and changes are to be ascribed to the Will of the Absolute, occasions no offence to our ethical ideals. No important ethical objections arise when we postulate the self-consciousness of that Unitary Being which is the primal subject, the ultimate Ground, of the physical universe. The being and changes of things are known to the Absolute as its own self-consciously cognized states; the life of the world of things is the self-conscious life of the "World-Ground."

Ethics does not object to statements such as these. But when a similar affirmation is made concerning the being and action of self-conscious minds, our ethical conceptions and feelings must be tenderly dealt with, or they feel deeply wounded in vital parts. And yet how can we avoid that affirmation, to which the concurrent investigations of all the branches of philosophy point the way? The being and action of the mind of man has its Ground in that same Absolute whose self-conscious life is the reality of things. But does the Absolute lose its own self-consciousness when it serves — so to speak — as the Ground of the world of self-conscious finite minds? Are not the states and actions of these finite minds necessarily known to the Absolute as being — what, if the Absolute be a self-conscious Person, they certainly are — modes of its own self-conscious life? No consistent and tenable philosophical position is open to us but the affirmative answer to this question.

But our ethical conceptions and feelings at once raise an inquiry as to the consequences of the position which philosophy feels compelled to assume. How then, it inquires, shall we conceive of that reality of moral being, of responsibility and character, which is the most priceless possession of finite minds? Theology is also apt to take alarm at this position, and inquire: Would philosophy then make God the only sinner, the author of all sin? Speculative thinking, whether in ethics, theology, or philosophy, cannot give an entirely satisfactory answer to these inquiries, or wholly allay the feeling of alarm. Philosophy cannot, however, retract its tenet that the self-consciousness of the Absolute must be a consciousness of the being and action of all things and all minds, — as having their life and being in Itself, the universal "World-Ground." Various considerations soften the difficulties and allay the alarms occasioned by this tenet of the self-consciousness of the Absolute.

That finite minds are never, and in no wise, independent of God, is a proposition which is the very opposite of repugnant to religious belief. "In Him . . . we have our being," is a tenet of religion, as well as of philosophy. Having once accepted this principle, we cannot reasonably refuse to continue it in good faith, and in a comprehensive application of its truth. Of the constitution and activity of our bodies we need not hesitate for a moment to admit: it is all constantly and absolutely dependent upon the being of the Absolute. But by the postulate of religion, this being is a self-conscious life.

His self-conscious life is, then, no more to be excluded — as respects space, time, and causation — from the molecules of the human brain than from the interior of the densest lead ball. These molecules "live and move and have their being" in the Absolute. Nor need we hesitate to deny that the life of conscious sensation and ideation, which we justly call our own, is as truly and constantly interpenetrated by and dependent upon this universal self-conscious life. The conception of a co-etaneous self-consciousness of the Absolute for every act of our self-consciousness may be difficult or impossible to bring before the mind; but we are not justified, for that reason, in maintaining the impossibility of the reality to which the conception aims to correspond. On the contrary, all the general defences which philosophy builds about the self-consciousness of the Absolute are also defences against assaults upon this conception.

It is only when, by seemingly unavoidable inference, the responsibility for human choices, and for their result in human character, is removed from finite minds and laid, as it were, upon the universal Will, that theology and ethics more positively and intelligently object. But that activity of its own which the finite mind cognizes in self-conscious volition or free choice is, like every other activity, dependent on the being and action, in the finite mind, of the Absolute. Such activity is therefore known to the Absolute, if known at all, as being what it really is; namely, as a manifestation of its own being and action, a self-consciously recognized change in itself, the alone primary and fundamental cause of all physical and psychical life. But how can this be, and yet the finite mind remain "free" and "responsible," in the meaning of those important adjectives which ethics seems to require? This is a question which all systems of philosophy are powerless satisfactorily to answer. But then it is a question which every form of theology, and all religious faith, is even more powerless to answer. It is the old and ever-unsolved problem: How can real personal and ethical finite being co-exist in the same universe with absolute Personal Being? In more distinctively theological form: How can God be infinite, and finite man be responsible and free?

In dealing with this insolvable problem philosophy may take one of several possible courses. It may deny that man is responsible and free, that he is indeed a really ethical being. It is difficult briefly to sketch the consequences upon all the departments of reflective thinking which logically follow from this denial. It must suffice to say that, under its influence, the whole aspect of life and reality, not only as subjects of speculative treatment, but also as objects of practical endeavor, is profoundly changed. Those branches of philosophy which treat of the Ideals of Reason — the philosophy of morals, of æsthetics, and of religion — suffer most. The change involves their theoretical completeness and their power to supply rational principles for conduct. But even in the sphere of metaphysics important changes become necessary. Moreover, such a denial is obviously opposed to a large class of facts which, although they have that indefinite and elusive character which belongs to all facts of emotion, aspiration, and belief in ideals, are among the most stubborn and influential factors of human experience.

In its endeavors to escape the intellectual difficulties which arise from admitting the co-existence and reciprocal action of finite personality and a self-conscious Absolute, philosophy may deny that the Absolute is self-conscious personality. The ultimate philosophical position then becomes that of materialism, pantheism, or agnosticism. But such a denial is accustomed, and indeed almost compelled, to include also the freedom and real ethical being of finite minds. In the interests then of a supposed speculative consistency it, too, sacrifices many of the most pressing claims of the ethical, æsthetical, and religious nature of man. Moreover, it may be convicted of a vicious or incomplete metaphysics, in so far as we are able to show that there are positive reasons for affirming the self-conscious personality of the so-called "World-Ground."

In the face of these supreme difficulties, the only course remaining for the philosophy of religion is the only defensible course. It consists, first, in maintaining, on rational grounds, *both* the reality of man's ethical personality and the absoluteness of the self-conscious Life in which this finite personality has its ground. It requires, next, the effort so to frame the conception and statement of these two great truths as to free them from the contradictions which they seem, at first sight, to involve. That this effort is accompanied by a progress in approximation to complete success, we believe the history of this branch of philosophy will prove. To this end both descriptive and speculative psychology are constantly making certain contributions; and so is the discussion, current in treatises on ethics and theology. This end the philosophy of religion will more nearly attain when it is ready faithfully and candidly to avail itself of the conclusions of psychological science and of the indications derived from the history of philosophy.

But, finally, it must be admitted that we are utterly unable to satisfy the demand for a comprehensive knowledge of *the manner* of that reciprocal action which constantly takes place in reality between finite personality and the personal Absolute. But "the manner" of all ultimate connection between the really existent beings of even the finite world is hidden from our sight. The fact of any connection at all appears to us an ultimate and incomprehensible fact. This is true of that connection which physical science assumes among all the elements and aggregations of elements that constitute the world of things with which it deals. At least equally mysterious is the connection between things and finite minds. How can matter act on mind, and mind on matter? This is a question which has been the puzzle of the ages. Knowledge, ordinary or scientific, does not depend on our being able to answer the question:

How is any action of one real thing on another possible? It rather assumes such action as a fact, and endeavors to discover the terms, or uniform sequences, of the admitted action.

In raising the inquiries, *How* the self-conscious Absolute can act, not only upon, but — since we are speaking of the Absolute and of its self-consciousness — also in and through finite personality; and, *How* this Absolute can be conscious of the being and action of finite personality as, not simply the being and action of that which is other than itself, but also as being and action of which it is itself the ultimate "Ground," — we have reached the utmost limit of the tether of human reason. Properly speaking, neither science nor philosophy (but then also neither theology, nor religious imagination, nor revelation, nor faith) can answer these inquiries. In the conceptions with which the inquiries deal lie those mysteries which are part of the secret of the Being and Life of the Absolute. The effort of philosophy is to clear from contradictions these conceptions, and definitively to limit the sphere of ultimate mystery. This effort involves the handling of the most difficult and delicate of all philosophical problems.

Positive arguments for the self-consciousness of the "World-Ground," may be divided into two classes. These are the more distinctively metaphysical, and the more distinctively ethical and æsthetical. The former endeavor to show that the most rational, if not the only intelligible, determination of the admitted characteristics of the Absolute, implies self-conscious personality. Such characteristics are chiefly those expressed in the terms Unity, Reality, Subject of States, Ground of activity that manifests Finality, etc. Upon this question we find the two extreme positions taken, on the one hand by writers like Hartmann, and, on the other, by those who sympathize with the metaphysical conclusions of Lotze.

The predicate of "Will," as applied to the Absolute, seems to imply self-conscious personality. Now, Schopenhauer and Hartmann both affirm that the word "Will" is far better fitted to give intelligible expression to the essence of the Absolute than is the word "Force." What it is really to will — say they — we know in concrete self-conscious experience: what it is really to be a "force," or to exert "force," or to conserve "force," — if it be somewhat essentially different from our experience in being wills, — we cannot even form the faintest conception. "Will," then, is a term confessedly representing a generalization from concrete *self-conscious* experience. Blind or unconscious Will, on the contrary, is a synonym for Force. Accordingly, when we deny to this "moment" in the life of the Absolute the determination of self-consciousness, we only fall back, under a new and illusive term (namely, "Will"), upon the same confessedly unrealizable conception (namely, "Force"). For Mr. Herbert Spencer's Unity of "Force," which the universe of phenomena manifests to us, we may fitly substitute a Unity of "Will;" but in doing this, we really advance a reason for affirming the self-consciousness of the "World-Ground."

Somewhat similar must our conclusions be when we attempt clearly to analyze what is meant by speaking of the "Unity" of the Absolute. Is not the rational, self-conscious life of mind only the type and norm of all unity, the form inclusive of the essence of whatever is really One? In what conceivable sense, we may ask, can things be unitary beings to us, unless we cognize them as such in the uniting act of self-conscious life? How, moreover, do we become "one" to ourselves, and set ourselves as unitary beings over against all beings not-ourselves (not *one* with us), except in and through the same process of self-conscious cognition? If, then, by the Unity of the Absolute we mean anything more than the unity of mental representation for ourselves which the picture of the Absolute has must not this Unity realize itself in the only conceivable form of an actual self-conscious Life? "Transfigured Realism," as it seems to us, must either be so transfigured as no longer to be realism, or else it must give an intelligible character to the unity in reality which we affirm of the Absolute, in the form of a unity of self-conscious Mind.

It is the contention of a certain development of German speculative thinking that no being can have reality (in the only highest and truly defensible meaning of the term) which is not capable of being something more than an object for the cognition of other being; which is not indeed capable of being subject-object, object to itself (of having "For-Self-Being," *Für-sich-sein*). Thus Lotze is fond of affirming that self-conscious spiritual Life is the only true reality. On this principle, the only real being which "Things" can have, is their being in the self-conscious life of the Absolute; and, furthermore, the only satisfactory claim to the highest reality, which the Absolute can make, depends upon the postulate that the Absolute is an actual Life of self-consciousness in an eternal self-realizing as Spirit and Idea. Views concerning this contested point are among those which the philosophy of religion borrows from metaphysics. In this connection, then, we recall how philosophical analysis shows that all reality is given to us only as implicated in the process of self-conscious cognition. Implicated in this process are those obscure beliefs and indefinable postulates which cluster, as it were, about reality. And as separable from these *momenta* of the self-conscious process we can attach no meaning at all to the term "reality." The fundamental choice of metaphysics appears then to lie between affirming the self-consciousness of the supreme Reality, and the untenable position of scepticism toward the fundamental postulates of all knowledge.

That the conception of the Absolute as the real Subject or Ground of the changes which happen in reality compels us to affirm the self-consciousness of the Absolute, is a proposition required, we believe, by all thorough psychological and philosophical analysis.

The second set of considerations which influence us to conclude that the "World-Ground" is self-conscious and personal, are more difficult to put into the form of argument. They are, however, no less cogent on this account. They are derived from the ethical and æsthetical, and especially from the more distinctively religious, feeling of mankind. Ethical human nature shrinks back, bewildered, before a philosophical system which finds the World-Ground in blind, unconscious (and therefore unfeeling and unethical) Force. Æsthetical human nature seeks to realize its ideas of the beautiful in that act of imagination which projects a beauty of self-conscious and rational life into the ultimate Reality. And the life of religious faith and conduct finds it exceedingly difficult, if not quite impossible, to maintain itself at all, in the face of the conclusion that its object of belief, adoration and obedience, is devoid of all which it esteems of most value, — in brief, of self-conscious life. In this sphere of feeling — ethical, æsthetical, and religious — lie many considerations, therefore, which carry great positive weight in determining the question: Is the Absolute an unconscious Force, or a rational and self-conscious Life?

On these and similar grounds, and in spite of all the inherent difficulties and objections, the philosophy of religion is warranted in affirming the self-consciousness of the Absolute.

The grave and difficult question which next arises concerns the ethical being of the Absolute. Is the "World-Ground" a *moral* personality? In searching for an answer to this important inquiry, the appeal to the physical and natural sciences is suggestive but unsatisfying. Physical nature can only very imperfectly be shown to rest upon an ethical basis. The appearance of rational order, which the World has been held by the majority of thoughtful observers to possess, is indeed suggestive of a *quasi*-moral "World-Ground." Nor do the explanations of a mechanical theory as to how, in fact, this order came to establish itself, deprive the suggestion of its force. On the contrary, the mechanical theory, even in any one of the several forms given to it by the disciples of evolution, adds certain important elements to the general suggestion. It hints, at least, at the possibility that further knowledge of the necessities of the case, so to speak, and of the final outcome of the stern application of these necessities, when made to all sentient life, would remove the impression of the *un*-morality, or the immorality, of much of nature's action. But the most favorable interpretation of the working of physical forces and natural laws, which it is fair or rational to make, leaves much that is difficult to reconcile with the ethical being of the "World-Ground."

It is, therefore, rather to human nature and to history that we turn for so-called arguments by which to prove the ethical being of the Absolute. On this field, it cannot be denied that philosophy can make out a much clearer case. Yet even on this field disputes arise which are not easy of settlement.

All satisfactory philosophical account of the existence of distinctively ethical human nature seems to us definitely to indicate, if it does not completely prove, the ethical being of the One in whom this nature has its explanation and ground. This conclusion can be maintained after candidly weighing all the efforts of evolutionary science to describe the stages by which man's moral nature has attained its present development.

The genesis and the significance of those unique ideas and feelings which we call "moral" seem plainly to require an ethical and — as it were — a sympathetic "Ground." How a merely physical evolution, or an orderly play of blind, unconscious forces, can result in the manifestation of *such* ideas and feelings, with their characteristics of universality and unconditioned value, it is quite impossible to conceive. But it is not less impossible to conceive how an Absolute, that is essentially self-conscious personality, could be the primal cause in reality of other ethical life without itself being an ethical Life. Does, then, the Absolute, as the admitted ground of moral nature in man, represent to itself these ideas of the Right, the Ought, and the ethically well- or ill-deserving, as universal and of unconditional value, without manifesting its own real being therein? An affirmative answer to this question seems to us inconceivable. Probably no system of ethical philosophy has maintained that the Absolute is the *self-conscious* and primal source of all ethical ideating and feeling in man, and yet is itself devoid of ethical life. As a matter of fact, the denial of the self-conscious personality, and the denial of the moral personality of the Absolute, stand or fall together.

This more distinctively metaphysical argument may be supplemented by considerations drawn from the phenomena of ethical, æsthetical, and religious feeling. That ethical finite being should be dependent, for its destiny, upon an unethical ground, can never be otherwise than offensive and distressful to ethical feeling. So do certain strong spontaneous responses which æsthetical human nature makes to the encitement furnished by the perception of natural objects, by the intercourse of society and the contemplation of phenomena of history, impel the mind to belief in the moral personality of the Absolute. The feeling of genuine awe, as distinguished from the feeling of personal fear, may be regarded as one of those vague but potent æsthetical bonds which exist between the heart of man and the moral being of the "World-Ground." Nor can that limitless capacity for admiration, for reverence, for affection, which human nature develops — since the capacity finds its rational correlate in no finite object to call forth its full measure — fail to be regarded as indicative of the soul's instinctive feeling after the moral personality "whom faith calls God." The tendency of men to adore and to obey that which they conceive of as morally good and great, points in the same direction. In fine, the threads of that web of unformulated arguments which the capacities and inclinations of man's emotional nature weaves around the concept of an ethical Absolute, are invisible and delicate, yet tenacious and effective. As craving is the spur which nature thrusts into the side of all living beings, from the amœba to the highest of the mammals, so insatiable longing after good, and unceasing dissatisfaction with the finite, are the cry of the human soul after an ethical and æsthetical "World-Ground."

> "In die Welt hinausgestossen
> Steht der Mensch verlassen da."

An impersonal and unethical Cosmos furnishes cold food for this craving. This "deep-seated craving" it was which led Augustine to the true knowledge of God, when he had been for some time "hunting after the emptiness of popular praise, down even to theatrical applauses, and poetic prizes, and strifes for grassy garlands, and the follies of shows, and the intemperance of desires." "Justice," says George Eliot, "is like the kingdom of God, — it is not without as a fact, it is within us as a great yearning." "Justice," and all the other moral predicates which religion ascribes to the Absolute, are esteemed to be without as a fact, because in fact they are within us as a "great yearning."

It is without doubt difficult to formulate reasons for conclusions reached under pressure from the ethical, æsthetical, and religious feelings. It is none the less true, however, that these feelings in fact exist, and do actually impel men to faith in the real existence of God as an object needed for their completer satisfaction.

That self-conscious and ethical personal Absolute, which philosophy postulates as the "Ground" of other nature, but especially of human nature, we are entitled to call *God*. When this supreme synthesis as to the being of the Absolute is reached, the so-called "proofs" for the existence of God have done their appointed work. We cannot, however, attain the same rational confidence with regard to all the definite ethical predicates which theology is wont to ascribe to God. Here emerges in the path of the progress of religious philosophy the fierce and dreadful conflict between Pessimism and Optimism. The most cautious analysis and the boldest but wisest synthesis prevent the student of philosophy from rashly handing in his adherence to either of these conflicting parties. Certainly none of the many forms of an easy-going Optimism can find acceptance with penetrating and thoughtful minds. The profound reality and mysterious significance of physical and moral evil hang like a thick cloud over every direct path by which we try to reach the proof that perfect justice and perfect goodness belong to God. The discoveries of modern science peremptorily reject the traditional argument of theology by which the entire weight of the world's physical evil is hung upon the sinful choice of finite minds. That wrong-doing necessarily produces misery, and that much of the misery of men is actually produced by their wrong-doing, are propositions from which no system of ethics dissents. But, on the other hand, the phenomena appealed to by pessimistic systems like those of Schopenhauer and Hartmann are unmistakable enough; and the domain covered by such phenomena is probably being increased rather than diminished by the discoveries of modern physiology and psychology. Every new form of disease-producing microbe, with its distribution of its products, like the rain, upon the just and the unjust, is a startling additional fact thrown into the scale which Pessimism is interested in weighting heavily. Nor is the depressing evidence confined to the sphere of physics alone. That manifestation of the Power not-ourselves "which makes for righteousness" in human history is far from being such as to enable the holders of optimistic views readily to triumph over their opponents.

On the other hand, Hartmann's elaborate attempt to raise the widespread pessimistic feeling and judgment of the age to the dignity of a philosophical system, on the compound basis of psychological analysis and induction from facts of history, is a failure; and — from the very nature of the case — a dismal failure.[1] It overestimates the relative number and significance of the facts on which it relies; it underestimates the number and significance of those facts to which the opposed theory can

[1] Comp. Hartmann, Philosophy of the Unconscious, Coupland's translation, vol. iii.; and Zur Geschichte und Begründung des Pessimismus, Berlin, 1880, by the same author; also, Der moderne Pessimismus, by Dr. Ludwig von Golther, Leipzig, 1878; and Sully, Pessimism: A History and a Criticism, London, 1877.

point. It fails to show — as it aims to do — that pain is a necessary factor of all conscious life, and an increasingly large factor as the development of the higher and more rational forms of life goes on, rather than a temporary condition in the evolution of these higher forms. It treats far too cavalierly (and therefore unphilosophically) those fears, faiths, and hopes, which extend the continuity and significance of the life of the individual, and of the community, into other times and spheres than those whose facts can be made the basis of a scientific induction; and, finally, it loses much of its support from other more fundamental principles in the philosophical system of which it forms a part, when its proposition that the being of the Absolute is *un*conscious and *un*ethical, is successfully disproved. Historically considered, Hartmann's views on this subject are a fleeting product of the worst temper of the present age. On this point we agree with the observation of Dr. Edmund Pfleiderer.[1] "We should honor too highly that mode of wisdom called Pessimism, if we assented to the multitude and considered it as anything more than an apparent systematizing of that bad humor which afflicts the many *blasé* minds of our highly nervous century,— as being a really new and epoch-making view of the Universe at large. The moral disease to which our age is subject, an indolent eudæmonism, has found expression in it. This, and this alone, is the reason for that wealth of applause from a multitude of like-minded men, of which this tendency in thinking loves complacently to boast."

In the face of two contradictory conclusions suggested by induction from two sets of facts, it is not of the nature of human reason to remain at rest. The philosophy of religion, from a survey of all the phenomena, does not confidently derive the conclusion that the world is, ethically or æsthetically, the best conceivable or the best possible; or that the "World-Ground" is perfectly wise, just, and good. Much less, however, does it

[1] Die Aufgabe der Philosophie in unserer Zeit, Rede zur Feier des Geburtstages seiner Majestät . . . Wilhelm I., etc. Kiel, 1874.

derive in this way the contradictory of these conclusions. In the conflict of mental tendencies which is occasioned by the attempt to make a rational choice between the two conflicting systems of philosophical conclusions, the ancient principle of Becoming, or rather the more modern principle of a rational evolution of the world, is a helpful resource. As the vastness — in respect to space, time, and complexity and number of objects and interests — of the application of this principle becomes apparent, the lesson of that patient, wise, and cautious spirit which philosophy should cherish, is enforced by the most tremendous sanctions. Philosophy finds little satisfaction in the current theological theodicies, whether they consider the facts of the present and the past, and predict the future, from the predominatingly optimistic, or the predominatingly pessimistic point of view. Even more unsatisfactory, however, seem all the recent attempts to explain the world's being and progress without attributing it to an ethical and self-conscious "Ground."

At this point those facts with which the study of the history of civilization makes us familiar offer their assistance to the synthesis of philosophy. On the whole they show — we believe — some firmly secured progress of the race toward the supreme ethical and æsthetical Good. In spite of all that the pessimism of Hartmann has to offer, the claims to an increase of every important form of well-being by the struggles of the race through the centuries can be established on historical grounds.

It is, however, only when we contemplate the phenomena of the religious life, and especially of Christianity — that most historical and inherently progressive of all religions — that the more convincing form of obtainable evidence is presented to the mind. The conceptions of a progressive redemption of the race, of the final triumph of the supreme Good over all that we call evil, and of the union of all ultimate forms of the Good — happiness, beauty, and righteousness — in the blessed life of a community known as the perfected "Kingdom of God," largely determine our attitude toward the debated question of Optimism or Pessimism. That these conceptions originate and flourish chiefly in the domain of one form of religion called "revealed" constitutes no reason whatever why philosophy should refuse or hesitate to make use of them.

The proposition that the Absolute is a *perfect* self-conscious ethical life — that One who is not only all-wise but infinitely just and good exists as the "World-Ground" — does not admit of "proof," in the stricter sense of this word. It may be said, however, to be the most reasonable hope and faith of the sanest and ethically and æsthetically most symmetrical minds. It is a proposition which, received as a postulate, is far indeed from explaining everything, or even from immediately introducing the appearance of harmony among all the facts. It is a proposition, the truth of which seems to be progressively accumulating as the advance of the race affords more and more of historical ground on which the proposition may be based. That it is a proposition which the ethical and æsthetical emotions tend to regard with a high degree of favor, there can be no doubt. Indeed, this statement falls far enough below the truth. It is not those who have actually suffered most who have found in life, and in their reflections thereon, most reason for the pessimistic frame of mind. The tried and tortured heroes of the race have, for the most part, ranged themselves, to the last extremity of personal suffering, on the side of optimistic faith and hope. Only a philosophy which has made up its mind from the beginning rigorously to exclude some of the choicest facts of human experience, because it cannot explain — not to say appreciate — them, will fail to take the testimony of these emotions into its account.

From the moment when the conclusion is reached, that the nature of the "World-Ground" is the highest self-conscious, rational, ethical, and æsthetical Life, the progress of the philosophy of religion becomes comparatively easy, rapid, and sure. To the determination of this great and inclusive problem all its other problems are subordinate. If reason can effectively command the light of this Life to arise upon the world's system of finite things and minds, then how great is that Light! Thus does the supreme synthesis of philosophy aim to give a profounder interpretation and a new significance to all the particular facts and truths of the positive sciences.

The God whom philosophy seeks and finds is not a Being to be described by the fewest and most abstract terms possible. The rather is He the most concrete, real, and individual, and yet most varied and comprehensive Life. To that Unity of Reality which He is, the philosophy of nature and the philosophy of mind alike ascribe all the entities, forces, laws, and final purposes, which are introduced to them by those particular sciences on which their synthesis is built. In Him is the being of that which has mass and extension, and which displays manifold immanent and transeunt energies of various degrees. In Him is the ground of the permanency and unchangeableness of the *quantum* of the world's "matter" so-called; in Him the ground also of the conservation and correlation of energy. It is the Unity of His Reality that explains the reciprocal being and action of all things; and the same is the bond in reality between all bodies and their correlated minds. In His own abounding ethical and æsthetical Life, with its joy in all the reality of the beautiful and the morally good, do we also find that ultimate objective basis for human ethical and æsthetical development which philosophy seeks.

The degrees of confidence with which we make these and other similar statements are various; and the grounds for the existence of confidence in the statements themselves are not all alike secure. But the analysis which provides the factors for this synthesis, and the comprehensiveness and certainty of the resulting synthesis, are both — we believe — constantly winning their way in the history of reflective thought.

Additional evidence for the necessity of postulating self-conscious and ethical personality of the Absolute may be derived from the failure of those philosophical systems which deny the truth of this postulate. Metaphysically considered, these systems may all be said to be lacking in a sufficient and effective *principium individuationis.* This is manifestly a chief fault of Schopenhauer's philosophy. He leaps to the generalization that the world as "Thing-in-itself" is Will, by means of an indescribable and fictitious psychological process. But in order deductively to explain the world from this principle of Will, he is obliged to introduce into his philosophy a quite unintelligible view of the Platonic ideas. These "ideas" must somehow serve the Absolute, instead of its own self-conscious personal life, as a ground of diversifying itself into the world of phenomena. So, too, does Hartmann, by an elaborate process of induction, so called, succeed in adding — so he thinks — "Idea" to Will, as belonging to the essence of the Absolute. But Hartmann also can get no work, no actuality of a world-being and a world-process, out of his Absolute, without adding thereto at least certain elements of conscious life. Accordingly, he selects these elements from the lowest and least worthy forms of life. The Absolute is a "clairvoyant," we are told; the Absolute needs, in order to start it upon the process of self-manifestation, at least a certain amount of blind but painful feeling of unrest. The "*single transcendent consciousness* of the All-One . . . has for sole content the *absolutely indefinite transcendent pain or unblessedness* of the void infinite will."[1]

Similar fault might justly be found with all the positive conclusions of other systems of philosophy which, like the systems of Schopenhauer and Hartmann, deny to the Absolute a self-conscious and ethical life. Their Absolute fails to meet the demands of reason as a satisfactory and really effective "World-Ground." It needs some other transcendent being than itself, or some actual admixture of the very elements theoretically denied to it, in order to make it capable of manifesting itself after the fashion of the world of our experience, — not to say, capable of manifesting itself at all. What is true of Hart-

[1] Philosophy of the Unconscious, Coupland's Translation, ii. 257.

mann's "The Unconscious" is — as has frequently been shown — true as well of the "Unknowable" of Mr. Spencer.

The subordinate problems of the philosophy of religion may be divided into two groups; of these, one concerns the predicates or attributes of God, and the other concerns His relations to finite things and minds. All the predicates of God are to be more precisely determined in accordance with the conception which has already been established; namely, He is a self-conscious, rational, and ethical Absolute. His Unity is to be understood as, in kind, the unity of a personal life; and since this personal life is that of the Absolute, we affirm that God is *one* God, the "alone" God, and besides Him is no other. His Unchangeableness is not "the monotony and rigidity of a perfect and unchanging self-likeness;" it is not inconsistent with the being subject of changeable inner states. It is rather that immanent and consistent adherence to the eternal principles of His own rational and ethical life, which is possible for the Absolute alone.

By the Omnipresence of God, it is meant to maintain, negatively, that the spatial limitations of finite being and action are inapplicable to Him; and, positively, that in the unknown *modus* of God's being and action within the world of finite things and minds lies the ground of the space-forming activity of our minds, as well as of the space-formed being of things.

By the Omnipotence of God it is meant to assert, negatively, that the limitations of causal activity, both in intensity and in scope, which characterize all finite beings, have no applicability to Him; and, positively, that all the action, and all the implied "power" or energy of things and minds, has its ground in Him alone.

By the Eternity of God, it is meant that the limitations of being and action in time which belong to the world of finite things and minds do not affect God; as well as that He is not subject to those conditions of the finite world which change in time. But it is also implied in the eternity predicated of

God that His self-conscious rational life is the permanent and unchanging Ground of all the being and action of things and minds, in time. Whether the predicate of "time" applies (in any meaning of the words, and, if at all, in what precise meaning of the words) to the life of the Absolute itself, is one of the most interesting and yet baffling of the subordinate problems of philosophy in the domain of theology and religion.

By the Omniscience of God, it is meant to deny that any of the limitations of knowledge to which finite minds are subject apply to God; it is meant also to affirm that, *somehow*, all that is knowable is immediately and certainly known by God. Reference has already been made to the many and great difficulties which encompass every attempt to form a clear mental picture of the *modus operandi* of the infinite knowledge of the self-conscious Absolute.

Of the more precise relations of God to the world, it is customary for philosophical theology to emphasize, chiefly, these three: creation, preservation, and government. Under the terms of that relation which the word "Creation" signifies we are justified only in affirming *a priori* the essential and absolute (*i. e.*, without limitations of time, space, or causal action) dependence of the world upon the wisdom and will of God. Under this general tenet a number of particular problems range themselves, for the attempted solution of which philosophy must acknowledge its dependence upon the conclusions of the particular sciences. How — in what order, by what stages and successive forms of the appearance of existent beings — did God create the world? Such answer as can be given to an inquiry like this must rely upon the consensus of those sciences which describe the evolution of all non-living and living beings, in their order and relations of dependence toward each other, in time. Are we to conceive of that relation between God and the world, which the word "creation" signifies, as eternal, or as having had a beginning in time? For the doubtful answer which is alone possible to this question, we need such help as psychology can furnish by an analysis of the concept of "time," supplemented by such contributions as physical science can make touching the probable past duration of the system of finite things. Other inquiries — such as, Why did God create the World at all? or, Why create it at some particular time rather than another? or, How can we conceive of time as being when, as yet, the created world was not? — are speculative puzzles which belong, most fitly, to the play-time rather than to the serious work of the student of philosophy.

By the divine "Preservation" of the world, it is meant to assert that the world is continuously and ceaselessly dependent, for all its being and action, upon the immanent being and unceasingly active will of God. The more precise determination of this relation, as well as of the relation of creation, will be differently made by thinkers belonging to different schools of philosophy. What sort of being (of so-called reality or *substantiality*) does God impart to, and maintain in, finite things and finite minds? It is plain that, in the attempt to answer this question, the most fundamentally divergent views on the theory of knowledge, on metaphysics, ethics, and æsthetics, will make themselves strongly felt. But especially will the resources of speculative thinking be taxed to their utmost capacity in the effort to frame a consistent and tenable theory of the divine relation, in both creation and preservation, to finite minds. On the one hand, the "creation" of the soul cannot consist in the planting, as it were, within a body, of some undeveloped "mind-stuff" ready made; nor can its preservation be held to mean that, having been constituted "substantial," it continues to exist as long as God *preserves* it from the destructive force of physical agencies. Doubtless, it is as really true of minds as of things: In Him they live . . . and have their being. On the other hand, the principles of ethical self-consciousness cannot, safely or reasonably, be sacrificed to the desire of philosophy for a perfectly logical and deductive system of modes of operation, in reality, between God and finite minds. Here again do we stand on a field, within which philosophy can do little more than maintain a few great principles, clear their application as much as possible from the semblance of contradiction, and point out the present limitations of the powers of human reason itself.

"Government" is a term which we can most properly apply only to God's relation to finite personalities. At this point, then, the philosophy of religion refers to psychology and to the philosophy of mind for its conception of the personality of man, — the one who is to be "governed." It refers also to that conception of God as an ethical personality, which it has already attained, for the further determination of the nature of the relation which He, the "Ruler," sustains to finite personality. But it is especially from the philosophical study of human society and of human history that our doctrine of the divine government is to be derived. It is God immanent in human life, in its fundamental forms, its successive stages of development, its ideal and emotional springs, who is the Governor of men. All *government*, in the only true meaning of the word, implies the encitement, discipline, and control, of one person by another; and, in the case of the divine government, of course, the inspiration, illumining, and discipline, of all persons by the one Personal and ethical Absolute. Here, again, an appeal to the philosophy of the Ideal (the perfectly blessed, the perfectly beautiful, and the perfectly good) must be taken in order to suggest the nature of that goal, or end to be gained, which government implies.

The conceptions of revelation and inspiration are closely connected with the conception of divine government. A "manifestation" of that unity which the "World-Ground" is, the most pronounced agnosticism seems to find it necessary to suppose. But a *manifestation* is possible only between minds. That which is manifested is an idea; that to which the manifestation is made, is an ideating mind. Certainly, then, it is not a long or difficult step from the more indefinite and obscure conception of a manifestation of the Absolute to the more definite and clear conception of a revelation of God. Nor, if we regard God as the source of all life, and especially of all that spiritual life which is the essence of subjective religion, can the conception of inspiration fail to have a most valid and comprehensive use. As the objective factor, corresponding to inspiration, we find the "miracles" of revealed religion claiming a place in the historical manifestation of God. But the philosophy of religion is dependent upon metaphysics, in the two forms of the philosophy of nature and the philosophy of mind, for determining the *modus operandi* of the miracle, — so far as this is possible.

The more precise, detailed, and defensible exposition of all the predicates of God, and of all the manifold forms of relation in which He stands to the world, must be gained by philosophy in constant dependence upon the positive sciences. Among these sciences, the psychological and historical will necessarily hold the place of chief importance.

Whatever be his personal faith, the student of philosophy cannot regard as unimportant those facts, truths, faiths, and institutions, as well as that type of ethical and æsthetical character, which belong to historical Christianity. Those facts, truths, faiths, and institutions are of the greatest importance for determining the synthesis of philosophy. To neglect to give them in philosophy the place which they actually have in the life of the race, is to be guilty of an almost fatal neglect. By a "Christian" philosophy, we do not understand a system of dogmatic theology which accords with the prevalent orthodox type; we understand rather such a view of the world, the soul, and God, of the dignity and destiny of man, and of the goal of history, as gives to the Christian truths and facts the place which is their due. In this way can philosophy be of more real assistance to the progress of Christianity than by timorous and ill-considered efforts to resume its mediæval position of being ancillary to the dominant theology. In so far only as what men call Christianity is accordant with the deepest and most comprehensive rational, ethical, and æsthetical life of man, will it continue to win and hold the allegiance of the race. But it is precisely upon this, the nature of true religion, that philosophy most fondly and confidently dwells.

The value of that supreme synthesis, which the philosophy of religion makes, for the other departments of philosophy, and also for the particular sciences upon whose principles the synthesis is chiefly dependent, will doubtless be differently estimated by different minds. Certainly, from the conception of God — His being, predicates, and relations to the world — we cannot deduce the principles of the particular sciences. But it is our firm belief that they all gain inexpressibly in significance and value when they are considered in the light of this synthesis. This certified principle, or — if the objector prefer — this ennobling and captivating postulate, of a perfect ethical and æsthetical Life as the "Ground" of the world's being and progress, illumines and elevates the entire domain of human knowledge and human life.

It is only in the reasoned faith in such a principle that one can find that relative harmony of the scientific and the practical, the side of thought and the side of belief and emotion, which is the security of the religious life. Pure thinking, it is true, will not find God; neither will it satisfy conscience, or secure the redemption of the individual and of the race. But to do this, irrational and thoughtless feeling is also impotent, — whether called superstition or faith. Nor can busy doing and works done accomplish this salvation. For it is the life of reason, in all its variety and richness of content, which is according to the Life of the ever-living God.

CHAPTER XIV.

TENDENCIES AND SCHOOLS IN PHILOSOPHY.

THERE have been diversities of opinion, and divisions of thinkers into groups according to the character of their particular conclusions, from the beginning of speculative thinking until the present time. In truth, the manifestation of more or less definite tendencies and the formation of schools follow from the very nature of philosophy. The freedom of the philosophical spirit, employing the subtlest analysis and the most comprehensive synthesis for the solution of the ultimate problems of all Being and all Knowledge, necessarily results in division. The spirit, the method, and the character of the subject-matter, are all responsible for that variety of systems which the history of philosophy reveals.

The spirit of philosophy is freedom. From this it follows that each man's adherence to a particular tendency in philosophical discipline is largely a matter of choice. Or rather, the selection and formation of one's philosophical system are, in a peculiar way, the expression of one's whole rational and voluntary being. One may not, indeed, choose one's master or school in philosophy, and receive the content of one's speculative thinking, "ready made," as it were. On the contrary, to do this — however unwittingly — is to forfeit all favor from genuine philosophy. No other acquirement of the human mind is so improperly received without questioning from the hands of another. In attaining no other form of intellectual discipline, in reaching no other class of rational conclusions, are caution, patience, and willingness to await the growth of thought, so indispensable. At the same time philosophy, especially on its synthetic side, requires the commitment of the entire man as does no other form of reasoning and knowledge. It requires also that arousing of the ethical, æsthetical, and even of the religious nature, which has its ground in the life of the will.

The dependence of schools of philosophy, and of the adherence of the individual thinker to any particular system of philosophy, upon freedom of choice has been frequently observed. In discussing the definition of philosophy we found that its appeal to the will and its relation to character have been recognized in the very terms applied to it. This is true, not only of the figurative descriptions of Plato (see page 9 f.), but of the more exact and critical discussion of Kant. "The kind of philosophy which one chooses," says Fichte,[1] "depends on the kind of man one is. For a philosophical system is not a dead bit of furniture which one can take to one's self or dispose of, as one pleases; but it is endowed with a soul by the soul of the man who has it." "In the supreme and ultimate instance," says Schelling,[2] "there is no other Being than *Willing*. This is fundamental being, and to this all the predicates of such being conform. . . . The one effort of all philosophy is to find the highest expression for this." Herbart[3] goes so far as to declare that "the study of philosophy is a natural offspring of the totality we call 'the good Will;' this good Will is philosophy; only we must not confound the study of philosophy with philosophy itself." And less well-known names have in modern times declared themselves to the same effect. "To know the truth in spirit (by thought, or speculatively)," says one writer, "and to live in confiding intercourse with it, — this it is which the best of all philosophers have called 'to philosophize.'" The same view is expressed by another writer in

1 Comp. his words in the Darstellung der Wissenschaftslehre, Werke (ed. J. G. Fichte), ii. 155 f.

2 Philosoph. Untersuchungen der menschlichen Freiheit, Werke, vii. 350.

3 See also his remarks on the Practical Need of Philosophy, Kurze Encyklopädie, pp. 3–29.

the following language: "We have to distinguish two kinds of philosophy: the one manifests itself by the speech, and the other by the conduct, of the man. . . . This latter it is — the realization of wisdom by the man in his social intercourse — which has recently been brought, as philosophy in deed, to more general recognition."

However much allowance be made for exaggeration, through noble enthusiasm for one's favorite pursuit and through laudable desire to commend it, we cannot fail to recognize in the statements just quoted a most important truth. At bottom, philosophy implies the freedom of rational life. That diversity of the results of philosophizing, in which the different so-called schools of philosophy have their source, is due to this inherent freedom.

The necessary method of philosophy is also such as to occasion the rise in its general domain of diverging tendencies and of different systems of thought. Philosophy results from the movement of rational life, by more searching reflective analysis and progressively more complete synthesis, toward a harmony of the principles of all Being and all Knowledge. In this movement three characteristic attitudes of mind toward existing philosophical views are successively taken. Scepticism calls in question the tenets of the prevalent dogmatism; criticism strives to detect the errors or defects, and also the factors of truth, which are combined in these tenets; by a new synthesis, on the basis of this improved analysis, a new form of positive or dogmatic conclusions is obtained.

In the use of this indispensable "method" of all philosophy is to be found a reason for the origin of more or less well defined philosophical systems or schools. The reflective analysis of different thinkers will vary in the degrees of its penetration and comprehensiveness, — whether its application refer to the whole round of current philosophical problems or to some particular problem among them all. The analysis of no one thinker will be able to penetrate all the depths, or to extend to all the confines, of the world of things and minds. For the human mind is limited; but science is capable of unlimited growth, and reality is diversified and extended beyond all assignable bounds. It follows, then, that each adherent of a particular philosophical system, or of a particular solution to any great philosophical problem, will be one-sided or incomplete in his analysis. He will be compelled to stop short of the point where he can hold all the factors and principles of Being and Knowledge firmly in his mental grasp. Accordingly, and as a matter of necessity, his synthetic philosophy will be one-sided and defective. It will relatively exaggerate some thoughts; it will depress unduly, or wholly pass by, other important thoughts. Finally, the impetus toward system-making which belongs to the spirit and mission of philosophy will cause a further exaggeration of those limitations of human thinking that are expressed in the very existence of philosophical schools. The progress of reason in self-knowledge cannot be made secure by obtaining the common consent of thinkers to defer all system-making in philosophy until the analysis of the factors shall be complete. Each system, when broken into fragments by the blows of scepticism and criticism, affords some "rough-hewn" stones for the structures that are to follow. By its necessary method, philosophy is compelled never to attain the complete realization of the idea which it pursues. This is its glory, and not its shame. It is a never-finished rational life.

How variously might the foregoing reflections be illustrated by an appeal to the history of philosophical systems and tendencies! At one time a synthesis of principles, obtained by so-called "pure thinking" and independently of empirical generalizations, has dominated philosophy. Dialectic has thus been identified with reality; and a philosophical system consisting of abstractions has been the result. Deductive demonstration has at another time been employed as the only true philosophical method. Separated from all the constantly diversifying life with which inductive science deals, the most monstrous conclusions have thus been held to be "*proved*" beyond the possibility of doubt. The heart of living and concrete realities has been cruelly crushed under the heel of these despots in the use of the demonstrative methods. But new systems of so-called inductive philosophy have sprung forth from the bosom of modern science itself. And now all the problems of the universal life and the ultimate reality are to be solved — if solved at all — by observation and tabulating of phenomena. Then we are given to understand that the nature of the soul, and even of the Absolute, may be inductively established by considering how decapitated frogs and bisected insects behave; or how the *vis medicatrix* operates for the healing of a wounded crab or salamander. Then all analysis of psychological problems by introspection, and all effort to substitute tenable for untenable metaphysical views, are discredited. They are said to see "with the eyes of Peter Bell, which, seeing, see not," who fail to consider reflection and thought as means for penetrating the mysteries of the universe inferior to the study of the phenomena of "knee-jerk," or of the excited ganglionic nerve-cells of a cat or a dog.[1]

It is, however, the character of the subject-matter in philosophy which is chiefly responsible for the division of the tenets established into rival systems and schools. Psychology is, indeed, the indispensable propædeutic of philosophical discipline. But all the particular sciences also offer their presuppositions and discovered principles, in the form of problems, to the student of philosophy. The goal toward which he strives is the rational system of them all. But they all are constantly, and to a large extent, undergoing a process of development. How then, since they all furnish material to philosophy, can it escape the limitations and the necessity of change which they impose?

Yet more potent reasons for the occurrence of schools in

[1] Comp. Am. Journal of Psychology, Nov., 1887, p. 162.

philosophy may be derived from the consideration of the nature of its subject-matter. This consists wholly of problems, — of problems of the most profound and perplexing kind. All the more serious problems of each of the particular sciences concern that system of thinking which is philosophy. Even the principles which these sciences may take for granted become difficult *problems* for the student of philosophy. The clearest and most satisfactory solution of some of these problems may seem to involve conclusions directly contradictory of equally clear and satisfactory solutions of other problems. Witness the task which biology sets to philosophical ethics when it attempts to bring the psychical processes, including the process of choice, under the principle of a vital mechanism. How easy would the task of philosophical system become, if only one could pass by those presuppositions or unverified generalizations of the particular sciences which seem especially to need its harmonizing agency! One can frame a "system" in philosophy, if one will not be too particular about admitting unpleasant individual inquiries into membership in this system. We should all doubtless be of one school, if only Reality were not so varied and — shall we say? — inconsistent in its forms of manifestation.

Nor should it be forgotten that the ultimate problem of philosophy is no other than the problem of the Infinite, — the inquiry into the being, relations, and modes in manifestation, of God. Surely He is a great deep, and who can fathom Him? We obscurely feel the Presence, and hear the movement of His garments; but His hand veils our eyes. And when the hand is removed, we can see no more than the vesture which clothes His retreating form. Little wonder need be felt, then, if the approaches which are made toward the place where this problem can be clearly envisaged (not to say solved) are along diverging lines; or if the travellers on their way stop, in weariness or self-satisfaction, or because night has come, at places that lie distant from each other, and far removed from the goal.

The classification of the actually existing schools of philosophy follows from the very nature of philosophy and of its method. These may all be described under three most general heads. They are Realism, Idealism, and Dualism. Some of the other so-called schools or systems, such as dogmatism, scepticism, and criticism, are not (as has already been shown) properly to be so entitled at all. These are rather "moments" or tendencies in the spirit and method of all philosophy. And the undue emphasis of any of them, to the relative exclusion or suppression of the others, does not result in the formation of a school or system of philosophical tenets. Schools and systems, in philosophy as elsewhere, are to be classified — if at all — according to the divergent character of the positive tenets which constitute them. This is as true of those critical or sceptical propositions which sum up the results derived by the corresponding method of philosophical inquiry, as it is of the most extreme dogmatism.

Much less are agnosticism and eclecticism to be classed with idealism, realism, and dualism, as co-ordinate schools or systems of philosophy. Agnosticism, in so far as it remains agnostic, is not to be distinguished from the sceptical or critical attitude of mind. So far as the agnostic becomes positive, he is to be classified as an idealist, a realist, or an adherent of dualism. And the positive conclusions which enable us to classify him — if such conclusions are to be discovered in his thinking — may be tinged with more or less of either the dogmatic, the sceptical, or the critical spirit and method. Thus Mr. Spencer has the undoubted right to classify himself among the realists (with the distinction that his realism is evolutionary and "transfigured"), — albeit his position seems to many dogmatic rather than critical.

What, however, is the natural and necessary relation, as to position and development, which exists amongst the three schools or systems of philosophical thinking? In the attempt briefly to answer this question we shall expect to gain further verification for the conclusions which have already been reached, when considering the several principal problems in analytical and synthetic philosophy.

"Wherever," says Von Hartmann,[1] "we may look among the original philosophical or religious systems of the first rank, everywhere do we meet with the tendency to Monism; and it is only stars of the second or third magnitude which find satisfaction in an external dualism or still greater division." The same writer thinks that in all philosophies of the modern epoch we see "this tendency to Monism more or less perfectly realized in one fashion or another."[2] As an inquiry in the history of philosophy, there can be little doubt that a general assent must be accorded to these statements of Hartmann. The Unity of all Reality is, in some sort, a postulate of all modern philosophy; and this postulate, as a silent and sometimes sluggish assumption, enters into the organization of all experience as the task is attempted by the particular sciences. Moreover, that growing conviction as to the unity of the universe of phenomena, which expresses itself in the assumption of a universal "reign of law," in admitted principles of all physical science, in the attempt to establish on scientific grounds a theory of psycho-physics and of the general relations of body and mind, and in the gradual drawing together of all the sciences, affords support to a monistic philosophy. Dualism, as a claimant for the position of a rational and consistent system of thinking, is undoubtedly being discredited by the progress of the age.

It is further to be noted that Dualism arises — at least in modern times — almost altogether as a protest against some form of Monism, which is deemed extreme or dangerous. It is chiefly fear of the logical consequences of monistic conclusions which induces the modern student of philosophy even to consider the dualistic hypothesis. In the ancient times the world, from

[1] Philosophy of the Unconscious, Coupland's Translation, ii. 234.

[2] Ibid., p. 239.

lack of scientific knowledge, seemed to men too diverse to be accounted for as the manifestation or revelation of a single principle. The search after a unity of the "World-Ground," which belongs to the very nature of reason itself, was therefore limited in its range. Knowledge was limited as regards the laws and modes of energy which connect together the world of real beings. Imagination was limited in its flight. But it was those peoples who felt most keenly, though in a *naïve* and unreasoning way, certain great divergencies in the manifestations of reality, among which the first dualistic systems arose. Two fundamental and irremovable distinctions, on which indeed all our experience is based, gave occasion to these systems. They are the distinction between matter and mind, and the distinction between moral good and moral evil.

It is the fear that these two distinctions will be lost or marred, and the fear of the theoretical or practical consequences of such an event, which impels many minds even now away from philosophical Monism. On the contrary, all the instincts of the philosophical mind, all the tendencies of modern scientific discovery and modern speculative thinking, all the influences from the example of the greatest thinkers (materialistic, idealistic, pantheistic, theistic), are committed to the cause of monistic philosophy. Every attempt to establish two ultimate principles of all Knowledge and all Being, and every attempt to deal with any of the subordinate philosophical problems in a manner implying the existence of two such principles, is opposed to our modern thought. In conflict with the most tenable of the dualistic systems no fairly consistent monistic system can fail to secure the "prejudice" of philosophical thinking. In conflict with all dualistic systems, some form of a monistic system will ultimately maintain the supremacy.

But why, it may be asked, if this is so, does Dualism continue (at least — if we accept Hartmann's estimate — "among the stars of the second or third magnitude") so persistently as a third system opposed to both of the other two? Chiefly because of the failure of current systems of Monism so to answer the problems of philosophy as to avoid contradicting certain apparently obvious facts and important truths. These facts and truths — we repeat — concern, first, the nature and relations in reality of the body and the mind; and, second, the nature and relations of the morally good and the morally evil, as well as the ground which good and evil have in ultimate reality. Forms of Monism, which virtually contradict the distinction between the reality, *me,* and the reality that is *not-me,* cannot succeed in preventing the persistent recurrence of rival dualistic schemes. Monism must so construct its tenets as to preserve, or, at least, as not to contradict and destroy the truths implicated in this distinction; otherwise, it cannot remain in possession of the rightful domain of philosophy. But even more imperative, and far more difficult, is the task imposed upon Monism by those dualistic considerations which emerge on ethical grounds. To blur, or reduce, or deny, valid ethical distinctions is to furnish an elixir of life to an expiring Dualism; it is even to equip it with an all-conquering sword. No form of Monism can persistently maintain itself which erects its system upon the ruins of fundamental ethical principles and ideas.

The science of mind, whether pursued from the experimental and physiological, or from the more purely philosophical point of view, has during the last half-century made rapid progress. A new form — if not of a science, at least of scientific research looking toward the establishment of a verifiable body of science — has been originated and pursued with ardor and brilliant results. This is psycho-physics, or physiological psychology. The very existence of such an attempt at science is indicative of a strong monistic tendency. Its conclusions, so far as it can be said to have established conclusions, favor a monistic philosophy. But what kind of a monistic philosophy? Not such a kind, we believe, as denies the derived and dependent reality of either the body or the mind. Certainly not that modern and most captivating form of materialism, which refuses to recognize a real subject of the psychical states, but regards them all as only phenomenal and expressive of the complicated molecular and chemical relations and changes that belong to the atoms of the material organism. Against this form of Monism, psychology and philosophy will continue to erect the barriers of a scientific Dualism. Body *and* mind, — both will continue to hand in their irresistible claims to recognition as belonging to the world of finite reality. Nor will the scientific comprehension of the nature and laws of either one of these two kinds of reality be furthered by refusing to recognize the facts. Each of the two is real, because each of the two maintains its place as capable of that reciprocally conditionating change of states which is indicative of all finite reality.

But some form of philosophical Monism is indicated, we have already said, by the researches of psycho-physics and by that philosophy of mind which builds upon the principles ascertained by these researches. Realities correlated as are the body and the mind must have, as it were, common "ground." This conclusion is not based upon the false expectation that some *one* bond or connection between them will ever be envisaged as really existing. It is rather a conclusion constantly strengthened by increasing information as to how infinitely varied, subtle, and comprehensive are the ties of reciprocal action which unite the two. They have their reality in the ultimate One Reality; they have their interrelated lives as expressive of the one Life which is immanent in the two. Only by this supposition can we satisfy all that the antiquated theories of Occasionalism or Pre-existent Harmony were invented to explain, as well as all the wondrous facts which modern psychology is bringing to the light.

Doubtless the most difficult and serious work, which any true monistic system will have to achieve in overcoming the inconsistencies of a dualistic philosophy, lies on ethical ground. We have already indicated what some of these difficulties are. All attempted solutions of them end largely in a confession of ignorance and of mental inability to explain. But then this is a confession which Dualism has to make no less than Monism. We do not the better explain the genesis of moral evil — real, and in a world of reality — either by positing an eternal Principle of such evil over against God, or by denying the constant dependence of all finite personality upon the Life of God. On the contrary, Dualism increases our difficulties; for it either admits an eternal schism in the very Being of Absolute Good, or else it attributes to the creature such an independence as sacrifices the infiniteness of the Divine Personality.

Dualism may therefore be regarded as the guardian of the interests which are jeoparded by either a materialistic Realism or an Idealism that resolves the *extra*-mental reality of the world of things into merely a series of objectifying psychical processes. It has a certain use and value in defending the rights of scientific physics against an incomplete philosophical analysis. It may also defend the rights of psychology against the unwarrantable encroachments of a materialistic view of nature. Whenever we are inclined to hasty generalizations concerning the relations of the "World-Ground" to finite minds, in the supposed interests of its unity and absoluteness, Dualism interposes grave objections derived from universal and valid ethical distinctions. It is thus both a warning and an incitement to philosophical Monism. But it contributes nothing of positive and lasting value to a true solution of cosmothetic problems; nor can it ever so shape itself as to become a satisfactory philosophical system. In being consistently and persistently *philosophical* we are always seeking some form of monistic system.

We give credence to Dualism, accordingly, only in order to be more cautious and penetrating in all our philosophical analysis, more patient and comprehensive in our attempts at a final philosophical synthesis. But as itself a claimant for adherence it can meet with little intelligent favor. It is scarcely too much to say that in the development of rational self-knowledge, and in the growth of philosophical system, this form of thinking is constantly being relegated to an inferior position. Doubtless its extinction will come when, but only when, Monism shall have made full room in its syntheses for those facts and principles upon which Dualism has hitherto maintained its partial conclusions.

But if we are to look for a satisfactory philosophy in some form of Monism alone, to which of its two principal forms shall it be, — to Realism, or to Idealism? The answer from history seems to us inevitable. To neither of these two forms, with exclusion of the considerations upon which the other is based. So often as Realism rears its structure of philosophical tenets in disregard of idealistic principles and postulates, so often does Idealism find it easy to pull this structure — with scorn for its shallow analysis and its ignorance of psychology and the history of philosophy — down to the ground. But, on the other hand, so often as Idealism pushes its conclusions to their logical issue in disregard of the principles and postulates to which Realism appeals, so often does it find itself confuted by the "common-sense" of mankind, by the presuppositions of all science, and by the plainest ethical and æsthetical, as well as metaphysical, principles. Only some form of Monism that shall satisfy the facts and truths to which both Realism and Idealism appeal can occupy the place of true and final philosophy.

An analysis of the primary act of knowledge has shown us the reality of knowing subject and of object known as implicated in that act. The actuality of the act of knowledge, with all that is implicated in it, is the common point of starting for both Realism and Idealism. But the disregard or relative depreciation of either of these two sets of factors is the source in which these rival views originate. The extreme conclusions of both constitute a call to a new and more fundamental analysis of knowledge; and to another and more successful attempt to treat, by the process of reflection, all that knowledge implicates.

Each extreme, moreover, contains, to some extent, the corrective for the other. The history of speculative thinking and of its results in the formation of philosophical system, shows this process of reciprocal limitation and correction constantly going on. The clear self-conscious effort of modern philosophy is directed toward a re-examination of the ground so as to secure, in a more complete and tenable form, the statement of the results of analysis. But it also aims at ultimately combining and systematizing these results so as to attain a true and comprehensive view of the principles of all Knowledge and all Being. Some form of Monism which shall incorporate both Realism and Idealism is, therefore, at present, the intelligent and avowed aim of philosophy. The tendency of modern thought toward a form of speculative thinking that is (if the compound may be pardoned) a "Real-Idealism" or an "Ideal-Realism," is unmistakable.

This tendency may be enforced and illustrated by considering how the realistic and the idealistic conclusions supplement and correct each other at every stage of philosophical development. The same thing may also be accomplished by showing how both Realism and Idealism, as two exclusive systems, conceal each other's postulates within themselves and perish by having their inner life consumed thereby.

Realism in its most primitive and crude (its boorish or savage) form assumes, without reflection or criticism, the existence of "Things" ready made. With this form of thinking, knowledge of things is likened to some sort of copying-off, by impressions made and received of these ready-made things. Only scanty reflection is needed to show that the so-called "impressions" of some of the senses cannot possibly stand the test of this assumed correspondence to *extra*-mental reality. Thus crude natural Realism is forced to permit of an important change. Idealism then establishes itself in possession of a certain field won from its rival view of the world of things.

But Realism next retreats upon the proposition that *some at least* of the senses convey, under all ordinary and normal conditions, impressions which are truly representative of the qualities and relations of things, as these things exist external and ready made. The distinction between primary and secondary qualities of matter is therefore introduced. This distinction, instead of simply being recognized as helpful in psychological analysis and in the organization of experience with a world of phenomena, is assumed to be inherent in the very *extra*-mental reality of things. It is then said that "Things" may *seem* sweet or sour, ill-smelling or of pleasant odor, high or low in pitch, colored with this shade or that; but they *are* really extended and impenetrable, ponderous, etc. For the assurance that this statement is true, the last appeal may be made to touch and muscular "impressions." But the distinction in qualities, as immediately and indubitably involving the claims of this form of Realism, is dissolved at once by the conclusions both of physical and of psychological science. Physics shows us — so it thinks — that the only real and *extra*-mental things are the atoms; and the impressions of things — the "Things" hitherto assumed to be in some sort immediately known as they really are — come far short of representing the reality, even as respects its so-called primary qualities. While psychology points out on what conditions and by what processes the immediate cognition of extended and impenetrable and external things is developed, under the laws of the mind's life. Thus is new territory brought within the conquests of Idealism.

Just at this point realistic thinking is accustomed, being hard pressed by idealistic truths, to make a kind of dash sideways, and take refuge in the thinnest shell of a critical conclusion. To change the figure of speech, it mixes a smattering of physiology with an imperfect psychological and philosophical analysis, and so compounds a new kind of Realism. But this new tenet can make no successful appeal to "common-sense," for it has departed too far along the sceptical and critical road from the accepted beliefs of unreflecting mankind. And it also lacks justification from science and philosophy, because it has prematurely and unwarrantably called a halt in the journey along this road. Realism now admits that we have no immediate knowledge of any really external thing. But what we do immediately know, it claims, is our own excited and sentient organism. Here physiology and psychology combine to show that the excited organism is precisely what no man ever immediately knows. By sight, for example, the external parts of our own bodies are no more immediately known than are the objects separable from our bodies. And by sight no man ever immediately knew his own sentient retina, or the organism concerned in vision (optic nerve-tracts and chiasm, corpora-quadrigemina, and upper occipital lobe) posterior and superior thereto. How far we are from such immediate knowledge through the skin is made perfectly obvious by the modern experimental researches into the development of that wonderful organ and of the knowledge of which it is the organ. And yet this kind of Realism characterizes all of the modified Scotch school, including even Sir William Hamilton, who vacillated between it and another equally untenable view. It is now practically driven from the field by the appropriate idealistic considerations.

And now a yet more lordly form of Realism appears, and in the name of physical science claims to erect itself upon foundations quite unassailable by philosophical Idealism. It calls itself "physical Realism," in honor of its assumed derivation from the kind of science whose name it bears.[1] It consists of a system of inferences, from "data of sense," to "physical objects of science." It authoritatively describes the world of *extra-mental* reality in the well-known terms of "atoms," "energy"

[1] See, for example, a work bearing this title: "Physical Realism: Being an Analytical Philosophy from the Physical Objects of Science to the Physical Data of Sense," by Thomas Case, M.A. London, 1889. The author of this volume seems to hold both the last two realistic hypotheses as to the nature of the object known as really existent, by the mind. A new philosophy is proposed by this author, which infers physical objects without from "physical data within;" and the physical *data* within are the known physical parts of the nervous system.

potential and kinetic, physical "causation" and "law," etc. Thus is disclosed to us a world that really is widely and wonderfully different from the world that appears to us. It even involves many assumed realities that, judging by all the data of sense only, cannot possibly have being at all.

But the considerations upon which the rival idealistic view relies follow pitilessly this form of Realism as it retreats from the natural and universal interpretation of the data of sense into a sphere of imagination and inference where only expert students of the particular sciences have any success in the attempt to follow. Idealism, by a further process of analysis, dissolves these "objects of science" into a content and a form, both of which are ascribed to the constitution of the mind, but cannot be representative of ready-made and *extra*-mental reality. For the content — namely, the "data of sense" — is to be regarded as states of the conscious mind; and by calling it "physical" or "objective" we do not escape this conclusion. And "inferences" from these data to "physical objects of science" are subjective activities which, in themselves, can never take us out of the realm of mental form and mental law. But if scientific Realism falls back upon the immediate cognition or belief, which is attached to the "data of sense," it becomes of all forms of Realism the most difficult to defend against the attacks of Idealism. For what is "given" in the "data of sense," whether in the form of knowledge or belief, is as far as possible removed from the world of realities in which physical science lives and moves. *This* world is distinctly *not* immediately known by any one; nor is it believed in with certainty of conviction by every one. It is rather a hypothetical world, resulting from the trained imagination and from the subtle, difficult, and often exceedingly doubtful, inferences of a very few minds.

It may be said, to be sure, that the knowledge of the world is constantly being more firmly established by the exercise of all that power of prediction and explanation in which physical science rejoices. But of itself — Idealism may answer — this only proves the logical consistency of the scientific ideas, the well-grounded but still subjective validity of the propositions we have learned to make concerning certain objects of knowledge. Of itself, it does not answer any of our inquiries concerning the genesis, nature, and validity of our so-called perceptions, representative images, and conceptions of "Things."

The debate between these two great schools of philosophy cannot be settled by an appeal to physical science. The legitimate conclusions of physical science will remain unchanged within their own sphere, whether Idealism or Realism shall obtain the upper hand in the domain of philosophy. Nor can a "new" third philosophy of the realistic order be founded, in the name of physical science, which shall resist with peculiar success the attacks of the subtler forms of the idealistic theory.

Finally, Realism — perhaps growing desperate and losing some of the semblance of self-control — may rest its case, as against Idealism, upon moral and religious faith. It may cry out: "What! would you do away with the reality of moral distinctions? Would you resolve God into a shadowy mental image, or into a mere conception somewhat more consistently and elaborately formed? That there is force and meaning in this outcry, however much it resembles the confession of a cause that is lost in the field where the cold steel of ratiocination carries the day, we do not doubt. But Idealism, in its turn, may reply with a similar appeal to prejudice. It may cry out against Realism as materialistic. For it, too, has not infrequently appeared in history as the champion of orthodoxy of morals and religion.

In spite of the prevalence of Aristotelianism, as the authorized philosophy of the Church in the Middle Ages, there were not wanting occasions when Platonism gained the ascendency in ecclesiastical circles. The extreme Idealism of the disciples of Descartes was propounded in the interests of religious faith. Berkeley avowedly promulgated his theory of sense-perception, and then extended his conclusions from it into the realm of the philosophy of nature, as an antidote for the prevalent materialism of his day. By far the greatest of all American theologians, Jonathan Edwards, seems obviously to have been in philosophy a "cosmothetic Idealist" of the most pronounced sort. If the dangers of Idealism are great, and lie in the direction of Pantheism, no less great are the dangers of Realism in the direction of Materialism.

In every form of Realism, then, the considerations on which Idealism relies can be effectively used to annul all the conclusions which leave these considerations out of the account. The history of philosophy, and the very nature of the philosophical method, evince the truth of this remark.

On the other hand, something similar may be shown to hold true of all the "pure" or extreme positions of Idealism. They, too, may be proved either to have been taken in disregard of certain primary facts and indubitable principles, or else to hold concealed within them certain realistic postulates which finally work the change of the positions themselves.

We have already seen how even the most primary act of knowledge, on analysis, postulates among the "data of sense" the reality of that object which is given as *not*-me, to the knowing mind. To insist, as Idealism rightly does, upon the truth that the object cannot be given to the mind without an activity of the being *to* whom it is given, according to constitutional laws of its being, does not destroy the bearing of the supplementary fact. It is impossible for the mind to regard this object, thus given, otherwise than as an *extra*-mental being. Nor is this "impossibility" to be satisfied by resolving it into an impotency. The knowledge of the *not*-me is rather, primarily, a potency of the mind to apprehend being other than itself, — a potency of the knowledge of the reality of the "Thing" known.

Furthermore, the fact that the knowledge of things, when compared with the mere having of sensations or other mental states, must be regarded as a complex and later development of the mind, does not annul or weaken the force of the postulates that are implicated in all knowledge. This process of *becoming able* to know belongs to the growth of reason itself. What reason is, however, and what it guarantees, — these are questions that cannot be settled merely by giving an historical description of the factors and stages of its growth. The postulated reality of the "Thing" known is a result of rational activity that cannot be left out of the account. And so often as, in the effort to account for this result, Idealism refers to the admitted fact that the mind, which is active in perceiving, is also active in postulating, so often will Realism have occasion to refer to the other fact, that the object perceived is postulated as a reality *not*-myself.

It is only by recognizing a similar postulate, already in force, that Idealism itself can reach any knowledge of a mind, which may serve as the subject of changing psychical states. Every claim to dispense with this postulate and, at the same time, secure an immediate and sure knowledge of mental reality, is psychologically indefensible. Thus the scepticism which Idealism displays toward the *extra*-mental reality of the external object is turned against the ideating mind. It is equally powerful there. As to the actuality of the individual mental state, there can be, of course, no doubt. As little doubt can there be that every mental state is necessarily thought of as referable to a subject of all the states, — to a mind. But the reference is itself a mental act; and the necessity of thinking all mental acts and states as referable to a subject of them all, may itself be called by the sceptical critic an impotency of thought. Thus is Idealism, after it has denied the *extra*-mental reality of the external object, forced by scepticism to question also the *extra*-mental reality of the so-called subject of the ideas. Nothing but absolute Solipsism (the bare affirmation of the truth, As I think, I am thinking, and there is nothing known to be actual besides my thinking) seems inevitable. But reason cannot thus abjure its confidence in itself. It revolts from this extreme conclusion of a sceptical Idealism. It affirms again its original postulate, as implicated in its own act of knowledge, and as applicable both to itself and to its own external object. This is equivalent to the realistic affirmation; in some sort, both "I" and the "Things" of my knowledge are real. But it belongs to further metaphysical analysis to tell, if possible, precisely how much must be included in this statement.

The progressive organization of experience involves a constant application and extension, as it were, of the same realistic postulate. In one sense of the words it may be said that, as we gain experience, we more clearly and certainly know that things really and *extra*-mentally are, and that we ourselves are real psychical existences, subjects of a developing psychical life. On the other hand, it must also be admitted that the progressive organization of experience gives us no new means of knowing the truth of our fundamental postulate. We certainly can be said to gain vastly in knowledge of the modes of action and the changing relations of real beings. Perhaps there is no objection to saying that our conviction of the *extra*-mental reality of things, and of other minds, is deepened and confirmed with the progressive organization of experience. But neither ordinary knowledge nor accumulations of scientific truth can serve to "*prove*" anew such a reality for that which is given to my mind as *not*-me,—whether material things or other minds. Inferences cannot get behind or beneath the postulate, to confirm or to support it. Inferences all imply the postulate. They can only apply it. By the application the self-conscious reason becomes more familiar, as it were, with its own fundamental laws. When we reason up to it, or down to it, we find the postulate there.

Accordingly, any form of Idealism which leaves the realistic factors and postulates out of the account ends in conclusions which reason deems absurd. It fails in the attempts to explain the progressive organization of experience. This organization of experience necessarily implies the existence of other minds than mine. In whatever sense I am real, in that same sense they are equally real. Thus much is implied in all intercourse of man with his fellows, — intellectual, social, political, religious. The most "Egoistical Idealism" will not venture to deny to you that you, in some sort, really exist.

But the only bridge of knowledge I have from myself to the reality of other minds is laid, as it were, over their material bodies. By inferences — subtle, repeated, remote, and often doubtful — one mind may be said to know that other minds are; that they as really *are* as it is itself, and are really, in essential qualities, *as* itself. All of these inferences are based upon the knowledge of the "Things" which we call the bodies inhabited by other minds. If, then, Idealism will not fling itself out upon this realistic postulate, it cannot logically arrive at the conclusion that other minds have an existence *extra*-mental to its own. The postulate makes a safe and logical passage only when it includes the *extra*-mental reality of the bodily things, from whose changes the existence of the minds is inferred.

It would be quite too absurd, however, to hold that no other minds than ourselves exist, — that there is nought, even of that sort of being we call a soul, except our own poor example of such being. For at this point Idealism seems to cut ethics, æsthetics, and religion, up by the roots. Without real minds, existing in relations of intercommunication through really existent material means, no conduct or ethical law of conduct is possible. In other connection (page 186 f.) we have seen how the postulate of practical reason which Kant proposes implies the existence in *extra*-mental reality of a whole scheme of metaphysical entities and relations. "Pure" Idealism cannot even say, in the language attributed to Omar Khayyám, —

> "We are no other than a moving row
> Of Magic Shadow-shapes that come and go;"

for there is no knowledge, or chance for knowledge, that *we* exist, except as an imaging process of the individual *Ego*.

Doubtless the successful appeal of polemical Realism to æsthetical or religious prejudices rests upon a certain basis of truth. The only perfectly "pure" and logical form of Idealism is a sceptical Solipsism which has gone to the lengths of denying all cognition of reality except, or beyond, the actuality of the self-consciously recognized psychical state belonging here and now to the individual subject. Such Idealism is, of course, inconsistent with the recognition of any real beauty in nature, or of any really beautiful and good Absolute One, whom we may worship as *not*-ourselves, as indeed God.

Those devoted to the pursuit of the physical sciences are accustomed to imagine that they are dealing with objects which have some peculiar claim to escape from the ravages of a thorough idealistic construction of philosophy. There could not well be a greater mistake. To be sure, such a philosophy would reduce the body of physical science, and the universe which is its object of research and discovery, to the similitude of a dream. But why should any peculiarly strong objection be felt to this? If our own bodies are dreams, we need not mourn the dream-like and phantasmagorical character of the heavenly bodies. We know nothing of the latter except through changes in the former. We need care nothing as to their reality except as they affect the happiness of our dream. As dream-objects they serve their purpose as well as they would were they those vast and distant *extra*-mental realities which science assumes them to be. If we are to lose from knowledge the reality of friend and foe, of wife and mother and child, and yet the dream continues pleasant, we can easily dispense with the reality of the fixed stars. All that physical science can claim, or aim to secure, as compared with ordinary knowledge, is a superior consistency and comprehensiveness for its dream.

And, indeed, the reasons why we recoil from regarding all external nature as purely phantasmagorical are not *scientific* at all. Besides the one metaphysical reason, they are rather ethical, æsthetical, and religious. The mind, indeed, insists on carrying this postulate which enters into the more primary acts of cognition over into the complex, inferential, and derived knowledge of the physical sciences. Idealism, as well as Realism, feels itself compelled to recognize the force of this impulse. It therefore takes the form sometimes called cosmothetic; or it becomes of the absolute and metaphysical kind. It, too, affirms as the final conclusion of all philosophical searching the existence, *extra*-mentally, of a Unity of Reality. Only it considers this alone real Being that is *not*-me, to be some Ideal, some frankly or secretly assumed spiritual Unity.

The conclusion derived from the foregoing brief sketch of the antagonistic positions of Idealism and Realism, as inherent in the contrasted solutions which they give to the different philosophical problems, might be confirmed by an appeal to the history of philosophy. History shows the two engaged in the process of correcting each other's faults, and supplying each other's deficiencies, from the beginning of speculative thinking until now. The process has resulted in enriching the content of the ideas held by both classes of schools. It has impelled each of the two onward in the effort to be more comprehensive, so as to admit into itself all the true data and conclusions of the other. History, therefore, shows the two rival systems approaching a common ground of standing. And that ground of standing can be no other than such a monistic philosophy as shall hold in harmony all the truths upon which both Realism and Idealism rely.

In fact, a purely realistic or a purely idealistic system of philosophy cannot be maintained. Any position approaching more or less nearly that of complete and uncompromising Realism, or the same kind of Idealism, is tenable only as a point of momentary standing. It is reached and held only as a step in the larger progress of synthetic philosophy. Every such position, whether taken in the name of Realism or in the name of Idealism, is but a point marked in the progress of the human mind toward a final and satisfactory Monism. This Monism must find the Unity of all Being and Knowledge, the World-Ground, in an ideal Reality, a realized Ideal. Such an One is nothing else than some rational, self-conscious, and personal Life.

But — it may be asked — after we have come to this somewhat barren conclusion, what remains for philosophy to do? And in case we accept the conclusion, what better off are we in respect to affording a solution of the separate philosophical problems, — those "riddles by which our mind is oppressed in life, and about which we are forcibly compelled to some view or other, in order to be able really to live at all"? The answer to the last of these two questions is: "Much every way;" and the answer to the first of them is: "Much in many ways."

After the supreme task of philosophy has been, as it were provisionally, performed, every particular problem in the domain of philosophy requires the same detailed examination upon an inductive basis and by the method which is peculiar to philosophy, as before. But the significance of every problem is enlarged and heightened by our possession of the truth of this supreme synthesis. Every problem also, as it becomes more clearly understood, contributes something new and persuasive toward the proof of the synthesis itself. To speak from the point of view of religion, all things have their meaning made deeper and broader by a rational faith in God; and, on the other hand, the understanding of all things else adds support and clearness to our faith in God.

Even of the detailed problems of psychology and philosophy the remark just made holds true. It is true, for example, of the problem of sense-perception. The vision of the Absolute is not, indeed, to be attained through the eye of sense; neither is it the ear of flesh and bone which hears and recognizes His voice. But to one who considers the experience of knowledge by the senses, from the higher philosophical point of view, the presence of the Absolute, the real Being that is the reality of all things and the validation of all knowledge, is to be recognized even here. From the beginning of philosophical speculation upon this problem until the present time, the infinite mystery of existence which it involves has been recognized. And what is true of this problem of sense-perception is certainly true of all the problems of philosophy.

We find then a proof of the substantial truthfulness of the conclusions reached by our examination, in the continued recurrence and constant but gradually softening antagonisms of the main philosophical schools and tendencies. Dualism is yielding, in history and in the judgment-halls of reason, to a monistic philosophy. Realism and Idealism are — starting from divergent points of view and contesting all along the way a series of antagonistic positions — approaching the goal of such a Monism as shall include the truth of both. It is *this* philosophy to which the physical and the psychological sciences point the way. In the same direction we are urged by the necessities that flow from our ethical, æsthetical, and religious ideals.

The cry has recently been raised in our ears for the forming of a distinctively "American" philosophy. Such a cry can never be understood as other than, in large measure, *ad captandum*. Yet its existence as a fact, and the audience it receives, are most encouraging to those engaged in the study of philosophy. The cry is a recognition of an awakening interest, throughout our land, in philosophical pursuits. But this awakening of interest is not peculiar to us. The earnest pursuit and rapid progress of those particular sciences, on which philosophy depends, have not been without result in behalf of her larger interests and higher development. A hand, held out to philosophy by the students of these sciences, is plainly visible in every land where it and they have been dwelling together, — not always in unity. But a real unity of interests belongs to both. And by the combined and persistent efforts of investigators in these sciences, and of those who have felt that impulse toward philosophy which Plato called *Eros*, a wonderful development in the self-knowledge of reason may be expected to result. But an "American" philosophy we may no more seek than an American science or an American theology. A true and lofty philosophical thinking, based upon all the results inductively established by all the world's science, and "ancillary" to theology in another than the scholastic way, shall be our aim. That it can scarcely lead to a new form of Dualism, the teaching of historical tendencies, and the very profoundest call of reason, should make sufficiently plain.

INDEX.

THE END.